MW00811609

NATALIE CURTIS BURLIN

Natalie Curtis Burlin

a LIFE in NATIVE and
AFRICAN AMERICAN MUSIC

Michelle Wick Patterson

UNIVERSITY OF NEBRASKA PRESS
LINCOLN AND LONDON

Library of Congress Cataloging-
in-Publication Data
Patterson, Michelle Wick, 1973–
Natalie Curtis Burlin: a life in
Native and African American music
/ Michelle Wick Patterson.
p. cm.
Includes bibliographical
references and index.
ISBN 978-0-8032-3757-5
(cloth : alkaline paper)
1. Burlin, Natalie Curtis, 1875–1921.
2. Ethnomusicologists — United
States — Biography. 3. African
Americans — Music — History
and criticism. 4. Indians of North
America — Music — History
and criticism. I. Title.
ML423.B87P37 2010
780.92 — dc22
[B]   2009038145

Set in Arno by Bob Reitz.
Designed by Nathan Putens.

Dedicated to my grandmothers:
Alice Wick and Josephine Smith,
who each, in her own way,
encouraged and inspired me.

CONTENTS

ILLUSTRATIONS

ACKNOWLEDGMENTS

I would like to thank the many people who deserve credit for their invaluable assistance and support during the writing of this book. My work here grew out of my dissertation research at Purdue University, and I would first like to thank the members of my committee. Donald L. Parman serves as a model scholar for me, and I deeply appreciate all of his encouragement, advice, and superb editing skills. His generosity (including the many lunches we shared at Little Mexico II), both when I was his student and after I graduated, has meant a great deal to me. Without his support I am not sure this book would have made it to press. Nancy Gabin has also been a wonderful source of support, and I greatly appreciate her advice, insights, careful editing, and sense of humor. She was always willing to lend a sympathetic ear during the research and writing process, and I truly value the time we spent together. Susan Curtis contributed to this project from its early stages, helping me define the important questions, and offered invaluable advice throughout the writing process. Vernon Williams provided useful insights into the project and helped me frame important issues. I am fortunate to have enjoyed the aid of such a tremendous group of people.

I am also grateful for the assistance of many archivists and librarians, who are essential to our work as historians. First I would like to express my heartfelt gratitude to Alfred Bredenberg. The overseer of the Natalie Curtis Burlin Archives and a researcher on Curtis in his own right (see his Web site: nataliecurtis.org), Bredenberg was extremely generous and helpful. He invited me into his home to conduct research, offered advice on other sources on Curtis, and fully supported my work. The archivists at the Hampton University Archives must be thanked for their willingness to dig through their collections and provide me with a broad range of resources. The librarians at the reading rooms of the Library of Congress were very helpful as well. I would also like to thank the librarians and staff at the American Folklife Center, especially the Performing Arts Reading Room, for their assistance in finding sources. The archivists and staff at the National Anthropological Archives deserve my gratitude for their help locating photographs and other material, and I greatly appreciate the assistance I received at the archives at the Denver Art Museum. The librarians and archivists at the Archives of American Art, the Southwest Museum's Braun Research Library, UCLA's Special Collections, and the Archives of Traditional Music at Indiana University were generous and helpful. Finally, I extend my sincere thanks to the staff at the libraries at Purdue University. Their willingness to pull material out of storage, find sources through interlibrary loan, and support my research in other countless ways is greatly appreciated.

During the research and writing of this book I relied heavily on fellow Purdue graduate students, who helped shape my work in our courses together and in our many conversations, both on the fourth floor of Recitation Hall and at many social gatherings. I would especially like to thank Aram Goudsouzian for reading early chapters. I also enjoyed the advice and support of Ryan Anderson, Amy Bosworth, Cullen Chandler, Art Leighton, Yesuk Son, Adam Stanley, Steve Stofferhan, and Dave Welky. I greatly appreciate the congenial and supportive atmosphere among the graduate students at Purdue.

I am fortunate to have maintained these support networks as I moved on in my career and continued to revise and develop this book. I'd like to thank my former Earlham College colleagues, especially Sandrine Sanos, for their advice and support. I also particularly want to acknowledge the members of the Mount St. Mary's University Department of History for their encouragement and support as

I finished this project. My colleagues in the Mount Faculty Writing Group offered excellent advice, particularly on ways to rework the fourth chapter, and I am grateful for all their help. Additionally, I owe a great deal to Sherry Smith for her advice on ways to transform this work from a dissertation into a book and for her suggestions on how to situate Curtis within her contemporary context. Margaret Jacobs offered valuable advice on revision and generously shared her own research with me. Unnamed reviewers of the manuscript for the University of Nebraska Press must also be thanked for their careful reading and their thoughtful suggestions for revision. All of these people have done much to strengthen my work.

My research would not have been possible without the financial support that allowed me to travel to archives and to find the needed time for reading, writing, and revising. I would like to thank the Purdue Research Foundation for two years of support while I was finishing my graduate degree. Additionally, Earlham College's summer faculty development grant allowed me to spend a summer navigating the arduous process of turning a dissertation into a book.

I would like to thank my friends and family for their support, encouragement, and assistance. Many high school and college friends provided me with a place to stay and some human contact while I visited various archives around the country. My family has always encouraged me in my work, and I owe them a huge debt of gratitude. My mother fostered my love of reading and writing from an early age, particularly my passion for history. She has always been my biggest supporter, and I love and respect her for that. My father has also been a constant source of love and support. His greatest gift to me is the drive to work hard. His advice to "just get it done," which I received during our many hours of basketball drills in the barn of Wick's Almost Heaven Farm, has served as a constant encouragement. My sister deserves special credit not just for her support but also for her delightful companionship on several research trips. My brother and his family have always encouraged me and offered me a welcome respite from the strains of the academy. Other family members — grandparents, aunts, uncles, cousins — have also been part of this support network, and I am very thankful for them. Finally, I would like to thank my husband, Garth, for his belief in my abilities and his unceasing support throughout the research and writing of this book. He endured countless hours of discussion about Curtis and allayed my frequent concerns that this project would never be completed with the good humor and confidence that make him such a remarkable guy. I never would have completed this book without him.

NATALIE CURTIS BURLIN

Introduction

Why Remember Natalie Curtis?

IN A PARIS CEMETERY ON ALL SAINTS' DAY IN 1921, A SMALL group of American and French artists and musicians joined the throngs of people marking the holiday to honor a recently deceased American woman they wanted to remember as saintly. The group met to honor Natalie Curtis, an amateur ethnomusicologist and writer on Native American and African American music who had died after being struck by an automobile after descending from a Paris streetcar. Her husband, the modernist painter Paul Burlin, described his sense of this gathering, a "strange indescribable *feeling*, hard to put into words." As thousands "stood in reverence" in the cemetery, he recalled, "a sense of awe came over me, that we were following a saint!" Ideas of "sainthood" permeated the remainder of the memorial service. Alexandre Mercereau, a writer on art with an interest in "primitive" cultures, asked, "For in what does real saintliness consist if not in carrying without despair, throughout the long cavalry of life, the heavy cross of goodness, of perfection, of love." Curtis had become a "permanent source of serenity amidst the terrible struggle of existence, of peace amidst the belligerent

instincts of man, of belief amidst hundred-headed fanaticisms";
she had been a "spiritual ray amidst the darkness of materialism,
a perpetual torch of the ideal, of pure happiness amidst the base
pleasures which satisfy the majority." Mercereau admired her for
her stance against prejudice and hypocrisy and for her willingness
to question the very notion of "civilization." Mercereau believed
that in the United States "red men and black men" would venerate
Curtis and concluded with the hope that "if there is a happiness
more infinite than that of non-existence" that one could reach "by
sublime personal virtues and by the ardent prayers of those who
knew you on earth," then the door to this happiness had already
been opened for Curtis.[1]

Indeed, several groups of Americans met to honor and remember
Curtis's life, work, and spirit. In Santa Fe, her adopted Southwestern
home, a group of women writers, including Carol Stanley, Alice
Corbin Henderson, and Elsie (Elizabeth) Sergeant, met to celebrate
her life. Stanley insisted, "Every one of us who loved her must feel
keen personal joy over her part in our lives, but her influence was
too intense for us to dream of mourning her passing." Instead of
grieving the women vowed to continue Curtis's work and hoped
to dedicate a new music room or even a building to her somewhere
in Santa Fe. In fact, this group of women, in their writing and creative endeavors throughout the 1920s and 1930s, did indeed build
upon and extend the work Curtis had begun two decades earlier.[2]
Stanley further observed that a Hopi man, upon hearing of Curtis's
death, replied: "But she cannot die. She is singing now—somewhere
with her Hopi friends." The man then softly sang songs Curtis had
taught him. He remarked, "She sang like Indian, have to have spirit
of Indian for white woman to sing that way."[3]

In Curtis's hometown of New York City yet another group met
to honor her. In 1923 African American musicians held a service
for her and for Henry Krehbiel, a music critic and scholar of Negro
spirituals. The mostly black gathering (the only white faces belonged

to the deceased musicians' families), held in the basement of a public library, praised Curtis's and Krehbiel's studies of African American music. The room contained a chair holding Krehbiel's picture, two of his books underneath it, while another chair displayed a photograph of Curtis at the piano, as well as her books. Curtis's brother Bridgham found that the "very simplicity of [the service] made it the more touching." He was moved to witness a young girl place roses beneath his sister's picture and to hear the kind words spoken by Columbus Kamba Simango, an African informant who had shared songs with Curtis, and by Harry T. Burleigh, an African American musician. The group concluded their service with calls for a more permanent memorial to Curtis's life work.[4]

Yet another memorial to Curtis helped bring this group's desires to fruition. Officials of Hampton Institute, a black industrial school, held a memorial for Curtis in conjunction with one of its most important annual celebrations, Founder's Day, in January 1926. A large audience gathered at the school's museum, including Curtis's mother, Augusta, and her four surviving siblings. Hampton proposed to honor Curtis's memory by granting a "Natalie Curtis Scholarship" to a deserving Native American or African American student, preferably one with musical inclinations. Hampton also presented a bronze statuette created by an American sculptor entitled *The Buffalo*, which depicted an African American soldier from the recent war. The statuette was dedicated to Curtis, "beloved of many of different races and colors." Upon presenting the sculpture, which would be placed in the school's library, Simango's wife quoted an African proverb: "Gratitude is best shown, not by much talk, but by lighting another fire."[5]

Curtis's good friend Elbridge Adams, a New York lawyer, delivered the memorial address, commemorating Curtis as "a loyal friend of Hampton as well as of the American Negro and American Indian." He noted her unforgettable "strong and vivid personality" and declared his belief that no one who had known her could ever really forget her, especially the "countless thousands of her black-and red-skinned friends." Adams portrayed Curtis as "the most tolerant person I have ever known." He claimed that she possessed a marked ability to understand and sympathize with the oppressed and simply could not countenance prejudice, an attitude that allowed Curtis to "look into the heart and soul of a human being" and to understand "the joys and sorrows, the hopes and fears" of others almost instinctively. Curtis, Adams declared, always looked for the best in others, only seeing the virtues in her friends. This openness, he observed, shaped her work. She did not record Native American music "in an impersonal, detached way," but instead "made herself one of the people" she studied. She wanted to do more than just collect Indian songs; she hoped to "understand and reveal the inner life of a primitive race."[6]

Curtis's work with Native Americans and her positive outlook on life, Adams concluded, prepared her especially for work with African Americans. "She brought to this work," he claimed, "the same loving care and sympathy that characterized all her labor for the black race." Curtis, he said, never believed in racial inferiority, arguing instead that although blacks lacked the intellectual development of whites, they had their own unique gifts to bestow on American culture. Adams finished by reasserting the power of Curtis's legacy in the world of music: "The most competent musical critics have pronounced that the work of Natalie Curtis in the field of native American folksong is the work of a masterly genius and will endure forever." He grieved that Curtis had died just as she began receiving much-deserved international recognition for her work.[7]

Others joined in the chorus of praise for Curtis's ability to sympathetically record the music of African Americans and Native Americans. Curtis's friend Kurt Schindler, a musician, recalled accompanying Curtis on a collecting trip among the Hopi. Her willingness to sit on a rough dirt floor in happy contentment among "her beloved Indians," persuading them to "talk and sing to her and explain the mysteries of their legends," had deeply impressed Schindler. He pronounced Curtis a "genius" for the "strange mixture of child and woman in her" that allowed her to accomplish much more than any "wise man or 'mere musician'" could. Her work with African Americans particularly moved him: "I never had a chance before to state publicly . . . what a deep and educating influence this remarkable woman has had upon the shaping and moulding of my own ideals [and] . . . how she held up the beaconlight of her own idealism to inspire me to serve only the highest art; how she made me believe in the American public." Schindler promised that her memory would "live like a sacred flame in my heart to my life's end and, if it may be willed so, through my work to other generations."[8]

The final speaker at the Hampton memorial service, Father Winfred Douglas, who knew Curtis from her visits to the West, echoed the other speakers' appraisal of her as a gifted, tolerant, and vibrant person. Douglas commented on her sympathy: "This is perhaps the supreme human gift: the power of spirituality sharing the joys, the sorrows, the hopes, the aspirations of others and thereby comforting, encouraging, inspiring the helped soul to its best achievement." Like her memorializers in Paris, Douglas also alluded to the saintlike qualities Curtis possessed. She seemed to him "a person wholly devoted to the good of others for the love of God." Douglas noted that "Tawimana" (the "Song Maid" in Hopi) had thrived among her Native American friends and found in their mythology an apt metaphor for Curtis. "Natalie was like the desert rain," he asserted, "reviving the thirsty, refreshing the withered, bringing new growth from the seed, making the desert bloom and bear fruit."[9]

As these memorials suggest, Natalie Curtis's family, friends, and colleagues remembered her as a sincere and sympathetic friend of Native Americans and African Americans and as an able interpreter of their musical traditions. These characterizations are not surprising, given that many of these memorialists shared in her research and in her ideas about American music and culture, but they are not wholly accurate. Although Curtis had an obvious concern for the groups she studied and wanted to improve their conditions, she remained wedded to ideas of primitivism and white superiority that colored her research efforts. Her life, like many lives, represents a great deal of ambiguity, but within this ambiguity much may be discovered.

Born in 1875 to a well-to-do family in New York City, Curtis trained as a classical musician in the United States and Europe. Prepared for a career as a composer and pianist, Curtis visited the American Southwest around 1900 and was captivated by Indian music. She devoted herself to its study, publishing articles in a number of popular magazines. Her first lengthy work on this music, *Songs of Ancient America*, came out in 1905. Two years later she produced *The Indians' Book*, a collection of more than two hundred transcribed songs from eighteen tribes accompanied by artwork, photographs, and folklore. Curtis's work led her to Hampton Institute, a school for African Americans that at the time offered training to Indian students. While researching there Curtis, unlike many other scholars of Indian music, expanded her interest to the songs of African Americans and Africans. She published *Negro Folk Songs* (1918–19) and *Songs and Tales from the Dark Continent* (1920) to preserve this music and to offer it as inspiration for Americans. Curtis insisted that composers might use the sounds and spirit of these traditions to develop a distinctively American musical idiom and create a national cultural expression. Curtis understood music as a language of interracial discourse and as a means to generate reform for Native Americans and African Americans. In 1917 she married Paul Burlin, an artist who also incorporated Indian and black subject matter into his work, and eventually joined him as an expatriate in Paris in 1921. There, after she delivered an address to the International

Congress of Art History in October 1921, Curtis's career and life were tragically cut short at age forty-six by a car accident.

Few Americans today remember Natalie Curtis at all. Her name is occasionally mentioned in histories of Native American and African American music or in works on women anthropologists and folklorists of the early twentieth century. Often she is criticized for her racial essentialism, which clouded her accomplishments as a folk music collector. Like other amateur female ethnomusicologists and anthropologists she has been dismissed as sentimental or "unscientific" for her approach and her presentation of folk music. Her tragic death at an early age means that she missed opportunities to refine her viewpoints or publicly reflect on her career and its meanings. Nor did she get to witness the full blossoming of the seeds she had planted: she did not live to see the rise of respect for black folk traditions during the Harlem Renaissance of the 1920s or the period of greater respect for Indian cultures during the New Deal of the 1930s.[10]

Because of the role Curtis played in preserving the musical histories of these groups, and because of her search for a personal and American identity during these pivotal years, Curtis's life story deserves to be told. As the many memorials to her suggest, her career touched on a number of important themes in the late nineteenth and early twentieth centuries, a period of sweeping economic, social, and cultural change. Because of these themes one must resist the temptation to dismiss Curtis as a minor figure in the history of ethnomusicology and American thought. Her life story has much to tell us about the role of women in music, anthropology, and Indian reform. It also reveals a great deal about the multifaceted roles played by images of Native and African Americans in American culture and in the search for an American identity. This is the first full-scale biography of Curtis, and as interesting as Curtis's story is in itself, its broader significance lies in the issues with which it engages.

As a "New Woman" Curtis faced a world of possibilities and anxieties. She embraced the new opportunities for women to study and perform music, and she expanded the boundaries confining female musicians and researchers in her efforts at composition and ethnomusicology.[11] In the Southwest she, like other white women, experienced the tensions between increased opportunities in the fields of anthropology and ethnomusicology and lingering gendered restrictions on women's opportunities. She capitalized on her position as a privileged white woman to gain access to informants and to attract audiences to her writing and reform efforts. Many women followed Curtis to the Southwest, especially in the period following World War I; she paved the way for younger generations of politically active and culturally engaged women to work in the Southwest.[12]

Curtis also served as a transitional figure within the field of Indian policy and reform. Her work bridged the late-nineteenth-century era of forced assimilation and allotment and the cultural pluralism and appreciation for Native American lifeways of John Collier's Indian New Deal in the 1930s. Although still paternalistic, the Indian New Deal did reverse the harshest elements of the previous era and plant seeds for political and cultural self-determination for Native people.[13] Curtis's refusal to abandon the nineteenth-century evolutionary rhetoric of the "vanishing Indian" and her tendency to speak on behalf of Native Americans coexisted with her calls for white Americans to listen to Indian voices, accept Native cultures on their own terms, and reject the policy of complete assimilation. The transitional nature of her work — seen, for example, in her reliance on federal boarding schools for her research while simultaneously calling for an end to these schools' harsh assimilationist policies — helps us understand a significant change within official Indian policy, the move from assimilation to cultural pluralism.[14]

Curtis's research among Native Americans also raises questions about the response of Native people to efforts to preserve and study their cultural institutions. Curtis stressed, particularly in *The Indians'*

Book, that the songs and stories she recorded were "the direct utterance of the Indians themselves."[15] Her portrayal of Native Americans as collaborators and joint participants in the preservation process raises difficult questions about the process of collaboration and cultural brokerage between informants and researchers.[16] Curtis may have believed that she allowed Native American informants to speak unimpeded by her interference, but she clearly shaped material to meet her own needs and those of her audiences. Her research reveals the functioning of an American Orientalism, a fascination with a primitive Other located on American soil.[17] Native Americans have long served as symbols of American identity.[18] Curtis's insistence on presenting an "authentic" Indian voice played into turn-of-the-century desires to locate a national identity in response to the turmoil resulting from a modernizing America.

Although Curtis is better known for her works on Indian music and folklore, her efforts in African American music are equally significant. Few students of Indian music also studied black song. Curtis's work is particularly significant because Curtis also turned to African Americans in her quest for a cultural American identity. This phase of Curtis's career reflects similar tensions between essentializing a "primitive" Other and making sincere efforts to use music as a means for racial uplift. The influence of Hampton Institute and the role of Curtis's patrons in this research bring these tensions to the surface. *Negro Folk Songs* and *Songs and Tales from the Dark Continent*, both products of her fieldwork in conjunction with Hampton, reveal Curtis's inability to divorce herself from racialist notions of human development even as her research opened the possibilities for interracial understanding and discourse. Curtis is often noted for her accomplishments in recording the harmonization in Negro spirituals, while being dismissed for her racialist thinking. Her efforts to use music to help African Americans — through a music settlement in Harlem, for example, or her efforts to promote black composers — complicate this image of her life and work.[19]

Many disaffected Americans at the turn of the twentieth century sought in primitive or folk cultures remedies for the maladies of modern life. Curtis joined composers seeking to produce an American musical expression with Native American and African American songs, who argued that the true spirit of America lay not in the factory and large city, but in the American West, in the romantic South, and among the true "folk" of the United States. Curtis incorporated Native American and African American themes into the Arts and Crafts movement in an effort to find alternative ways of living and working in the modern, industrial world. Curtis joined other thinkers, often termed antimodernists, who appropriated medieval, Oriental, or martial cultures as a way of achieving "authentic" experiences in their own lives. Although these Americans are often criticized for the self-centered nature of their appropriations, Curtis's work reveals that not all antimodernists — particularly not those attracted to Native Americans in the West — ignored the needs of the groups from which they appropriated cultural elements for their own uses.[20]

Natalie Curtis's career centered on the theme of her search for an identity as an American. Throughout her life she constantly engaged in a process of defining an identity for herself and her fellow Americans. Beginning with her youthful passion for the piano and Wagner, she adopted the language of music as a means to express and understand herself. In her encounters with Native Americans and African Americans she drew on this language to make sense of her increasingly diverse, urban, industrial, and modern America. Natalie Curtis's life story shows one way in which an American woman came to terms with the compelling issues of her day and encouraged others to adopt her vision for an America different from the one in which she lived.

THIS RESEARCH DRAWS FROM A VARIETY OF PUBLISHED AND unpublished primary sources. Curtis wrote three major works, composed over fifteen songs, and penned over eighty articles in popular magazines, journals, and newspapers. Because of her many years of involvement at Hampton University, its archives contain correspondence between Curtis, school officials, and others interested in her work, as well as pamphlets from music programs, songs, student records, and other useful material. Curtis also corresponded with a number of important figures in anthropology and politics, including Theodore Roosevelt, the philanthropist George Foster Peabody, and the anthropologists Aleš Hrdlička and Franz Boas. The Library of Congress contains copies of manuscripts, recordings, and musical compositions by Curtis, as well as material from fellow musicians, especially David Mannes and Percy Grainger. Recordings of Native American and African Americans songs by Curtis are located at the Archives of Traditional Music at Indiana University. Correspondence and other material kept at the Southwest Museum's Braun Library; the diaries of Curtis's brother George, held in Special Collections at the University of California, Los Angeles; and Curtis's field notebooks, housed at the Denver Art Museum, provided previously unknown perspectives on Curtis's work. Finally, the Natalie Curtis Burlin Archives, in the possession of Alfred and Virginia Bredenberg, proved extremely useful. This collection includes correspondence, clippings, photographs, artwork, and a plethora of useful material on Curtis found nowhere else. These primary sources, taken together, helped reconstruct Curtis's life and career, providing useful insights into her social and cultural world.

This book is divided into seven chapters. The first two examine the impact Curtis's early life and training had on the formulation of her later ideas and career. Chapter 1 explores the privileged cultural legacy Curtis gained from her family. The Curtises epitomized major social and economic transitions of the nineteenth century, changes that led to the arrival of modernity during Curtis's lifetime. The first chapter thus paints a picture of the upper-middle-class society into which Curtis was born and the influence this upbringing, especially

Transcendentalism and abolitionism, had on her life. The second chapter examines Curtis's teenage years and musical education. Music provided Curtis with a language that allowed her to discuss her artistic, spiritual, and feminist anxieties within a largely female world. Her training in classical music, her participation in the vibrant musical scene of 1890s New York City, her passion for the operas of Richard Wagner, and her early efforts to compose American music all prepared, but did not dictate, her path toward the study of Native American and African American music.

The next three chapters focus on Curtis's Native American research, writing, and reform efforts. Chapter 3 examines Curtis's initial attraction as a woman and a musician to the Southwest and to the music of its Native peoples. As Curtis collected music on Indian reservations, at boarding schools, and at the 1904 St. Louis World's Fair, she functioned as both a colonizer appropriating Native music and a potential reformer hoping to ameliorate the poor conditions of her informants. In her early writings on the Southwest and Native American music she presented the region as an American Orient open to Americans searching for authentic identities. Chapter 4 interrogates Curtis's claim that she merely served as the "pencil in the hand of the Indian" in *The Indians' Book* and other writings. This claim is largely false; Curtis's work represents her desire for authenticity and fascination with the "primitive" more than an accurate record of Indian music and folklore or the actual words of her informants. However, Curtis's claim that she was presenting a genuine Indian voice opened a space in which Native Americans might speak. Furthermore, her intention to dispel harmful stereotypes, increase white understanding, and help Indian youth cope with their difficult transition to the modern world does not lose its significance because of her interventions in these texts. Chapter 5 further develops these themes by arguing that Curtis used white interest in Native American music to pursue reform, especially within federal Indian schools. Working apart from other

Indian reformers, she represents a shift in Indian policy in the early twentieth century.

Chapter 6 explores Curtis's work collecting and popularizing African and African American music while researching at Hampton Institute and other sites in the South, as well as her work with the Music School Settlement for Colored People in Harlem. It examines her problematic portrayal of blacks as primitives capable of redeeming a soulless American culture. This portrayal, however, coexisted with Curtis's advocacy for African American music and civil rights and with her ability to collect a variety of African American folk songs and capture the harmonies found in their music. This chapter also examines the contradictory influences of Curtis's patrons on her thinking about culture and race, ranging from the racialist attitudes of her patrons associated with Hampton, to the primitivism of her patron Charlotte Osgood Mason, to the nascent cultural pluralism of Franz Boas.

The final chapter places Curtis within a broader cultural context and examines the ways her ideas fit in a variety of different, yet related, movements. Her participation in the Arts and Crafts movement, her role as a member of the artists' colony in Santa Fe, and her contributions to "Indianist" and "Negro" movements in classical music demonstrate the multifaceted scope of antimodernist discourse, particularly through the inclusion of race in these discussions. The language of music shaped a personal and particularly American identity for Curtis, one she believed other Americans could and should adopt.

1

An "Atmosphere of Culture and High Purpose"

Family Influences in a Changing America

NATALIE CURTIS, AN "ATTRACTIVE AND AMIABLE CHILD WITH large frank blue eyes, pink cheeks and golden hair," was born in New York City on April 26, 1876, the fourth of six children of Edward and Augusta Curtis.[1] Natalie and her siblings, Julia, Constance, George De Clyver, Bridgham, and Marian, grew up in a period of significant transformation in American life. Indeed, Curtis's family epitomized many of the changes Americans underwent in the second half of the nineteenth century. The experiences and aspirations of her grandfather George Curtis, her paternal uncle George William Curtis, and her father, Edward, reveal the effects of the social, cultural, economic, and political changes that Americans both celebrated and feared.

Curtis's family influenced her later search for an American identity and shaped the ways she would try, like many other Americans, to understand her changing world. The close emotional and personal ties Curtis maintained with many family members, along with the financial and social resources of a connected and moderately well-to-do family, provided her with a basis of support and encouragement throughout her life. Curtis was an heir of "old" New England families, many of whom had actively identified with the Transcendentalist movement and abolitionist reform, who had recently completed the transition to the New York cultural and social scene, and who advanced progressive reforms. Her later work with Native American and African American music is understandable in light of her family's influence.

Curtis's father's side of the family traced its lineage back to colonial New England, where Henry Curtis and May Guy Curtis arrived in Sudbury, Massachusetts, in 1636.[2] Curtis's grandfather George Curtis (1796–1856), an ambitious banker in Providence, Rhode Island, helped bring about the shift of financial and cultural capital from New England to New York. He helped modernize American commerce and business as he advanced his family into the new urban elite. After several promotions at his bank he married into the socially and politically connected Burrill family. His young bride, Mary, was the daughter of James Burrill, the chief justice of the Rhode Island Supreme Court and a senator in the U.S. Congress (1817–20). Her uncle Tristram Burgess served in the state supreme court and in the U.S. Congress. In addition to such crucial social and political connections, Mary, described as "one of the most beautiful and accomplished ladies of the period," enhanced the cultural and educational life of the family.[3] The union produced two sons, James Burrill and George William, but proved to be a short-lived one when Mary died in 1826.

George cared for the motherless boys as best he could, alternately sending them off to school and placing them in the care of relatives. In 1835 he remarried into another prominent Providence family. Julia Bridgham, age twenty-four, was the daughter of Samuel Willard Bridgham, a noted lawyer and the first mayor of Providence. This marriage further cemented George's social standing. As one historian comments, the "Curtises, Burrills, and Bridghams were among a circle of the most politically and socially prominent families in

Rhode Island."[4] Julia, only twelve years older than the eldest Curtis son, took on the role of companion rather than mother to the two boys. Commentators described Natalie Curtis's grandmother as a "charming and talented" woman who "read widely and wrote poetry with skill and was possessed of a fund of good sense and of a great vivacity."[5] George and Julia had four sons: Natalie's father, Edward; John Green, a New York physician; Samuel, who died shortly after the Civil War; and Joseph, who died in the war.

Although Providence offered the Curtis family many opportunities, notably a rich cultural life infused with the spirit of the Transcendentalists and chances for civic office holding, New York City lured an ambitious George Curtis to relocate in February 1839. The city attracted talented men like him because of the opportunities presented by the rapid expansion of trade and manufacturing. George accepted a position at the newly organized Bank of Commerce and gained a reputation as an able banker, leading to his presidency of the Continental Bank of New York in 1844. A biographer asserts that George was "characterized by shrewd business ability, coupled with an outstanding reputation for honesty and trustworthiness." His reputation opened other doors in the financial world to him, allowing him to purchase a fashionable home at 27 Washington Place. This area had recently become the home of wealthy New York City families escaping the increased commercial development in other areas of the city (Henry James was born at 21 Washington Place, and Cornelius Vanderbilt owned a home at 10). The Washington Square neighborhood, "bound by social, family, and business ties," became "*the* place to be," according to one historian of the area.[6] Upon retirement George moved to Jackson, Florida, because of failing health and died there in 1856. Julia then returned to New York City to be close to her children.[7]

Natalie Curtis never knew her grandfather, but she certainly reaped the benefits of his success. George provided the family with financial security, and the freedom that accompanied it, and with business, social, and political connections. Curtis would later draw on these family resources to fund her education and travels. Both George and Julia provided their family with a sense of social responsibility and an appreciation for art and culture. Although Curtis shared in this inheritance from her grandparents, it was her father and uncles who benefited most directly. Her father, Edward, and his brother John Green both relied on family resources while they trained to become physicians. The eldest Curtis boys, George William and James Burrill, reaped the benefits of their father's business acumen. Both enjoyed opportunities to advance their studies at home and abroad. The younger of the two, George William, used family wealth and cultural capital to become a well-known orator, writer, and civil service activist. His ideals had a profound impact on his niece.

George William Curtis (1824–1892) represents another facet of the transformations that marked the late nineteenth century. His political activities within and without the Republican Party and his opinions on suffrage and especially race relations demonstrate the widespread influence of Transcendentalist and abolitionist ideas. He initially attempted to follow his father into the world of business and commerce but found it distasteful. In 1842 he and his older brother, Burrill, began an eighteen-month stay at Brook Farm, the utopian Transcendentalist community. Although he never fully accepted this community's goals, George remained an earnest sympathizer with its members, and his experience with Transcendentalists profoundly influenced his life. At Brook Farm he communed with Ralph Waldo Emerson, Henry David Thoreau, and Margaret Fuller and honed his love of nature and music. One biographer argues for the strength of the Transcendentalist influence on George William: "Without Brook Farm, Transcendentalists, and Emerson, it is quite safe to say that the life of Curtis would have been less worthy of our admiration."[8] Transcendentalist ideas, such as the notion that in the natural world individuals could transcend ordinary life, deeply marked the Curtis family for generations to come.

In 1846 the two brothers embarked on a "Grand Tour" of Europe and parts of the Middle East. This experience instilled a greater sense of cosmopolitanism in young George William and jump-started his literary career.[9] The publication of *Nile Notes of a Howadji* (1851) and *The Howadji in Syria* (1852) established George as a writer and helped land him a spot as the author of "The Easy Chair" column at *Harper's Monthly Magazine.*

One historian places George William Curtis in the "new knowledge elite of journalists, academics, and other professionals that developed in the second half of the nineteenth century." This group saw their role as "sentinels and tribunes of the 'public interest'" and sought to shape public opinion in order to create the "good society."[10] Curtis in particular used his superb oratorical ability, skillful writing, and editorial opinions to shape the views and direct the actions of his audiences. As part of the intellectual elite he maintained ties with other leading thinkers of his day. The constant stream of notable intellectuals that flowed through his Staten Island home had a marked impact on his family, as did the inheritance of Transcendentalist and abolitionist ideals.

Uncle George exerted a profound influence on young Natalie Curtis. The Curtis family was close-knit, with many members exchanging visits between their homes in the greater New York City area. George took an active role in the lives and careers of his younger brothers. He and his wife, Anna, often entertained guests in both their Staten Island home and their summer house in Ashfield, Massachusetts.[11] Curtis and her uncle shared a close relationship. She admired his stature as a well-known writer and orator and absorbed his opinions on equal rights for blacks and women. The two also enjoyed music together. Family members were encouraged to study music and to play an instrument. Natalie and her cousin Lizzie often entertained the family together at the piano, and Uncle George and Natalie shared an enthusiasm for German opera, especially the works of Richard Wagner. Natalie deeply cared for him and expressed a profound sense of loss upon his death in 1892. "It is *too* terrible!" she wept to her childhood friend Bessie Day upon her uncle's death. "I can not bear to think of it. My heart aches so for Lizzie and Aunt Anna in their fearful sorrow."[12] Clearly, Uncle George meant a great deal to Curtis.

The Transcendentalist ideas George acquired as a young man particularly shaped the youth of his family. From his experiences at Brook Farm George developed a sincere appreciation for music, particularly for the influence it could have on society. In his mind music, emotion, and the intellect fused together, creating a virtuous person who had a duty to create the "good society." Transcendentalist ideas of the perfectibility of humankind and his own sense of "moral enthusiasm" shaped George William into a civic-minded reformer. His encounter with many of the leading lights of Transcendentalism also bred in him a sincere appreciation for nature and a notion that the best education involved a balance of mind and body. These themes, undoubtedly stressed to the youngest members of the Curtis family, recurred in the writings and reform agenda of the adult Natalie Curtis.[13]

Similarly, Curtis's uncle's abolitionist legacy molded her thinking about race relations in America. George became embroiled in the growing sectional crisis of the 1850s. His commitment to abolitionism was cemented by his 1856 marriage to Anna Shaw of Staten Island, a member of a well-off abolitionist family. In addition to his social and political views, economic responsibilities to his family pushed George toward the lecture circuit. In 1856 he began his career as an orator, delivering his first address, "The Duty of the American Scholar to Politics and the Times." In this speech he justified his involvement in politics, arguing that the intellectual was not a "closeted specialist, but that 'priest of the mind' dedicated to the elevation of public thought and action" and devoted to community interests and to humankind.[14] Other orations, such as "Political Infidelity" and "The Present Aspect of the Slavery Question," focused on the political tensions besetting America on the eve of civil war. Family influence partly accounted for his strong antislavery views and his belief that African Americans deserved equal rights, but no special favors, as American citizens. George's brother-in-law Robert Shaw led the Massachusetts 54th, a famous all-black regiment. His stepmother, Julia, "a woman of firm spirit and definite anti-slavery conviction," urged George to "stump it" in support of the war and its goals. With his brothers Sam, Joe, and Edward serving in the Union Army, George's sense of urgency to fulfill the moral aim of emancipation gained new meaning.[15] Occasionally he risked his own safety in expressing his opinions. During a lecture in Philadelphia in 1860 hostile crowds hurled bottles and bricks as George tried to convince them to support black rights, even at the risk of the Union. His niece later admiringly wrote of the "moral courage that sustained Mr. Curtis when he was mobbed for his antislavery speeches during the Civil War."[16] Natalie Curtis further recalled how her uncle's views on race relations influenced her ideas on this issue and how she respected his courage in the face of hostility.

Following the war's conclusion George Curtis continued to call for African American rights, eventually supporting the Radical Republican agenda because of its stance toward freed people. He pushed for black voting rights and especially championed education as the solution to social and economic inequality. One biographer noted that he "evinced a sincere, intense aversion to racial prejudice and discrimination of any kind."[17] One may suspect, however, that George also espoused a paternalistic and romantic view of black Americans. A number of former abolitionists argued that black emotionalism and gifts for music could contribute to American culture and, in some areas, made African Americans superior to whites.[18] George's support for educational institutions such as Hampton Institute, an industrial school for blacks located in Virginia, and the Peabody Fund, a Northern philanthropy that aided Southern

schools, suggests that he adopted an accommodationist approach
to race relations, if not a romantic one. His niece's research on
African Americans at Hampton exhibited a similar blending of
paternalism with an earnest desire to improve the conditions of
African Americans.

In the decades following the Civil War former abolitionists,
as James McPherson observes, continued their involvement in
various reform efforts. Although McPherson contends that many
abolitionists and their descendents ("neo-abolitionists," he labels
them) continued to advocate for African American citizenship and
civil rights, George William Curtis's devotion to the freed people
wavered, especially in the final years of Reconstruction. Republican Party politics and civil service reform gradually outweighed
his commitment to black rights. He was "as much Republican as
abolitionist," remarks McPherson. Although once a defender of
Reconstruction policies, claiming he "preferred 'the party of thieves
to the party of murderers,'" by 1875 George had become convinced
that a "policy of force must give way to a policy of conciliation."
Like a number of former abolitionists he increasingly advanced a
"formula of time, education, and hope" as the solution to American
race relations.[19]

Abolitionists and neo-abolitionists also turned toward other
causes. For instance, George William, fearful of "swarms of Poles,
Bohemians, Hungarians, Russians, and Italians," supported restrictions on immigration. This "refuse population of semi-civilized or
barbarous lands," he warned, threatened the "sturdy, intelligent,
industrious, moral people sprung of English stock." As McPherson
argues, George William Curtis "retreated further than ever from his
one-time egalitarianism." Although Curtis was not representative
of most abolitionists in his nativistic views, he shared with them
his support for women's suffrage.[20]

Supporters of women's suffrage vacillated between calling for
the universal right to vote and arguing that the ballot be granted to

those deemed most competent to use it. In general, suffrage advocates adopted a policy of disassociating suffrage from African American rights or using racist assumptions and arguments to campaign for white women's right to vote. George Curtis more often discussed suffrage in terms of women's rights as citizens than by making racial arguments. He used his position at *Harper's* to promote suffrage, and he considered women an intelligent part of his readership. In a truly civilized society, he argued, women would have the right to vote and opportunities for higher education. Women deserved the vote, he contended, because suffrage was a natural right of citizens. Society would benefit from women's political participation, and the vote would also directly help women. Curtis challenged the prevalent notion of "separate spheres," believing it to be a creation solely benefiting men. He championed full equality between the sexes in all aspects of society and urged freedom for women to develop as individuals. Access to higher education was high on Curtis's list, and he pushed for coeducational facilities and for equal educational opportunities for women of all classes. He also advocated equal pay for equal work. Curtis's views inspired his daughter Elizabeth to become an active worker in the New York suffrage movement and his niece Natalie to support suffrage and pursue an independent career.[21]

Natalie Curtis and Lizzie Curtis had a close relationship, and her cousin's lifework deeply affected Natalie. Upon Lizzie's death in 1914 Curtis penned a revealing tribute to her deceased cousin that demonstrated the intimacy the two women shared and the respect Curtis felt for her family.[22] Curtis credited her cousin's support for suffrage to her involvement in charity work. Indeed, many suffrage supporters in the 1890s stressed women's role as moral guardians as a rationale for allowing them the vote. Curtis attributed the family devotion to literature, music, and public-spiritedness to her cousin's dedication to her cause. She recalled the days Elizabeth Curtis spent in the "wisteria-covered house" surrounded by the "atmosphere of culture and high purpose that characterized her home." Curtis credited both of Elizabeth's parents with imparting "a spirit of service to the community" to their daughter, who carried on her parents' legacy long after their deaths. Curtis expressed admiration for her cousin's strong convictions, her lack of prejudice, her "gift for oratory," and her ability to empathize with others easily, traits she tried to emulate.[23]

Although Curtis admired her cousin's beliefs, their more personal bonds coalesced around a shared love for music and the piano. "With her little cousins she generously played duets," Curtis reminisced. She remarked that Elizabeth had a "brilliant faculty" for music and that listeners often pressed her to play concerts, accompany soloists, and train groups of amateurs for performance. Curtis seemed especially struck by Elizabeth's willingness to play for anyone. She noted that her cousin "played as gladly for working girls to dance as for some professional violinists to practice Brahms."[24] Perhaps her cousin's life and reform work sparked something in Curtis. It may have suggested intimate connections among music, the arts, and reform, connections Curtis would later demonstrate in her work with Native American and African American music and folklore.

Like her cousin Curtis grew up in a home that inspired her intellectually and artistically. Although he did not attain the stature of his half-brother, Edward Curtis created a comfortable home for his wife, Augusta, and their children in New York City. Edward Curtis, or "Bogey," as his children often called him, was born in Providence to George Curtis and Julia Bridgham Curtis in June 1838. Upon the family's move to New York City Edward attended a "select private school" to prepare him for entrance into Harvard.[25] Sons of bankers and merchants, like Edward, often pursued professional careers, especially in law or medicine, in the mid-nineteenth century. This was perhaps a self-conscious strategy adopted by members of this class to diversify their capital and their skills. A career in the professions also served as an opportunity for these sons, who chose not to participate in the family business, to maintain ties to elite social networks and live off their fathers' fortunes in respectable ways.[26]

After graduation from Harvard in 1859 Edward Curtis returned to New York City for his medical training at the College of Physicians and Surgeons. He volunteered in the Union Army as a dresser and later as a medical cadet at Georgetown. He served in a number of theaters, and in May 1863 the army appointed him to acting assistant surgeon in the microscopy department of the Army Medical Museum in Washington. He earned his medical degree the following year from the University of Pennsylvania and soon after received a commission for a field assignment as an assistant surgeon with the Army of the Potomac. He married Augusta Lawler Stacey in Chester, Pennsylvania, on November 16, 1864, and returned to the museum. His talents and service led to his selection in 1865 to assist the surgeon general in the autopsy of President Abraham Lincoln. He continued his research appointment in the army, conducting research on bovine bacterial disease and telescope photography until February 1870, when he returned to New York to open a private practice.[27]

The New York Edward Curtis returned to significantly differed from the one he had left. For one thing the population of the city had grown. In 1860, not too long after Curtis departed, roughly 805,000 people lived in the city. Upon his return just a decade later the number had risen to around 943,000, and some estimated that the number reached 1.5 million during the workday. Not only had the population increased, but the makeup of New Yorkers had also changed. In 1870 roughly 419,000 of the residents counted in the census were foreign born, with that number increasing each year.[28] The city was also in the midst of economic and social changes. New York underwent dramatic transitions in the last decades of the nineteenth century, changes Edward Curtis's father had helped initiate. Corporate managers and manufacturers replaced merchants as city business leaders. The financial and business centers of the city expanded rapidly, and capital diversified. The city benefited culturally from these changes, as more capital for publishing houses led the city to eclipse Boston as the literary center of the United States. White-collar and semiskilled jobs increased and brought more people into the middle and upper classes.[29]

These changes triggered social transformations as well. A rapidly growing and more diverse population meant that religious and ethnic differences created divisions among many groups, including elites. The traditional Anglo-Protestant elite now found itself sharing leadership with German Catholics and Jews, while the rest of the city experienced increasing levels of segregation based on class and ethnicity. The historian David Hammack remarks, "Gradually but unmistakably the region's economic, social, cultural, and political resources were becoming more widely dispersed among its population as a whole." Although Hammack perceives divisions, especially within the powerful class to which the Curtis family belonged, other historians question the extent and consequences of this diversification of the elite classes. Sven Beckert notes the same types of transformations as Hammack but argues that elites found ways to consolidate their power despite their internal divisions. Beckert asserts that a "self-conscious upper class" coalesced following the Civil War. This elite forged "dense social networks, to create powerful social institutions and to articulate an increasingly coherent view of the world."[30] Edward Curtis, the son of an influential banker, an up-and-coming physician with degrees from Harvard and the University of Pennsylvania, and a member of several prominent organizations and clubs, surely claimed membership in the group described by Beckert. His status within New York City's upper middle class affected his daughter's experiences, opportunities, and options as certainly as it shaped her character and ideals.

Professionalization within the field of medicine allowed Edward Curtis to forge important social and economic ties within the elite networks of the city without directly following in his father's footsteps. He benefited from, and perhaps helped shape, changes in the medical profession in the late nineteenth century. The medical field stratified sharply in these years, with doctors like Curtis gaining access to the best schools, appointments, and medical societies. His specialized training enabled Edward Curtis, and others like him, to control entry into the profession and claim the high fees their specializations could demand. Elite physicians enjoyed the latest scientific developments and facilities and rose above their peers in terms of wealth, social prestige, and influence.[31]

Edward Curtis's medical career clearly demonstrates how he benefited from professionalization. Curtis received several important appointments in the city and taught at the College of Physicians and Surgeons. He also belonged to important medical societies at the national and local levels, memberships deemed "essential to an unequivocal professional status" that showed that a physician was "orthodox" in his practices. His appointment to the city's board of health, for example, allowed him to maintain his professional standing and strengthened his ties with political and business networks within the city.[32]

Curtis enhanced his participation in these networks by accepting employment at the Equitable Life Assurance Society as its medical director in the fall of 1876. The Equitable provided Curtis with additional income and security. Through founder Henry Baldwin Hyde's innovative policy plans and aggressive marketing techniques, the Equitable grew in just thirty years into the largest company of its kind.[33] Curtis's work there soon dominated his career, leading him to resign most of his positions in the medical field. His annual salary at the Equitable of $15,000, in addition to possible family resources from his father's estate, would have provided a comfortable, if not extravagant, lifestyle.[34]

The society in which Edward and Augusta raised their family was shaped by Edward's professional aspirations, his family ties, and the social life in which they participated. Clubs were integral to social aspiration in late-nineteenth-century New York City. New Yorkers could find clubs to suit every lifestyle and interest. Certain social clubs, however, catered to elites, served as status symbols, and fostered business connections. Professionals like Edward Curtis, who were not among the wealthiest of the city, could still gain entrance into elite worlds through such associations. Curtis belonged to the "fashionable and famous" Century, Harvard, Lawyer's, and Rockaway Hunting clubs. He also held memberships in Phi Beta Kappa, the New York County Medical Society, the Roman Medical Society, the Military Order of the Loyal Legion of the U.S., the Sons of the Revolution, the American Institute, and the Academy of Natural Sciences in Philadelphia.[35] Club life was important because, as Beckert writes, "cultural identifications would increasingly provide the glue that kept an expanded bourgeoisie together." Clubs provided "institutionalized networks" that united professionals with manufacturers, bankers, and other elite groups in the city. Membership overlapped among clubs, and members often socialized in outside settings, thus expanding social networks.[36]

Club membership, while just one facet of Curtis family life, provided a broad and complex network of social and cultural interaction in New York. By joining the Century Club, for example, Edward Curtis gained admission to a prestigious organization that promoted literature and the arts. Members included "most of the distinguished artists, authors and journalists" of the city and those in "professions akin to these pursuits." The Harvard Club helped to "promote social intercourse among the alumni resident in New York and vicinity," and the Lawyer's Club, a social group housed in the Equitable Building where Curtis worked, offered members a meeting room, a lunchroom, and a library. Besides social and cultural groups, Curtis joined organizations related to his professional and personal interests.[37] His club memberships solidified ties to other social and political elites and may have opened doors for other family members as well.

The home life of the Curtis family provided opportunities and experiences that allowed them to pursue lives unavailable to thousands of other New York residents. In the late nineteenth century traditional residential patterns, in which rich and poor lived in the same communities, gave way to more homogenous neighborhoods based on class. In New York exclusive neighborhoods developed, in part, because of the efforts of the middle and upper classes to distinguish themselves from their less affluent neighbors, surely part of the reason George Curtis elected to move his family to Washington Square. The Curtises resided in the family home at 27 Washington Place, an area considered a fashionable place for middle- and upper-class families to live.[38] Although the Washington Square area had declined by the 1870s from its former opulence as an enclave of the very wealthy, it still maintained an aura of respectability and refinement. Henry James commented that "this portion of New York appears to many persons the most delectable. It has a kind of established repose which is not of frequent occurrence in other quarters of the long, shrill city; it has a riper, richer, more honorable look than any of the upper ramifications of the great longitudinal thoroughfare — the look of having had something of a social history."[39] Observers found "a character peculiar to itself" as a refuge for "New York society" that had been driven from other areas of town by the lower classes. Washington Square contained rows of old-fashioned brick homes on the north side; the east side housed the University of the City of New York, a hospital, and homes of artists. A series of small shops for residents, old houses, and apartments constituted the south side, and "fine private residences and apartment-hotels," the Washington Memorial Arch, and a park marked the west side. During Natalie Curtis's childhood Washington Square was already taking on the artistic and bohemian characteristics for which the area would later be known.[40] This neighborhood, then, retained a certain nostalgia for its past, along with premonitions of a different sort of future, when the

Curtis family returned to Edward Curtis's childhood home. This mixture of conservative tradition and modernist tendencies surely influenced Natalie Curtis's development.

While her Washington Square home certainly shaped young Curtis's worldview, she could not avoid experiencing the crises posed by the broad transformations in American life during her early years. In fact, the year of Curtis's birth, 1876, marked a number of significant events emblematic of a changing American society. In this year Americans gathered in Philadelphia to celebrate their centennial and the progress, particularly technological and industrial, they had made in the last one hundred years. Underlying this celebratory mood, however, were growing concerns about the stability of their social, political, and economic order. The Centennial Exposition, as the historian Robert Rydell argues, "promised a diversion from endless accounts of political corruption in Washington, collapse of financial and mercantile establishments, and stories of working-class discontentment with the industrial system" and served as a "calculated response to these conditions."[41] In the years following the Civil War the United States underwent what some have called a "Second Industrial Revolution." These decades experienced pronounced economic growth that transformed American life. The nation made a significant transition from agrarian and small-shop manufacturing to a full-scale modern industrial economy. More Americans became wage earners, and fewer worked in agricultural enterprises. More and more workers moved from small, close-knit communities to large, anonymous urban centers. During these years the economy proved largely unstable, marked by a number of dramatic downturns, most notably the depression that began in 1873 and lasted until the late 1890s. The growing separation of the wealthy and the poor (and the concomitant fear of class warfare), the growing corruption and scandal in national and local politics, epitomized by New York's Boss Tweed, and the increase in ruthless business competition caused many Americans to fear the decline of their democratic traditions and worry that something was profoundly wrong with their society.

Organizers of the Centennial Exposition sought to alleviate these concerns through the fair's themes of progress, order, and patriotism. The elaborate opening ceremonies, which featured copious displays of American symbols, emphasized national unity, progress, and America's status as a chosen nation. Rydell describes the appeal of the fairgrounds, with their blend of exhibition halls (described as "colossal edifices"), fountains, and other displays, as "at once pastoral and heroic." Exhibits on American progress appealed to the very traditions many feared industrialization was displacing. The magnificent Corliss engine, which powered the Machinery Building, served as a symbol of future progress. Fair promoters clearly had economic priorities in mind as they designed exhibits that linked together the celebration of American greatness with the notion of continued economic development and social stability. Organizers not only addressed middle-class audiences but tried to attract members of the working classes to the fair. They hoped that by witnessing comparisons between the United States and other nations, workers would develop a greater appreciation for their relatively better status. The emphasis on progress and the future greatness of the American people was designed to mute rising concerns about the state of the nation's political, economic, and social standing.[42]

The Philadelphia exposition echoed the dominant mood toward nonwhite Americans and helped further solidify it. Displays from other nations, organized by race, privileged the countries of Western Europe. More significantly, exhibits featuring Native Americans reinforced ideas of savagery and decline. Rydell contends that organizers like Otis Mason, a professor at Columbia University in charge of the Smithsonian exhibit, reinforced the central belief that Native Americans "belonged to the interminable wasteland of humanity's dark and stormy beginnings." Mason and others deemed Indians useful only as counterparts to American society, the "antithesis to the forces of progress."[43] Fairgoers observed artifacts and living Native Americans through a hierarchical lens that placed tribal people perpetually in the past, excluded by evolutionary forces from participation in the modern world. Indians needed to vanish so they would no longer impede the material and commercial progress of white Americans. While Native Americans were on display at the fair, African Americans found few opportunities to participate. Organizers excluded black Americans from the planning process, refused requests for exhibits or displays, and discriminated against workers. The most prominent representations of African Americans associated them with displays of the American South and presented them as "old time plantation darkies" in singing groups. African Americans, the exhibits suggested, were childlike members of the human race and happy working in the South in their new economic and social position.[44] Other nonwhite peoples of the world found themselves similarly displayed. The fair reinforced racial hierarchies and linked them to themes of American economic progress.

Although the Centennial Exposition sought to allay rising concerns about the condition of the nation, many Americans continued to worry about America's future. Other significant events also marked the year of Curtis's birth, particularly in terms of race relations. The defeat in June of General George Armstrong Custer's troops by a contingent of Sioux and Cheyenne at the Battle of Little Big Horn shook the confidence of many. However, the Native American victory proved short-lived as the army and the so-called friends of the Indian continued the process of eradicating Indian land ownership and attempting to destroy tribal customs and practices. The passage of the 1887 Dawes Act expedited the assimilationist agenda of the government and reformers, and the massacre of Ghost Dancers at Wounded Knee in December 1890 ended Native military resistance.

The year 1876 also marked a transition for African American rights.

The presidential election, which pitted the Republican Rutherford B. Hayes against the Democrat Samuel J. Tilden, resulted in the infamous "Bargain of 1877," in which Hayes won the presidency and white Southern Democrats received promises of federal indifference toward their plans to end so-called black rule in their states. Northern Republicans, including Natalie Curtis's uncle George William, increasingly ignored the rights of African Americans in the South, choosing instead to focus on economic progress. Growing racism in the North and rising violence and terror against blacks in the South have led commentators to label this period the beginning of "the nadir" for black Americans.[45]

The historian John Higham observes that the tensions of the late nineteenth century were manifest both in popular culture and among American intellectuals. The movement toward increased physicality, expansiveness, and appreciation of nature, he argues, comprised the American response to the sense of psychological and spiritual decay supposedly resulting from the rise of an incorporated world.[46] Americans in the late nineteenth century struggled to come to terms with this changing world in a variety of ways. Although it may be a truism to say that each generation struggles to find its identity, the one into which Natalie Curtis was born faced a number of significant challenges in its attempts to make sense of national and personal identities. In Curtis's case she, like a number of her contemporaries, both drew from and challenged the ideas and examples of her family.

Although scholars have portrayed Natalie Curtis's generation as engaged in an effort to defy or even destroy the Victorian world of their parents, Curtis did not share fully in this project, at least not on a personal level.[47] As a young woman she fostered close bonds with each of her parents. She and "Bogey" developed a warm relationship. When Curtis was a young girl, her father took her to see the Italian operas he loved so much and the German operas she adored. He encouraged her musical inclinations on the piano and provided her

with the means for advanced study. Upon his death in 1912 friends
and relatives of the family expressed their understanding of the close-
ness Curtis and Edward shared. Katherine Chapin, a good friend
of Curtis, wrote about her recognition of the "vital part" Edward
played in his daughter's world and the "big place he held in your
life." Chapin understood the sacrifices Curtis had made to care for
her father before his death, "when the little girl he has taught and
loved could come back to comfort and understand him."[48] Curtis
had an even closer relationship with her mother. Augusta Lawler
Stacey Curtis, or "Mimsey," as her children affectionately called her,
played a significant role in all of her children's lives, but particularly
in Natalie's. Augusta hailed from a respected and well-connected
family in Chester, Pennsylvania, the great-granddaughter of a hero
of the Revolutionary War and the descendant of well-educated
and connected lawyers and politicians.[49] Augusta probably met her
husband while he attended medical school at the nearby University
of Pennsylvania. The two married on November 16, 1864, in her
hometown of Chester. Augusta shared a special relationship with
her sisters — Jeanette, Constance, and Natalie — and named two of
her daughters after them. Aunt Nat, as young Natalie Curtis knew
Natalie Stacey, pursued a career as a composer and as a pianist.
She encouraged her namesake in her musical ambitions. Natalie
Curtis's mother and her family remained a constant source of support and encouragement for young Curtis, particularly regarding
her musical inclinations.

The relationships between individual members of Curtis's family
profoundly affected her. She drew from examples set by her older
relatives and used their ideals as a foundation for her own life. Until
her death in 1921 she regularly corresponded and even traveled with
"Mimsey" and her siblings. Her family imparted in her a sense of
purpose and high ideals, especially a liberal outlook on race and
gender issues. They instilled in her a sense of responsibility to defend
the rights of oppressed peoples, especially African Americans and

women. Her family's Transcendentalist leanings encouraged her to look to other cultures and traditions for answers to her questions of spirituality and personal identity. Curtis also learned how music and art could affect lives and change society by witnessing her family's use of the written word and music to express political and social ideas. She grew up with the awareness of being a member of a privileged elite class, with all the attendant benefits and responsibilities. The America in which she was born faced unprecedented economic, social, and cultural transitions that provoked many questions but few concrete answers. The city of her youth served as an epicenter of these changes, its residents contending with these transformations on a greater scale than other Americans. For many these changes provoked a crisis of identity. Natalie Curtis came of age with these questions very much on her mind. Her nuclear and extended family experienced these transitions and drew upon the traditions and resources of earlier generations. While these experiences impacted Curtis profoundly, music always remained central to how she approached the concerns of her world.

2

"They Don't Know What Bliss Is!"

Curtis's Musical Adolescence

NATALIE CURTIS CAME OF AGE IN THE LAST TWO DECADES OF the nineteenth century. One is tempted to look at these formative years to discover clues as to why a privileged young woman from New York City would choose to study and promote the music of Native Americans and African Americans. Why did Curtis forsake a career in classical music to devote herself to musical traditions so unlike those of her youth? Were there seeds of change already planted and taking root while she was young? What experiences prepared her to embrace the music of America's marginalized "folk"? Although it is important to address these questions, if one were to focus solely on their answers, a significant part of her story would be lost. Curtis enjoyed a most interesting musical adolescence. Her passion for music allowed her to explore different facets of herself; the musical world gave her a means and a language through which to shape her identity as a young woman in the late nineteenth century.

Scholars seeking to understand the lives of young women in this period have raised important questions concerning how they shaped their identities and made choices. Helen L. Horowitz, in her study of the educator M. Carey Thomas, explores the impact reading had on Thomas as a youth: "Through reading she shaped an identity that . . . guided her personal relationships for the rest of her life. Through reading, M. Carey Thomas created herself."[1] Reading allowed Thomas to explore alternative paths otherwise unavailable to the young Quaker woman and gave her an outlet to express her aesthetic and personal passions. Thomas's reading, further, took place with her female peers, with whom she discussed and wrote about the new ideas she encountered. In much the same way Natalie Curtis's adolescence was shaped by her passion for music. Music became a means for Curtis to express her innermost feelings and explore facets of her identity. An examination of young Curtis's musical life therefore opens new ways for historians to understand identity formation among women of her generation.

In the same way that contemporaries like Thomas forged an identity through their reading, Natalie Curtis created and re-created herself through music. By sharing her musical experiences with her female peers Curtis found a means to express ideas about her gender, sexuality, spirituality, and intellect. Her intense devotion to the piano, her close association with the intellectual ideas of her instructors, and her avid participation in New York City's musical scene, as well as her opportunities to study music and travel abroad, all shaped Curtis's identity as a young American woman. Through the language of music she created ways to express her deepest thoughts, and she did this within a primarily female world. Her search for a personal identity as a young female musician eventually blended with a larger cultural search for an American musical expression in her earliest compositions. Her musical training and experiences prepared Curtis for her career as an ethnomusicologist, but they did not necessarily predict this path for her. Instead these formative events in her life provided Curtis with many options, many other roads she might have traveled instead. Her turn to Native American and African American music was not so much a departure from her earliest search for an American identity as an extension of it.

NATALIE CURTIS SPENT HER ADOLESCENCE AT THE "OLD family home" at 27 Washington Place in New York City, guided by her family's influence. Curtis's family members established a foundation for her that encouraged her to think broadly and act boldly, and they provided the financial and emotional support for her undertakings. She attended the Brearly School, a female private institution that offered a college-preparatory curriculum. She also studied music, took lessons in piano and singing, and participated in the city's musical scene. Her family shared Curtis's love of music, even if it occasionally interfered with her schoolwork. She and her father, "Bogey," who unlike his daughter preferred the Italian operas so popular during his youth, attended German musical dramas at the Metropolitan Opera House. Curtis's brother George recalled his sister's passion for this music. "A lameness in one knee at the time caused her to use a crutch," he remembered, "and often her enthusiasm led her to pound out applause so long and vehemently that her father had to take the crutch out of her hands." At times Curtis would be so overcome with emotional exertion from a night at the opera that she could not attend school the next day.[2]

She also shared her musical experiences with close friends, particularly a fellow New Yorker named Elizabeth Day, or Bessie, as she preferred. Even after Day's family moved to New Haven in 1888 the two young women shared a number of golden days in New York's concert halls and opera houses and in each other's homes. The Curtis family embraced Day (Edward insisted she call him "Uncle Ned"), and the girls' friendship was perhaps strengthened through their frequent correspondence between 1889 and 1893. Their mutual passion for Wagner, their adolescent infatuations with leading conductors and performers in the city, and their mutually supportive friendship bound the two women together. To an extent

Bessie Day and Natalie Curtis's bond epitomizes the female relationships described by Caroll Smith-Rosenberg. The two young women
shared a close relationship and often strongly expressed their love
for each other. They inhabited a world of women: although they
often interacted with men on their forays into New York's musical
scene, they did so within groups of women. In Curtis's case this
occurred either with friends like Day or with older relatives like
Aunt Natalie or "Mimsey," as she called her mother, Augusta. Quite
often these relationships were bound together by correspondence.[3]
Bessie Day and Natalie Curtis, further, were "New Women," and
their correspondence reveals the passions, anxieties, and questions
typical of their generation. Music allowed them to discuss their
changing world and helped them articulate personal identities.

Like Curtis, Bessie Day took music lessons, and the two took
pleasure in exchanging stories of their tribulations and triumphs.
Musical training at the time often began as early as age four or five,
with educational guides recommending that children this young
begin to learn the basics of rhythm, tone, and melody. After age six
children possessing the desire to take up music, and the good health
to pursue it, were encouraged to begin a plan of study that developed
proper techniques and instilled a deeper understanding of music
theory. Music educators recommended finding the proper teacher
and offered advice on making this difficult decision. These guides
promoted piano study for all beginning music students. Age five or
six was considered an acceptable time to begin to study the piano,
and educators urged parents to combine this with harmony lessons
and performances for friends and family.[4] Considering the pieces
of music Natalie Curtis attempted as a teenager and the caliber of
her music teachers, Edward and Augusta must have heeded such
advice when Curtis began to study music at an early age.

Considered an important social grace for upper- and middle-
class girls, the piano became a fixture in many Victorian homes.
Ideas about the piano were directly tied to the prevalent domestic

ideology; piano-playing women were expected to "instill a love for culture" in their homes and to uplift their families with their music. As Craig Roell asserts, people "associated [the piano] with the virtues attributed to music as medicine for the soul" and further linked it to the Victorian values of "toil, sacrifice, and perseverance."[5] Women were expected to play the piano because it properly molded their character and enhanced their role as society's nurturers. Piano playing, while hard work, brought happiness into the home and served as an acceptable outlet for women's artistic ambitions.

Natalie Curtis's dedication to the piano and her ambition to achieve professional mastery fell both within and outside of the established norms for young women at the time. Middle-class Victorians expected their daughters to play the piano, their facility considered a social grace. The almost torturous practice schedules foisted upon young women, however, made little distinction between "whether the pupil aspired to a concert career or [to] merely enhanced social graces."[6] The predominant method of teaching, the "Klavier Schule," required several hours of practice daily. In a culture that valued hard work, even in leisure, hours of piano practice were accepted as a fitting way to instill proper values and impart a skill to young women.

Curtis's devotion to the piano, however, went much deeper than this. She did not learn to play in order to snag the best husband, uplift her family, or develop an appreciation for hard work. Perhaps her parents initially agreed to piano lessons because they seemed proper for a young lady of their social class, but Curtis's devotion to music led her to pursue much more rigorous study. Developments in music education for women in the last few decades of the nineteenth century aided Curtis in her pursuits. As women in greater numbers demanded music education, the quality of their instruction improved. Private teachers and conservatories began offering more advanced courses in theory, harmony, counterpoint, ensemble singing, and music history. The successful tours of European female musicians, such as the "Swedish Nightingale" Jenny Lind, helped establish a new pattern of early training in the United States and study and a debut in Europe, followed by a return to America.[7] As a teenager Curtis studied with private instructors and attended conservatories in the United States and Europe. Clearly her devotion to music was strong, and the training she acquired served her well her entire life.

The arduous practice schedule that Curtis adopted for herself far exceeded the demands or goals of standard piano instruction. A typical summer day for Curtis consisted of several hours of practice: one hour on the first two pages of a Liszt waltz, one hour on Bach, another hour working on special exercises, and yet another hour playing for friends. Curtis practiced so often that she had to get a clavier — a keyboard instrument that produced a more muted sound — to appease her family, who grew weary of her constant playing. Curtis indeed practiced "so much that the family have '*struck*'" and greeted her piano playing with "wild whoops from upstairs and voices shrieking 'You are driving me perfectly *crazy*! Do stop!'" During the 1892–93 season Curtis practiced so hard that she coerced her younger sister into taking dictation so she could still play while composing letters to her friend. Curtis later purchased a techniphone, a practice keyboard that made only soft clicks and probably kept the rest of the Curtis family sane. Her incessant practice, although an occasional annoyance to her family, clearly demonstrated her commitment to mastering her instrument.[8]

Her desire for a career as a musician explains Curtis's intense devotion to her practice schedule. Curtis was not alone; other young women also studied music because it offered one of the few outlets for a career. Music critics recommended five to ten hours of daily practice for women desiring to become professionals. Several styles of playing were deemed a must, as was one or two years of study at a seminary.[9] Others had paved the way for Curtis to pursue a professional music career. Amy Fay, the author of *Music-Study in*

Germany, took piano training in Germany in the 1870s. In her letters from this period Fay wrote of practicing for five or six hours daily, only cutting back to three or four while vacationing. Fay's typical day resembled Curtis's: four hours of piano practice in the morning, a brief meal, several hours of instruction at the studio of Franz Liszt, and occasional recitals for friends and family.[10]

The often limited opportunities for a young woman to have a career as a professional musician may have caused Curtis's family to question her choice to postpone marriage and family for the uncertainties of a musician's life, but Curtis could turn to Bessie Day to contemplate her concerns with a sympathetic friend. These two confidantes shared their ideas about the proper role of women in society and as musicians. Undoubtedly they were influenced by the rise of the "New Woman" at the end of the nineteenth century, when many Americans debated the role women should play in modern society. Music commentators wondered how the "New Woman" would shape American music. Could women compose art music or merely parlor tunes? Could respectable women perform publicly? Should married women continue a career in music? Some even pondered whether a woman could play the cello without losing her virtue.

Curtis devised her own answers to these questions. As she intensified her musical studies and began to plan for her future, she confided to Day:

> I don't know myself, but I want to have a kind of profession just as a man would, so that I could be perfectly independent. Don't you think that it would be awful to feel as some girls do that they *must* marry? Just as though they were so many cows! And not only that, but as Clara Lincoln [a family friend] said, "What can you do if you *don't* marry? Why your life is blank! It is different with you though," she added, "because you have your music, and if all your family died, even you wouldn't be lonely." I think every girl ought to have

something — study a sort of profession, as it were, even though she need never practice it, don't you?[11]

Her belief that a young woman had the right, even the duty, to maintain an independent lifestyle emboldened her to pursue a rigorous course of study in music and to later maintain that independence through her writing and research on Native American and African American music. Her ideas on the relationship between music and gender encouraged her to broaden her music education.

Curtis rounded out her musical training through voice study and lessons in music theory. She sang in local choral ensembles and practiced singing regularly. For instance, in the winter of 1891–92 Curtis auditioned for Anton Seidl's festival chorus, which would sing at the celebration of the New York Philharmonic's fiftieth anniversary. Seidl's secretary informed Curtis that she possessed a lovely voice and gave her a spot in the chorus. She also landed a solo at the pupils' concert at the National Conservatory, where she took lessons. Curtis felt elated and lucky, remarking to Day, "All I need now is to fall in love to accomplish the final combustions." She had apparently overcome earlier voice problems. Previously she had informed Day of throat treatments administered by a Dr. Asch, "who is burning, spraying, and hacking me to pieces by degrees." She maintained a strenuous schedule the following year, with two harmony lessons a week, a choral singing class, practice for the Conservatory Chorus, and a regular four or five hours of piano practice each day, plus tickets "for almost all the concerts and *countless* other engagements." She often played for friends and family, including an evening at a Mrs. Coriswald's during which Curtis "banged the box for the edification of a vast multitude of fashionables and professionals."[12]

Amy Fay recommended that the aspiring professional study with several different teachers, and she herself sought out the best instructors she could find. Curtis followed Fay's advice. She began study under William Semnacher, a German pianist who had begun teaching in America in the late 1860s after extensive training in Europe. He briefly held a professorship at the New York Conservatory, but after 1879 he focused exclusively on private instruction. The *American Art Journal* praised Curtis's teacher, remarking, "Mr. Semnacher has been imminently successful by adapting his method to the individuality of his pupils, who consequently make thorough and rapid progress."[13] A noted teacher, perhaps, but not a virtuoso performer, he catered to the needs of upper- and middle-class families who mainly wanted their daughters to acquire a valued social grace. Since Curtis instead aspired for professional mastery of the piano, she, like Fay, began to seek out better-known piano instructors who would provide her with the skills and prestige needed to enter the realm of professional music.

Curtis, then, was thrilled at the prospect of studying with Arthur Friedham, a German pianist, composer, and teacher who was touted as the best interpreter of the works of Franz Liszt. Prior to beginning lessons with Friedham, Curtis, along with several friends, attended one of his recitals. She confided later to Day that she had worked herself up to a state of "nervous prostration when Friedham came on" and that she clutched her friend Angela throughout his performance. Curtis also complained that Mimsey and a family friend "had the giggles all the way through" Friedham's performance. The giggles did not prevent Curtis from enjoying the recital. She felt that Friedham played beautifully but that the composition was beneath his real abilities. She seemed relieved that he had played well and thankful to Angela for helping her endure the emotional intensity of the recital.[14] Curtis left feeling a bit more confident in her decision to begin study with her new teacher.

She spent her first summer of study under Friedham commuting to his studio from the family's summer home. For the summer of 1892 the Curtises packed up their Washington Square home and headed for their summerhouse, "The Moorings," in Far Rockaway on Long

Island. In the second half of the nineteenth century improved ferry and train services allowed more upper- and middle-class families to spend their summers and vacations on the shores of Long Island. Far Rockaway had long been home to one of the few nineteenth-century resort hotels in the United States. The development of leisure activities in the area, such as fox hunting (Edward Curtis belonged to the Rockaway Hunting Club) and other equestrian activities, golfing, and yachting, drew many to the island. Residents could, according to one historian, "experience country life without losing contact with developments in the city and office."[15] The entire Curtis family spent their summers in Rockaway and participated fully in the social and cultural life of the area. As she readied the house for their departure, Natalie Curtis discussed her summer plans with Bessie Day. Foremost among her thoughts were the upcoming piano lessons with Friedham and her incessant fears that she would disappoint the noted pianist.

Curtis devoted much of the summer to developing her skills on the piano through her lessons with Friedham and the demanding practice schedule she adopted. Fortunately she made a favorable impression on Friedham at their first meeting. She and Mimsey arrived at his apartment for her first lesson and waited for him in the music room. "It is very good of you to give me lessons," Curtis greeted him modestly. "I am only a beginner." Friedham's shocked expression prompted Mimsey to explain that Natalie was not a beginner, but only thought of herself as one. Friedham continued to look nervous, talking rapidly, his eyes flitting about the room, until Mimsey suggested that Natalie play for him. Curtis later boasted that "down I sat, never more cool and self-possessed in my life." As she played Friedham came over, leaned on the piano with a pencil in his mouth, and nodded or grunted an occasional approval. Finally he uttered, "Very nice." He asked Curtis to play something modern. She played a work by Ignace Paderewski with the same level of self-possession. Friedham assured Curtis at the lesson's end that she certainly was not a beginner and promised to give her lots of work that summer.[16]

Curtis devoted herself to an arduous practice schedule under Friedham. On some days she would practice for six to seven hours. Although Curtis seemed satisfied with Friedham's methods of instruction, she occasionally suffered from bouts of illness and self-doubt that threatened to impede her musical progress. At times she was too weak to play and feared falling behind in her lessons. She continued to practice anyway, despite her father's fears that a summer cold could worsen into something more serious. Once her mother intervened — "the Bird struck," Curtis complained as she was sent off to the Berkshire Hills to recuperate. At other times Curtis managed to practice and attend lessons by dosing "myself with brandy and strong coffee" before a lesson. Curtis occasionally complained of her perceived lack of progress as Friedham's pupil. She lamented to Day, "If there is anything discouraging it is to have him play a thing for you and then have to sit down and play it yourself *just* afterwards." Curtis aspired to achieve the skill of her teacher but despaired, "Why is it that I can never get things to sound finished and artistic, that every little point should stick out and all my crescendos and diminuendos sound exaggerated and unnatural?" She found Friedham very particular and exacting, not letting a single mistake go unnoticed. Before Curtis had felt as if she "slobbered over things so," but with Friedham's high standards she could feel herself turning into an artist. She told Day: "When I'm at my lessons . . . I am not Natalie Curtis at all, but just a medium for F[riedham]'s mind. His individuality is so strong, that I seem merged with it completely." Curtis believed that she played differently when with her teacher, and she especially enjoyed the moments when he played selections for her.[17]

As Friedham piled on the work Curtis came to respect him and his opinions even more. His assertion that "a musician nowadays must be an *educated man*" struck Curtis as particularly important.

Friedham had a significant impact on her development technically as a pianist but also, more generally, as an artist. Curtis often related to Day her interesting talks with her teacher about French art, modern impressionism, Franz Liszt, politics, and literature. She took to heart his admonition that to be a modern musician one must acquire a broad education, especially if one were to grasp the philosophical meanings in the works of composers like Liszt and Wagner. Curtis often mentioned to Day the books or articles she was reading, sending them to her so the two could discuss them. Curtis read Goethe, Tennyson, and Keats, among others, and even tackled the works of the philosopher Arthur Schopenhauer, who had influenced Wagner's dramatic ideas. During that summer and others she expanded her intellectual horizons by reading widely and conversing with a diverse group of people. Although Curtis believed she had improved her piano playing over the summer, she continued to feel like a beginner in many ways. When some friends related the gossip that Friedham only took a few talented students and that he had praised her at a recent social function, Curtis was overjoyed. "I was just beginning to be frightfully discouraged," she wrote Day, "and I was sure that F[riedham] thought me a *perfect fool!*" Relieved by this news Curtis delved into her practice with renewed vigor: "I feel that I am *learning, learning, learning,* and I am *happy, happy, happy!*"[18]

Her happiness seemed to go far deeper than receiving Friedham's approval. It had a great deal to do with being able to see herself as an artist with her own talents, ideas, and identity. Her next music teacher, Ferruccio Busoni, continued where Friedham left off. Busoni, a friend of Friedham and a fellow pupil of Franz Liszt, was an Italian pianist and composer who lived in the United States from 1891 to 1894 and returned later for concert tours. He has been described as "one of the towering pianists of the era" and as "a moderate progressive artist during the stylistic transition between the late romantic era to the early twentieth century." The dominant German influence in America made study with Busoni attractive.

In 1891 he began teaching at the New England Conservatory but became frustrated and resigned in the fall of 1892. Lacking funds to return to Europe, Busoni moved to New York City in 1893 and began teaching and performing. He privately taught a number of students and gave harmony lessons to Curtis.[19]

Busoni became recognized as an important, if rather unconventional, music teacher. Between 1888 and 1924 "generations of rising pianists and composers passed through his hands, people of various nationalities and different mentalities, both men and women." His students shared a powerful devotion to music and other arts. They were "musicians of very high intellectual standards, often conspicuously creative themselves, many of them scholars and writers whose accounts and reminiscences have considerable literary value." To be a Busoni student it was "not enough to play the piano exceedingly well or to be technically good at composition. One had to become an artist in his sense of the word." This meant achieving a unity of feeling for all aspects of art, music, and literature. Busoni expected his students to understand music as artists and stressed the nontechnical aspects of the discipline. "Phrasing, tone-color and tone quality were always Busoni's main concern," one student remembered.[20]

Busoni's focus on the intellectual and emotional aspects of music appealed to Curtis. Busoni taught, according to one biographer, because "teaching, more than any other professional activity, fulfilled a basic need to communicate."[21] Curtis's close relationship with Friedham suggests that she appreciated and flourished under this type of instruction. Busoni, who tended to prefer independent students who would benefit from his emphasis on the abstract over the technical, must have appreciated a hardworking and intelligent pupil like Curtis. Later in their lives the two corresponded regularly on Curtis's work collecting Native American music, and Busoni composed Indianist compositions based on her collections, which he dedicated to his former student.

While Curtis benefited from her musical training under Friedham and Busoni, her participation in New York's musical world also contributed to her ideas about her identity as a woman and an artist. Her formal training was enhanced, and often surpassed, by her enthusiastic participation in the city's musical scene. Here, particularly through her response to Wagner's musical dramas and close relationships with New York's leading musicians, Curtis further developed her sense of self and found ways to use the language of music to contemplate important issues, particularly those related to gender and spirituality. Curtis's boundless enthusiasm for the New York music scene also shaped her relationships with family and friends. As the 1890 musical season geared up, Curtis could barely contain her excitement at the prospect of seeing and hearing the music she loved so well. She pleaded with Bessie Day repeatedly to visit so they could take in these musical delights together. Curtis possessed a keen knowledge of the dates of concerts and opera performances, ticket information, and train schedules and continually attempted to make plans with her friend. A typical enticement Curtis offered went as follows:

WEDNESDAY AFTERNOON — symphony lectures
WEDNESDAY EVENING — "Siegfried"
THURSDAY AFTERNOON — de Pachmann
THURSDAY EVENING — maybe rehearsal
    of "The Damnation of Faust"
FRIDAY AFTERNOON — public rehearsal of symphony
FRIDAY EVENING — free
SATURDAY AFTERNOON — Siegfried
SATURDAY EVENING — symphony concert

"This is for the first week," Curtis tempted her friend, "*can* you resist?"[22]

It certainly would have been difficult for Curtis or Day to resist all that the city's musicians had to offer. The second half of the nineteenth century was an exciting time of growth and development for New York's music scene. The city's musical life had grown up along with the city. As New York's population expanded in the 1820s, more immigrants arrived who appreciated music and wanted to ply their skills as musicians. The numbers of theater musicians and music teachers thus multiplied over the course of the century. When European refugees of the upheavals of 1848 arrived, they brought along the classical works of Beethoven and Mendelssohn, as well as more modern works by Wagner and Liszt. Individual conductors like Theodore Thomas and Leopold Damrosch labored to raise American standards but were often forced to rely on the support of wealthy patrons when box office sales did not cover the expenses of their undertakings. Influential musicians and their benefactors created many important institutions, like the New York Symphony (1878) and the Metropolitan Opera House (1883), in the three decades prior to 1900.[23]

As New York attracted a growing number of talented musicians, Curtis seemed quite capable of meeting and even befriending them. In fact, she once remarked to Day, after speaking with Anton Seidl after a rehearsal, "You know I don't get a bit trembly at musicians anymore — I think I'm getting used to them." Letters to Day also mentioned meeting other famous or significant figures in the New York musical scene. Curtis spoke to the pianist Amy Fay on the street and sent flowers and letters to the opera star Lilli Lehmann. She even barged into the dressing room of the operatic bass Jean de Rezke to discuss a young Italian tenor in whose career Curtis had taken a sudden interest.[24] In another instance Curtis's meeting with a musician while on a family vacation at "the Moorings" proved eye-opening. During the summer of 1890 Curtis met Gertrude Cowdin, a fellow pianist, who studied with Francis Alexander Korbay, a Hungarian tenor, pianist, and composer and a student of Franz Liszt. Korbay had arrived in America in 1871 and survived mainly as a piano and voice teacher and as an occasional recital performer.

Cowdin invited Curtis to the home of Mrs. Draper for dinner and for the opportunity to meet Korbay and Vladimir de Pachmann, as well. The Russian pianist Pachmann was known for his "velvety touch" and for his skillful rendition of Chopin's works. He was also rumored to have an eccentric personality, and in his meeting with Curtis he did not disappoint. After dinner she was scandalized to learn that Pachmann did not even care for the works of Chopin but only played them to please the public. He, like Korbay (who, Curtis gossiped to Day, was "said by some to be his [Liszt's] son"), favored Liszt. Korbay's wife also played the piano, and Pachmann insisted that she play a Liszt song. Dragging her to the piano, Pachmann forced her to play but was unsatisfied with her performance. Much to Curtis's horror and amazement, Pachmann screamed that he could not bear to hear "such trash!" A violent argument ensued in which Pachmann was so unruly and foulmouthed that the others locked him in a room.[25] As Curtis recounted the excitement of that night to Day, she seemed simultaneously thrilled and appalled to have witnessed such a scene. This incident, along with others, added both to Curtis's understanding and to her questioning of the nature of the musical world.

As an aspiring musician interacting with some of the better-known artists of her day, Curtis shared her developing insights with Day: "I think that if I were great, I should be tempted not to defile my mind by coarse or uncongenial surroundings but, as Emerson says, shut myself up along with my own mind in order to give it pure and perfect expression." Perhaps the Pachmann debacle prompted Curtis to ponder the relationship between art and ethics. "You would think that an artist of any kind would be a person of the highest moral standard," Curtis wrote. "But they are not; and as a rule they are the most immoral lot. If you are an artist you have no morals. And if you are strictly moral you are either a dry old parson or a prig[gish?] old man with no art in you." These experiences prodded Curtis to question her own identity as a musician.[26]

As Curtis grew more accustomed to New York's musical world, she found a critical voice in which to discuss it. Music provided her with a language through which she could assert her authority as a musician and express her ideas as an artist. She took the study and critique of music quite seriously, carrying a blank notebook to concerts and operas to record her impressions during intermissions and between acts. Although Curtis felt that her jottings were often "the most ridiculous things to read over afterwards," she nevertheless offered to share her notes with Day. A sampling of Curtis's reactions to the operas and concerts she attended reveal the sharpening of her critical facilities. She deemed Baron Alberto Franchetti's *Asrael*, at the Metropolitan, which premiered on November 26, 1890, the "weirdest, most mixed-up sort of thing I have ever heard," an assessment shared by the professional critic Henry Krehbiel, who deemed it a "sup of horrors."[27] Later that season Curtis warned Day that if she wanted "to endure an evening of anguish, go and hear Mielke *try* to sing Brünnhilde in *Götterdämmerung*." Her performance was "simply flat, stupid, and rank!" Curtis complained. She found Emil Fischer, a German operatic bass, to be a "thorough artist" who helped assuage some of her disappointment. She saw Fischer again in *Parsifal*, Wagner's opera about medieval knights of the Holy Grail, which Curtis deemed "divine," except again for the unsatisfactory performance by Antonia Mielke. She and Mimsey heard the Boston Symphony Orchestra in January 1891, a performance that thoroughly fulfilled Curtis's high expectations. Curtis admired the style of Arthur Nikisch, the Hungarian conductor of the Boston orchestra between 1889 and 1893, who was "all suppressed passion" as he conducted. She found the Polish violinist Timothie Adamowski a beautiful player but could not resist gossiping to Day that he was "quite a society man and an inveterate flirt." Curtis's attendance at *L'Africaine* again afforded her the chance to hone her critical skills. "What rot!" she exclaimed. "It was so exactly like a circus." The performances by the baritone Reichmann and the bass

Fischer were good, but Minnie Hawk's "high-notes were just like a cat's," and a duet in the fourth act was "simply ridiculous." Although often harshly critical of performances she disliked, Curtis used these experiences to articulate her own artistic voice.[28]

Curtis's developing critical sense that season may have been inspired by a chance meeting with the music critic Henry Krehbiel. Krehbiel, an author, editor, and lecturer, wrote for the *New York Tribune* and championed the works of composers such as Brahms, Tchaikovsky, Wagner, and Dvořák. His well-known lectures and program annotations helped the public better understand and appreciate art music. One historian writes of Krehbiel, "No subsequent New York critic played so influential a role within the city's community of artists — and no subsequent critic so deserved such a role."[29] Curtis and her mother attended one of Krehbiel's lectures on the New York Philharmonic's program, Wagner's *Parsifal*, and the Grail myths. After the lecture the two Curtis women were presented to Krehbiel, and Natalie Curtis mentioned her piano lessons with Arthur Friedham. The esteemed music critic responded, "Are *you* the little Miss Curtis?" Curtis was mortified. "He must think I'm about two!" she cried to Day. The conversation improved when Krehbiel mentioned Friedham's enthusiasm about Curtis's progress. After their next meeting with Krehbiel, Curtis remarked, "Mimsey and I like him *so* much."[30]

Meeting Krehbiel excited Curtis and allowed her to envision herself, perhaps in the near future, as a professional musician. Spending time with well-known artists nourished her feelings of artistic maturity. These expanded in November 1891 when Curtis gushed to Day, "Just think, Bessie! I've *met him*! Did you ever hear of such luck?"[31] She had met Ignace Paderewski, a Polish composer and virtuoso pianist who made his American debut in Carnegie Hall on November 17, 1891. He had gained renown in European cities for his enthralling style and stunning appearance. His music excited listeners and reminded some of older masters like Liszt and Rubenstein.

Commentators described his piano as sounding "like an orchestra," declaring that "the notes seem to come from different places of the hall" and that the piano would "sing and a human voice seems to rise from it." Paderewski sported a large bush of reddish yellow hair and affected an appearance that "looked artistic but not Bohemian." American audiences responded enthusiastically to the pianist. He gave 18 recitals in New York City and another 117 elsewhere on his first American tour. Paderewski charmed his audiences, and the "custom of women rushing to the platform and surrounding him, inaugurated in London, was also adopted in New York." His charm, frankness, intellect, and optimism made people "almost as eager to converse with him as to listen to his playing."[32]

Curtis had been eager to experience Paderewski's playing and to meet him in person. "I almost *died* at Paderewski last night and after it was over I was simply sick with emotion," she reported to Day. After the encore Curtis spied the conductor Walter Damrosch making a beeline for a little door that led to the dressing rooms that were already filling with Paderewski's admirers. Curtis purposefully walked past the door and sighed, "Oh! How I should like to meet him!" Her aunt Natalie suggested that she ask Damrosch to make the introduction, but Curtis suddenly lost heart and decided to leave. Her aunt called her a "darned fool" because she missed Damrosch's attempts to make eye contact with them. As the house lights dimmed and they neared the exit, "a spirit of desperation seized" Curtis, and she decided to return. Aunt Nat, frustrated with the emotional whims of her niece, suggested they just go home. Once Curtis made up her mind, though, there was no stopping her. Curtis "grabbed *hold* of her and dragged her back into the hall again by the hair of her head. As I said I was *desperate* and so excited that I hardly knew what I was doing." Curtis braced herself for the big moment as she entered the room. Damrosch greeted her warmly and agreed to introduce her to Paderewski. Holding Curtis's hand, much to her youthful excitement, Damrosch said to the pianist, "I want to present to you a *most talented* young lady." They shook hands, bowed, and Curtis addressed him in German. She confessed to Day, "I hardly knew what I was saying; it was somebody else talking." She then thanked Damrosch for the introduction, "flung myself upon Aunt Nat, ecstacized [*sic*] all the way home and couldn't remember when I reached the house, *which* side the bell was on to save my life."[33]

Curtis raved to Day about her experiences with Paderewski and especially the impact of his playing. "He plays me *sick*, every time I go to hear him," she swooned. After his performance Curtis felt "as used up as though my whole fat body had been dragged through the eye of a needle." Curtis and Mimsey attended another Paderewski recital a few days later in which he "played like a *god*." After the performance they spied Paderewski drinking beer in a separate room with other men. Upon learning that the room was not just for men the two Curtis women boldly entered and asked to be presented to the virtuoso. Paderewski eyed Curtis up and down before asking, "You also, are very fond of music, are you not?" "I am devoted to it," Curtis gushed, "but when I hear you play, I don't want to even touch the *pedals* again!" Curtis, relieved that Paderewski remembered her, discussed with him music and her trip to Bayreuth that summer.[34]

As much as Curtis gloried in her meeting with Paderewski, her greatest passion was for Wagner's musical dramas and the conductors who brought them to the American public. Opera was central to young Curtis's musical enjoyment and became an important facet of New York's musical climate in the 1880s and 1890s. New Yorkers had enjoyed English, French, and Italian operas since the late 1830s, but by the 1880s German-language operas were performed more often. German opera became more popular in New York for many reasons. For one thing, German immigrants brought with them rich cultural traditions and pride in their German heritage and by the 1860s had firmly ensconced German opera in their communities.

Occasional German operas were performed for non-German audiences at Niblo's Garden and the Stadt Theater. Further, with the rise of new money and the creation of vast fortunes that accompanied the growth of New York industry and commerce, a new leisure class formed that found an appropriate highbrow outlet in opera. The New York Academy of Music initially provided the wealthy with a place to see and be seen, but the "old" money was reluctant to share space with the newly rich. The newly rich responded by constructing their own opera house, the Metropolitan, with twice as many boxes, in which they could freely express their conspicuous consumption. The music historian John Dizikes notes: "Musically, it [New York's plutocracy] barely supported one opera house. Socially, it needed two." The Met did not fare well in the mid-1880s until, under the inspiration of Leopold Damrosch and later Anton Seidl, it began offering full seasons of German opera. By this time the public had begun to demand entire performances of Wagner's works.[35]

In the late 1880s and early 1890s New York City offered a feast to fans of the composer. The Metropolitan Opera House began offering German operas in 1884, when Leopold Damrosch organized and recruited the most talented Wagnerian performers. His hard work favorably reversed the fortunes of the Metropolitan and brought a new audience of "musically knowledgeable, serious listeners" like young Natalie Curtis and Bessie Day. The strain of his successful endeavor proved too much for Damrosch, who died of pneumonia in February of 1885. His son, Walter, took his place and helped the Metropolitan recruit Seidl as its new conductor. Seidl, a Hungarian conductor and Wagnerite, arrived in the United States in 1885. In addition to conducting he participated in the largely female-sponsored Seidl Society, which provided affordable concerts by the seashore that Curtis often attended. Although the orchestra played lighter fare for the summer, Seidl firmly held to his conviction to introduce the public to high-quality works and modern pieces. Among other things he enjoyed tremendous success dur-

ing the next six years at the Metropolitan staging performances of
Wagner's music dramas.[36]

Wagner's works and ideas were first introduced to Americans
through print — in debates over his operatic ideas — not through
actual performances. Americans "identified Wagner with something
profound," according to Dizikes. Americans related to Wagner's efforts
to stake out new territory in the musical world. Wagner wanted to
change the nature of opera by stressing the primacy of words before
music through his concept of the musical drama. He harkened back
to the Greeks for inspiration, believing that they drew "on myth
while celebrating human life" and that they combined all the arts
into a cohesive wholeness. Wagner argued that his works reintegrated
the arts, went beyond mere entertainment, and could become a
new religion. Dizikes explains that in Wagner's work "music and
words combine indissolubly." There are "no more songs, duets,
quartets breaking up the drama. No more vitriolic display." These
are replaced by a drama of "unbroken exposition, unbroken melody,
not contemptible mere tunes." Everything becomes "a seamless
fabric, with the orchestra woven into the center."[37]

Wagnerian operas also became popular because Wagner's works
spoke to Americans undergoing rapid change and discontinuity in
their society. Joseph Horowitz writes, "If Wagnerism had a core, it
was a core of disillusionment with the status quo, with the industrial
revolution and its legacy of science, technology, and allegedly sterile
rationality." He further argues that the Gilded Age's "custodians
of culture" helped Americanize Wagner in such a way that he was
not perceived, as he was in Europe, as "decadent, modernist, or
politically risqué." In the United States his music instead became
"distinctively humanist, an antidote to materialism, scientism and
urban anomie."[38] This understanding of Wagner sheds light on his
appeal to young Curtis, who later engaged in a similar search for
antidotes to American modernism.

Curtis counted herself among the adherents of this new religion of Wagner and joined the audience of serious, knowledgeable opera-goers who flocked to performances of his work. In America, women constituted a much larger proportion of Wagner's audiences than in Europe. Some have contended that women's interest in Wagner's operas in New York had a great deal to do with the personal mag-netism of Wagner's best-known conductor, Seidl. Always "poised and mysterious, undemonstrative and impassioned," Seidl cut a striking figure with his "Gothic features, and flowing hair." Walter Damrosch, another popular Wagnerian conductor, also attracted the attention of women audience members. As much as some would have liked to dismiss women's devotion to Wagner performances in New York as just so much obsession and emotionality, the appeal of his works went much deeper. Women at Wagner performances sat "transfixed and transformed" as they partook of one of the few "intense experiences" available to them. In the darkened opera hall the "bad effects of husband and bedroom were silenced by a musical-dramatic orgasm as explicit and complete as any mortal intercourse," writes Horowitz. The ritual of attending a Wagnerian musical drama provided American women with a powerful emo-tional outlet denied them in other areas of their lives. The characters themselves seemed to speak directly to Wagner's women fans. As Horowitz comments, "In sum, Wagner's powerfully and compassion-ately drawn women — muses and helpmates, scourges and heroines, victims and saviors — conflate aspects of Romantic sentimentality with intimations of the new modernism."[39] Gilded Age women sought to reconcile Victorian domestic ideology with the role of the "New Woman." Wagner provided a language in which young women like Curtis and Day could formulate their identities.

Curtis often mingled her passion for Wagner with her feelings toward Walter Damrosch. She and Day used "It," as they secretly called Damrosch, as a way to clandestinely discuss more forbidden topics like sexuality. When the Metropolitan appointed Seidl to replace Walter Damrosch's father and left young Walter in a secondary role as Seidl's assistant, he felt "great sorrow and anguish of heart."[40] Walter managed to retain a place for himself by conducting, lecturing, and composing. Although Curtis adored him, not everyone shared her assessment. As Horowitz writes, "While his poise was admired, and while his podium career would span six decades, Walter Damrosch was never a major conductor, and his rise was rapidly squelched."[41] This of course lay in the future, and at the time Curtis knew him best Damrosch commanded respect and influence in many circles. His handsome appearance was often cited as the reason for his support among women audience members. The *Musical Courier*, for example, reviewed his conducting: "No more amusing sight can be imagined," the reviewer intoned, "than this youthful Adonis sitting for a quarter of an hour between each rising of the curtain in the conductor's chair and leering at the ladies in the boxes and making the most of his opportunities for demonstrating his personal vanity." Perhaps the *Musical Courier* was too harsh, but Damrosch, according to George Martin, was "young, charming, handsome, [and] full of energy" and was later rumored to have had affairs with noted artists.[42] Certainly, Damrosch cut a striking figure for young Natalie Curtis, both physically and musically.

Curtis shared with Day one of her most treasured meetings with this "youthful Adonis." "It" was "looking *so* handsome," she told Day, and had such "wonderful eyes." Curtis and "It" spent a delightful train ride one evening discussing her rehearsals for the Seidl concert and her vocal training. Their conversation turned to the proper role of the artist in society and to Curtis's disregard for fashion, of which Damrosch approved. They discussed upcoming concerts, Lilli Lehmann, and Curtis's trip to Bayreuth. They practiced their German together, concocting a silly rhyme to help them learn the language. As Curtis concluded her trip home, she told Day, "all I could see were those gleaming, almost glittering eyes fixed upon me."[43] Walter Damrosch was ten years Curtis's elder and a married man, but Curtis could not always contain her girlish infatuation with the famous conductor. In Curtis's relationship with Damrosch her young hormones combined with her sincere devotion to becoming a musical artist. Certainly her reference to him as "It" carried sexual connotations. With Damrosch she found an acceptable way to blend her adolescent yearnings with her love of music.

The two young women extended their infatuation with Damrosch into their response to Wagner's works. In similar ways discussions of Wagner framed Curtis and Day's deeper discussions of love, passion, friendship, and spirituality. Their mutual appreciation for the composer allowed the friends to share their feelings for one another. While attending a "Popular Wagner Concert" on August 31, 1890, Curtis deeply missed her companion. "I longed for you," Curtis wrote her friend. "I was sitting quite near, in the balcony and in such a way that I could see [possibly Anton Seidl's] face all the time. He always has such a noble, inspired kind of look when he is leading, that I love to sit where I can see his face." The heavenly concert could only have been improved by the presence of her dear friend, who shared Curtis's devotion. "Some days when you look back on them, seem sort of golden. Such was the case with that concert," Curtis reminisced to Day.[44]

On other occasions Curtis shared moments of musical ecstasy and transport with her sympathetic friend. "I have just been playing, and weeping over Tristan," she told Day. Wagner's musical drama about unrequited love left Curtis "nearly dead." As she pored over the score Curtis relived other operas she had attended and especially recalled the singer who played the female lead Isolde in *Tristan*. Lilli Lehmann, or the "goddess," as Curtis and Day adoringly called her, achieved great stature singing this role in America. The two girls obsessively followed Lehmann's career, attending numerous performances, sending her gifts, and exchanging photographs of their beloved soprano. Lehmann had enjoyed modest success singing minor roles in Europe. Upon her arrival in the United States to sing at the Metropolitan Opera House under Leopold Damrosch, her career blossomed. Best noted for her performances as Isolde in *Tristan* and Brünnhilde in *Siegfried* and *Götterdämmerung*, Lehmann gained many admirers. Ill health forced her to return to Europe after the 1891–92 season, but she made periodic trips back to the United States.[45] Curtis admitted to Day that she had dreamed of the "goddess" in a flower-filled garden and prayed for sleep so she could again enjoy "such *blissful* dreams." Writing to her friend late at night in her room, Curtis confessed that she "should simply love to go to Tristan tonight, and have my heart torn out of me. It is ready to be torn out — in fact it is pretty nearly out already." Her emotions overwhelmed her as she wrote, "Oh! Lehmann! Tristan! Isolde! I am simply *wild*," and concluded the letter with "I shall die!"[46]

The following spring Curtis relived these feelings at a concert and lecture on *Tristan*. She had just listened to a lecture by the singer Theodor Reichmann on his conception of this work. Harkening back to her summer rapture over *Tristan* and thinking of her beloved Lehmann, Curtis was swept away: "I could just *feel* the man next to me looking at me in utter amazement. I was all grieving inside and so dreadfully *sehnsuchty* [from *sehnsuchtig*, German for yearning or longing], that I felt that I should do something very rash, if I did not keep my self-control." By the end of the performance Curtis's legs were weak. It was the first time, she revealed to Day, that she had been "really *moved* this winter."[47]

Curtis relished finding others who agreed with her views on music and shared her enthusiasm and devotion. Day was probably the most congenial person to accompany Curtis, for the two often discussed how to appreciate music. The proper atmosphere especially mattered to Curtis. She preferred sitting among the true devotees and music lovers whenever she attended the theater or concert hall. Curtis tested this assertion in January 1891 when some family friends, the Lincolns, invited her to join them at the symphony in a box belonging to the wealthy Astor family. Curtis remarked that the accommodations were, "of course, very magnificent, though I felt decidedly out of place amid such luxury at a concert." Despite the sumptuous surroundings Curtis complained that she could not hear as well and did not experience the musical atmosphere to which she was accustomed. "Give me the Family Circle, with its dirt, swells, and blind men," she told Day, "and the Astors can keep their purple and fine linen." While surroundings were important to Curtis's musical experience, the people who accompanied her also mattered. She often complained of people sleeping next to her or of "unrefined" sorts who could not appreciate good music. "I always have a kind of jarred feeling if I know the person next to me is feeling bored," she confided to Day. "It makes such a difference to me whom I am with at a concert. . . . If I feel a person is in sympathy with me, I enjoy anything ten times as much."[48]

Later in the 1891 season Curtis had a chance to experience music the way she preferred. She enthusiastically described to Day a concert conducted by Seidl that featured six soloists and was full of "the most enthusiastic Germans and Jews." Arthur Friedham won Curtis over with his renditions of Liszt's work. Friedham, the pianist Franz Rummell, the Prussian composer and conductor Max Spicker, and other Germans "sat together with their arms over the backs of each others [sic] chairs, listening attentively during the music, talking and laughing in the intervals, and going out for their *bier* during the intermission."[49] Curtis appreciated their intense interest in the performances, but also the good-natured camaraderie that resulted from a shared love of music.

Her deep passion helped form her sense of self, but the intensity of her feelings led her to question the effects this had on her character. Her father had shared his reservations about Curtis's whole-hearted devotion to her art. "Papa says that music is a bad habit with me and that I am nothing more nor less than a musical drunkard," Curtis confided to Day. Her father's criticism gave Curtis pause and forced her to reconsider the course she followed.

She wondered to Day if perhaps she was too infatuated with music and musicians or if her extreme emotional reactions to music were normal. Curtis worried that others did not share the intensity of her response to music and that perhaps people found her odd.

> I wonder why I am always so funny? Do I cut a very ridiculous figure? People always laugh at me the moment I open my mouth. Pad. and WD [Ignace Paderewski and Walter Damrosch] were amused at me the other night. Crazy as I was, I could see that they were. Not rudely but just inwardly and quietly amused. Papa says he should think that people would die of laughing when I "slop-bucket" all over them, as he elegantly expresses it. He enjoys all my adventures as much as I do myself really, although he calls me "emotional slush." Connie says I'm a fool! But I don't despair, but walk in and blissfulize while I can. Poor creatures. They don't know what bliss is![50]

The stares and barely concealed smiles that Curtis encountered in the throes of her enthusiasm, however, could not dissuade her from pursing her real love. The purpose, the "bliss," that she found for herself in music simply surpassed any other emotions.

Music did not just provide Curtis with feelings of elation; it also opened her mind to spiritual contemplation. As she and Day discussed their musical ideas they also ventured into discourses on their religious and ethical beliefs, particularly as they reached early adulthood. During the summer of 1893 Day became quite ill. Her ailment provoked a sort of spiritual crisis for both young women and led Day to ask Curtis about her own beliefs. Curtis began her reply cautiously: "I always feel that if by stating our beliefs we hurt those nearest and closest [to] us, it is best to keep them to ourselves." Curtis conceded that in the interests of social harmony she could allow others to think that she believed as they did, but she then asserted, "I shall never *deny* the truth — what I felt to be Truth — no matter if it made a social outcast of me." Her acceptance of herself as a "musical drunkard" also applied to her spiritual beliefs. Curtis wanted to be certain of her beliefs before she clarified them for the world. Day, though, could be privy to her friend's inmost thoughts:

> That there is a great *cause*, of which we are the effect, that there is great and universal *good* manifested thro' all Creation; that the Vital Power, the Life, the Cause, the Essence of all things is God — that we are all parts of one great whole which is God and that our nature is spiritual, unchanging, and eternal, being God. I accept the divinity of Christ in the sense that he is the fullest expression or rather manifestation of the divinity in man, and I think that it is possible for us all to attain that perfection — in fact we *must* attain it, if not in this state of consciousness, then in some future one. I think that the noblest thing in the world is Love of Good; for Good's sake, and a desire to be good, thro' love of Good. A wish for a reward, either here or hereafter, is utterly debasing to our higher nature.[51]

Curtis's somewhat unorthodox views of religion reflect the influence of new spiritual ideas circulating at the end of the nineteenth century. Both Curtis and Day had met Charlotte Osgood Mason, who would later become Curtis's patron, and whom Curtis described as "broader than the average Christian."[52] Mason was intensely interested in mystical and psychic phenomenon and shared with her husband, Rufus, an interest in hypnosis and telepathy. Reflecting on the death of her spouse Mason argued that death should not be feared, but seen as "a bridge of light, a rainbow over which humanity may pass to its Walhalla." She encouraged others to embrace life and death and to use their present lives to improve themselves spiritually and to prepare for their eventual rebirth.[53]

Many others joined Mason, Curtis, and Day in their search for a spirituality outside the bounds of established Christianity. Mainline Protestant churches slowly and painfully adapted to the new needs of an urban industrial society and often found their teachings at odds with new scientific developments, particularly the theory of evolution. Movements outside the mainstream, such as Christian Science, New Thought, and Spiritualism, offered adherents appealing alternatives to established religion.[54] Although Victorians looked to alternative spiritual paths, particularly in Asian religions, they did not fully reject the dominant values of their own society, as the historian Thomas Tweed argues. Instead they selected and adapted ideas and concepts that best fit their needs. People found these religious alternatives appealing for a variety of reasons. Tweed identifies three types of people attracted to Buddhism in the second half of the nineteenth century — rationalists, romantics, and esoterics. "Rationalists" focused on the logic and reason they perceived in Buddhism and stressed its continuity with new scientific discoveries, as well as its emphasis on toleration. Curtis identified more with "romantic" adherents or supporters of Asian traditions. Tweed characterizes this group as "the intellectual descendents of German Romantics like Goethe and American Romantics like Emerson." Although some romantics found the spiritual teachings alluring, they were primarily attracted by the overall aesthetic cultures of these religions. The third type, "esoterics," focused more on the spiritual and secretive teachings of Buddhism and other Asian religions. New spiritual movements, particularly Theosophy, helped popularize these ideas in the United States. Curtis attended several Theosophist meetings as a young woman. Her identification with these teachings and other non-Western spiritual alternatives solidified during this period.[55]

Theosophy stressed the return to ancient forms of knowledge and made claims to have bridged the gap between religion and science. Theosophy, meaning "divine wisdom," drew inspiration from Asian religions and was based on the esoteric teachings of its founder, Helen P. Blavatsky, who offered what she considered a scientific, philosophical, and spiritual system that held the truth behind all religions. Theosophists believed in three fundamental truths: that a god exists, is good, and is the life-giver dwelling within every person;

that humans are immortal and face a future of limitless glory; and that divine laws of justice govern the universe. The Theosophical Society aimed to form a nucleus of "Universal Brotherhood"; to encourage the study of comparative religion, philosophy, and science; and to pursue the study of the unexplained laws of nature and the secret "powers latent in man." Theosophists discussed notions of karma, reincarnation, vegetarianism, and other traditions from Eastern philosophy. Since the 1880s the society had active chapters in New York that held meetings and lectures and published theosophical materials.[56]

Theosophy grew out of the Spiritualist movement that thrived in the mid-nineteenth century. Scholars have examined the links between Spiritualism and women, particularly the ways in which the religious movement fostered women's rights. "Not all feminists were Spiritualists," writes historian Ann Braude, "but all Spiritualists advocated women's rights, and women were in fact equal to men within Spiritualist practice, polity, and ideology."[57] Both Spiritualism and Theosophy asserted that individuals had direct access to divine truth, allowing women to participate equally with men in these movements. Women served in leading positions and often used religious platforms to address feminist issues. Theosophy probably appealed to Curtis as much for the role it accorded women as for the other teachings it advanced.

Curtis attended Theosophy meetings and contemplated the movement's spiritual teachings. In September 1893 she persuaded her mother to attend a meeting and reported, "We were both glad afterwards that we had not let the opportunity of hearing the two Indians [who spoke at the meeting] slip through our fingers." The first speaker, a Buddhist from Ceylon, "looked like some curious lizard, with his long hair and tight skirt," leaning and twisting on the table as he spoke. The Buddhist speaker briefly described how he had consecrated himself to "the great Excuse of all Life" and pledged not to take life, not to steal, lie, or speak idly. Buddhists, he argued, believed in one god and tolerated other religions, "recognizing the fact that there is some truth in all of them." This religion, Curtis reported, also "preaches above all, love for one's fellow men, and a hatred of war and violence."[58]

The second speaker was a high-caste Brahmin from India who described his beliefs and daily practices. "What he said was so beautiful," exclaimed Curtis, "and couched in such exquisite language!" He stressed that religion and civilization came from the East and that the duty of a Brahmin was to shut himself from the world spiritually without neglecting his duties to others. Curtis concluded, "*Renunciation* seems to be the keynote of this religion." After the speakers finished, William Q. Judge, one of the founders of the Theosophical Society, asked the audience what they thought of these "two heathens," and the crowd emitted a "shriek of laughter." Judge compared their teachings with those of modern Christianity, or "churchianity," and contended that the Indian beliefs better represented the teachings of Jesus. Curtis affirmed this, saying, "It was true — Christ is supposed, you know, to have drawn many of his teachings from old Indian sources."[59]

Although Curtis may not have joined the Theosophical Society, its teachings certainly colored her own beliefs. She admitted to Bessie Day her reluctance to share her ideas because "I am ashamed to own it, I thought you would be *shocked!*" "I hope the Indians have not worried you," she continued.[60] Curtis's interest in alternative spirituality also reflected the influence of her family. It is significant that Mimsey accompanied her daughter to these lectures and supported her unorthodox ideas. Furthermore, the prevalence of Transcendentalist ideas within her family prepared Curtis to be open to spiritual views outside the Western tradition. One historian comments, "That virtually all Transcendentalists were fascinated by Asian religions is without doubt." Many believed that "Christ was not the only way to salvation, that Hinduism, Buddhism, and other world religions also were divine revelations." Surely this openness to and even acceptance of non-Western worldviews made Curtis more willing to look to other cultures for answers to her own spiritual dilemmas. She found the Indian speakers and their ideas beautiful and intriguing and accepted that they could be as valid to her as the teachings of Christianity. Non-Western people had something valuable to offer to her personally and to the world in general. This receptivity to, or perhaps even preference for, ideas outside the American mainstream guided Curtis's later work and helped shape her adult identity.[61]

Curtis's acceptance of these spiritual ideas often coalesced with her passion for Wagner. Her earnest desire to experience his work in the proper emotional and spiritual atmosphere reached fruition in two trips to Europe, in 1890–91 and in 1896–97, during which she had the chance to visit the home of her beloved composer. On these trips to Europe she combined her appreciation for Wagner with her aspirations to become a professional musician. Although Curtis studied with some of the era's finest piano and composition instructors, the allure of study in Europe remained strong. To many Americans a musician could not become successful without some European training. It had almost become required that music students, particularly young women, make the journey across the Atlantic to advance their studies. Amy Fay in her account of her year abroad, *Music-Study in Germany*, warned other young women: "Unless people have an enthusiasm for art I don't see the least use in their coming abroad. If they cannot appreciate the *culture* of Europe they are much better off in America." Her writings on the musical atmosphere of Europe, however, caused many to follow in her footsteps.[62]

The Curtis family traveled to Europe early in the 1890s. Throughout the 1890–91 season Curtis had excitedly planned this trip. Her family decided to tour the continent and to spend part of their vacation in Bayreuth, Germany. This small town housed the theater Wagner had specially designed for the performances of his musical dramas and held an annual festival that had become a mecca for Wagner enthusiasts. As the summer approached Curtis found it difficult to contain herself. In late April Natalie, Mimsey, and Marian Curtis visited the boat in which they would cross the Atlantic. Natalie's older sister Connie had already left for Europe by then, and her letters home only further whetted Natalie's appetite to go. Curtis had heard that Walter Damrosch might be in Europe that summer and wondered to Bessie Day "if we shall meet *It* at Bayreuth?" Curtis wrote her aunt Nat to tell her she had purchased tickets for Bayreuth and that "the dream might be coming true." Upon Mimsey's insistence Curtis quoted an article about her trip from the *American Art Journal*: "Miss Natalie Curtis, daughter of Dr. Curtis, who has had four years training at the piano under the excellent master Mr. William Semnacher will visit Bayreuth this summer and return in the fall. Miss Curtis' large and beautiful tone production and musical intelligence have won for her no little reputation in social circles."[63] Although Curtis seemed a bit embarrassed to quote the journal, she obviously exhibited some pride in this recognition and a great deal of excitement regarding the opportunity.

Natalie Curtis and the rest of her family must have taken the trip, although no letters to Bessie Day from Europe have survived. One can only imagine the rapture Curtis must have felt as she silently took her seat in the temple of Wagner's art and participated in the almost ritualistic viewing of his operas. The Curtises likely also visited other European nations during their tour abroad, experiences that must have further broadened Natalie Curtis's worldview. If anything, this initial trip to Europe only increased Curtis's desire for a life of music and probably led her to consider returning for more formal training.

After additional years of instruction in the United States, Curtis pondered a longer, more intensive course of study in Europe. She confessed to Day that her demanding schedule under Friedham left her "rather seedy and shaky" from overwork. Although she had enjoyed her last trip to Europe and knew that the road to success in American music often went through the continent, Curtis expressed her doubts to Day. "I feel very well that my place is at home, in my family," she began. "I know that Papa would feel my absence tremendously and I owe him *so much* that I can never pay him that the least I can do is to stay with him if my presence gives him any pleasure." She realized that her parents would allow her to study abroad and would make any sacrifice to provide her with the advantages of European training, but she would feel like an "ungrateful hog" to leave Bogey and Mimsey.[64]

Alongside Curtis's concern for her family were nagging doubts about her own abilities. She confided in Day: "If I were a great genius I should feel that the developing of that God-power within me would be the most important thing. . . . But the very moderate amount of talent" she had could be fully developed in the United States. Curtis broached the topic with Friedham at their next lesson. As Natalie mopped her face after finishing a trying etude, Mimsey asked Friedham point-blank if her daughter could study in Europe. Apparently Augusta did not share Natalie's opinion that study in Europe would be detrimental to Curtis family life. Augusta inquired if Natalie had enough talent to study with the Polish pianist and teacher of Paderewski, Theodor Leschetizky. "Cer-tain-ly!" replied Friedham. "No doubt about it!" Mimsey then informed Friedham that Natalie felt discouraged by her progress and had even considered giving up the piano. Friedham assured Natalie that she could handle European study and that she would probably impress some of Leschetizky's pupils with her playing. Curtis's "heart gave a great *leap* of joy" and propelled her into an excited conversation with Friedham about whom she should consider for a teacher in Europe. Curtis's doubts about her musical future and ability slowly evaporated.[65]

The encouragement of her instructors, plus the active support of her mother, pushed Curtis toward study abroad. In 1896 Curtis and her brother George traveled to Europe, visiting London, Paris, Italy, and the Rhine region. That winter Curtis studied at the prestigious Paris Conservatory. One of her teachers was Alfred-Auguste Giraudet, a dramatic bass and vocal instructor. Giraudet had debuted in Paris at the Theatre-Lyrique as Mephistopheles in 1868 and sung other operatic roles until his retirement as a performer in 1883. He taught in Paris and later in New York City. Curtis suffered from a severe attack of appendicitis that winter, prompting Augusta to come to her daughter's aid. After a month-long visit to Switzerland the two Curtis women traveled to Bayreuth. Natalie Curtis enrolled in the school there, and they formed a "close friendship" with the surviving family members of the deceased Richard Wagner.[66]

Sensing the importance of this period in both their lives, Augusta recorded her reminiscences of their stay at Bayreuth. She explained that Natalie, "who had always desired to study the dramas [of Wagner] at first hand, had in visiting Bayreuth during the previous summer made arrangements with Herr [Julius] Kneise to take private lessons of him in the Autumn."[67] Kneise, a German conductor and composer, had taught singing in schools throughout Europe and had arrived in Bayreuth in 1882 to work as chorus master for the festival operas. In 1890 he became the director of the Preparatory School for Stage Singers, associated with the Wagner festival. The school attracted only seventeen pupils in 1892 and by 1898 had only five. Many left because of the strict regimen foisted upon the students, but of those who remained several became talented singers. After lessons with Kneise, Natalie Curtis, according to Augusta, "had the very great privilege of becoming a pupil of the school as well — a very rare and interesting musical experience."[68]

Curtis joined a class of six to eight pupils that winter and adopted the demanding schedule expected of all students. She played over scores with Kneise in the mornings, then attended classes at the school in the afternoons. She studied German declamation and the roles of several Wagnerian characters. Kneise and an assistant taught students different parts and drilled them in various aspects of performance. Wagner's widow, Cosima, oversaw the school and attempted to influence and encourage the students. "But it was Frau Wagner's inspiring touch," Augusta asserted, "that at last gave style and finish to the work of the students." Curtis and her mother defended Cosima against charges that she was too controlling and domineering by pointing to the superior results she achieved at the festivals.[69]

The Wagner Festival drew thousands to Bayreuth every year for the annual cycle of operas. Wagner had chosen the somewhat isolated town to stage his musical dramas so that audiences would have nothing to distract them. Augusta affirmed, "To Wagner the theater was not to be the place where man should be *diverted*, but where he should be *converted*." By the 1890s large numbers of the converted converged upon the sleepy town to partake of not just the stage but the "Bayreuth spirit," as well. According to festival historian Frederic Spotts, the rituals surrounding attendance led people to "sense that to participate in the Festival is the greatest privilege one can have." Augusta remarked, "Of the many memories of Bayreuth I recall nothing more delightful than the pleasure of being one of the procession that made its way to the theater under the trees of the shaded road, knowing that for some hours one would lose oneself to the exterior world, and live in the beauties of 'Rheingold,' 'Siegfried,' or 'Parsifal.'"[70]

Other attractions also occupied Natalie and her mother during their stay in Bayreuth. School excursions into the surrounding countryside and evenings at "Wahnfried," the Wagner family home, stood out in Augusta's mind. On Wednesday evenings students and visiting singers performed parts from Wagner's works. The Wagners even invited Natalie and Augusta to celebrate Christmas with them. The students prepared a surprise for Cosima, singing Bach's Christmas Oratorio to her with one of Cosima's daughters.

Natalie Curtis joined in the singing and shared her songbook with the surprise guest. The Curtises returned to Wahnfried for the New Year's Eve celebration and again for the birthday party for Wagner's son Siegfried. They deemed themselves especially lucky to be asked to join in the remembrances of Franz Liszt's death because only "a few chosen friends are invited to the Villa . . . to gather in quiet memory" of the great composer. They believed that they had "shared in an intimate memorial" that evening and that their entire visit to Bayreuth was shrouded with a sense of something special, even holy.[71]

Curtis returned from her pilgrimage to Wagner's home and her European training prepared to fully embrace her identity as a musician and artist. The New York musical scene continued to hold its allure for Curtis, but now no longer an adolescent, she began to consider her future. Eschewing marriage and a life of domesticity, Curtis desired a professional musical career. Women in turn-of-the-century America had opportunities to become professional musicians, but their options were limited by the dominant gender ideology. A commentator in the *Etude* remarked that by the end of the 1890s the stage and the church, once closed to women's musical participation, now regularly included female performers, especially as pianists. Although the greatest pianists remained men, the writer contended, women had made the piano their instrument, and some could even make a living as full-time performers. Despite this optimistic outlook for women the writer concluded with a rather limited vision for women musicians — perhaps one day there would be all-female orchestras. The idea of women participating as equals in the profession was beyond the mental grasp of even this relatively liberal observer.[72]

Despite a half century of progress toward greater inclusion, women musicians were still limited by gendered notions about the proper role for women in music. Another article in the *Etude* observed a sense of restlessness among female musicians and noted that many chafed under the restrictions holding them back. After contending that some women deserved the same pay as male musicians, the author felt compelled to justify women's participation by assuring readers that teaching or performing did not detract from a woman's femininity: "The best type of woman musician is, indeed, a woman still. Her heart throbs with passion; her soul cries out for sympathy and with sympathy, but she puts her shoulder to the wheel and goes into her profession with all the bravery of a man."[73]

The concern that female musicians not lose their femininity limited their options as musicians. Although more women, like Curtis, continued to receive formal musical training and wanted a career, or at least a brief opportunity to practice their art before marriage, relatively few could make a decent living as professionals. Teaching music, increasingly seen as an acceptable occupation for women, offered an outlet. Many middle- and upper-class women formed music clubs that provided women a chance for "self-development and the betterment of their communities, as well as a means of overcoming their isolation at home." Some women tried to specialize in a particular instrument or composer to create a niche for their talents. Others banded together in all-female orchestras, relying on the novelty of such groups to attract audiences but still not challenging the mores that prevented their full participation as professional musicians.[74]

Musicians like Curtis underwent years of musical training and struggled to create a place where they could use their talents. Despite years of arduous practice on the piano and study under noted instructors, Curtis decided not to pursue a career as a pianist. She never publicly explained her choice to give up the concert stage. Her brother claimed that a "strained hand, due to over-zealous piano practice," prevented her from pursuing this path, one for which she most assuredly was prepared.[75] Or perhaps lingering doubts about her abilities kept her from professional performance. Certainly she recognized the limited range of options from which she could select. Curtis lacked the temperament to teach piano, and it would have been difficult for her to restrain her talents and enthusiasm to occasional participation in a women's musical club. Composition, which she had dabbled in as a teenager, offered her a chance to work as a professional musician. It provided her with the challenges and stimulation she craved and allowed her to address the broader concerns about American music so prevalent among the nation's composers.

Female composers faced many challenges. In the 1890s a growing number of women wrote orchestral music, songs, and smaller works. Their efforts sparked public controversy over the question, "Could or should women compose and could they ever equal the creative work of men?"[76] This debate, and the social tensions it evoked, shaped the conditions under which women composed and by which their work was judged. It also affected the type of music women wrote. Composition posed a challenge to any musician because of the amount of schooling required to compose, the need for money to support one's efforts, and the difficulty of getting works published and advertised. Women faced additional burdens, including lack of encouragement and outright opposition, as well as denials of talent and condescension.[77] Opponents of female composition argued that women lacked the innate ability or drive to compose well, that they could not handle the rigors of the composer's life, and that composition would strip women of their femininity.

Despite these hardships many women became composers. To some composition became a feminist issue; they linked their musical work with arguments for the expansion of women's rights and challenges to sexual stereotypes. Others, like Amy Beach, the most famous female composer of the period, denied any discrimination and contended that equal opportunities existed. They may have, but they were narrow ones. The music historian Alan Levy argues that the notion of "the 'paucity' of female composers is more image than fact" and that indeed many women worked as composers in the early twentieth century. The barriers erected against them, however, shaped the type of music they wrote. "With the parlor accessible and the concert stage forbidding," Levy remarks, women mostly composed songs, ballads, and solo piano and ensemble pieces. This type of music, rarely performed in public settings, was considered appropriate for women but kept even the most talented female composers invisible. The historian Judith Tick adds that this situation also placed women in a double bind. "When they composed in the smaller 'feminine' forms such as songs and piano pieces," Tick notes, "they were thereby demonstrating their sexually derived inadequacies to think in the larger abstract forms. If, on the other hand, they attempted these forms, they were betraying their sexual identities by writing 'man-tone' music."[78]

These ideas assuredly had an impact on Curtis's decision to compose, and like many other women Curtis opted for songs rather than large-scale works. G. Schirmer published Curtis's "Dearest, Where Thy Shadow Falls," a song for voice and piano, in 1898; "Song from Pippa Passes" in 1899; and, the next year, "An den Fruehling" (Spring Song). In 1902 the Wa-Wan Press, a musical publishing house dedicated to promoting American musicians, issued her most substantial composition, *Songs from a Child's Garden of Verses*. At first glance these compositions may seem like insignificant and limited attempts by Curtis to become a professional composer. Upon further consideration, however, these songs demonstrate the influence of her training, especially her study in Germany, and her attempts to contribute to the creation of "American" music. They also partly explain her eventual attraction to Native American and African American "folk" music.

Curtis's studies in Germany and her infatuation with the music of this nation suggest that she was influenced by the tradition of composing lieder, songs based on poetry in which the composer sought to blend together the words and music into a unified whole.

The German lied developed during the nineteenth century and was greatly influenced by Romanticism. Composers like Franz Schubert and Friedrich Schiller based their songs on the works of national poets, such as Johann Goethe, or on German folk traditions. Nature and the "primitive" attracted many of these Romantic composers, who appreciated the "untamed and irregular" nature of folk poetry, as well as its "simplicity, naïveté, and spontaneity."[79] Curtis admired many lieder composers and even read the poetry of Goethe as an adolescent. Their influence appears in her early compositions. "An den Fruehling," with its German title, clearly demonstrates these connections. This poem set to music exalts in the joy of spring and in love for a young maiden. "Song from Pippa Passes," based on a Robert Browning poem, also celebrates nature. Curtis applied the German lieder tradition to English poetry and music in this compositional effort. Both songs demonstrate how Curtis blended German ideas about music with her American conceptions of song and culture.

Nationalist musical movements at home and abroad also affected Curtis as a composer. In the formative years of her training musicians in the United States hotly debated the notion of an "American" music. Sparked by the visit of Czech composer Antonín Dvořák in the 1890s and his call for American composers to create a national music based on Native American and African American themes, musicians struggled to develop a distinctive national sound. Considering her connections to and knowledge of the music world, Curtis must have participated in this discourse. She had studied in Europe at a time when rising nationalist concerns led many musicians to incorporate folk song and dance into art music. Her early compositions reflect the influence of nationalism in music. *Songs from a Child's Garden of Verses*, a collection of Robert Louis Stevenson poems set to music, was obviously not an "American" composition. However, the publisher of this piece, the Wa-Wan Press, actively promoted the works of American composers. Arthur Farwell, the press's founder, sought out music that expressed national themes, many of which used Indian and black motifs. Curtis's association with Wa-Wan suggests the high level of awareness she had regarding this search for an American musical sound. Her "Dearest, Where Thy Shadow Falls" probably best demonstrates her efforts to compose American music in the German lieder tradition. This song, based on a poem by Ralph Waldo Emerson, reflects the strong influence Transcendentalist thought exerted on her, through her family and through her appreciation of Romanticism. By choosing this poet, who also contended for the creation of an American art form and appreciated the influence of nature on the nation's cultural life, Curtis attempted to contribute to the search for an American musical identity.[80]

Although Curtis did not yet draw on the folk traditions she later espoused, her early works demonstrate her inclination toward developing a national music. She had other models from her training that would also lead her to seek out an American "folk." Her beloved Richard Wagner, for instance, based many of his musical dramas on traditional German myths. Many of his works critiqued the modern world by celebrating primitivism and the "natural man." Curtis deeply admired Franz Liszt for his Hungarian compositions. She wrote that the composer "preserved in art form the strange music of the strangest race in history — the gypsies." Curtis further noted the impact of his work. "Liszt in his treatment of Hungarian melodies is a lasting example," she wrote, "to those who may follow in other fields of folk-lore."[81]

NATALIE CURTIS'S DECISION TO COLLECT, PRESERVE, AND popularize Native American music, while remarkable, was not as dramatic a departure from her training and ideals as one might initially suspect. Ideas about national music and the use of folk traditions may have predisposed her to seek out America's own folk in Native Americans and later African Americans. Her travels to the Southwest in the early years of the twentieth century helped lead her down this path. New opportunities for white women in the region and the limits she faced as a female composer served to bolster her decision to reject a career in the world of classical music for one as a folklorist among the nation's "primitive" peoples.

3

"I Am Full of Plans"

Curtis Discovers Native Americans and Their Music

IN THE SUMMER OF 1903 NATALIE CURTIS EXCITEDLY WROTE President Theodore Roosevelt to share her enthusiasm for Native American music and art and her proposal to preserve and promote these valuable treasures with "all educated persons." Thanking the president for supporting her endeavors, Curtis exclaimed, "I am full of plans." Her plans included collecting, preserving, and popularizing Indian music for the benefit of Indians and all Americans. Believing she shared in the president's "clarity of purpose and promptness of action," Curtis yearned to fulfill her new vision for American music.[1] Evincing the same enthusiasm for her new undertakings as she earlier had for Wagner and the musical world of New York, Curtis again threw herself into her work. This time, however, her labor did not consist of hours of practice at the piano or poring over Wagnerian opera scores. Now Curtis devoted her efforts to the collection and popularization of Native American music. She found herself transported from the stylish music halls of New York City to a desolate government building in an isolated Hopi village, yet her enthusiasm for music and its potential for human betterment only increased as her physical comfort subsided. Beginning in 1903 Curtis published a number of articles on Native American music and culture, particularly from the Southwest. After the 1907 publication of *The Indians' Book* she portrayed herself as an advocate of Native American rights, particularly regarding their music, poetry, and arts. What accounts for Curtis's transformation from a classically trained pianist and devotee of Wagner and highbrow music to a spokesperson for Indian song and folklore?

This transformation can be accounted for in part by the experiences of Curtis's youth. Her family's relatively liberal values regarding gender, race, and culture, as well as their emotional and financial support, certainly provided some basis for her decision to study Native American music. Family ties also led her to important patrons who encouraged and financed her research in the West. The Curtis family's Transcendentalist heritage and openness to non-Western ideas as a source of personal identity could also have paved the way for her newfound interests. Her earlier attempts to create Americanist music as a composer of small parlor pieces may also have led Curtis to seek out alternatives. Importantly, in Curtis's youth music provided her with a sense of personal identity and fulfillment, as well as a means for engagement with the broader world. In Native American music she found even greater promise.

In this quest for new ways of understanding herself and her world Curtis joined other Easterners, particularly upper- and middle-class educated white women, in traveling to the American Southwest. Like other women she discovered that chances to work on behalf of Native Americans were becoming increasingly available. First as a travel writer reporting on the West and then as a self-appointed mediator between Native Americans and Eastern audiences, Curtis found people and places to fulfill her search for meaning and purpose in life and the desire and means to share this with others. In her discovery of Native American music Curtis found an identity for herself as a woman, a musician, and an American.

Some time around 1900 Curtis's younger brother George, after graduating from Harvard and working briefly as a librarian in New York, moved to the Southwest. George suffered from ill health, and the Curtises hoped that the Western climate would help. Like other young men from well-established and well-connected Eastern families George Curtis may have had additional reasons for his journey west. Other young men in similar circumstances, such as Theodore Roosevelt, Frederic Remington, and Owen Wister, also went west as they bridged the gap between adolescence and adulthood. These young men viewed the West — as their fathers and grandfathers had often viewed the "Grand Tour" of Europe — as a place of temporary refuge from the maladies of their increasingly industrialized and specialized worlds. For this new generation the West became more than a place for young men to renew their health; it also provided an outlet for cultural and artistic talents that the modern industrial order no longer provided. It became a place for them to articulate an identity and even begin new lives. For George and other young men the West could also serve as a place to display their manhood in ways the East no longer allowed.[2] George worked on a ranch, probably in Arizona (although later he permanently lived on his own ranch in southern California), and frequently sent letters and photographs to the family in New York.

His enthusiasm for the region proved contagious enough to entice his sister to join him for a visit. Throughout her life Natalie Curtis had enjoyed new experiences and travel, and perhaps the romantic allure of the region, just then enticing the East Coast, encouraged her to go. At some point during her visit Curtis heard an Indian song that changed her life. Although she never formally recounted just exactly what she heard, this strange, enticing music drew her in and completely captured her heart and soul.

Between 1903 and 1906 Curtis threw herself into her new work, traveling to a number of Western communities, reservations, schools, and expositions and publishing numerous articles on Native American art and music and the people and places of the Southwest. These writings established Curtis as a popularizer of the region and an advocate for the preservation and perpetuation of Indian cultures. Curtis found herself within the emerging field of research and writing on Southwestern Indians, placed in the vanguard of authors who began popularizing this region and its peoples as an "American Orient." Curtis became in many respects a transitional figure between the moralizing and assimilationist attitudes of the Victorian period and the cultural pluralism of the modern era.

THE SOUTHWEST THAT CURTIS FIRST VISITED, AND LATER came to love, had only recently begun attracting Eastern European Americans. Historians of the Southwest note that in many ways it is not just a physical, geographic place, but "a region of the imagination," as Leah Dilworth terms it. Outsiders, and some insiders, have often portrayed it as a special area within the nation that offers Americans unique and exciting opportunities. Although Americans had engaged in trade within the region since the early nineteenth century and increased their military and economic presence after annexation in 1848, it was not until the final decades of the century that European Americans really poured into the Southwest. The increased availability of travel to the region helped bring new visitors more easily. The Atchison, Topeka and Santa Fe Railroad attracted customers to the "Great Southwest" through its popular lithographs, and tours led by the "Harvey girls" of the Fred Harvey Company further increased the region's appeal. Promoters of tourism presented a vision of the Southwest as a place "inhabited by peaceful, pastoral people, 'living ruins' from the childhood of civilization." Their brand of tourism accentuated the exotic nature of the region, while making it accessible to Eastern tourists. Hotels and commercial outlets organized by its promoters resembled expositions at world fairs, educating visitors on the region, its peoples, and its cultures. The Southwest soon became home to numerous American artists, writers, anthropologists, and adventurers who joined Curtis in the belief that the region offered something unique, something unlike anything that could be found in the staid old cities of the East Coast or in Europe.[3] Like her brother George, Natalie Curtis found in the Southwest a place to express her creative and artistic talents; also like her brother, whose education seemed ill-suited for a career in the East, she found a space in which she could use her training and expertise in meaningful ways.

Curtis joined other European American women in finding such a space in the Southwest. Barbara Babcock and Nancy Parezo, in *Daughters of the Desert*, contend that "'restless and rebellious' women seeking freedom from their stays and from the drawing-room domesticity of Boston and New York found in the Southwest not only topographical and psychological space, but an otherness that intrigued and nurtured." These women, many relying on the wealth and influence of their families in the East, managed to make new lives for themselves through their work and discovered their ability to influence public opinion, science, and government policy concerning the region and its inhabitants. The appeal, as Babcock and Parezo note, lay in "the combination of an open, unspoiled landscape and a settled, agrarian, highly-developed Native American population," which "made for a timeless, edenic image that contrasted sharply with the unhealthy, aggressive, industrial culture of the eastern and mid-western United States." The Southwest especially attracted women with education and talent who felt their ambitions limited in the East. Many travelers to the region were college educated, unmarried, ambitious, and desirous of influence with the public sphere. As Molly H. Mullin notes in her study of European American women in the Southwest art market, the West provided women a place in which to "abandon constraining social conventions" and gain authority. Mullin contends that because these women operated on a "relatively underdeveloped periphery and [found] value where others had not, they had a chance of commanding greater public influence and authority than if they had remained in the Northeast."[4]

Many women shared their experiences with audiences in the East through letters, articles, and books or the artifacts they brought home. These texts at times resemble those produced by their European counterparts who visited the "Orient" in their focus on exotic or primitive aspects of the region. Women who wrote about colonized regions, like the Orient or the American Southwest, felt the pressure of multiple discourses, particularly of femininity and imperialism, on their writing. Female writers "negotiated complicated questions of authority, power, and ideology," placing themselves in spaces deemed unfit for white women but going to these regions as privileged members of the dominant group.[5]

Curtis encountered these tensions in her earliest writing on the Southwest, which unexpectedly did not explicitly focus on Native American music or folklore, but on an Arizona penitentiary and her misadventures as an inexperienced Easterner in the West. In the *New York Evening Post* Curtis shared her observations of the territorial prison in Yuma with a man she identified only as "Texan." This character, who blushed "under his bronze skin" each time he spoke to Curtis, proved a trustworthy and capable companion, able to translate Western ways to his Eastern guest, despite his awkwardness in a female presence. Initially stunned by a prison that appeared to her more like a Spanish castle than an American jail, Curtis wrote, "In the land of glaring color there is none of the dingy despair that we associate with prison life." Once inside the facility Curtis viewed it through an Orientalist lens: "There are an open court and a patch of grass where palms are spreading out their tropic beauty in the glare of the Arizona sun. Can this be an American prison? Surely it is a fortress of medieval Spain. These dark-faced men in striped clothes are not Americans; to my fancy they are the Spanish retainers and men-at-arms of the lord of his castle." Although she viewed the prison as exotic, even romantic, she justified the American colonial presence in the region because it brought law and order. "It is a world of peace, of law, system, cleanliness, of ceaseless activity and healthful toil," she confirmed. Her survey of the prisoners further reinforced the need for American control. She described most prisoners as "Mexicans," with only a few "Americans" present. Most frightening, however, were "the Apaches," mostly there for murder. Exposing her racial views Curtis mused: "What does an Apache know of the sacredness of human life? His warlike race is still in the same stage of development as were our own ancient forefathers. The Apache holds his own life cheaply and to him the life of man is no more than the life of an animal or insect." Thankfully, Uncle Sam was trying to reform these dark criminals through a system of work, order, and cleanliness. During the tour the warden pointed out work rooms where trades were taught, a chapel, a schoolroom, and a library — all agents of middle-class Eastern civilization. Curtis next took her readers through the men's cells, including places for solitary confinement and dark pits "where men are starved into obedience." As their tour progressed, however, her sympathy for the inmates grew. Only by seeing the prison as a "training school for life" was she able to reconcile her views of the penitentiary. The warden confirmed that the Mexicans imprisoned within his walls were much better off than before and that American civilization would take root in the region eventually. Thanking him for this tour Curtis supported American paternalism: "Well, I think Uncle Sam is a good and wise father to his erring children." As she left the compound, smugly content with the idea that the prison served as a force for positive change, "Texan" disagreed with her and offered a Westerner's view of the situation. "You seem to think that soap and water constitutes the New Jerusalem!" he harangued her. "I tell yer, Miss New York . . . you can't appreciate what it is to them fellows to be corralled like that the hull time. Yer don't know what agony four walls can be to a man. Gee-whiz!"[6] Curtis eventually agreed with him, admitting her lack of proper perspective as an uninformed Easterner. By conceding to the Texan she adopted a self-effacing posture that allowed her to relate to her readers who would have held similar views and showed how her experiences in the West had changed her.

She continued this stance in another article in the *Post* in which she recounted her quest to secure a burro, her "little white Bonita," to "spirit me out into the tinted wilderness" with just her notebook and a picnic lunch. In this accounting of her misadventures with Bonita, Curtis, like other colonial travel writers, poked fun at her overconfident, naive expectations regarding the romantic adventures she hoped to have with her new burro. By again taking on an attitude of self-effacement, Curtis could set readers at ease regarding her challenge to gender norms as a woman alone in the West, and she could project an aura of innocence even as she was taking full benefit of her position within the dominant class. She began her tale with the arrival of a beautiful white burro who, in exchange for a regular supply of hay, would accompany her on trips to the desert. Through the voices of Mr. Landlord and her friend from the prison, Texan, she revealed that Easterners like herself had much to learn in the desert. The two men questioned her plans and pointed out her misguided assumptions about burro travel. At the same time that she acquiesced to their superior knowledge, though, Curtis asserted her feminist attitudes and her authority as a female colonizer. She wanted the donkey, after all, to give her freedom of movement. Bonita, she hoped, would take her alone into the desert, away from the watchful eyes of the town and her hosts. She further asserted her feminist ideals in her insistence that she ride astride the burro rather than in the more ladylike sidesaddle position. As the uncooperative animal dragged Curtis through Yuma's streets, she ordered the "Babe" ("the biggest Indian in Yuma") to hold Bonita while she attempted to mount the animal. Later she demanded that "a squaw" help shoo the stubborn beast off the railroad tracks.[7] In these relations with Native Americans Curtis assumed the position of colonial authority. With other European Americans, though, she more carefully negotiated this authority by downplaying her abilities while still asserting her feminist desire for freedom. In the Southwest women like Curtis could assume different identities to suit their needs.

Having found a space in the West in which to assert herself, Curtis invited other Americans to visit the region she increasingly viewed as an exotic, even primitive place. She urged her readers "who flock to Europe to see the relics of antiquity" to instead "turn your faces to the great Southwest of our own continent. There are ruins, historic towns and folklife as interesting as anything the Old World has to offer." A European American traveler, for instance, could view the women selling pottery at Laguna Pueblo to catch a glimpse of the "American Orient." These women balanced large earthen jars on their heads and wrapped themselves in bright shawls as they bartered trays of their handcrafted wares. "It seemed impossible to believe that this bright bit of picturesque life was America," Curtis commented. "The brilliancy, and indeed the whole suggestiveness of the scene was oriental." Curtis's portrayal of Pueblo women as Oriental Others represents an approach commonly taken by writers on the Southwest. Barbara Babcock argues that Pueblo women, particularly the "olla maidens" whom Curtis described, had become part of Western nostalgia, valued "if only in . . . imaginary projections, outside history." Curtis indeed imagined these women and their community as both apart from and a part of America. The women in the "scene" fulfilled her expectations of "the Orient," and all that it implied, but as Curtis reminded her readers, this "Orient" existed within America's borders. Easterners could now easily reach this region and claim their authority over it.[8]

As she spent more time in the Southwest and deepened her interest in Native Americans and their music, her presentations of Native people and their land became more nuanced. Curtis acknowledged that she had not initially understood or appreciated the people or the music of the region (and one may question if she ever fully did). A trip to the village of Oraibi, home of the "peace-loving Hopis," changed her mind forever. Before coming West, Curtis admitted, "I had the vague idea that all Indian music was a monotonous, barbaric chanting without form, with no beginning and no end." In her ignorance of Native Americans she lumped them together as a "race of savage people in the same primitive grade of development." After seeing the Hopi with her own eyes and realizing their vast differences from other Indians, Curtis rejected her earlier generalizations. She confessed that she "was not prepared to find a people with such definite art-forms, such elaborate and detailed ceremonials, such crystallized traditions, beliefs, and customs." Their music especially astounded her. "I felt that I had come in search of gold and had found diamonds," Curtis remarked. "The Hopis' every act of life seems to be a ceremonial rite, containing a symbol, a poetic significance known only to those outsiders who have dwelt long in Hopi land and are deeply-versed in Hopi lore."[9] She had a similar realization about Native American music while part of a delegation of a "few privileged palefaces" that brought thirty Navajos to the annual Tournament of Roses festival in Pasadena, California, on New Year's Day of 1903. The "privileged palefaces" showed the Navajos around Los Angeles, exchanging "war-cries" with the residents, enjoying the marvels of modern technology, and visiting popular tourist attractions. One evening, as the Navajos camped (probably at Charles Lummis's El Alisal), Curtis approached the interpreter and asked, "If I sing for them will they sing for me?" Because of her stereotyped and misinformed ideas about Indian music, she sang a piece of the song of the Valkyries from a Wagner opera, "for I imagined that Brünnhilde's wild cry would be something like the Indians' own music." The Navajos replied by singing songs in "a strange, low, nasal chant" that had the "monotony of Nature's music" and a strong spiritual essence. Curtis realized that her selection was far "more barbarous" than the music of the Navajos.[10] As she came to concentrate more exclusively on Indian song, she shifted her role from a popularizer of the region to one she envisioned as a mediator between Native American singers and Eastern audiences. She transformed herself from a regionalist travel writer to an amateur anthropologist and ethnomusicologist.

Among the Hopi at Oraibi, Curtis believed, she had truly found her calling — a way to use her talents as a musician; a means to contribute to public discourse on music, art, and American identity; and a space in which she might find personal fulfillment. Curtis believed herself specially suited to the task of recording Indian songs, often with only pen and paper, in challenging situations. Her brother George, who often accompanied Curtis as she collected, commented that "Natalie's ear for music was so marvelous that she could set down, without the help of a phonograph, the strange melodies and rhythms that are so different from the white man's music."[11] Finally she found that her skills as a musician and recorder could be employed for what she understood as a useful and noble cause.

Curtis believed that her training and "ear" for music had prepared her for this new course of study. Other commentators of her day might have added her feminine attributes to this list of qualifications. European American women in the late nineteenth and early twentieth centuries found the field of anthropology, particularly in the Southwest, more open to them than other professions. Anthropology was only just becoming a professional discipline and had yet to develop the credentials, such as formal academic training, that normally worked to restrict women's participation. Further, as historians Nancy Lurie and Nancy Parezo argue, some men in the field welcomed women, believing that their special nature enabled them to collect field data men could not obtain, that white women could relate to Native Americans in ways men could not, and that they could discern different anthropological insights from Indian life.[12]

A number of white, middle-class women entered the field of anthropology in the American Southwest in this period, and many shared the notion that they could make special contributions as women. Members of the Women's Anthropological Association, as Lurie notes, believed they provided "special information which would enrich a defined discipline." Matilda Coxe Stevenson, a founder of this organization, serves as an example of how women created spaces for themselves in Southwestern anthropology. She began researching at Zuni in the 1880s under the direction of her husband, James, who worked for the U.S. Geological Survey. Stevenson initially collected data from Zuni women, a reflection of the notion that her gender would grant her better access to this material. She used this research as a means, however, to explore other aspects of Zuni life, especially religion. Although generally seen as having good relationships with individual informants, Stevenson believed Indians had a moral obligation to share their culture with her whether they liked it or not. As Parezo argues, Stevenson remained ambivalent in her views of Native Americans, capable of seeing much of value in their cultures but not able to overcome evolutionary views of human development and racial hierarchy or her sense of entitlement. Upon the death of her husband Stevenson struggled to assert her authority as an anthropologist and chafed under the restrictions on women in the field.[13]

Notions about women's special role, as Matilda Stevenson learned, could also limit the work of women researchers. Parezo asserts that although more women could participate in the field, they could do so only within a "narrow range of womanly activities." Women were limited to "soft, delicate, emotional, noncompetitive, and nurturing kinds of behavior," while men partook of the "real" scientific work with its "tough, rigorous, impersonal, competitive, rational, and unemotional" attributes. Parezo and Babcock conclude that it was "not accidental that much southwestern women's research has concentrated on arts and crafts, on culture and personality, on childraising and acculturation, on music and literature."[14] Curtis, like other female anthropologists and ethnomusicologists, found notions of gender both promising and limiting when she began collecting Native American music.

Her interest in Indian music developed into a more formalized desire to understand, study, and eventually record the songs she first heard on the windswept deserts of Arizona. Curtis joined other European American researchers who had also "discovered" Native American music. Beginning in the late 1870s the Southwest served as a site for ethnologists and other researchers interested in documenting various aspects of Native American cultures. Most famously, Frank Hamilton Cushing, under the aegis of the Bureau of American Ethnology (BAE), lived among the Zuni for over four years, attempting to learn the intimate details of their culture. His experiences, as well as his self-promotion, set a precedent for the expansion and development of further research in the Southwest.[15] One aspect of this research was the study of music. The earliest music study began upon contact between Europeans and Native Americans in the seventeenth century. Between the 1880s and the 1930s "a unique confluence of artistic, social, educational, and academic concerns led to a florescence in writing American Indian music."[16] The German musician Theodore Baker's *On the Music of the American Indians* (1882) is often cited as the monograph that opened the way for American researchers, who began to collect music out of a shared urgency to preserve these forms before they vanished along with their producers. Some anthropologists, like James Mooney, for example, learned Indian songs and later sang them to musicians. The adaptation of the phonograph under Jessie W. Fewkes marked an important advance because it allowed scholars to record and check their transcriptions. Musicians entered the field as well. Frances Densmore, a conservatory-trained musician working for the BAE, collected over 2,100 cylinders of music (3,591 sound recordings) from tribes across the United States from the

1900s to the 1930s.[17] She published her findings in over 140 popular and scholarly journals, books, and BAE reports. The anthropologist Alice Fletcher studied music, as well as other aspects of Native American culture. In 1893 she published *A Study of Omaha Indian Music*, the first major American study of tribal music. She later published a more general work on Indian music, *Indian Story and Song from North America* (1900).[18] Her partner, Francis LaFlesche (Omaha), published his own research on music as well. Frederick R. Burton, as musical specialist in the ethnological departments of the American Museum of Natural History in New York and the Field Museum in Chicago, studied the music of Northern tribes, particularly the Ojibway, and published *American Primitive Music* in 1909. Many students of Indian music hoped to use their findings to advance scholarship on music in general and to help develop an American musical idiom. John Comfort Fillmore, for instance, developed a theory of musical evolution from his studies of tribal songs. The musicians Benjamin Ives Gilman and Jaime de Angulo, arguing that the standard Western scale could not accommodate the range of sounds in Indian music, each created new forms of notation adapted to the songs they collected. Composers such as Charles Cadman and Arthur Farwell, who established the Wa-Wan Press to encourage American composers, hoped Native music would provide inspiration for Americanist compositions.[19] Curtis therefore found herself amid a diverse group of professionals and amateurs, scientists and musicians, men and women, who undertook their collection of Native American music for a variety of reasons, some of which she shared and others beyond her scope of interest.

Curtis collected songs among Hopi and Navajo informants as early as January 1902. By the spring of 1903 she had obtained an Edison cylinder phonograph and now began recording Hopi songs on the Third Mesa of their reservation.[20] Earlier students of Indian music, such as Fewkes, had experimented with the phonograph as a means of preserving and studying Native American language and songs. Like Curtis, Fewkes sought out those groups most isolated from white society and preserved songs "in their primitive form." In 1890 Fewkes encouraged researchers to enter "the almost illimitable field for research" in Native American song, insisting that "now is the time to collect material before all is lost." He further advised researchers like Curtis that the phonograph offered "a practical and efficient way for immediate preservation."[21] In May 1903 Curtis recorded several songs by Hopis living in Oraibi, the largest and most prominent village on Third Mesa. She also kept a notebook in which she recorded songs by hand in order to compare these with the phonograph recordings. Curtis managed to meet the village chief, or *kikmongwi*, Lololomai, and received permission to record songs in his home. She even convinced Lololomai's daughter Noya-soya and his sister Ponianomsi to contribute songs to her growing collection. Several Hopi men sang dance and kachina songs to the accompaniment of rattles.[22] Songs from the Powamu ceremonial, the Flute Dance, and the Antelope society were recorded, as were grinding songs and lullabies. Navajos, whose reservation surrounded the Hopis, also sang several songs for Curtis. Curtis recorded several melodies in nearby Canyon Diablo, perhaps to escape the scrutiny of government officials on the reservation.[23]

Although Curtis convinced some Hopis to share songs with her, many remained reluctant. The Hopis likely desired to protect their sacred music from being shared with uninitiated outsiders or were rightly suspicious of white Americans. Curtis, however, assumed that their reluctance resulted from fear of reprisals from the reservation agent or other government officials. The federal government's official policy toward Native Americans in this period stressed the need for Indians to assimilate to American ways by adopting American ideas, goods, and lifestyles and eliminating Native cultures and tribal ties. Government officials and teachers, as well as Christian missionaries, waged a campaign to eradicate Native cultures and tried to suppress Indian dances and ceremonies. On the Hopi reservation this policy was strictly, even brutally, enforced by the school superintendent, Charles Burton. He had arrived on the reservation in July 1899 to take over the superintendent position at Keams Canyon School. He zealously pushed the official assimilationist policy by using force to "persuade" Hopi parents to enroll their children and blamed a group of conservative Hopis, traditionally labeled the "Hostiles," for hindering the tribe's progress by clinging to "their ancient and heathenish customs."[24]

Burton became notorious for his enforcement of the so-called hair-cutting order issued by Commissioner of Indian Affairs William Jones in 1902. Jones issued a circular to reservation agents and school superintendents urging them to put a stop to traditional Indian customs such as body painting and long hair. As an ambitious young man desiring to impress his supervisors, Burton forced Hopi men into compliance with the order, disregarding the important cultural meanings they associated with long hair. He desired to go even further, asking for permission to destroy kivas (underground ceremonial chambers) and to prohibit anthropologists from studying the tribe. Even after public outcry led Jones to modify the original order, Burton argued that "their long hair is the last tie that binds them to their old customs of savagery, and the sooner it is cut, Gordian like, the better it will be for them. I am fully in sympathy with the original order and only regret that there was any backward step taken in the matter; it has resulted in harm." Burton came under public scrutiny from the Sequoya League, an Indian reform group headed by Charles Lummis, an eccentric, feisty writer and promoter of the Southwest. The league charged the superintendent with misconduct regarding the treatment of Hopi children in the reservation schools. Charges of raids into Hopi homes to capture children, of severe whippings of students, and of poor food, medical care, and living conditions were leveled against Burton. Based on a secret investigation by the reformer Gertrude Gates and the testimony of Belle Axtell Kolp, a former Oraibi day-school teacher,

Lummis publicly attacked Burton and his policies and won a formal government investigation of the superintendent.[25]

Although Burton was cleared of most charges of wrongdoing and faced only minor reprimands, the accusations suggest that the Hopi reservation was not a welcoming place for Curtis and her phonograph. Considering the climate of distrust and suspicion that reigned among the Hopis during these years, it is little wonder that Curtis's Native informants felt reluctant to speak with her or to share songs. Many Hopis must have distrusted whites, no matter their professions of goodwill. Curtis, though, firmly believed that the struggles she faced in getting Hopis' cooperation stemmed from government policies that sought to wipe out the Native cultural traditions she eagerly sought to preserve.

After her initial struggles to record music in Oraibi, Curtis returned to her New York home in 1903, frustrated and disheartened by the opposition she had encountered. She complained that the Bureau of Indian Affairs "engaged in a work of well-meaning iconoclasm parallel to that of the conquering Spaniards of the sixteenth century, who in their zeal for Christianizing had made bonfires of the sacred glyphic books of the Mayas and Incas, whose civilization was in some respects higher than their own." These attitudes forced her to work in secret for fear of being expelled from the reservation. The policies at the Indian schools particularly galled Curtis. She was appalled that Hopi children could not sing or even speak in their native tongues and called the policy a form of "race suicide." Drawing on a "hereditary friendship" between the Curtis and Roosevelt families, Curtis expressed these sentiments in a letter to the president and asked for his help in overturning the destructive policies of the Indian Office.[26]

Curtis captured Roosevelt's attention by sending him one of the songs she had collected, music that he found "most striking" and "very interesting." The song opened the door for a meeting in which Curtis persuaded the president to take immediate action on her behalf. Curtis voiced many of the same arguments she would repeat throughout her career, arguments that bridged the span between the assimilationists of the late nineteenth century and the cultural pluralism of reformers like John Collier two decades later. She shared with the president the insights of a Native American she had met on her trip who told her, "The white man thinks that no people in the world can be any good unless they talk his language, swear like him, pray like him, and wear his ugly and uncomfortable clothes." She was not, however, calling for full acceptance of Native American culture as it then stood. Instead she argued that Indian officials needed to be more discerning as they sought to assimilate their charges to white ways. She asserted that to "educate a primitive race the would-be educators should first study the native life in order to preserve and build upon what is worthy in the native culture." Not only would preservation of desirable traits provide Native peoples with the self-respect necessary for their development, she argued, but their "racial gifts" would assuredly enrich the culture of white Americans.[27]

Curtis's proposal had its intended impact on the president. Within hours of their meeting Roosevelt provided her with the necessary letters to research on Western reservations free from official interference. Roosevelt wrote to Secretary of the Interior Ethan Allen Hitchcock that "a young lady who is particularly interested in the semi-civilized Indians of the Southwest" had impressed him with her ideas about the preservation of the "artistic side of the life of the Indian." He told Hitchcock that he fully agreed with Curtis's proposals to develop and preserve Indian songs and poetry and to reform education policies, so that teachers could "do everything possible to develop the Indians' artistic capacity along their own lines." Roosevelt instructed Hitchcock to speak with William Jones, the commissioner of Indian affairs, and have him "confer with Miss Curtis" and discuss the matter with Hamlin Garland and George Bird Grinnell, both members of Roosevelt's informal cabinet of

Indian advisors. Roosevelt concluded with the directive, "I should like every possible facility given Miss Curtis for exhaustive investigation on the reservations in question."[28]

President Roosevelt's support bolstered Curtis's confidence and encouraged her to carry out her plans to soften the harsh edges of existing assimilation policy. Thanking Roosevelt for his prompt and insightful assistance, Curtis planned to carry out "more thorough investigations of schools and societies connected with Indian matters in the East." She felt a sense of urgency, fearing future presidents would not share his "enlightened" views on reforming Indian policy. "Therefore," Curtis rather naively remarked, "I think the Indian question should be set right if possible during your administration."[29] Emboldened by presidential support, Curtis reached out to other prominent people connected with Indian affairs and resumed collecting Native music in the Southwest.

Curtis shared the basis of her research agenda in a 1903 article in *Harper's*. She portrayed her arrival in Oraibi from the viewpoint of her Hopi guests: "What has the *Pahana* [Hopi for a white person or an American] come for, how long is she going to stay, and what are in all those boxes?" Curtis imagined Hopis raising these queries as she settled into a government house at the foot of the mesa. Once established she remained a source of curiosity for the villagers, especially after she set up the phonograph and tried to entice them to sing for her. She remarked that at her makeshift studio "the Indians collected daily with true Hopi curiosity to peek in at the windows, to stare at the 'Pahana' and to join in the fun and excitement of singing into the machine." Curtis claimed she could not leave the house without being followed by an entourage of Hopis.[30]

She recorded the visits, several clandestine, of Hopi singers who for a variety of reasons wanted her to record their music. She met the composer Tawakwaptiwa after overhearing a group of men sing one of his songs at the local trading post. Using the aid of an interpreter Curtis hummed his song and asked him how he had composed it. Tawakwaptiwa joined Curtis in the singing, providing "vivid gestures" to describe the song about "butterfly maidens" chasing one another through the "virgin corn." The song, like many of the Hopi tunes Curtis collected, reflected the almost universal Hopi preoccupation with rain for their crops. After meeting Tawakwaptiwa and learning about his artistic and composing abilities, Curtis exclaimed, "Here was a genius, one in whom the joy of life sparkled like living water, overflowing in picture, poetry and song, spontaneous as a leaping fountain."[31] Another Hopi singer, Poliyeshwa, followed Curtis to her studio during a windstorm, sang for her, and asked her if she wanted to record his song. Although claiming he wanted to share his song, Poliyeshwa proved reluctant to do so in the presence of other Hopis. After the recording an older Hopi woman arrived, forcefully invited herself into Curtis's home, and asked her to play Poliyeshwa's song. Unhappy with this version the old woman retrieved an English-speaking girl to voice her opinions to Curtis, who then convinced the woman to sing her own version of the song.[32] Curtis used these accounts of recording to bolster her argument that Native people wanted their music preserved and understood.

Although women anthropologists of the region were often consigned to "feminine" topics and women informants, Curtis worked with both men and women. Most of the informants she distinguished by name were in fact men. Like many other women researchers Curtis collected material from daily life, but her interests generally transcended the domestic realm. She collected lullabies and corn-grinding songs from women, but also men's work songs and ceremonial music. Her interest in the spiritual nature of the songs, the way that singers used the music to integrate life and work, outweighed discussions of gender roles, even in songs collected from women. For example, when she visited the New Mexican pueblo of Laguna to inquire into the Spanish influence on Native songs, she collected music primarily from women. As she walked the "picturesque" streets she heard strains of music drifting down from a rooftop. A group of women, a few of whom spoke some English, sang as they ground corn. Curtis learned that the songs reflected the need for rain and provided the women with a rhythm for their labors. She promised them that she would write down their songs on paper so "people will know that Indian songs are beautiful, and the songs will never wholly be lost, or forgotten."[33] Although she occasionally discussed women's domestic roles and motherhood, her concerns reflect a more general interest in preservation and in understanding the song's meaning. She continued this pattern of collecting as she visited other Southwestern tribes.

From these interactions with Native informants Curtis articulated her ideas on the relationship between music collector and singer, one involving a "reciprocal interchange of ideas." Recorders of Indian music needed to be cautious in their use of this material, she warned. They must recognize the ideas upon which the music rested and understand the connections between Indian society and music. White researchers must be willing to learn from their Native informants. She stressed the importance of recording songs exactly as Native people sang them. "Instead of harmonizing the songs," she asked later in her career, "would not the Indian Office more wisely lay particular stress on their accurate transmission from the old Indians to the Indians of to-day?"[34] Like many whites who feared Indians were "vanishing," she also desired to preserve this music for future generations. Other collectors of Native American music at the time, such as Alice Fletcher and "Indianist" composers like Charles Cadman, believed Indian music needed to be harmonized or "idealized" by the collector.[35] Curtis opted for a different approach. "Many have said truly that the songs of the negro and the American Indian contain a wealth of musical material for the composer," Curtis noted. "But I sought the Indian songs solely that I might reverently record and preserve what I could of an art that is now fast passing away beneath the influence of the Moody and Sankey hymn tunes and patriotic songs taught the Indians in the government schools."[36] Indian songs, she argued, needed to be recorded with exacting detail and in their original format.

Most important to Curtis, recorders of Indian music needed to understand and sympathize with Native Americans, even to the point of adopting an Indian persona. In a visit to a government classroom she claimed to have learned how to properly and effectively interact with Native people. The students, because of repressive educational practices, had learned to hide their cultural expressions from any white person. By singing Indian songs to the children and showing them that she "respected and loved the things that were dear to them," Curtis drew out their tribal songs. "Though I had a white face I was somehow 'Indian inside,'" she remarked, seeing her attempts to be "Indian" as the key to the successful collection of Native American music. Adopting an Indian persona, as several scholars have noted, became a means of creating an American identity and a way to achieve authenticity. Further, it allowed white Americans to alleviate the guilt surrounding the brutality of their collective history with American Indians and to then form more secure relationships with Native people.[37]

Bonds between informant and collector, Curtis believed, formed in their struggle to comprehend one another. She recounted her experiences with Koianimptiwa, an educated Hopi who spoke some English and dressed in American clothing. He approached Curtis one afternoon saying, "I want to sing. . . . I want to sing my song." The Hopi composer struggled to express his ideas in English so that Curtis could really understand. His efforts inspired her. The young man explained that he had composed the entire song the day before and intended it for an upcoming kachina dance. He wanted Curtis to record it before anyone else heard it. "I gazed at Koianimptiwa and saw him in a new light," Curtis wrote. "I had often watched him hauling wood, but now I wondered that I had never before thought of him as a poet." Curtis continued: "I was filled with the poetry of the song, and I looked at my Indian guest with something like awe. I longed to know how the creative impulse had stirred his fancy to activity. I longed to know the workings of the Indian mind when roused by the call of genius." Curtis hired Koianimptiwa to drive her to a camp across the desert and used the time to try to learn the kachina song. As the Hopi singer sang Curtis tried unsuccessfully to imitate him. She almost gave up: "Ah Koianimptiwa, I am stupid and your song seems very difficult to me!" As the day wore on, and the two struggled to communicate with one another, Curtis finally grasped the music as she observed how the song seemed to embody "the very spirit of the desert." At the end of the day she took the Hopi's hand and made a promise to him, a vow she felt she made to all of her informants:

> I have learned your song and I am going to take it to my people, the Pahanas, who live near the great, great water. I want them to know that the Indian songs are beautiful. They have never heard any Hopi music; you have never seen the great waters near which my people live. The Pahanas will listen to your song, and it will be as new, as strange and wonderful to them as the big salt ocean would be to you. And when they have listened and wondered, I will say to them: "This is Koianimptiwa's song. May it bring rain to his fields!"[38]

Curtis took on the mantle of mediator between Indians and Americans like herself. She had come to believe that the bonds she forged with informants like Koianimptiwa qualified her to speak on their behalf. Helen Carr's work on writers engaging with Native American topics provides insight into Curtis's need to connect with her informants. Carr points out that many writers identified strongly with their Native American subjects and tried to use this identification to disassociate themselves from the "aggressiveness, destructiveness and materialism of the present, and identify with the Indians' difference from this." This portrayal, Carr asserts, often manifested itself in writers engaged in some form of ethnographic fieldwork. Curtis set herself forth "as someone with the unusual gift of gaining the love and respect of the observed group, who then offers trusting confidences."[39] Curtis demonstrated to her readers that she had indeed gained the trust of her informants through her efforts not just to record their music, but to painstakingly learn their songs and share them with others. Through her efforts, Curtis contended, she had earned the right to speak on behalf of Native peoples.

BY THE FALL OF 1904, BELIEVING THAT SHE HAD CREATED important ties with Native American singers and having recorded a number of songs in the Southwest, Curtis began articulating plans for a larger collection of Indian music, one for which she would become a scribe on behalf of the Native people she had visited. Although she had published some of the songs she had collected, she planned a more comprehensive book comprising Indian song and story.[40] Even though the Curtis family was relatively well-off, Edward and Augusta could not financially support their daughter's ambitions. Natalie Curtis, therefore, acquired the financial and philosophical support of Charlotte Osgood Mason. Mason, described by Curtis as a woman "well known for her warm interest in human problems and her charity of heart," had befriended Curtis during her spiritual searching as an adolescent. A wealthy widow with an avowed interest in the "primitive," Mason became Curtis's patron and benefactor and traveled with her on research trips in the West.[41] Curtis found another sponsor in the wealthy philanthropist George Foster Peabody. Peabody had made millions as an investment banker with Spencer Trask and Company, but he had grown uneasy over the widening gap between the rich and the poor and devoted himself to full-time philanthropy. He especially supported peace movements and the education of Southern African Americans. Curtis met the philanthropist through either family connections or Mason and interested him in her work. Peabody offered to support a research trip to gather material for what Curtis described as "some form of a book [that] may be used in the Government Schools." Although this project excited Curtis, she feared sharing her ideas with too many people. She explained to Peabody her "feeling that something of the force of the purpose is dissipated if it is too widely shared before the flame has had its chance to kindle the blaze for which it was struck." Thanking him for the thousand dollars he had just sent, Curtis told Peabody that this "flame" had been ignited when the "woes of a helpless people stirred my whole soul to desire for helpfulness." She continued, "Now you have made it possible for me to do that which I have daily and nightly asked to do, and to do it as we have dreamed and hoped it might be done." Curtis's "we" referred to Mason and the ideals she held up for Curtis in her work, including an appreciation for the spiritual as well as the musical and artistic aspects of Indian music. Both Mason and Peabody enabled Curtis to carry out the grandiose task they envisioned. She wrote Peabody that she felt her work to be "the Indians' song" and implored, "Let me do my small part as scribe in the still hour before the dawn, and then let the work speak, and the silent people give at last their message of simplicity and truth."[42]

Having assumed the role of "scribe" for the unheard Native peoples of America, Curtis expanded her knowledge of the nation's many Indian groups. One of the main outlets she chose, interestingly enough, was an Eastern boarding school for Native students. Even though Curtis often criticized Indian education policies, she chose to work closely with officials at Hampton Institute, a school established for African Americans soon after the Civil War that had initiated an Indian program in 1877. Curtis became connected with Hampton soon after her initial foray into collecting Native American music. Her patrons may have introduced her to school officials — Peabody actively supported the school, and Mason had

invited Curtis to accompany her on visits to the institution — or
her family might have had connections, particularly through her
uncle George William Curtis. Curtis supported Hampton's mission
to prepare blacks and Indians to become teachers, farmers, and
skilled laborers without losing every aspect of their "traditional"
cultures. She especially endorsed its policy of preserving the music
and folklore of its students. Donal Lindsey argues, in a study of the
school's Indian program, that Hampton's interest in the study of
Native cultures worked to "reinforce both its stance on education
and its training methods, fitting the student for a life of service to
his community but not for advancement in a rapidly modernizing
white nation." Although criticized for what appeared to be limited
aspirations for its students, Hampton leaders countered that "racial
traits" could not be changed easily or quickly, so the school best
served its students by preparing them to return to reservation communities. Studying their cultural traditions, they argued, would give
students pride in their heritage and ease their transition back into
Indian society. Cultural preservation further benefited the school by
attracting the support of Northern and Southern whites interested
in Native American art and music.[43]

Curtis and her patrons were drawn to Hampton in part because
of its programs in musical preservation. In a 1904 article Curtis
praised Hampton's "noble task" of preserving Indian music and for
encouraging its graduates to return home and collect tribal songs.
She argued that incorporating Native music and art into the students' manual skills training would not detract from the school's
aim. Because "primitive man expresses his aspirations in his religion
and art," she argued, any effort to suppress this would result in the
"degradation of the real man." In a 1905 article, "Hampton's "Double
Mission," Curtis commended the school's tradition of encouraging
its African American pupils to sing and preserve spirituals, which
allowed "the colored people [to give] to our country something we
had not before." Now the opportunity to do the same for Native

Americans at Hampton presented itself. These efforts went beyond saving songs — they saved the singers as well. If citizenship is based on self-respect, Curtis reasoned, then how could one have self-respect if taught to despise one's own race? Hampton produced an African American or Native American graduate who "is not an imitation white man but the best kind of Negro and Indian," who will "make the best kind of American citizen he is capable of making." Curtis urged Hampton to continue to pursue this course, adding, "where Hampton leads, may all Indian schools follow."[44] Curtis clearly did not agree with critics of Hampton's policy regarding its supposedly limited (and perhaps racist) aspirations for its students.

Her vocal support for the school's mission paid handsome dividends for Curtis. The *Southern Workman*, the school's periodical, published her articles on the value of Indian music, as well as short songs she had collected.[45] School officials allowed her to record music from its Native students, and Curtis kept a notebook of songs specifically for publication in the *Southern Workman*. She fostered a close relationship with Hampton leaders, particularly Principal Hollis B. Frissell. The two regularly corresponded to plan meetings and discuss Curtis's work. Through Frissell's influence school presentations became a platform for Curtis to express her ideas about the value of collecting Native American music. For example, in April 1904 she participated in Hampton's anniversary celebration, which offered Indian music as a new feature on its program. Curtis "seized upon the spirit of the moment," pointing out the value of Native American music and poetry, which were rapidly vanishing. She organized an Indian entertainment for Hampton's 1905 "Virginia Day," spending several weeks at the school "inspiring and rehearsing" students for their presentation. Curtis's remarks at this performance about the value of Indian music to American national music were interspersed with Pawnee, Arapaho, and Hopi songs.[46] The following year she wrote to Frissell about the importance of the musical presentation: "I feel very strongly with you that the

Indians should be thus represented at our meeting. I will gladly do my utmost to come and help."[47] She planned a commencement program in which the students would "appear in costume and sing," as their "appearance could be made a very attractive and pleasing incident on the program." The *Southern Workman* informed readers about Curtis's work, arguing that "the time was right for making an impression" about the worth and dignity of Native music. Leaders at Hampton, acknowledging the school's interest "in the preservation of the folk-lore and folk-songs of the races to which its pupils belong," urged its students to write out, preserve, study, and contribute their songs to scholars like Curtis.[48]

During visits to the East Coast Curtis worked on her project of collecting music from a larger number of Native American groups. She visited with Passamaquoddy and Penobscot tribal members in eastern Maine and transcribed their war, dance, and love songs.[49] She also sought assistance from many noted scholars of Indian languages and societies. She wrote to Matilda Coxe Stevenson for advice on the translations of Zuni song titles and remarked that her work with the Zuni tribe had become "a growing pleasure." She also wrote to James Mooney, a noted BAE anthropologist who knew several Native languages, had conducted fieldwork among tribes in Oklahoma, and was best known for his work on the Ghost Dance religion. She sent him some Kiowa "song-words" that she had collected from students at Hampton, hoping that he would examine and correct them for her. Curtis also contacted other scholars, including J. Dynely Prince for help with New England tribes, the anthropologist Franz Boas for assistance with the Kwakiutl, and the missionary H. R. Voth for help with the Hopi. Curtis further drew from the work of other experts, notably Alice Fletcher, Francis LaFlesche, Washington Matthews, Frank Cushing, and James Stevenson. She kept voluminous notebooks containing multiple versions of songs, questions to ask various professionals, and notes on translations and the meanings of songs and stories.[50]

A promising opportunity to encounter additional groups of Native Americans presented itself at the Louisiana Purchase International Exposition in St. Louis late in 1904. Concentrated groups of Native peoples provided Curtis with the chance to directly observe and compare their art, music, and dance. Beginning in 1876 the United States joined Europe in hosting international expositions celebrating industrial achievement and the "progress" of the white upper and middle classes. The St. Louis fair, the "largest, most spectacular fair the country had yet seen," celebrated the centennial of the Louisiana Purchase. Sprawled across a 1,272-acre site, the exposition boasted eight neoclassical buildings, numerous foreign pavilions, an Olympic stadium, and a commercial entertainment zone known as the "Pike."[51]

Besides the "normal array of commercial and technological exhibits" in the main buildings, fair planners had also amassed the "most extensive anthropological exhibit of any world's fair," under the anthropologist W. J. McGee. Other ethnological exhibits included a Filipino village and a model Indian schoolhouse, both arranged by the federal government. Along the Pike visitors witnessed daily reenactments of the Boer War, visited the Fair Japan concession, or strolled through the re-created streets of Jerusalem. Even the Olympic games, held in conjunction with the exposition, sponsored "Anthropology Days," featuring various indigenous peoples from around the world competing in traditional Olympic events and demonstrating their own special talents (the highlight for fairgoers being a Pygmy mud fight).[52] Fair planners depicted Native Americans in three venues: along the Pike, in Wild West Shows and the "Cliff Dwellers" and "Alaska" exhibits; in informative installations supported by agencies of the federal government; and in exhibits such as the Indian school that were intended to draw a sharp contrast between the "savagery" of the past and the "civilization" of the future.[53]

Curtis, who had attended the previous major American fair in

Chicago in 1893, arrived in St. Louis in the fall of 1904 prepared to view the ethnological exhibits.[54] Like other fairgoers Curtis probably wanted to partake of the many sights and sounds before the fair closed forever, but her main focus was a comparative study of the music of the "primitive races" on display.[55] Accompanied and aided by her brother George, Curtis accomplished much at the fair: she gathered material for an article on the "primitive" music of "many lands," she photographed several Native peoples for later research, she collected music and folklore from different tribes of Native Americans, and she established important new contacts for subsequent collecting. George helped his sister by jotting down stories, recording the names and tribal information of informants, and noting information useful for future fieldwork.[56] The songs and stories mainly dealt with tribal creation myths or dances and ceremonials. One Navajo informant, Basante, provided the Curtises with a version of a tribal creation song and described the mountains sacred to his people. Curtis wrote in her notebook that Basante was "very glad to have [the] song written down for he says that nowadays the youth are . . . careless of the old songs and changes are apt to come to them." Basante also shared a "very sacred" song with Curtis, a song so holy that he silenced her when she asked him to sing it while he was working with other Navajos. A man identified as Charlie Kwakiutl shared a story about how a Kwakiutl man received a special dance through supernatural means. The Curtises also collected explanations of ceremonials and tribal legends, like a Klalish totem pole story and a Crow tale of twelve brothers. Many of the informants were schoolchildren. The Indian Office had recruited pupils to participate in the model school and to serve as interpreters, and it only seems reasonable that the Curtises would have relied more heavily on English-speaking informants. George listed many of their informants by name, such as Ida Turningbear, a fifth-grader from Yankton, South Dakota, who shared "How the Indians Live," and Floyd Young Hairy Wolf, who recounted a Crow legend. Some of the informants later became well-known. James Murie, a Pawnee who explained ceremonials to Curtis and assisted her with subsequent fieldwork, became an anthropologist, and Jacob C. Morgan, an interpreter and contributor of a creation story who had attended Hampton Institute, became a Navajo tribal leader.[57] Perhaps the most famous informant was the captured Chiricahua Apache leader Geronimo, whom organizers persuaded to participate in the fair by allowing him to sell his autograph and photographs to fairgoers. Curtis persuaded the Apache to share and explain his medicine song for her growing collection.[58] Curtis and her brother visited anthropological exhibits of other "primitives," as well. They saw the Ainu of Japan; Patagonians from South America; African Pygmies; Moros, Igorots, and Negritos from the Philippines; and Native American tribes including the Cocopa, Kwakiutl, Pima, Navajo, Cheyenne, and Pawnee.[59] The pair observed Native people's public performances of dances and songs and found opportunities to speak with them and other attendees.

Scholars of world's fairs stress the importance of examining the messages fair planners intended for their expositions. The historian Robert Rydell has characterized the St. Louis fair as an "overarching effort by local and national elites to issue a manifesto of racial and material progress and national harmony" that used an "anthropologically validated landscape" to justify both the conquest of the former Louisiana Purchase and the more recent acquisition of the Philippines. This theme was particularly borne out in the exhibits prepared by W. J. McGee of the different "types" of races that occupied each one of his four stages of development — savagery, barbarism, civilization, and enlightenment. A former member of the BAE, McGee arranged his living exhibits around his theory of racial hierarchy and sought to showcase different "types" representing stages of human development. The historian Paul Kramer concurs that the St. Louis fair was an "advertisement for an expanding industrial capitalist order that sought to justify both foreign commerce and military intervention to their respective publics through lurid racist imagery." He further argues for the importance of considering the effect the colonized could have upon their representations. The historian Frederick Hoxie places the St. Louis fair within the context of changing public perceptions of Native Americans. He argues that two very different ideas about Indians competed for public acceptance. The notion that Indians were "members of an exotic race with little connection to modern America" vied with the idea that Indians, through education and "progress," could become assimilated to white American ways. The St. Louis fair, Hoxie argues, helped resolve this dilemma — the idea of Native Americans as "primitives" became the dominant theme in popular representations. America's Native peoples joined other "backward races" assembled in St. Louis to serve as entertainment and "education" for fairgoers.[60]

Curtis's activities at the fair reflect both her acceptance of and her challenge to the dominant racial and imperialist discourses of the fair's organizers. On one hand, she accepted many aspects of the official philosophy about human development and race. She readily placed nonwhite peoples into the category of "primitive" and "backward" and even offered her own ranking of their development. Nor did she question the notion that people could be placed on display for the personal edification of white Americans. In a *New York Times* article comparing the music of "primitive" peoples she ranked and judged these groups according to standards similar to McGee's classification. Curtis favored Native American music over other forms of "primitive" song. Chinese music she deemed less interesting or useful because, "after centuries of development, [it] now is crystallized," although the orchestra performance at the Chinese theater intrigued her. Recognizing increased interest in the peoples of the Philippines, Curtis reported on the different music styles of the islands. She found the Igorots fascinating despite their songs, which "scarcely can be called music at all." Like other fairgoers she found the native people of Japan, the Ainu, an "ethnological puzzle" because of their light complexions but "primitive" traits. Their music "is so different from all others as scarcely to sound human," she reported, but their "sweet and simple living" appealed to her. Curtis was indifferent to Japanese music, preferring other Japanese arts. However, she did find Japanese absorption of Ainu music and art into their national culture an important model for Americans. Curtis concluded her article with an assertion that of all primitive people Native Americans were the most artistic. "It may come as a surprise to many to learn that the Indian is a man of great possibilities in mind and character," Curtis wrote. "He is also a poet." Because of their potential contributions Curtis asked her readers, "Should not the lesson of Japan and the Ainu make us stop and think what our own art and literature might become if we should harken to the Indian's song?" As she had earlier rejoiced in locating America's "Orient" in the Southwest, Curtis now celebrated the treasure of folk music to be discovered among Native Americans. She described various types of song, ascribing differences to the characters and environments of different tribes but assuring her readers that all these songs contained a "wealth of musical inspiration." This treasury of song, however, could soon vanish because of misguided assimilation policies. Curtis commented, "The intelligent listener turns sorrowfully from this abuse of valuable material to seek in the older Indians the real Indian music, alas, so rapidly vanishing before the efforts of the schools."[61] From these comments it is clear that Curtis absorbed many of the fair's messages about a hierarchy of human development and the commodification of "the primitive" for white American consumption.

Although one cannot deny the impact of the intended messages of the fair, fairgoers like Curtis interpreted and understood the exhibits and entertainment they witnessed in St. Louis on their own terms as well. At the fair Curtis incorporated her own observations and expectations with the dominant discourse of the fair planners, particularly in her response to the anthropological exhibits.[62] She dismissed the goal of assimilation to white ways by complaining that Indian school bands played "only our own commonplace tunes." Curtis did not fully embrace the idea that "primitive" cultures at best could only provide "civilized" Americans with a few thrills and some laughs but had nothing of substance (besides their land and labor) to offer the Western world. Curtis challenged this notion by calling Native American songs "poetry" and contending that, like the Japanese, Americans could benefit from making Native cultures part of their national identity. Curtis further refused to accept McGee's presentation of Native peoples as mere "types" for the study of human evolution. She took note of the names of her informants, tried to learn something of their personal and tribal histories, and valued their contributions.

Curtis also questioned the goals of complete assimilation as presented by the federal government's exhibits. As Hoxie contends, some Americans in the early twentieth century came to see Indians as "primitives" incapable of complete civilization, and some, like Curtis, worried that valuable artistic material would be lost if Native Americans totally accepted white ways. The historian Robert Trennert notes that the fair helped increase appreciation for Native arts and crafts in general and in the Southwest in particular.[63] Curtis, and others like her, helped generate public appreciation for the artistic and musical side of Indian life through their research at the fair and subsequent efforts inspired by the exposition. In particular her time in St. Louis broadened Curtis's goals to include other Indians in her musical studies and bolstered her plans for *The Indians' Book*. On a more practical level the fair provided significant contacts on several reservations. Indeed, shortly after leaving the fair the Curtis siblings traveled west to continue this research.

George Curtis and Natalie Curtis left St. Louis in early November and headed north to Wisconsin to begin a four-month tour of Western reservations, agencies, and boarding schools. Curtis went to collect material for her book; George, although vitally interested in his sister's goals, probably went to experience Western life (and to serve as a proper chaperone for his sister).[64] Their first stop was the Winnebago Agency, where they visited the school and met with individuals willing to share songs and stories. The letters of endorsement from Roosevelt may have eased the process, prompting superintendents and teachers to cooperate. By November 15 they had reached the Pine Ridge Agency in South Dakota and established themselves in a local hotel that served as a meeting place, as well as a home base for their excursions out to the reservation and the surrounding area. The superintendent allowed them to visit boarding and day schools, and they contracted with interpreters to aid them in their research. The Curtises sought out Sioux band leaders, whom they believed could best share the tribe's music with them. They even paid some, such as Short Bull, for songs. At Pine Ridge, as at other reservations, Curtis relied on Native interpreters as well as the local white missionary for assistance in interpreting and translating the material she collected. At their next stop, the Rosebud Agency, she immediately sought out a missionary for help with the language and relied on a "half-breed catechist" for interpreting.[65]

Curtis established relationships with individuals who shared their own material and also introduced her to other potential contributors. At Rosebud Curtis met Little Horse and his wife, "old St. Louis friends," who assisted her with her project.[66] At the Pawnee Agency in Oklahoma another St. Louis connection, James Murie, met with the Curtises. Murie taught Curtis a hand-game song and took her to witness a Ghost Dance. Perhaps the most important informant Curtis met on this trip was a Southern Cheyenne policeman whom she encountered on a train to Oklahoma City. This Southern Cheyenne, known as Hiamovi, or High Chief, became a major contributor to *The Indians' Book*. He shared hand-game, Sun Dance, and peyote songs with Curtis. He also introduced the

Curtises to informants from his and other tribes. The Curtises spent nearly a month with High Chief, traveling across the countryside, meeting in the lodges, teepees, and homes of several Native Americans willing to share parts of their cultures.

Curtis also maintained her reliance on the contributions of schoolchildren. Curtis's concern with reforming the education system brought her to many schools, and she found the children willing to sing, tell stories, and provide artwork. She traveled to reservation schools as well as prominent off-reservation institutions, such as Chilocco in Oklahoma, Albuquerque in New Mexico, and Phoenix in Arizona. Because students from many different tribes attended these schools — for example, at Phoenix Curtis worked with Hopi, Pima, Navajo, Yavapai, and Apache students — Curtis gained access to a greater variety of material without having to actually visit each tribe in person.[67]

Both George Curtis and Natalie Curtis relished their Western adventures. They collected a good deal of information for Curtis's book. They photographed many of the people they met, intending many of these pictures for the book, but also for their edification. The Curtises sent a number of pictures of themselves home to the family back in New York, especially photographs of both siblings with High Chief. George reported on some of their adventures — Natalie nearly falling from her horse, cold rides across wintry plains, clandestine meetings with Indians behind railroad embankments. He occasionally expressed annoyance with his sister's willingness to meet with any Indians who would talk with her. "N. passed the time of day with a few degenerate Indians," he complained, but at least, he conceded, she only bought them coffee when they asked her for drinking money.[68] George appreciated most of the sights and sounds of their trip. He gloried in the beauty of sunsets, the excitement of hand games, the mystery and solemnity of peyote services, the "ceremonious and beautiful" Ghost Dancing, and the charm of many of the informants.[69] In January the Curtises left the Plains region for the more familiar grounds of Arizona and New Mexico. Natalie Curtis kept a notebook of useful phrases to facilitate her research among Hopi informants. "Sing for me" and "thank you" were included, among other useful words.[70] The Curtises acquainted themselves with Zuni dancing, Navajo sand paintings, and many of the region's schools. By early March they returned to New York City, and Curtis began preparations for publicizing what she had gleaned about Native cultures on her trip.

IN A FEW YEARS CURTIS HAD REFASHIONED HERSELF FROM a classically trained pianist and composer to an active collector of Native American music and a major voice calling for its appreciation and preservation. Experiences in the Southwest and with Native music inspired her to extend herself in ways she might never have thought possible. She met with President Roosevelt, secured financial backing from two patrons, braved several tours of Western reservations, and wrote numerous articles on Indian music and her fieldwork. Her transformation from someone largely ignorant of Native people and their cultures to a forthright advocate for and self-proclaimed "expert" on Native Americans was truly remarkable. By 1905 Curtis focused her efforts on her opus, soon to be titled *The Indians' Book*, in which she fully expounded on her ideas about Native American music, art, and folklore and their relationship to Indians and to other Americans.

4

"The Pencil in the Hand of the Indian"

Curtis and *The Indians' Book*

"THIS IS THE INDIANS' BOOK," THE SOUTHERN CHEYENNE leader Hiamovi, or High Chief, began his foreword to Natalie Curtis's major work on Native American song and story. "Through this book," he implored, "may men know that the Indian people was [*sic*] made by the Great Mystery for a purpose." They had welcomed white "strangers" to the land divinely ordained for them and shared its bounty with them, as it "was meant by the Great Mystery that the Indian should give to all peoples." Hiamovi pointed out, however, that "the white man never has known the Indian. It is thus: there are two roads, the white man's road, and the Indians' road. Neither traveler knows the road of the other." Through the efforts of Curtis and Indians like himself Hiamovi hoped that this book would "help to make the Indian truly known in the time to come." It was important to the Southern Cheyenne leader, as it was to the white author, that the book represented the views of real Native people and fulfilled a purpose for whites and Indians alike. Hiamovi reiterated:

The Indian wise-speakers in this book are of the best men of their tribes. Only what is true is within this book. I want all Indians and white men to read and learn how the Indians lived and thought in the olden time, and may it bring holy-good upon the younger Indians to know of their fathers. A little while and the old Indians will no longer be, and the young will be even as white men. When I think, I know that it is in the mind of the Great Mystery that white men and Indians who fought together should now be one people.[1]

Curtis shared Hiamovi's view of her work and hoped to fulfill many of the same goals. She claimed that her book truly represented the words of the tribes she visited, arguing: "The Indians are the authors of this volume. The songs and stories are theirs; the drawings and title-pages were made by them. The work of the recorder has been but the collecting, editing, and arranging of the Indians' contributions." She intended her work to preserve the songs, stories, and art of a "primitive" people before they vanished in the face of white expansion and through the process of "civilization." Preservation of these valuable treasures would aid whites seeking an identity from the American environment and its own "folk" and also save the "racial inheritance" of the coming generation of Native Americans, who risked losing their cultures to assimilationist policies. Curtis also hoped that better understanding between the two groups would lessen conflict and ease the transition for Indians from "primitive" to "civilized."

The Indians of course were not the actual authors of this work. Curtis selected and shaped the material included in *The Indians' Book* for her own purposes, which may or may not have coincided with the needs and wants of tribal peoples. Further, she often presented Native Americans according to stereotypes and made broad generalizations about "the Indian." Her Indian often resembled the "noble savage," a timeless figure whose close contact with nature produced a childlike innocence and other qualities admired by industrialized white Americans. Curtis also accepted the equally widespread idea of the "vanishing Indian," a notion based on cultural evolutionism that held that Native peoples could not survive the process of modernization and would ultimately die out as a culture, if not as individuals. Closely related to this "vanishing Indian" were ideas about human evolutionary development in stages from "savagery" to "civilization"; these themes underlay her presentations of Indian music and folklore. Curtis's Indians were "primitives" to be studied to advance knowledge about human development. As primitives their options and abilities to participate in American society were limited by their racial evolutionary development. Curtis did not always see this "backwardness" as a negative, arguing that primitive people possessed innate abilities as artists and musicians and had a superior sense of spirituality compared to white Americans.

It is easy to criticize Curtis for views that today appear terribly misguided or even racist. By placing her motives and approach to collecting Indian songs in their proper context, however, her significance as a researcher becomes clearer. For all its stereotyping of Native Americans and questionable claims of Indian authorship, *The Indians' Book* differed from her contemporaries' collections of Native American music. It is important that Curtis presented Native viewpoints, attempted to engage in interracial dialogue with her informants, and claimed a moral responsibility to listen to Indian voices. Few other writers listed the names or included the words, however contrived, of those Indians who shared songs, told stories, or contributed drawings. Other researchers may have credited informants, but no other author claimed to be only a "recorder" or a "pencil in the hand of the Indian." Further, Curtis wrote for a popular audience of white readers while still attempting to address the scientific community. She made her presentation of Indian song and story accessible to the lay readers she hoped to influence while offering something to scholars of Indian life. Unlike some other writers on Indian cultures Curtis wanted her work to improve the conditions of contemporary Indian life. She used the informants in *The Indians' Book* to critique official government policy and to dispel popular negative views of Native cultures. Indians, she hoped, would benefit from the preservation process because they could incorporate the best of their old ways into their new modern lives. *The Indians' Book* offered a "new day" for young Native people; it held out the possibility of hope. Curtis therefore somewhat ambiguously straddled two approaches to the interpretation of Indian music — she fell into the trap of stereotyping and dehumanizing Native Americans, while she also attempted to provide a more human voice for an often silenced people.

The Indians' Book was Curtis's most important single contribution to the study of Native American music, although she shared her research in a number of other outlets, primarily those targeting a broader middle-class readership. Numerous magazine articles in *Harper's,* the *Outlook,* the *Craftsman,* and the *Southern Workman,* among other publications, and newspaper pieces in the *New York Evening Post* and the *Times* spread her work to a broad audience. Her writing for these popular outlets mirrors the efforts of other women involved in Southwestern anthropology, who often could not get their own research published in scholarly journals. "Popularizing and education were ways in which women were able to overcome their marginality," Shelby Tisdale asserts. Although their work came to be viewed as among "the most undervalued and underrewarded forms of anthropological discourse," Curtis and her fellow "popularizers" increased the public's understanding of the Southwest and Native Americans.[2]

Curtis's experiences, however, suggest that gender limitations alone did not lead her to publish in popular formats. She consistently sought to influence a broad audience more than a scientific one. Other members of her family, such as her uncle George William Curtis, an editor at *Harper's,* also turned to popular media to express their ideas. Furthermore, because anthropology had not yet become fully professionalized, many other amateurs and professionals also published in popular outlets. Curtis and other popularizers hoped to change average American views of Native Americans.

In her early writings she developed, elaborated, and reproduced the opinions and arguments that she later incorporated into *The Indians' Book*. Curtis's short publication *Songs of Ancient America* (1905) contained transcriptions and translations of three corn-grinding songs from Laguna Pueblo in New Mexico, along with Native artwork and Curtis's explanations of the material. She contended that the "Pueblo culture is of a high order on the primitive plane" and that the residents of Laguna were "small, gentle, and refined; natural potters and weavers; natural poets and song-makers," who accompanied every task with music. She maintained that these songs were very old, the "voice of ancient America," and that unless recorded by a sympathetic white friend, they would vanish along with the people of Laguna. To capture the songs, "as the Indians themselves sing them," Curtis had sought out the oldest women in the pueblo, who would know the "most authentic" versions of the songs. She stressed the importance of recording in the proper context, surrounded by Laguna women on their rooftops, singing and swaying rhythmically as they ground their daily corn in stone metates.[3] Curtis claimed that no matter the musical appeal, a song could only be understood fully when recorded in its original environment. *Songs of Ancient America*, unlike most of her other collections, presented Laguna songs in standard Western notation and in harmonization that was intended to reproduce the grinding sounds of the metates, which provided rhythm for the women as they sang. Curtis soon rejected harmonization, however, arguing that it detracted from "real" Indian music.

The absence of a Native "voice" in *Songs from Ancient America* differed from her approach in *The Indians' Book*. Curtis, like other researchers of Native American music, claimed authorship and authority over the material. She spoke as an expert on music and as

the interpreter of Native customs to a white audience. She followed
a similar approach in addressing a French audience in a short col-
lection of songs, "Chansons Indiennes. Tires du *The Indians' Book*"
(Indian Songs: Drawn from *The Indians' Book*), shortly before *The
Indians' Book* was published. This work, with its lack of an "Indian
voice," also represents an alternate approach to *The Indians' Book*.[4]
Curtis's experiences producing these shorter pieces prepared her for
The Indians' Book, in which she would instead present her subjects
as the authors and address the collection to a white as well as an
Indian audience

The Indians' Book became Curtis's best-known work and helped
establish her career in the study of Indian music. Readers responded
to its unique format and artistic character, which brought together
a diverse grouping of Native song, art, and story. The 1907 edition featured a stylish cover and colored typography throughout.[5]
A reader would first open to a brilliantly hued page of Southern
Cheyenne drawings of items from the "olden times" and would
then see the title page, complete with "Indianized" lettering and
a decorative border based on Native design. The foreword by the
Southern Cheyenne leader High Chief, which followed, included
a semblance of his handwritten signature and one of his drawings.[6]
Curtis then explained the presentation and transcription of the
music in the book and provided information on the drawings and
other artwork. Theodore Roosevelt's letter of endorsement came
next — "These songs cast a wholly new light on the depth and dignity of Indian thought, the simple beauty and strange charm — the
charm of a vanished elder world — of Indian poetry" — followed by
Curtis's introduction to the work, presenting her major themes and
ideas about Native Americans.[7] The introduction also explained the
purpose of the collection, the recording methods she had employed,
and her thoughts on the translation and transcription of Indian
music. A section on the current state of Indian life followed, and
then the main body of the book began.

Curtis presented the songs, stories, and artwork by tribe and followed a similar format for each group. She divided the material from eighteen tribes into six major groupings: Eastern (Wabanaki); Plains (Dakota, Pawnee, Cheyenne, Arapaho, Kiowa); Lake (Winnebago); Northwestern (Kwakiutl); Southwestern (Pima, Apache, Mojave-Apache, Yuma, Navajo); and Pueblo (Zuni, San Juan, Acoma, Laguna, Hopi). The major subsections sometimes contained additional material on a particular group, apart from sections on individual tribes. For example, under the "Plains" heading Curtis included subsections entitled "Organizations of the Plains Indians" and "The Holy Man or 'Medicine Man.'" Such subsections contained a separate piece on each tribe and included songs, stories, visual images, and music. Following the main body of text Curtis attached an appendix, which included a lengthy quote from John Fiske's *The Discovery of America* that justified the study of Native Americans and detailed interlinear translations of the songs from the main text for more serious researchers. In this section Curtis provided the Indian and English words for each song from the text, along with definitions and explanations of words and phrases. She expressed her hope that this work "may be of some aid in the comparative study of the linguistic stocks of the North American continent."[8] A list of "contributors" grouped informants by tribe and listed their Native names and an English name if they used one. A detailed index and a brief note about the lessons to be learned from "primitive man" concluded Curtis's work.

Each chapter had a similar format and served as a presentation on a particular tribe by its own members. Every tribal section had a title page that incorporated elements of design from artwork provided by someone in the tribe. For example, the Kwakiutl page featured the drawing of a killer whale that Curtis had collected from Charles James Newell at the St. Louis World's Fair. Even the lettering resembled tribal design. The Navajo title page's letters, for example, were meant to suggest the silverwork for which tribal members were well-known. Each chapter began with an ethnographic overview by Curtis in which she discussed the tribe's origins, environment, linguistics, history, and means of subsistence. She then explained the pronunciation of the tribe's language. Although the presentation in the tribal sections varied, all included pieces on customs, folklore, and songs. Curtis usually presented Native-language versions of the songs, along with English translations arranged in a lyrical fashion. Pictures and artwork of or by the participants were interspersed throughout each chapter. Each section concluded with handwritten transcriptions of the songs discussed in the main body.

An overview of one of the more significant chapters provides a good sense of what Curtis presented to her readers. The Cheyenne segment began with an informative ethnographic piece on the tribe, followed by a section on one of Curtis's main informants, High Chief, whose contribution "Cheyenne Life in the Olden Time" came next, along with a photograph of the leader. High Chief explained songs from the Sun Dance ceremony, songs for the Buffalo-Dance, and songs of the Red Fox Society. Another chief, Honihi-Wotoma (Wolf Robe), who was pictured on his horse, shared several songs as well. Curtis then included a piece called "The War-Path" that was followed by "Songs of Victory" contributed by Wolf Robe and Chief Nahios-si (Three Fingers). "An Old Tale," by Mochta-Wontz-tz (Starving Elk), explained the basis of the Cheyenne diet, and Three Fingers commented on a medicine song and a tune to be sung while swinging on buffalo-hide strips strung in tree boughs. A lullaby by a Southern Cheyenne identified as "Chief Woman" came next. Curtis included a photograph of High Chief smoking the "pipe of friendship" and then explained the popular "hand game" and its accompanying songs. The chapter concluded with a section explaining the basis for the peyote religion and a description of its ceremonies. Mowihaiz, a nephew of High Chief and a leader in the religion, contributed the final song of the chapter. In every chapter the songs appeared at the very end. Each had a handwritten appearance, as if transported directly from Curtis's field notes to the pages of *The Indians' Book*. Reproduced on a standard Western musical staff, the songs were not harmonized, although they contained directions for performance. Some songs, such as High Chief's "Buffalo Dance Song," contained only Cheyenne words, while others, such as Wolf Robe's "Song of Victory," provided English translations beneath the Native language.

THE FORMAT AND PRESENTATION OF *THE INDIANS' BOOK* reinforced the message that Native American cultures were disappearing and required the urgent attention of collectors like Curtis to salvage what still remained. These collectors asserted that Native American music needed to be preserved because of the benefits that would accrue to European American culture in the process. Curtis claimed that her informants specifically requested that she save their songs and stories, and she made a case for the reasons white readers would appreciate this material. The study of Native American music and culture would shed light on human development from savagery to barbarism to civilization, she argued, as well as provide insights into the evolution of Western music. Further, elements of Native American cultures could reinvigorate American society, possibly providing the nation with material and inspiration for an enriched cultural identity. These assumptions shaped how Curtis approached and processed the information she collected.

The Indians' Book's premise of the "vanishing Indian" was shared by other early twentieth-century Americans. The historian Brian Dippie remarks on the consistency of this theme in American history from the colonial period onward. Robert Berkhofer adds that because whites viewed Indians as savages and counterimages to civilization, they expected Indians to die out as European Americans expanded across the continent. By the second half of the nineteenth century notions of human evolution were added to this theme. Tribal peoples, scholars argued, would disappear as a "race" because their biological characteristics prevented them from adapting to the modern world. Evolutionist anthropologists contended that "races" evolved along a path from savagery to barbarism to civilization, exhibiting uniform characteristics at each stage. The study of human cultures, then, became an inquiry into the proper placement of groups into a hierarchy based on the notion that Western civilization stood at the apex and other "races" occupied levels below. Because characteristics at each stage were immutable, races would continue to occupy the same position on the evolutionary ladder and only "progress" very slowly. Although some commentators in the second half of the nineteenth century originally expressed optimism that all races progressed upward, and scholars like Franz Boas questioned this evolutionary scheme, by the 1890s many held "darker, more racist, more pessimistic views" of America's minorities. White Americans, according to Sherry Smith, defined Native Americans as "permanently peripheral, destined to economic dependence and political impotence."⁹

Throughout the nineteenth century white Americans expressed both self-righteous satisfaction and a sense of loss regarding such dire predictions for Native Americans. By the early twentieth century some had begun to lament the loss of Native cultures, especially as it would negatively impact the nation's sense of identity. In light of the many changes America faced in these decades, notably industrialization, immigration, and urbanization, the notion of the Indian as the "first American" fulfilled ideological and psychological needs. This "first American," Alan Trachtenberg argues, was increasingly made to take his "place in a revised version of the national character." Because they identified with Indians as the original Americans and saw them as their predecessors, Americans feared the consequences of Indians' disappearance. Brian Dippie asserts that the closing of the frontier, articulated by Frederick Jackson Turner in his famous 1893 address "Significance of the Frontier in American History," transformed the "Wild West into a treasured memory, a mythical embodiment of the nation's youth." Indians had ably served as symbols of a growing America, and their decline, no matter how inevitable, caused some to believe that "something precious, something basic to the nation's identity," was being lost.[10]

Curtis accepted this view of Indians and referred to Native Americans as "the most ancient of peoples" and as a "child race." Her informants often confirmed these views. After hearing stories about Dakota history Curtis explained to Short Bull, a leader in the Ghost Dance religion, that Dakotas were children on the cusp of becoming adults. "The old days will never be again, even as a man will never again be a child," she said. "Those days were the happy childhood of your race. Manhood brings sorrow and sorrow wisdom," she told the Dakota leader. Curtis also used stories to reinforce the notion of Indians as children. In "Hunting the Moose" the Wabanaki contributor Bedagi (Big Thunder) said: "The Great Spirit made all things; all men are his children. He made the Indians last of all, and so, since they are his youngest children, they are not as wise as the white men." This child race, Curtis contended, needed the time and space to evolve unimpeded. "The whole civilized world to-day faces this question," she wrote. "Is primitive man to retain his God-given right to evolution, or is he to be swept from off the earth before the imperious needs of civilized powers?"[11]

Curtis believed that the extinction of the first Americans would deprive the nation of a vital source of its identity and joined white writers, photographers, and anthropologists in a quest to preserve Native cultures. She was convinced that by writing down songs and stories from the oldest tribal people, she could best achieve these aims. She explained to her readers the process behind the making of *The Indians' Book*:

> By rail, by wagon, and by horse, over prairie and desert, the white friend journeyed from tribe to tribe, seeking the Indians with open friendship, and everywhere meeting their warm response. In nearly

every instance a chief was visited first and the purpose of the book explained to him. Would he and his people join in the making of a book to be the Indians' own — a book which should keep for all time the songs and stories of their race? The olden days were gone; the buffalo had vanished from the plains; even so would there soon be lost forever the songs and stories of the Indian. But there was a way to save them to the life and memory of their children, and that was to write them, even as the white man writes. The white friend had come to be the pencil in the hand of the Indian.[12]

Curtis claimed that Native Americans shared in white notions of the "vanishing" race, remarking that Indians responded to her requests for material with "enthusiasm that was touching in its gladness." Many elders had tried to "make some record of the songs" and "sought deeply to engrave the old tales upon the minds of a younger generation" because they recognized that "they walked in the sunset hour of their native life and that the night was soon to come."[13]

She stressed both the need and the willingness of tribal leaders to have their knowledge preserved. An elderly Navajo man replied to her request for a song by saying: "It is well that our songs should be written, and it is now time, indeed, that this should be done. . . . Unless the songs are written they will in time be forgotten." Having already realized this need the man remarked: "I have tried myself to find a way to record the songs, but I cannot write. Now you will write what I sing."[14] Another aged chief, a Pima, similarly told Curtis, "We are glad, indeed, to sing our songs for you." He feared the loss of the songs not only through the extermination of his people but also because of white prohibitions against singing Pima songs. "It is as you say — soon all the songs will be forgotten," the chief lamented. "White people do not like us to sing Indian songs."[15]

Native leaders not only recognized the need for preservation but, according to Curtis, warmly accepted her offer to preserve their music for them. She re-created her initial meeting with the Hopi leader Lololomai in Oraibi, when she explained her purpose in collecting Hopi music and received Lololomai's consent. Curtis told the Hopi leader that because children were attending school, they were "learning new ways and are singing new songs — American songs instead of Hopi." She feared that the children would never learn the beautiful Hopi music, and so it would be forgotten. Lololomai, Curtis reported, nodded his head slowly and replied, "Hao, hao (Even so, even so)." She further explained that because the Hopi lacked books, their songs and even their language might disappear. Yet she offered him hope: "But if you could write, you could put your song into a book, and your people, even to the children of their children, could know your song as if you yourself were singing." Until the Hopi could do this, however, Curtis offered to take up the task. After hearing her proposition the "old chief turned to me pathetically. There was a wistful yearning in the aged eyes, a cloud of trouble on the wrinkled brow." He feared that the superintendent would prohibit them from recording Hopi music. Curtis reassured him that "the great chief in Washington" had granted her permission and that she hoped to use her recordings to change white attitudes about Indians and their songs. To this Lololomai responded, "Lolomai pas lolomai (good, very good)," and began to sing for Curtis. She carefully wrote the music down and explained to the Hopi chief "the mysterious tracings" she made on the paper. Upon the song's completion Lololomai again demonstrated his support. "Ancha-a, ikwatchi, ancha-a (It is well, my friend, it is well)," the aged Hopi man replied before leaving Curtis to pray, purportedly for the success of her undertaking."[16]

Native Americans were not the only beneficiaries of *The Indians' Book*; Curtis and her readers would also gain from the preservation of Lololomai's songs. Indians, as primitives, could serve a useful function for Americans seeking to understand their own racial pasts. Curtis argued that *The Indians' Book* would shed light on the white race thousands of years earlier, when they occupied the same stage of development. "The child race of a by-gone age has left no written record of its thoughts. Silent through the ages has passed barbaric man," Curtis wrote, but her study would give them voice. She claimed, "Of value, then, to the history of the human race, as well as the history of America, are the written utterances of this primitive people." In the appendix she quoted from John Fiske's *The Discovery of America*: "Aboriginal America is the richest field in the world for the study of barbarism. . . . Until we have become familiar with ancient American society, and so long as our view is confined to the phases of progress in the Old World, the demarcation between civilized and uncivilized seems too abrupt and sudden." The continuity of human development, Fiske believed, could be witnessed in the study of Indian life at the present.[17]

    Although Fiske was more concerned with the broad outlines of human development, other scholars focused on how Indian songs would provide insights into the evolution of music. Alice Fletcher, for instance, hoped that her collection of Native music in *Indian Story and Song* would shed light on the history of music, "for these songs take us back to a stage of development antecedent to that in which culture music appeared among the ancients, and reveal to us something of the foundations upon which rests the art of music as we know it to-day." The musician John Comfort Fillmore also believed his studies of Native American songs would enlighten scholars about the evolution of music, because they revealed how current Western music, especially the basic elements of rhythm, harmony, and melody, had developed from primitive forms. Curtis traced a similar path, arguing that primitive Indian song lacked harmony, which she suggested might be supplied by the natural environments of the singers. However, the other two components of song, rhythm and melody, were highly developed in Indian music. Curtis also found Native songs to contain intriguing vocal expressions and use of symbolism. *The Indians' Book* revealed the ways in which music evolved and changed technically, emotionally, and spiritually.[18]

Curtis's positive representation of Indian traits fell into the category of ideas and attitudes often labeled "primitivism." In her mind the cultures of Native Americans had much to offer modern America precisely because they were expressions of a primitive people. Marianna Torgovnick understands primitivism as a set of tropes, images, and ideas "through which we view primitive societies, draw lines and establish relations of power between us and them." She contends that "the needs of the present determine the value and nature of the primitive," making the primitive "infinitely docile and malleable, as what we want shifts and changes." Primitivism, defined by Leah Dilworth as "a belief in the superiority of seemingly simpler ways of life," served as a "reactionary response" to modern, industrial life. Dilworth notes that people like Curtis viewed Native American cultures as more real and authentic alternatives to their own lives and believed them to be a panacea for the problems of their own society. Dilworth further argues that between 1880 and 1920 these visions of Native Americans shifted from Indians as the "vanishing race" to the Indian as "the ideal American artist." Although Dilworth sees a definite shift in imaginings of Indians in this period, Curtis's primitives remained quite flexible. Although she too represented Indians as model artisans, she also drew from older white notions of primitivism embodied in the notion of the noble savage.[19]

The idea of the noble savage had a long history, and Americans in the early twentieth century found appealing ideas of the Indian as a primitive living in a "golden age," as a "man of nature" in touch with his emotions and living by the rhythms of the natural world. The noble savage was brave, honest, heroic, spiritual, and in possession of a simpler way of life. This view, however, deprived Native people "of a historical reality apart from white projections." The noble savage belonged in the past, occupying what anthropologists have called the "ethnographic present." These Indians had no history; they had always lived in their current state, and because the outer world had changed, they were fated to vanish. Scott Vickers notes that the noble savage was "a departing visionary, a wise and retiring nobleman of the plains or forest." Curtis's portrayal of Native Americans reflected nostalgia for an irretrievable past and demonstrated white needs for an alternative way of life.[20]

Throughout *The Indians' Book* Native Americans functioned as noble savages who had much to offer white Americans. Many informants' accounts focused on the glories of the past — or "olden times," as Curtis often phrased it — prior to white intrusion. Curtis featured informants who were supposed to be the oldest members of their tribes, hoping they would appear to her readers as the most "authentic." These informants bolstered her proposition that the "Indians are the authors of this volume," that *The Indians' Book* represented "the direct utterance of the Indians themselves. The red man dictated and the white friend recorded." Curtis's focus on the oldest informants, like Lololomai and the Pima and Navajo leaders, the most "Indian" speakers in her book, fulfilled readers' expectations that noble savages be nearly dying and isolated from mainstream America both physically and socially. To many whites in this period the only "real" Indian was one who appeared to live in the same primitive fashion as Native people did when Europeans first arrived in the Americas. Other writers, like Washington Matthews, Frank Hamilton Cushing, and Franz Boas, also claimed to have relied on the oldest and therefore most authentic tribal members they could find. Curtis hoped that this representation of her informants would lead readers to view her collection of music and folklore as authentic.[21]

This quest for authenticity often led researchers to stage, alter, or manipulate their representations of Native Americans. The photographer Edward S. Curtis (no relation to Natalie) occasionally retouched his photographs or provided sitters with "authentic" objects to wear or display for *The North American Indian*.[22] As with Natalie Curtis, the appeal of the primitive merged with and reinforced the desire for authenticity. She also manipulated images to meet her primitivist goals. For instance, she refashioned the Navajos into the very Orientalist "Bedouins of America," characterizing them as "industrious, independent, and fearless," combining "the strength of the warrior and the simplicity of the shepherd." Navajos became the "true sons" of the desert. Similarly, she described the Kwakiutls of the Pacific Northwest as "sinewy, strong, and of keen and fearless imagination." Like the Navajo they possessed a special connection with their environment, earning from Curtis the appellation "the sea-kings of America." Curtis often physically manipulated images to fit these notions. She reworked photographs of Kwakiutl men in ceremonial dress at the St. Louis exposition, for example. One man posed in front of a decorated canoe with a nondescript background behind him. Curtis carefully painted over anything that would suggest the modern world, preferring to present the Kwakiutl as unconnected with contemporary life. Pieces of Indian artwork contained directions in Curtis's hand explaining how to properly reproduce them. Curtis provided instructions for cropping and altering parts of photographs as well.[23] Regardless of evidence to the contrary, she presented many of the tribes in *The Indians' Book* as primitives residing in a noble past.

Although Curtis presented Native Americans as sharing a uniform primitive culture, her stereotyping distinguished between tribes. Plains Indians, for instance, were often represented as fearless warriors, in touch with the spiritual world. In a section entitled "The War-Path" Curtis drew on images of Plains warriors as stoic, brave, honorable, and spiritual. She consistently posed Plains leaders in war bonnets, either sitting atop a horse or staring off into the distance. Like the Kwakiutl photographs many of the pictures of Plains Indians appear to have been touched up by Curtis to remove anything that would detract from the image of the noble savage. The Southern Cheyenne leader High Chief, whom she called "the noble Indian who has helped so greatly in the making of this book," embodies her view of the valuable traits of Indians. High Chief, according to Curtis, came from aristocratic stock; he was a good leader and a faithful servant as a policeman. He devoted himself to spiritual matters, never lied, and had a proper appreciation for "the olden time." A photograph of him standing alone on the prairie with a single feather in his hair, or one of him smoking the "pipe of friendship," captured Curtis's idea of Plains Indians as primitives to be admired.[24]

Pueblo Indians presented a variant on Curtis's theme of the noble savage, one more in keeping with the ideal artisan image. "The Pueblo Indians have ever been a peaceful agricultural folk," Curtis asserted, noting that they had "their own ancient industries" and a full religious life. She presented Southwestern tribes as ancient people, still able to live according to their own ideals. Their dismissals of European American culture especially appealed to Curtis, as did their ability to blend religion, art, and work in their daily lives.[25] Curtis imagined Pueblos as natural artists and poets, as did other European American commentators. Photographs of artisans like Nampayo, a Hopi-Tewa potter, and several drawings of Pueblo ceremonial life reinforced this image of the Southwestern primitive.[26] Unlike the Plains Indians, whose recent history of warfare and removal to reservations Curtis discussed, Pueblos lived in a timeless world. They not only served as ideal makers of art but provided inspiration as objects of art as well. In her descriptions of her informants Curtis often commented on their artistically inspiring appearances. She was struck, for example, by the incredibly "picturesque figure" of the Hopi singer Koianimptiwa, as he sang into her phonograph: "He was a study in black and white for an artist. His high, broad shoulders, lithe frame, and slim, sinewy muscles were sharply outlined beneath a tight-fitting black jersey. He wore duck overalls and a broad black felt hat, which fastened under his chin with a cord. He resembled more a study by Velasquez than our common idea of an American Indian." Another

Hopi singer, Poliyeshwa, "looked as though he had been blocked out by a Michelangelo. [He seemed] an unfinished study in human anatomy."[27] Curtis described other Pueblo informants in similar fashion, focusing on their physicality and their surroundings to demonstrate that art for the Pueblos was so natural that their very bodies exuded it.

Despite minor Spanish influences she believed that Pueblos still lived according to ancient ways, untainted by contact with whites. Her portrayal of her Hopi informants Lololomai and his nephew Tawakwaptiwa especially reveal this. Curtis introduced Lololomai as "the watchful father of his people," who "bore himself with the dignity of the chieftaincy" for the last eighty years. What Curtis does not tell the reader — an omission for which she is criticized by William Clements — is that Lololomai was the leader of a faction of Hopis called the "Friendlies" or the "Progressives" by white officials on the reservation because of their acceptance of government schools and other aspects of white culture.[28] While Curtis was visiting Oraibi the tribe became so factionalized that the "Friendlies" and their opponents, the "Hostiles" or "Conservatives," each carried out their own ceremonies. In 1906 the "Friendlies" ousted the "Hostiles" from the village. Lololomai's nephew Tawakwaptiwa was the leader of his uncle's faction during the infamous Oraibi split. Curtis could not have been unaware of these tensions or of the tremendous impact they exerted on Hopi life and culture. Her commitment to presenting the Hopis as peaceful poets and artists would not permit her to discuss these contemporary issues in *The Indians' Book*. Instead she described Tawakwaptiwa as "a Hopi untouched by foreign influence, the child of natural environment, spontaneous, alert, full of life and laughter."[29] Again Curtis portrayed Indians in ways that fit her own conceptions of primitivism.

Curtis suggested that the noble traits she discovered among the tribes she visited could serve the needs of white American society, particularly in the realms of music and art. Native Americans here became a "folk" from whom the country could draw inspiration for a national culture, much like European nations had turned to their own folk traditions for artistic and musical material. In her introduction Curtis explained her views:

> Like all folk-music, the music of the Indian is the spontaneous and sincere expression of the soul of a people. It springs from our own continent, and is thus, of all music, distinctively American. If Indian song be encouraged with Indians, and recognition of it awakened among our own people, America may one day contribute a unique music to the world of art. Not that the musical art of America can ever be founded on Indian melodies; for the art of the Aryan must be Aryan to be the true expression of his race. But the folk-music of any land is a soil from which genius draws sustenance for fresh growth, and the stimulus to the creative mind through contact with this native art should give to America a new and vigorous art impulse.[30]

Curtis argued that American composers and artists could find a distinctly American identity and culture through contact with indigenous societies. She hoped that her collection of songs and stories would inaugurate this movement because she believed the United States lacked unique artistic expression. "We are a people of great mechanical and inventive genius," she argued, "but we are not naturally song-makers, poets, or designers." She asked if the nation could "afford to lose from our country any sincere and spontaneous art impulse, however crude." The "undeveloped talents" showcased in *The Indians' Book* were "precisely those in which the Anglo-Saxon American is deficient."[31] Her book, filled with evidence of this poetry and artistry, could be used to spark creativity and provide a means to create America's own music and art.

Other writers and students of Native American cultures shared Curtis's hopes of providing Native material for white musicians. Washington Matthews expected "poets, novelists, travelers, and compilers" to use the material collected in *Navaho Legends*. Frederick Burton hoped that his collection of Ojibway music would provide composers with themes and "color" in their compositions and would contribute to a nationalist music.[32] Within the next ten years (as will be discussed in chapter 7) more musicians and artists began heeding the advice of collectors of Native song and story, like Curtis, composing "Indianist" works derived from their own conceptions of Native American life and music.

Curtis also hoped to encourage Native artists to contribute their "natural" talents to a national cultural expression. The work of the Winnebago artist Angel DeCora on the lettering and design of the tribal title pages awakened Curtis to the special talents of Indian artists. She had asked DeCora, a graduate of Hampton Institute, to create the design for the Winnebago section. The design and lettering were so beautiful and original that Curtis's publishers wanted all the title pages to resemble DeCora's. When Curtis asked a white designer to copy the Winnebago lettering, he replied: "Whoever did that lettering is a genius! Don't ask *me* to make anything like it!"[33] Native Americans, they believed, could best produce this type of artwork and only needed encouragement from "white friends" to do so.

DeCora, who later taught Native design at Carlisle Indian School, expressed similar opinions about Indian art. She too believed that Indians possessed latent artistic abilities that only needed the proper stimulus to blossom. DeCora prodded her students to "adapt our Indian talents to the daily needs and uses of modern life" and to make their own special mark on the nation. DeCora also shared with Curtis a proclivity to romanticize Native life, often producing generic Indians and resorting to themes expected by white audiences. This pattern of patronizing support for Native American musicians and artists, of encouraging or even forcing Indian artists to produce according to white aesthetic demands, accelerated in the coming years. Curtis could be commended for her desire to help Native artists, but her insistence that they conform to her notions of primitivism and the noble savage was dehumanizing, limited their work, and denied artists and musicians credit for their actual achievements.[34]

Not only did Curtis hope to use *The Indians' Book* to create a new American music and art; she wanted to revitalize the nation spiritually. Her Indians were all deeply religious and offered whites valuable lessons on integrating spirituality into all aspects of life. Native Americans possessed ties to the natural world that Curtis believed most whites in the industrial, urban United States lacked. She directed her readers: "Let us pause in the stress of our modern life to listen to the ancient lore of our own land. From the heart of the nature-world speaks the voice of man proclaiming deity. The Indian's religious thought, uttered in every form of life, and his conception of an omnipotent and all-pervading divine power is entirely spiritual and impersonal. The Indian has a message for the seekers after truth who welcome, whatsoever its form, the recognition of God by man."[35] In nearly every chapter Curtis highlighted Native spirituality. She described beliefs, rituals, and myths in an appreciative fashion, occasionally drawing positive parallels with Christian thought. Songs accompanied every action, she argued, and allowed Indians to include religion in everything. In the Southwest, she believed, Pueblo peoples' hard work and constant prayers for rain, as well as their appreciation for the beautiful, created an ideal society. "The white visitor learns many a simple lesson from the life of these most ancient inhabited towns of the United States, the pueblos of the Southwest," Curtis asserted.[36] The supposedly simple and spiritually integrated nature of Native life strongly appealed to her.

Curtis's view of Native Americans as ultra-spiritual beings whom whites should emulate undoubtedly reflected the influence of her patron Charlotte Mason. Curtis lived with Mason while she prepared the manuscript for *The Indians' Book*, and Mason accompanied

Curtis on her Western trips. Mason's late husband, Rufus, was an authority on psychic healing and research, and after his death she turned to non-Western spiritual ideas for solace. Mason contended, as Ann Douglas writes, that "primitive" people with their "life of 'pagan' rituals and 'spiritual' consciousness could save or succeed the sterilities of white civilization now 'in the throes of death.'" Mason would later claim that her time spent among the Plains Indians allowed her "to absorb their spirituality," which drew upon their close contact with nature. She urged her African American protégés in the 1920s to emulate the spirituality of Indians. Zora Neale Hurston recalled that Mason had "collected a beautiful book of Indian lore" and would often "take the book from the shelf and read me something of Indian beauty and restraint." Mason, known for her domineering personality and strongly held beliefs about the nature of primitive people, surely influenced Curtis's representations of Native American religiosity.[37]

Curtis was not the only white writer to admire Native American societies for their spirituality. A few writers began to question the desirability of eradicating Native religions, and some investigated Native belief systems more deeply. These writers often shared Curtis's desire to emulate Indian spirituality themselves, as well as her belief that whites could learn much from Indians artistically.[38] George Wharton James, in *What the White Race May Learn from the Indian*, devoted a chapter to Native art, encouraging whites to tie their work to the natural world as Indians did. James stressed outdoor living, hard work, and a natural diet as Indian lessons for whites. Sherry Smith contends that James emphasized the "supposed universal artistic and spiritual aspects of Southwestern Indian lives, pushing for recognition of their place in the 'family of man' on that basis." The notion that Native Americans possessed a better-integrated life and could seamlessly combine work with spirituality appealed to many in industrializing America. For example, Carlos Troyer, a musician and student of Indian song, admired the Zuni for their "simple life, peaceful and contented, always happy in the enjoyment of their daily work." Although some white writers began to express these ideas in the early twentieth century, it was still at least another decade before they gained wider acceptance and popularity.[39] Curtis, then, might be viewed as a transitional figure in the development of these views.

Even though Curtis's positive views of Native Americans could generate improved attitudes and treatment of them, her reliance on stereotypes and generalizations dehumanized Native people and forced them to live in a "primitive" mold in order to be accepted as Indians. "The Indian" became a malleable symbol in Curtis's search for a personal and national identity.[40] Curtis's Indians addressed her own needs and desires. By portraying her collaborators as being intensely religious or possessing natural artistic abilities, Curtis said more about her own concerns for America as a secular society without a national culture than she did about Indian lives. No matter how sincere her desire to provide the voice of Native peoples, Curtis's representations of Native Americans were often her own imaginings, created to fulfill her needs. Her claims for "authenticity" and Indian authorship were belied by her textual intrusions, which reflected Curtis's desires as much as the thoughts of Native American people.

Her imagined Indians had to be seen as authentic voices — hence her insistence on presenting her role as the "pencil in the hand of the Indian." Therefore Curtis took liberties with the texts of her informants that belie her rhetoric about being merely a mouthpiece for vanishing Indians. Curtis's claims to have only recorded the words of her informants were misleading. She played an active role by shaping the type of material contributed, remaining heavily involved in the collecting and editing process, selecting the most "authentic" artwork to include, and capturing on film images that catered to her notions of Indianness. The proposition that Native Americans directly contributed to *The Indians' Book* is undermined by an examination of those texts purported to be the actual words of Indian people. Curtis's voice frequently intrudes into the supposedly "direct utterances" of Native informants. Curtis often cited a tribal member as the author of a segment of a chapter, but within a given section the language shifted from first to third person, leaving the reader unsure of the speaker. For example, in the Dakota chapter Chief Maza-Blaska (Flat-Iron) explained the song of the Dog-Feast. "Behold, it was thus," he began and continued to narrate a story of the feast's origins, liberally sprinkling "Indian" phrases like "lo" into his tale. Then the story shifted suddenly away from the chief's voice, and the reader was informed that "the grandfather of Maza-Blaska" originated the feast, rather than the expected "my grandfather."[41] Curtis obviously paraphrased and combined material she collected and then presented it as the work of one or two people. The introduction by High Chief, for instance, was reworked by Curtis from notes she had jotted down from an interpreter while the Southern Cheyenne leader delivered an address. At other times she did not bother to hide this, as in the Winnebago chapter, in which she presented stories of a cultural hero as "told by Chash-chunk-a (Wave), Nek-hu-wi-ka (South Wind), and other Winnebagos of Nebraska and Wisconsin."[42]

Any anthropological researcher shapes the agenda for the collection and presentation of data, and although Curtis probably did not intend to be deceitful or disguise her own participation in the creation of the book, twenty-first-century perspectives require us to consider her role as an editor of a work claiming to be of and by Indians. Certainly her approach raises questions about what material Curtis left out or why she included the kinds of songs and stories she did. For example, nearly every tribe in this collection provided creation stories. Would so many informants have done this unless specifically asked for this type of material? Would they have desired to include different types of stories that Curtis deemed unworthy of inclusion in her book because they may have not fit into her ideas about Indians? She occasionally noted that informants asked her to place certain songs in specific parts of the text, but she never explained the many other decisions she must have made while compiling the book on the East Coast, far from the Western reservations and tribal lands where she collected the material.[43]

It is in her translations and transcriptions of Native songs that one best sees how Curtis shaped the material according to her own needs and ideas. Although she voiced concerns about correctly presenting Native languages, she worked harder to express the beauty and meaning of Native American music for white readers. Her translations of Indian songs include their "real" meaning, as well as a "literal" interpretation. Other students of Native music had faced this challenge before her. Washington Matthews, an army physician and part-time anthropologist, remarked on the difficulty of re-creating Navajo music within its proper context for a white audience. He solved this problem by not confining himself to "a close literal translation," because readers would not understand it, and it would be uninteresting as well. Alice Fletcher, another influence on Curtis, similarly offered "free" translations in *Indian Story and Song*.[44] Curtis relied on these more established authorities to guide her. In a letter to James Mooney asking for help with a Kiowa song, Curtis remarked that she had to make "the translations very free in order that they might fit the music, but of course I do not want to take unwarrantable liberties with the text."[45]

Curtis had her Native collaborators justify her transformation of their music into poetic forms that would seem familiar to white readers. She wrote, "Indians feel that, in the English rendering of their verse, justice is not done to the poetry when there is given only a bare and literal translation of the symbolic word instead of a full expression of the meaning." Curtis intended for the translations to be "as literal as possible" but wanted the "real meaning" to "truthfully flash through the English words" with the "fragrance, the color, and above all, the spirit of the original" retained.[46] For example, in the chapter on the Pawnee, Eagle Chief provided a song from the Bear Society. Curtis reproduced the song in English with a "literal translation," followed on the next page with a "free metrical translation — the hidden meaning revealed." The literal translation

> Yonder coming,
> Yonder coming,
> Lo, the many yonder, he —
>> Yo!
>
> Mine, too might have been a triumph
> Like the many yonder, he —
>> Yo!

became

> They are coming,
> They are coming
> Lo, the victor hosts, ya he —
>> Yo!
>
> Forth to meet them go the women
> With the rising sun, ya he —
>> Yo![47]

Curtis felt free to change the words and even added vocables, syllables that have no literal meaning but are important to the song, to the original text. She repeated this pattern in several other places, providing the "real" translation based on her own understanding of Indian thought. Later scholars have called Curtis to task for liberties she took with the interpretation and translation of the language of Native songs. Her translation of a Hopi lullaby has been criticized by several students of Native American linguistics for the changes she made within the text. In this song, "Puwuch Tawi," Curtis likened

Hopi children sleeping in cradleboards to blind beetles that carry one another on their backs. Commentators have argued that her attempts to reveal the hidden meaning of the song in her translation misrepresented Hopi ideas. The song was meant to reproduce the movements leading up to sleep and would not have suggested blindness, nor would it have been understood as poetry.[48] Curtis, though, had few apparent problems adding or omitting material from the original "authors" of the book, especially if a modification would better serve her ideas about Native Americans.

Curtis faced a dilemma familiar to translators of Indian music for a Western audience. Arnold Krupat, a scholar of Native American language and song, suggests that "all translations must situate themselves in relation to the principles of Identity and Difference (Sameness and Otherness, Likeness and Unlikeness, Ours and Theirs)." He contends that translators tend to stress one category more than others. Curtis, he argues, falls within the "esthetic/accessible axis of translation."[49] She was more concerned with making her translations familiar to her audience by presenting them in a format they would have recognized. Poetic styles of contemporary European American poets suited her better than the songs as Indians actually conceived them. She further stressed the songs' artistic, creative element — the "hidden meaning revealed" — over their literal meaning. Curtis never questioned the liberties she took with the songs provided by her informants. Many other white commentators on tribal peoples shared this attitude. Sherry Smith points out that writers like Curtis represent just one group of non-Indians trying to claim the right to construct Native identities. Lawyers, judges, journalists, educators, reformers, and anthropologists all claimed "the right to speak on behalf of Indians." Because most Native Americans were only beginning to obtain the skills needed to reach a white audience, people like Curtis could present Native cultures uncontested.[50]

Curtis also believed she could speak for Native Americans because as a fellow American she occupied the same natural environment.

She continually insisted that Indian music developed from the environment they inhabited. Because Indians shared the land with white Americans like herself, all Americans could rightfully appropriate Native cultural elements they deemed valuable. Indians served as guideposts for whites seeking to express American identity rooted in the nation's soil. Comparing Hopi music to the wind, Curtis wrote, "As the gusts lash the flying sand into eddying columns they sing a ceaseless song." Walking through a sandstorm with her "trusted Hopi guide," Curtis listened to the song of protection the man began to sing. "It seemed the soul of the wind had died at sunset," Curtis remarked. "And as the refrain rose again and again, I too felt my spirit captured, swayed, and borne out in song."[51] The effect of the Southwestern environment on Indian art and song became a favorite theme for Curtis. By linking Native creativity with nature rather than Indian culture, Curtis allowed herself to lay claim to the region and especially to Native American song. She concluded: "The Hopi is the voice of the silent desert; he wakes his world to melody, but at night all is still, and the ancient town sleeps in the white light of the moon. We look off over the endless stretch of desert and the thought sweeps over us — vast is this continent of ours, yet this is my country and these strange, poetic people are my neighbors. My joy in all this beauty is my right."[52] Simply by witnessing "the endless stretch of desert" before her and imagining the Hopis as her "neighbors," Curtis believed she had a right to use Indian music for her own needs.

In addition to her liberties with the texts she collected, Curtis suffered from other shortcomings in her efforts to serve as a "pencil in the hand of the Indian." That Curtis did not speak any of the Native languages of her informants but included translations of their contributions raises additional questions about the authorship of *The Indians' Book*. One wonders how she arrived at her translations and what liberties she took during the process of translation and transcription. Curtis admitted her shortcomings in this respect, noting her reliance upon Western-educated Indians and white scholars for translating the material. She often worked with Native-language speakers after meeting with her informants, leaving one to question how accurately she represented the statements originally given by contributors. Curtis did labor to present her translations with some degree of accuracy. Her field notebooks contained numerous versions of songs and demonstrate the great efforts she made to capture the meanings of her informants.[53]

Transcribing non-Western music into a format understandable to her American readers also presented a challenge. Curtis confessed that this was "a task of no small difficulty," especially because she often wrote the songs "by the light of the tipi fire or under the glare of the desert sun." While Curtis recorded Lololomai's song, the Hopi asked her why she took so long to transcribe the music onto paper. Curtis replied: "Lololomai, you know that when the Hopi sets a trap for the blackbird, sometimes it is long before he can catch his fluttering prey. Your song is a wild blackbird to me, and it may be that the sun will move far along the sky before I have captured it." Curtis faced a similar struggle during her previously mentioned journey across the desert with Koianimptiwa, who sang to Curtis as he drove her wagon. Although she later learned Koianimptiwa's song, her struggle to capture songs by Hopi singers, the tribe with which she was most familiar, might prompt concern. However, many ethnomusicologists of her time shared in the difficulty of "objectively stating on paper what happens in sound," as the ethnomusicologist Bruno Nettl terms it in his discussion of transcription. Transcription proved even more difficult for non-Western musical forms that contain sounds not accounted for by Western musical notation. Curtis may not have accurately recorded every song in *The Indians' Book*, but she did labor, as other ethnomusicologists did, to present Indian music as best she could with the limited resources at her disposal.[54]

ALTHOUGH CURTIS USED INDIAN IMAGES FOR HER OWN ENDS and often painted Native people in the romantic hues of the noble savage, at times she sincerely attempted to let her informants speak in *The Indians' Book*. She strongly believed that if Native peoples' stories and songs were heard, whites would better understand Indians. Music, she contended, revealed the "inner life" of any people, and she expected her book to help both whites and Indians. She also believed that music was a language that could transcend racial, cultural, and linguistic barriers. It could help correct dangerous misconceptions about Native American life, especially concerning warfare and religion. Once myths and wrong ideas about Indians were properly challenged, Curtis believed, Indian policy, particularly the push for complete assimilation, would change for the betterment of Native peoples. *The Indians' Book* sought to address the needs of Native Americans caught between traditional ways and the modern world. Curtis hoped to establish an interracial dialogue between European Americans and Native Americans.

Regardless of questions about the actual authorship of *The Indians' Book*, Curtis's approach is significant because it gave Native informants a far more prominent role than did many other works on Indian cultures. Many popular writers and anthropologists relied on Native informers in their work, and some even credited individual Native Americans, but no one else granted them authorship in their collections. Alice Fletcher, who served as a model for Curtis in many ways, used informants in much of her research, including her works for a popular audience. She dedicated *Indian Story and Song* to her "Indian Friends" who had shared material with her and mentioned the efforts of informants Francis LaFlesche (Omaha) and James Murie (Pawnee) in this and other works. Her collaborators, however, rarely received credit for authoring any works with Fletcher, even though they often did the bulk of the fieldwork themselves. Her partner LaFlesche in fact struggled for years to gain recognition for the substantial contributions he made as an anthropologist in his own right.[55] Anthropologists working in the Southwest, such as Matilda Coxe Stevenson and Frank Hamilton

Cushing, also mentioned some of their informants by name in their reports, but they never credited them with more than contributing some data or allowing the scientists to observe their behavior. Curtis adopted a very different approach that, while it may have been self-serving, intended to place Native Americans in a more equal role with herself and her readers.

Curtis firmly believed that she offered Native Americans chances to speak for themselves, and she therefore let her informants play a role in shaping the volume. She hoped that her work would inspire educated Indians to take up this task, much like Hampton Institute encouraged its students to participate in folklore studies. She recognized that Native researchers had "access to their people's holiest rites" and argued that "their understanding of Indian thought" would create an "exposition of Indian religious life" superior to any white work. Until graduates of the educational system were ready, Curtis would have to encourage their tribal members to contribute to her research.[56] Curtis insisted that Native people could teach whites more about their cultures than whites could ever learn on their own. She later cautioned researchers that in the study of Native music "we white people must enter warily indeed, for truly we have here little to teach and much to learn." She further argued that researchers needed to relate to Native Americans on a personal level — they were not subjects, but human beings. Friends of Curtis remarked that "to observe her among her beloved Indians was to witness a miracle, for with her utter frankness and her beaming simplicity of approach she could make even the most reticent ones among them talk and sing to her and explain the mysteries of their legends."[57] In an era when anthropologists stole items of material culture from Native Americans, dug up graves, and expressed no qualms about barging into religious ceremonies to gather data, Curtis's willingness to allow Native people to voice their own thoughts seems especially significant.

A deeper examination of the contributions of two of Curtis's most important informants demonstrates how Native Americans could find their own voices as mediators between their world and white society. The two dominant figures in *The Indians' Book*, the Southern Cheyenne referred to as High Chief and the "Progressive" Hopi leader Lololomai, each had a rationale particular to his circumstances for participating in her project. They shared the problems of adapting to a rapidly changing world, lamented the loss of traditional practices, and believed in the necessity of adopting some aspects of white American society to survive. Early twentieth-century Native American leaders faced daunting challenges in this transitional period. As Margaret Connell Szasz notes in her collection of essays on "cultural brokers," events in the American West at the turn of the twentieth century placed Native people in increasingly constrained positions. Cultural brokers adopted a number of strategies to survive while still preserving their cultural traditions and land. They protected their cultures while helping anthropologists, taught in government schools while working to preserve their languages, and participated in Wild West shows while learning more about the outside world. The cultural brokers discussed in Szasz's collection, much like Lololomai and High Chief, were caught between "ethnocentric reformers and fledgling anthropologists" and tribal members "who were often of several minds about the passage of the old way."[58]

Lololomai, as the leader of the "Progressive" faction at Oraibi, used the political tactic of adopting those aspects of American culture that seemed most necessary for survival. In the past Lololomai had accepted off-reservation schools, English-language instruction, and American trade goods to insure Hopi survival. With Curtis he justified and continued his policy by accepting books and written musical notation to keep his songs from disappearing. In the process the Hopi leader used his contributions to critique the government's policy and to present his view of the situation at Oraibi. Members of his household, especially his soon-to-be successor and nephew,

Tawakwaptiwa, were directed to Curtis to contribute to *The Indians'
Book*. Lololomai shared material that he perhaps believed would
improve his circumstances in relation to federal officials, as well
as other Hopis.

The Southern Cheyenne leader known as High Chief, or Hiamovi,
shared many of the same concerns and solutions as Lololomai.
His reservation, like those of other Plains groups, was in the midst
of a transition from a communal, hunting, and warrior society to
a sedentary life of individual allotments, agriculture, and American law.[59] Like Lololomai, Hiamovi sought an accommodationist
path. As a police officer High Chief constantly negotiated a middle
ground between the demands of government agents and his personal desire to maintain significant parts of his culture. His special
role in society placed High Chief in a powerful position to shape
Curtis's research efforts. He used his special access to many informants to introduce her to other Indians who shared his opinions
and values, who would provide the types of songs and stories he
hoped would find inclusion in her book. He dictated which songs
he would share and even demanded that she publish them in a
particular arrangement.

In addition to her close relationship with Indian leaders like High
Chief and Lololomai, Curtis exhibited a genuine concern for the
welfare of the tribes she visited and wanted *The Indians' Book* to
help her readers understand Native Americans more fully, to see
through negative myths about Indians, and to develop positive
views of Native American cultures. Her informants, she argued,
believed that "the book 'speaks with the straight tongue'" and that
it would influence their lives in the future. "They look to it to tell
the white man that 'Indians are a good people,'" she asserted. Curtis believed that if she provided examples of positive Indian traits
and emphasized the human side of a people often portrayed as
savage killers or degraded beggars, then others would share her
sympathy for them.

The Indians' Book presented a more lighthearted side to Indian life than many of its readers may have expected. For example, the Hopi contributed songs used in a "playful sport" in which young women, the "butterfly-maidens" or "shower-maidens," would pour water on the "dawnlight-youths" from their rooftops early in the morning. Although conceived of as a "symbolic invocation for rain," a "little butterfly-maiden" explained that it was more about the fun and laughter it provoked.[60] Other amusements, such as a Wabanaki game of barter, a Cheyenne swinging song, or the hand games (team gambling games involving guessing the number of items the other team was holding) of many Plains groups, also worked to give a sense of Indian life as interesting and perhaps not too terribly dissimilar from the leisure time of readers.

Curtis also stressed the importance of romantic love and familial relations among tribal peoples. She presented courtship songs and practices from several different groups. The Dakota, for instance, contributed five modern love songs. "Many are the youths, many youths: / Thou alone art he who pleaseth me. / Over all I love thee. / Long shall be the years of parting!" sang Little Horse. Curtis described how Wabanaki youth arranged marriages and included the dance songs used at the celebrations, where the old people danced and wore "all their ancient Indian ornaments of silver, shell, or fur." More intimate family songs were also part of the collection. Contributors from the Southern Cheyenne sang this lullaby: "Little good baby, / he-ye, / Sleepy little baby. / A-ha, h'm." The Hopi explained their use of a cradleboard and the gentle rocking motion they used as they sang their children to sleep.[61] Curtis collected additional lullabies to show the "human, intimate side of Indian parentage." She stressed that Indian parents expressed the "strongest tie of affection" to their children, in spite of arguments to the contrary made by agents and school officials who sought to remove students from their family homes to attend school.[62] By highlighting personal relationships among Native Americans, ties to which white readers could certainly relate, Curtis challenged the notion that Indians were so different from whites that the two groups could not coexist and put a much more human face on the people featured in *The Indians' Book*.

Curtis challenged images of Indians as savage, bloodthirsty killers mindlessly waging war against innocent white women and children. She allowed her informants to share their conceptions of warfare and in particular to stress the religious ideas they carried into battle. Many informants, especially those among the Plains tribes, shared songs about war. Southern Cheyenne informants explained the "war-path," describing how a war party formed under various circumstances and stressing the potential honor as well as the hardships that came with it. Because of the serious nature of this undertaking, religious ceremonies prepared warriors to go into battle and secured "the protection of the Supreme Being." Curtis further explained in a note that "an Indian went upon the war-path in somewhat the spirit of a knight-errant setting out in search of adventure and glory." She compared Indians to European nobility in their desire for adventure and great deeds. Curtis tried to show that their reasons for fighting were understandable and even honorable. For example, in her introductory remarks on the Dakota she discussed the "great provocation to violence" tribal members faced in the late nineteenth century. "When forced to fight in defence of their hunting-grounds," she wrote, "the warriors proved themselves brave and skilful in battle." She also argued that "the massacres and depredations perpetrated by minorities of the tribe counterbalance the uprightness of the majority and the honor of the leaders." Indians known for their actions in war, such as Geronimo, contributed to *The Indians' Book* as well. Curtis described Geronimo as bearing himself "with the erectness of the Indian warrior," despite his seventy or eighty years. She wrote that the Apaches had "resisted with open hostility the encroachment of the whites" and that leaders like Geronimo "showed not only daring and cruelty, but also extraordinary skill and strategy in warfare, and endurance that seemed inexhaustible." Although white readers best knew the Apache leader in this role, Curtis included a medicine song from him rather than the expected war song. Geronimo explained that he sang it to go to "a holy place where Yusun [the Supreme Being] will give me power to do wonderful things."[63] Curtis made Native warfare, its causes and its course, accessible to whites, hoping to dispel negative notions whites may have held about Indians. She reasoned that as long as whites remained misinformed about these matters, Indians would continue to suffer for their supposed crimes against the United States.

Curtis also sought to dispel myths about Native American religions, particularly notions that Indians lacked systems of belief or that their current religious practices posed a danger to themselves and their white neighbors. The volume continually stressed the overriding religious nature of all aspects of Indian life. Indians prayed constantly, sang religious songs daily, and revered their deities in everything they did. Curtis noted the ways in which traditional rites, ceremonies, and songs continued to exert a profound influence on many tribes. Many ceremonies had been outlawed or discouraged by agents and missionaries for their supposed deleterious effects. Among many Plains tribes the Sun Dance, a dramatic, communal summer ceremony that served as the focus for social and religious life for many tribes, was outlawed in the late nineteenth century, particularly among groups that included some form of a flesh sacrifice.[64] Curtis's informants defended their religious ideas. High Chief, the Southern Cheyenne leader, explained that his people called this rite "the Offering" and that it was "an ancient religious ceremony, and through it is worshipped Macha-Mahaiyu, the Great Mystery, who rules the day by the sun and the night by the moon." He insisted that the opening Cheyenne song in *The Indians' Book* be the first song sung at the Sun Dance. "It is a prayer," he explained, "sung slowly four times while the dancers stand in a circle, with

outstretched hands, gazing upward. Sometimes tears will stream
from the upturned eyes in the intensity of prayer." They prayed that
evil would leave them and devoted themselves to the sanctity of
the ceremony. This was not some mindless opportunity to avoid
work or cause bodily harm, as government agents claimed, but a
religious activity of extreme importance to the individual and the
tribe.[65]

Native Americans in the Southwest faced similar suppression of
their religious ceremonies as the Plains tribes. Curtis allowed the
Pueblos to explain their rites and contribute the songs and stories
that accompanied them. Unlike most researchers on Southwestern
ceremonialism Curtis asked her informants for the meaning behind
their rituals. Others, like the missionary and anthropologist H. R.
Voth, focused on the minute details of Hopi rites but never bothered
to offer readers the Hopi's explanations. Voth's detailed descriptions of ceremonies, which were often littered with phrases such
as "I suppose" and "must mean," demonstrate his lack of interest
in Hopi perspectives on their religious practices. Curtis in contrast
described meeting with Hopis to learn more about their beliefs.
She asked Lololomai's family about the purposes of *bahoes*, which
she described as "emblematic prayer-sticks, into whose feathered
ends prayers are breathed," and asked that they make one for her. In
addition she shared informants' explanations of the Hopi Butterfly
Dance, Katzina dances, and the Flute Ceremony.[66]

The Navajo chapter focused almost exclusively on Navajo spiritual
beliefs and practices. Earlier studies of the tribe by the anthropologist Washington Matthews urged future researchers to comprehend
the spiritual allegories and symbolism of Navajo dances and the
religious songs and myths of the tribe by comparing them to major
religions. Curtis, who cited Matthews as a source, took up this task.
She encouraged informants to share their ideas on Navajo religion
in a comparative mode. "Our Hozhonji songs [holy songs] are
like the Psalms of David," explained a boarding school–educated

tribal member. "We sing them as a white man says his prayers. Our hero, Nayenezrani, is like the Bible hero, David. By our Holy Ones were the songs made, even as the Bible was made by holy people," he continued. It remains unclear whether Curtis or the Navajo informant initiated the comparison between Native beliefs and the Bible, but it reflects her overriding concern that Native American religious ideas be favorably compared with white ones. It also demonstrates her desire to create a "middle ground" for an interracial dialogue.[67]

Curtis defended traditional religious practices among the tribes she visited and also explained more modern spiritual beliefs, particularly the Ghost Dance religion and the use of peyote. As with the Sun Dance many agents had barred Plains tribes from Ghost Dance ceremonies out of fear that the dancing would excite tribal members into a warlike frenzy against neighboring white communities. The Ghost Dance spread to Plains tribes in the late 1880s as delegations returned from journeys west to meet with Wovoka, a Paiute known as Jack Wilson to whites, who proclaimed the coming of an Indian messiah. Adherents of this new religious movement believed that by dancing and singing proper songs they would usher in a new age — the buffalo would return, they would be reunited with dead friends and family, and the white intruders would vanish. Although most tribes performed the dance peacefully, reservation agents and local whites feared the dancing would generate new conflicts by encouraging Indians to fulfill the prophecy themselves. The Ghost Dance movement reached a deadly climax when whites acted on these fears and called in the Seventh Cavalry (General George Custer's former unit), which massacred nearly three hundred people, mostly women and children, at Wounded Knee Creek in December 1890. In spite of this horrific event several tribes continued to dance and to hope for a new age.[68]

Many of Curtis's informants adhered to the Ghost Dance teachings and willingly shared their ideas. She also relied on James

Mooney's report on the origins of this religious movement and the tragedy at Wounded Knee. Mooney, like Curtis, offered a sympathetic account, chronicling the circumstances that led the Plains tribes to accept Wovoka's teachings. Mooney and Curtis even shared many of the same collaborators — Short Bull, a Dakota leader in the movement; a Southern Arapaho named Sage who had brought the teachings to his tribe; and Apiatan, a Kiowa leader who rejected the doctrine. Curtis recounted the history of the movement based on her discussions with its leading figures. She first explained the cause. "It is hard for the white man to realize the suffering of the red man in the first sharp crisis of adjustment to the new life," she began. The wholesale slaughter of buffalo, the "white man's invasion of the plains," and the coming of the railroad had all brought death, disease, and despair to the Plains tribes. She described the origins of the Ghost Dance movement, its acceptance by other tribes, and the circumstances leading to the slaughter at Wounded Knee with sympathy and understanding for Native Americans. Curtis presented Short Bull as a dignified and committed leader of his people and allowed the Dakota to share his religious convictions in a section entitled "Short Bull's Narrative." "Who would have thought that dancing could make such trouble?" he asked. "We had no wish to make trouble, nor did we cause it ourselves," Short Bull asserted. He described his meeting with Wovoka and the message he received:

> It is true, all men should love one another. It is true, all men should live as brothers. Is it we who do not thus? What others demand of us, should they not themselves give? Is it just to expect one friend to give all the friendship? We are glad to live with white men as brothers. But we ask that they expect not the brotherhood and the love to come from the Indian alone.
>
> In this world the Great Father has given to the white man everything and to the Indian nothing. But it will not always be thus. In

another world the Indian shall be as the white man and the white man as the Indian. To the Indian will be given wisdom and power, and the white man shall be helpless and unknowing with only the bow and arrow. For ere long this world will be consumed in flame and pass away. Then, in the life after this, to the Indian shall all be given.[69]

This informant not only reasserted the universal spiritual nature of the Ghost Dance but reversed roles, taking on the position of moral superior and suggesting that in the end Native Americans would ultimately triumph.

Many contributors used *The Indians' Book* to defend and uphold the use of peyote, a religious practice that was eventually incorporated under the aegis of the Native American Church. As with other Native religions, government officials and missionaries on reservations and tribal lands objected to peyote because of the hallucinatory effects the drug produced and because the ceremonies often took entire nights to perform. Opponents of the new religion exaggerated the effects of the ceremonially used peyote and often confused it with the intoxicant mescal. (Although Curtis used these terms interchangeably, the ceremonies and songs she discussed concerned the use of peyote, not mescal.) Curtis's collaborators challenged the negative interpretations of the "mescal religion" and, by describing ceremonies and practices, offered their perceptions on the benefits of the new religion.[70]

A significant portion of the Cheyenne chapter discusses peyote and its positive influence. Curtis traced current practices to "a very ancient Indian faith" in South America that had changed somewhat as it spread to Oklahoma tribes. She correctly noted that younger Indians, "who have never known the old life of the buffalo-hunting days," tended to be the religion's adherents, attracted by their faith that it could cure tuberculosis and alcoholism. High Chief, whose nephew Mowihaiz (Magpie) was a leader in the religion, invited

Curtis to witness a ceremony, which she described in some detail. After explaining the objects used in the service and the consumption of the peyote buttons, Curtis remarked, "There is a solemnity in the atmosphere that awes the on-looker." She continued, "Intense concentration seems to burn like a holy fire." Followers of the peyote rite were not hopeless drug addicts seeking a hallucinatory thrill, Curtis contended, but sincere spiritual seekers hoping to improve their lives: "The poetry and mysticism of this cult supply to the modern Indian the spiritual uplift known in the old days to those who went apart to fast and learn of the spirits what should be their guiding 'medicine' through life." Like the Ghost Dance the peyote religion aided in the adjustment to a new life.[71]

Curtis allowed leaders of the peyote religion to share their beliefs with her readers. Magpie explained, "Other religions teach men what to believe, but in this religion each man learns truth for himself." God had provided Indians with peyote so that when a person ate it, "he sees all the truths of life and of the spirit." Magpie commented further on the positive aspects of his faith. "The mescal takes from us sickness and pain. It purifies us," he argued. "We eat the mescal because we want to see — we want to know — we want to know God." Few other white Americans shared Curtis's acceptance of the positive influence of peyotism in Native American life. Unlike them, Curtis argued that Native beliefs were strong, beneficial, and contained their own sense of logic and beauty and that if white officials only took the time to understand (and even support) them, Indian lives would improve.[72]

New Indian religions, Curtis contended, were products of the transition period and helped Native Americans adjust to their present conditions. In the same way she hoped that this collection of songs and stories would aid the coming generation of Indians as they adapted to their new world. She opposed complete assimilation for these young people, instead envisioning a melding of the old and the new. Curtis argued that Native Americans needed to thoughtfully integrate the best of their old lives into their new ways of living. She believed that Indians could no longer maintain traditional ways, but that did not mean they should completely discard every vestige of Native cultures, as many white reformers demanded. Instead she urged Indians to take pride in the noteworthy features of their former lives — as defined by her of course — and find ways to continue cultural practices. Through this blending of old and new, rather than the wholesale adoption of white Christian ways, Native Americans could survive the twentieth century. She used a Pawnee contributor, Eagle Chief, as an example of what she hoped other Indians would accomplish. This Pawnee leader lived in a modern house and raised cattle and horses. On his "American house" Eagle Chief had painted a white star with a blue background. The star, he explained, had become his emblem after he saw it in a trance. It decorated his house and served as his brand for his cattle. Curtis commented, "To infuse the new life of labor something of the old Indian poetry is an ideal for the future Indian working-man."[73]

Although most of *The Indians' Book* presents Indians in a timeless past, several songs and stories reflect the struggle of Native peoples to adapt their lives to changing circumstances. "In the present state of transition from the old life to the new," Curtis wrote in her chapter on the Dakota, Indian children were often educated at boarding schools and might not see their family for five years or more. She noted that the stay at school had become such "a distinct era in the life of the Indian" that songs had begun to accompany this experience. Julia Yellow-Hair, the granddaughter of a Dakota chief, contributed a love song associated with the trip to school. She sang:

For the last time, come greet me again,
Dear friend, I loved thee alone!
Now to school I'm going away;
For the last time greet me again,
For the last time, come take my hand!

Curtis collected a song from a Laguna man who, because of the changes in the local economy, had to work apart from his wife but still sang to her daily. He explained: "I sing to her though I am far away, and she too sings to me. The meaning of the song is this: 'I am here, working for you. All the while I work I think of you. Take care of yourself, and take care of the horses, and the sheep and the fields.'" New conditions had forced changes in Indian life, Curtis argued, but individuals continued to compose and sing songs that ordered and gave meaning to their world.[74]

Curtis offered other examples of individual Native Americans who found ways to maintain their cultures even while living under very new circumstances. She continually exhorted Indians, particularly young, educated ones, to do the same. In her introduction to the Winnebago tribe Curtis prayed that "an awakening of interest in the Indians" would encourage the tribe and that the "happy memories of past days, deeply planted in the hearts of the old people, may be to younger Winnebagos as seeds for growth in character and endurance that shall bring to their future the strength and virtue of their old lake life." Adaptation of traditional culture to the new life must be undertaken responsibly, Curtis cautioned. In her discussion of the Kiowa she recounted the hardships of the tribe and expressed optimism for their future: "It is to be hoped that discrimination in their absorption of new ways may help them to bring something of the old vigor into their new life." While hearing Short Bull explain his view on the Ghost Dance and express hope that things would change for all Indians, Curtis grasped the Dakota by his hands and offered him what she considered a message of hope: "I leave you with this word: Be of good heart. Even though the old days are gone, never to come again, still be of good heart. A better day will dawn for your people." She promised that Indians would mature, or evolve, into "manhood" as a race and that "the days of full maturity will be warm with sunshine." *The Indians' Book* offered Indians an alternative to complete assimilation — combining the best of their old lives with their new ones — and it promised hope. "May the Indians' Book echo to every Indian the message," Curtis proclaimed. "'Look for the new day!'"[75]

Curtis's concern for her collaborators differentiates her, in certain ways, from other collectors of Native American music. She sincerely wished for young Native Americans to read *The Indians' Book* because it could model a better life for them. Few students of Indian music contended that their work would have any effect on those who collaborated with them. Most believed their study of Indian music would benefit whites seeking to understand human nature or looking for a source of inspiration for their own cultures. Although Curtis made these same claims for her work, she also insisted that *The Indians' Book* would directly aid Native Americans. Despite her willingness to see Indians as belonging to a romanticized past, Curtis recognized that most occupied a difficult transitional stage. In her original introduction to the volume (which she never published) Curtis explained that one of her motives for collecting was to come to grips with the rapid changes of the twentieth century, changes affecting whites and Indians alike. Modern advances in transportation and the exchange of ideas meant that races in different stages of development now interacted. "The stone-age greets the age of electricity," she commented. She realized that past policies had demoralized Native Americans but believed that among the ashes of Indian cultures some "glowing embers" remained. She hoped that the spirit of the new century would breathe new life on these embers and mark the "signal fire of the Indian's rebirth."[76] She wanted her work to help individuals combine the best of their traditions with the demands of modern life, using material in *The Indians' Book* as a guide. Curtis offered Native Americans a message of hope that, although tinged with primitivism and evolutionary theories about racial development, promised a "new day" for Indians.

THE INDIANS' BOOK PROPELLED CURTIS INTO A CAREER OF advocacy for Native Americans. Invitations to speak on Indian music and publish additional works on their cultures occupied Curtis for the rest of her life. She, unlike many of her contemporaries in the field of ethnomusicology, took seriously her rhetoric about not just sympathizing with the people she studied but taking direct action on their behalf. The years surrounding the publication of *The Indians' Book* found Natalie Curtis hard at work for Native Americans.

1. Portrait of Natalie Curtis in her childhood. Courtesy of the Natalie Curtis
Burlin Archives, in the possession of Alfred and Virginia Bredenberg, Raleigh NC.

2. (*Left*) Natalie Curtis at Wagner's Bayreuth in August 1896, taken by her mother, Augusta. Courtesy of the Natalie Curtis Burlin Archives, in the possession of Alfred and Virginia Bredenberg, Raleigh NC.

3. (*Above*) Natalie Curtis, George Curtis, and High Chief playing a hand game at High Chief's camp, ca. 1905. Courtesy of the Natalie Curtis Burlin Archives, in the possession of Alfred and Virginia Bredenberg, Raleigh NC.

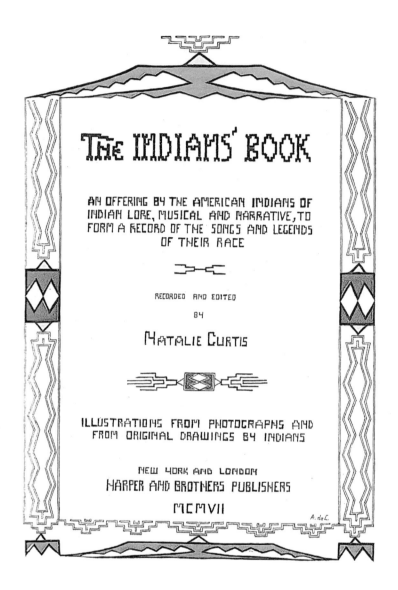

The INDIANS' BOOK

AN OFFERING BY THE AMERICAN INDIANS OF
INDIAN LORE, MUSICAL AND NARRATIVE, TO
FORM A RECORD OF THE SONGS AND LEGENDS
OF THEIR RACE

RECORDED AND EDITED

BY

Natalie Curtis

ILLUSTRATIONS FROM PHOTOGRAPHS AND
FROM ORIGINAL DRAWINGS BY INDIANS

NEW YORK AND LONDON
HARPER AND BROTHERS PUBLISHERS
MCMVII

A. de C.

4. The title page from *The Indians' Book.*

5. The title page from the Kwakiutl chapter of *The Indians' Book*.

6. (*Above*) A photograph of Kwakiutl men taken by Natalie Curtis at the Louisiana Purchase Exposition, St. Louis, 1904. Notice that the background has been darkened out on one half of the photograph. This altered image was included in *The Indians' Book*. Courtesy of the National Anthropological Archives, Smithsonian Institution, inventory no. 00073900, negative no. 77-10035.

7. (*Right*) "Puwach Tawi" lullaby, from the Hopi chapter of *The Indians' Book*.

Tašunke-Ciqala (Little Horse)

A Chief of the Olden Time (Chief Yellow-Hair)

8. (*Above*) Images of "Noble Savages": photos of Plains Indians from *The Indians' Book*.

9. (*Right*) First page of "Couldn't Hear Nobody Pray," from *Negro Folk Songs* (1919), showing Curtis's attempt to capture harmonization.

III
Couldn't hear nobody pray

* The melody is carried in the voice of the "Lead" (or Leader) printed in the piano-part in large type.

** The bass in this phrase, whenever repeated, comes well to the fore.

Department of Music

Under the Direct Supervision of J. Rosamond Johnson

PIANO

FACULTY

MISS ETHEL RICHARDSON
MISS FLORENCE HERBERT
MRS. STELLA HAWKINS
MR. WILLIAM H. BUTLER
MISS BEATRICE CAMPBELL
MR. J. ROSAMOND JOHNSON
MRS. EMMA DeLYON LEONARD

VIOLIN

MR. FELIX FOWLER WEIR
MISS GERTRUDE FIELDS
MR. WILLIAM H. BUTLER
MISS MARGARET UNDERHILL

CELLO

MR. LEONARD JETER
MR JACOB PEASE

VOICE CULTURE

MR. J. ROSAMOND JOHNSON
MR. G. H. BOLDEN
MRS. ELLEN FORD BROOKS

MANDOLIN, BANJO, GUITAR

MR. WILLIAM. H. BUTLER

FOLK DANCES & GAMES

MISS AMANDA E. KEMP, Director

MODERN DANCES

MRS. A. S. REED, Director

Lessons taught in Cornet, Trombone, Clarinet, Sight-Singing, Harmony and Composition.

TERMS:

Private Lessons, 50c   Lessons in Classes of 4, 25c

HOURS 10 A. M. TO 10 P. M.

Worthy pupils who cannot afford to pay for lessons will be given scholarships.
Special arrangements made for out of town pupils.
Scholars completing the Normal Course will be given positions as teachers.
All donations of $25.00 or more will entitle the giver the awarding of scholarships.

All communications should be sent to

Mrs. Emma Greene,

Registrar and Matron

4 and 6 W. 131st St.   Telephone 1079 Harlem

J. ROSAMOND JOHNSON, Gen'l. Supervisor

Sunday Afternoon

Music==Lecture Recitals

Music School Settlement

(For Colored People)

4 and 6 West 131st Street, New York City

TELEPHONE 1079 HARLEM

(3 Blocks from Lenox Avenue Subway Station; 2 Doors from 5th Avenue;

Near 5th Avenue Bus.)

THE NEW YORK AGE PRESS, 247 WEST 45TH STREET, NEW YORK CITY

10. Pamphlet for the Music School Settlement for Colored People. Courtesy of the Library of Congress, Performing Arts Reading Room, Mannes-Damrosch Collection.

11. Natalie Curtis in Santa Fe, 1917. Courtesy of the Natalie Curtis Burlin Archives, in the possession of Alfred and Virginia Bredenberg, Raleigh NC.

12. Portrait of Natalie Curtis. Courtesy of the Natalie Curtis Burlin Archives, in the possession of Alfred and Virginia Bredenberg, Raleigh NC.

5

"The White Friend"

Curtis and Indian Reform

THE *INDIANS' BOOK* DIFFERED FROM SIMILAR COLLECTIONS of music and folklore in its insistence that it be used as a tool to improve the lives of Native Americans. Curtis desired to encourage the administrators and teachers in the Indian school system to end their relentless attacks on students' cultures. She wanted government officials to better understand Indians and adapt their approaches to meet real needs, and she hoped that through appreciation for the beauty and charm of Indian songs white readers would support a more benign, less strictly assimilationist federal Indian policy. Curtis went beyond merely writing about the need for reform — she directly involved herself in the movement. She became in many ways a transitional figure in the Indian reform movement, a bridge between the unbending assimilationist policies of the late nineteenth century and the cultural pluralism that blossomed in the 1920s and 1930s.

Curtis differed from many of her contemporaries in the fields of anthropology and ethnomusicology in her pursuit of reform. Few students of Indian music and folklore connected their study of

Native cultures to critiques of Indian policy as strongly as she did. Many preferred to distance their work as scientists from any overt political context, often relying on government funding to support their work and conforming to notions of objectivity among their peers. Alice Fletcher, who collected music and studied the cultures of a number of Plains tribes, did use her position as an anthropologist to push for reform. Unlike Curtis, however, she supported the assimilationist agenda and helped implement allotment on several reservations.[1] Frances Densmore published primarily on Native music, not on bettering Indian conditions or granting Indians fair treatment. Densmore's desire to be seen as a serious researcher in the field of ethnomusicology prevented her, unlike Curtis, from engaging in work that would not have been deemed "objective" by her male peers. Matilda Coxe Stevenson gained access to Zuni society by befriending some of her informants, but even as she collected cultural artifacts she firmly believed the Zuni, like all primitive people, had no other option but assimilation. Like many other anthropologists she wrote about Zuni culture to salvage it from extinction, not, like Curtis, to improve Indian lives in a transitional stage.[2] Curtis made important connections between studying and appreciating Native music and folklore and the pursuit of reform. Music, she argued, provided insights into beliefs and cultures that could improve Indians affairs. Even if through the mediation of a "white friend" like Curtis, Indian voices should be heard and their ideas considered as Indians joined other Americans on the journey into the twentieth century.[3]

Indian reform, particularly "civilization" and Christianization, had been an object of Europeans from the onset of the invasion. American colonists proselytized among Indians on the East Coast and established missions and schools ostensibly for them, but Indian affairs were not as crucial to British colonization. U.S. missionary organizations, such as the American Board for Foreign Missions, worked among Indians in the antebellum and Civil War years. For

many, however, the needs of black slaves and freed people overrode concerns for Native Americans, who by the mid-nineteenth
century were psychologically and physically far removed from the
majority of reformers. With the demise of Reconstruction and the
implementation of a new approach to Indian affairs in the 1870s,
the so-called Peace Policy of President Grant, interest in Native
American reform grew.

The publicity surrounding the plight of a small group of Poncas
sparked interest in protecting and uplifting Native peoples. Standing Bear, a Ponca leader arrested (but later released, in the *Standing
Bear v. Crook* decision) for leading a small band out of Indian territory to their homeland along the Niobrara River in Nebraska in
early 1879, undertook an extensive tour of cities on the East Coast.
Along with the educated Poncas Susette ("Bright Eyes") and Joseph
LaFlesche, Standing Bear presented his case in Chicago, Boston,
New York, Philadelphia, and Washington. The trip was "carefully
orchestrated" by Thomas Henry Tibbles, the editor of the *Omaha
Herald*. The group condemned the current reservation system for
its corruption, violence, and abuses and called for constitutional
protections for Native Americans. The Poncas offered "Indian citizenship, education and the abolition of the reservation system . . .
as solutions for the present injustice." Tibbles appealed to former
abolitionists, people like Natalie's uncle George William Curtis,
for instance, and their nostalgia for the abolition movement as he
presented his case for Indian reform. Tibbles, Standing Bear, and
his entourage succeeded in generating that interest. As Frederick
Hoxie concludes, by 1880 "a central truth was becoming self-evident:
the government's policy was unworkable." Reformers increasingly
advocated for total assimilation and the end of the reservation system as solutions to the crises in Indian affairs.[4]

Many individuals personally responded to Standing Bear and
his pleas for reform. Helen Hunt Jackson, a writer living in Boston,
claimed to have experienced an epiphany during a presentation and

agitated for Indian rights the rest of her life. Her 1881 publication *A Century of Dishonor* railed against the history of abuses perpetuated on American Indians. She became "a veritable one-person reform movement," vociferously arguing for the end to mistreatment of Native Americans. Her sentimental novel *Ramona* (1884) dramatized the plight of the California Indians and was intended to "be another Uncle Tom's Cabin in the drive for racial justice." Although some have questioned Jackson's commitment to a policy of complete assimilation, in general she advanced an agenda similar to the majority of the newly organized reform societies.[5]

The majority of Indian reformers worked within these new organizations rather than individually. Members of these groups tended to be Protestants and professionals who viewed themselves as humanitarians. Reformers believed that Native Americans could quickly adopt white lifestyles and, as Thomas Holm argues, attempted "to reorient Indian societies and ideals" toward white, middle-class norms. Wilbert Ahern adds that reformers' "belief in the plasticity of all men" made them optimistic that Indians could easily and rapidly assimilate. Indians needed guidance, some prodding, and protection as they advanced upward toward civilization. Reformers advocated using federal control of tribal funds, rations, and annuities to force Indians to comply with their demands. They supported the Dawes Act of 1887 and stressed individualization, private property, education, and Christianity as tools to create American Indian citizens.[6]

A number of national groups supporting this agenda arose in the late nineteenth century. The Women's National Indian Association (WNIA), established in the spring of 1879 and led by Amelia S. Quinton, adopted home-oriented outreach to Native Americans, reflecting the group's "social feminism." Developing out of the WNIA, the Indian Rights Association (IRA), a male-dominated group, stressed a more businesslike approach to reform. Established in Philadelphia in 1882, the IRA maintained that Indians could indeed adapt to modern conditions and argued that government policies often worked against their progress. The IRA influenced government policy through its careful, firsthand investigations of conditions in Native communities. It established branches in major cities and kept lobbyists busy in Washington. The IRA cooperated with other reform groups, especially the "Friends of the Indian," which met annually at the Quaker Albert Smiley's upstate New York resort at Lake Mohonk. The Lake Mohonk conferences included mainly moderate reformers, drawn from the fields of education, missions, and government, who met to discuss important issues related to Indian affairs. Publications of the speeches, discussions, and addresses of conference attendees helped the "Friends" influence Indian policy.[7]

These late-nineteenth-century reformers, as Francis Paul Prucha contends, had established themselves "as the guardians of the Indians and the watchdogs and arbiters of national Indian policy" and succeeded in implementing their legislative programs by 1900. The Dawes Act (1887), with its privatization of Native American land, dissolution of tribal communities, and promises of citizenship, stood as the hallmark of their reform efforts. During the early years of the twentieth century, when Curtis became involved in Indian affairs, reformers experienced declining influence over government affairs. The passage of the Burke Act of 1906 and the Lacey Act of 1907, both modifications of the Dawes Act, against the wishes of most reform groups has been cited as evidence of their diminished power.[8] Reformers' tendency to see the Dawes Act as the panacea to the Indian problem might have contributed to this decline. Even as the expected impact of the Dawes Act failed to materialize, reformers doggedly stuck to their solution and made few efforts to push for alternate reforms. By the early twentieth century these reformers also faced new types of government officials whose emphasis on pragmatism in Indian affairs led them increasingly to view reformers as well-intentioned but uninformed sentimentalists.[9]

In addition to declining influence early twentieth-century reform-ers also underwent a shift in expectations and goals. Historians of Indian policy in the Progressive Era debate the extent of their change in policy and outlook. Some historians argue for continuity from the late nineteenth century through the early twentieth, arguing that reformers and government officials still optimistically expected Indians to blend into American society through the prescribed methods of education, dissolution of tribal ties, and individualized land holding. Francis Paul Prucha in *The Great Father,* his major work on federal Indian policy, argues for continuity of policy, with a shift only toward a more gradualist approach. He and other like-minded historians note that while overall goals remained constant, many began to doubt that Indians would assimilate as quickly as they initially expected. Under the administration of President Theodore Roosevelt government officials accepted a gradualist approach to Indian assimilation. They still believed that Indians would become a part of mainstream America, but not too quickly. Some have suggested that as reformers began appreciating Indian cultures it became easier for them to accept a more gradualist approach. The historian Kenneth O'Reilly concurs that optimism about Indian assimilation dominated policy as reform groups continued to defend their past goals and methods.[10]

Frederick Hoxie goes beyond this gradualist assessment and argues for a concrete shift in Indian policy in the early years of the twentieth century. Relying more on popular opinion about Indi-ans, expressed in magazine articles, fairs, and expositions, and on the works of social scientists than on Prucha's government docu-ments, Hoxie argues that the goals for Indians did change during the Progressive Era.[11] These "new" reformers used "science" to justify their policies. Evolutionary theory, Progressives argued, demon-strated that Native Americans could never expect to advance to the level of European Americans in such a short time. Reformers no longer expected Indians to assimilate completely into American culture and therefore educated them instead to take their proper place in society. This "place" meant marginalization, menial labor, and little hope for future advancement, much like the positions of other "dependent" minority groups. Some reformers espoused clearly racist ideas about Indians, while others believed they had the best interests of Indians at heart. Hoxie contends that Roosevelt's entrance into office marked a transition toward Western regional control of Indian affairs, especially through Roosevelt's "cowboy cabinet." Indian policy also changed because it became linked with ideas about imperialism abroad and segregation at home. As a result reformers assumed the "white man's burden" to help nonwhite dependents by teaching them to work in, but at the bottom of, an industrialized society.[12]

Curtis's research and reform agenda placed her in a transitional role, reflecting the older notions of the inevitability of the vanishing Indian and the paternalistic impulses of early reform groups and the newer appreciation for elements of Native American cultures and a willingness to allow or even encourage Indian traditions. Because she remained wed to evolutionary ideas of human development, Curtis believed that Indians must assimilate to many aspects of modern American life and that they needed guidance on their journey toward civilization. She never questioned the right of the government or of reformers like herself to dictate the path of the nation's wards. Instead she argued for a more culturally sensitive policy regarding the treatment of Indians, a less strident approach to assimilation. She never questioned the need for the Indian school system, for example, but wanted education that honored the best aspects of Native cultures and used Indian music and art to facilitate the transition toward modern, civilized life. Throughout her career Curtis urged a more gradualist approach, one that foreshadowed later developments in Indian affairs.

The difficulties she encountered in collecting Hopi and Navajo music in the Southwest sparked her earliest interest in Indian reform.

She blamed the oppressive policies of the Indian Office for informants' reticence in sharing songs with her. She expanded this into
a critique of missions and government schools, which she accused
of blindly and unfairly suppressing beautiful and significant music
and folklore. Drawing on family connections to President Theodore
Roosevelt, Curtis gained his permission and support to collect
Indian songs free from official interference. She continued to rely on
the president's support when she became involved in the efforts of
a small band of Arizona Indians, the Yavapais (mistakenly referred
to as the "Mohave Apache" by Curtis and most other commentators of this period), to secure their own reservation. Although this
issue was not directly linked to her area of expertise, Curtis sought
to exploit the president's interest in Indian arts to gain his approval
of a plan for a reservation for the Mohave Apache.

On a "stifling" August day in 1903 Natalie Curtis was summoned
"on a mysterious errand" from her family home on Long Island to the
New York City apartment of Charlotte Osgood Mason, her patron
with an avid interest in "primitive" spirituality. As she approached
Mason's Park Avenue apartment Curtis observed a crowd forming
on the street around a Native American man lugging an enormous
basket. She instantly recognized the white man accompanying him
as her "old friend" Frank Mead, who had arrived in the city "fresh
from the West." Mead, "an eccentric New York architect," had started
the New York branch of the Sequoya League, the same group that
had brought charges against Superintendent Charles Burton for
alleged abuses on the Hopi reservation. He had given up his practice in the spring of 1903 to head west and had befriended Curtis's
brother George and later Curtis herself.[13]

Mead soon explained why he was bringing a basket-laden Indian
to Mason's apartment and why he needed Curtis's help. Mead introduced the man accompanying him as Pelia, a "Mohave Apache"
(Yavapai) chief who had come east to make his case directly to
President Roosevelt. In the 1870s the federal government had placed

the Yavapai people on the San Carlos reservation, located along the Gila River in south central Arizona, along with the recently subdued Apaches. General George Crook, who disagreed with placing the Yavapai at San Carlos, had promised the tribe that if they remained peaceful and learned to live as whites, they could eventually return to their homeland in the Verde River Valley, 180 miles northwest of San Carlos, at the convergence of the Salt and Verde rivers. Dismal conditions at San Carlos in the 1890s prompted many Yavapais to leave the reservation to return to their homelands, with the permission of the agent. American and Mexican squatters in the meantime had moved into this region, forcing the Yavapais to live on the margins of their own homelands. A nearby abandoned military post, Camp McDowell, thus became the proposed site for the Yavapais' own reservation. The tribe had subsequently spent several fruitless years trying to compel the federal government to grant part of these lands to them.[14]

Even though the Yavapai had spent considerable time trying to obtain a reservation at Camp McDowell, Curtis portrayed these efforts as the work of white patrons on behalf of grateful but politically unsophisticated people. According to Curtis's dramatic version Mead had heard of their situation and visited the Yavapai. Despite threats from the non-Indian settlers Mead smuggled the chief out of the territory under a pile of blankets and brought him directly to the president to tell his tribe's story. In actuality the Indian Office had been trying to address the situation for at least two years and had even initiated a bill in Congress to secure the land for the Yavapai, and the Yavapai themselves had previously sent delegations to Washington.[15] In Curtis's view, however, the chance for the "white friends" to finally resolve the situation in Arizona now presented itself. She met with a cousin of Roosevelt vacationing near her family on Long Island and scheduled a meeting with the president, Pelia, and Mead.

Curtis prepared the Yavapai leader for his meeting with the president. Along with Mason she showed him the sights and sounds of white civilization in New York City, including skyscrapers, elevated trains, and a beach. Just prior to his engagement with Roosevelt, Mason made sure that the chief was "well soaped and combed" for his important meeting. Mead and Pelia made a successful pitch to Roosevelt that resulted in direct action toward the establishment of a Yavapai reservation at Fort McDowell. The chief presented the "Great White Father" with the large basket he had carried east and told his story "in a few simple words," earnestly trusting that Roosevelt would not leave his people homeless. After patiently allowing the Yavapai representative to have his say, Mead immediately took control of the meeting, impressing the president with his practical plan for resolving the situation. "Capital!" Roosevelt reportedly responded. "Mr. Mead, you get the Indians' land. Chief, tell your people that the White Chief will see that they have justice." Within days of the meeting Roosevelt appointed Mead as the special agent in charge of securing land for the Yavapai and dealing with the non-Indian squatters. Mead met with the groups involved and tried to establish a solution equitable to all parties. Although Curtis presented the solution as a quick fix, the reservation at Fort McDowell was not established until the end of the next year.[16]

Curtis may have contributed to Mead's appointment as special agent. She sent a letter to Roosevelt suggesting an even greater role in Indian politics for her friend. Without specifically mentioning the Yavapai case, except to comment on "the urgent matter of the starving Indians," Curtis applauded the merits of Frank Mead. She claimed that he could serve as "a channel for the carrying out of new and enlightened government methods regarding the Indian." She promised that he would not only develop Southwestern tribes industrially but would also "take care of the artistic and ethnological side without any talk or fuss or antagonism of missionaries." Curtis then subtly suggested that the investigations into the actions of the Hopi superintendent Charles Burton, a man "generally considered entirely inadequate to his position," might possibly leave a vacancy open for Mead. However, Curtis continued, Mead had so much to offer that perhaps a position as a supervisor of all Arizona agencies would be more appropriate for his talents and vision. She pictured Mead establishing a model agency, "a sort of modern Brook Farm," in which the traditional industries of the tribes could be developed, an experiment "of value not only to our country but to all nations who are struggling with the problems of colonization." Using the Transcendentalist experiment as a model reflected Curtis's family's influence and highlighted her belief that art could be used for reform. Curtis expressed her confidence in Roosevelt in a shameless attempt to win over the president, assuring him that by "your keen insight, your recognition of the 'right man' and how to use him, and, above all, by your directness of purpose, you are able to do in minutes what other men take years to accomplish." Although Curtis's efforts to replace Burton with Mead failed — Roosevelt replied that the charges against Burton "fall absolutely flat, in fact, comically so" — the president did grant a post to Mead.[17]

Roosevelt appointed Curtis's friend as the "Special Supervisor" to whom superintendents and agents from four states and two territories in the Southwest were to report on the development of industry on their reservations. More experienced voices questioned Mead's character. Hart Merriam, a member of Roosevelt's "Indian cabinet," expressed concerns regarding Mead's "mental ballast." The somewhat eccentric Charles Lummis responded that Mead "was 'a good deal saner than he looks, and I am inclined to trust him; but still would hardly vouch for his balance.'"[18] Regardless of his mental state or relation with others in Indian affairs, Mead maintained his contact with the women who had helped him and the Yavapai chief in August of 1903. Curtis and Mason later visited the tribe at its newly established reservation and participated in its celebrations, including a dance to honor Mead, its "savior," and to celebrate: "We have our land; . . . we are men again."[19]

In the years immediately following this episode Curtis mainly
agitated for change through her writing and lecturing, rather than
direct political activism. Although she never expressed her dissat-
isfaction, she may not have been fully pleased with the outcome
of this case. Although the Yavapai received their land, they continued to struggle for years to make the reservation sustainable
and to prevent the government from removing them to the Salt
River Pima Maricopa reservation.[20] In 1921 Curtis pleaded with
the American public to allow the Yavapai to retain their land at
Fort McDonnell and to prevent forced allotments on poor desert
tracts. She asked her readers, "Why should not the Mojave Apache
who still rightfully own their patch of fertile farming land be left
in peace?"[21] Curtis moreover found herself mostly relegated to a
secondary role in this case — mainly serving as a conduit for Mead
to meet Roosevelt — but in the future she found ways to assert her
ideas more forcefully and take a larger role in the reform process.
Curtis discovered that she could be a more effective advocate for
change, and have a more personally satisfying career, by combining
her desire for reform with collecting and sharing Native American
music and folklore.

While Curtis prepared the manuscript of *The Indians' Book* she
remained involved in Indian affairs. In May 1905 she resided in
Washington DC, with Mason. Living in the nation's capital kept
Curtis apprised of events related to Indian policy and in contact
with reformers and scholars who lived in the city. Events in "Indian
Country" tempted her away from the work of organizing the book,
but she continued to maintain her connections with important
figures in Indian affairs. For example, she met with the daughter of
Secretary Ethan Allen Hitchcock to encourage her to lobby Commissioner of Indian Affairs Francis Leupp on "the matter of the
clothing for the Indian children." Apparently Curtis hoped for some
compromise between Native and American clothing for Indian
students, telling George Foster Peabody that "we may have them

in hygienic moccasins" within a year. Peabody in turn kept Curtis
up to date on important events and issues, encouraging her to use
every opportunity to promote her work. He invited her to the Silver Bay Conference, a Presbyterian convention for missionaries
to Indians. A bit uneasy among this crowd because her views of
Indians differed from theirs, Curtis rejected his proposal to place
her on the official program. Even at this early stage of her career
she felt removed from the mainstream reform community. Still,
Curtis hoped that she could influence the missionaries' views of
Indians by finding ways to raise "the Indian matter before chosen
people here and there in conversation."[22] Curtis probably believed
that her mere words would not be enough to change attitudes. She
needed to find a more powerful, more effective means to advocate
for change.

Increasingly she believed that music, a medium that she often
considered a universal human language, could accomplish what
her words could not. By holding up the promise Indian songs held
for a national culture, and then warning sympathetic listeners that
this music was consciously being destroyed, she hoped to end the
policy of complete assimilation for Native Americans. She strongly
critiqued government policies that sought to replace Native values
and practices with those of the dominant American culture. Curtis
used a scene from Oraibi to criticize the government's assimilationist
goals. After collecting a song from the Oraibi leader Tawakwaptiwa
she watched Hopi children returning home from school and asked,
"And the picture made by this little band, was it the more pathetic or
the more grotesque?" The girls, she remarked, had lost the "butterfly
swirls" in their hair for plain braids and traded their bright Hopi
clothes for the colorless checked gingham of the school uniform.
The boys trod along in their heavy shoes and American suits of
cheap material. Worse yet, the children sang as they climbed the
path home ("for Hopis always sing"), not one of their beautiful
songs, but "Marching Through Georgia!" Just then Curtis happened

to spy Tawakwaptiwa dashing down the trail, "a glorious picture of glad, free life," and concluded:

> I stood still in my path. Behind me was the older Hopi, the poet, filled with the very essence of the people's life and thought. Before me was the coming generation, struggling upward, singing a song they could not understand, weighted in mind and body with the misfit garment of civilization. What part had such a dress, what place had such a song upon the limited wastes of the Hopis' desert home?
>
> As I stood between the old and the new, this question forced itself upon me: which type is the truer to the divine in man, these children of a so-called progress, or the child of natural development — Tawakwaptiwa, the shepherd poet?[23]

Similar observations further encouraged Curtis to question the policy of complete assimilation. She focused especially on ending educational policies that stripped children of their cultures. Previously Curtis had expressed these concerns in private correspondence to President Roosevelt, but now she voiced them to the larger public and adroitly used the words and actions of "real" Indians to punctuate her arguments. As she collected corn-grinding songs from the women of Laguna, one of them told Curtis: "Many songs are forgotten. Our people do not sing as they used. I do not hear the songs I heard before I went to school." Curtis also recounted a speech delivered to her by a Navajo leader she accompanied in Pasadena. He acknowledged, after witnessing the many splendors of modern American life, the necessity for his people to receive education to survive alongside whites. "But, why do the Americans," he inquired, "want to cut our hair and stop our dances and our songs? Will not the Big Chief in Washington forbid the Americans to keep forbidding us? We do no harm. It is well for the younger ones to learn new ways but leave the old ones to be happy with our dances and our songs." Curtis did not directly challenge the notion that Indians needed American education to cope with their changing world or question the foundation of federal Indian policy; she instead wanted to amend this policy to allow attractive elements of Native culture to survive into the twentieth century.[24]

She envisioned *The Indians' Book* as her contribution to reforming destructive federal Indian policies and hoped that intimate knowledge of Indians would lead others to agree with her views. In her introduction she explained: "The making of this record has been a consecrated work. Joy in the task has been shadowed by close contact with a struggling people in their need. It was impossible to live near to Indian life without being heart-wrung by the pathos of its tragedy — impossible to be among Indians without crying, 'Is there a people more deeply misunderstood?'"[25] Curtis intended to challenge current policy and to offer suggestions for a more humane, Indian-centered approach. Reviewers of *The Indians' Book* understood this as part of her purpose, one reviewer writing that the work should have "a shaming effect" on whites.[26]

Curtis began her critique of Indian policy in the area of her greatest expertise — the suppression of Native American music by government officials and missionaries. She complained about the loss of traditional culture because of the "effort to force all things Anglo-Saxon" upon tribal members and to prohibit expressions of traditional culture. An elderly Pima man thanked her for recording his song and appreciating his tribe's music. Whites, he told her, had forbidden his tribe from singing: "They think our songs are bad. We are glad you say they are good." Similarly the Hopi Lololomai initially feared the negative implications of sharing songs with Curtis. "White people try to stop our songs and dances," he explained to Curtis, "so I am fearful of your talk." Many tribal leaders shared her concern about the effects assimilationist policies at government schools would have on traditional music and art. Curtis hoped that her book as a whole would serve as a kind of indictment against the misguided, even cruel policy of suppressing music of such symbolism, beauty, and inspiration.[27]

Her opposition to the suppression of music led Curtis to criticize Indian policy and the treatment of Native Americans. She complained about whites who came into contact with the tribes — government officials, traders, teachers, missionaries, and local white neighbors. She outlined many of her criticisms in her introductory statements about individual tribes. For example, she chronicled the plight of the Winnebagos, who were forced "against their will and at their own expense from a prosperous home in Minnesota to a desolate Dakota agency."[28] The threat of "starvation, disease, and cold" on their new lands in Nebraska, along with the influx of white settlers after allotment, had created an "exhausted and discouraged tribe." Allotment had also had negative effects for the Kiowa in Oklahoma. "Ill-ventilated frame-houses," Curtis complained, "have replaced the tipi with its leaping fire and its open flap and smoke-hole." These changes in turn intensified the threat of tuberculosis. White pressure for land and disregard for Indian welfare had created dire conditions for the tribes Curtis visited. The Pawnee had barely recuperated from their removal to Indian Territory when "their new home was thrown open to white settlement." These whites, rather than providing models for civilized life, as proponents of allotment had promised, "brought to the Pawnee disease, discouragement, and vice." Despite these many setbacks, Curtis continually argued, Native Americans proved resilient and strong. Their strength often derived from their music, art, and religion, and therefore attempts to eradicate the last vestiges of Native life would prove disastrous.[29]

One of the strongest critiques of the treatment of Native Americans came from one of the few female leaders Curtis asked to contribute to her book. Chiparopai, a Yuma leader whose knowledge of English and Spanish enabled her to challenge an irrigation proposal that would have reduced her reservation to one-fifth its original size, shared songs and myths with Curtis. Chiparopai recounted her life story, commenting on the many changes she had witnessed as whites invaded her homeland. She noted a general weakening among her tribe and an increase in sickness, which she attributed to the adoption of white food and clothing. "Yes — we know that when you [whites] come, we die," she told Curtis. Curtis tried to reassure her that not all whites were evil and that "a better day will come," but the aged Yuma voiced her doubts:

> "Ah, well — white people do not mean to harm us — maybe. But you do not understand my people, and" she added slowly, "you never even try. You want to divide for us the little land that we may still call our own. You never ask us what we would like, or would not like. We are ruled by your laws and you never try to make plain to us what these laws mean. . . . You want our children to go to the schools that you have for us. Do you come to us old people first and tell us about the schools, and explain to us what the schools are for, so that we may understand? We Indians only know that schools will make our children like white people, and some of us — " she paused, then said quietly, "some of us do not like white people and their ways."[30]

Through the words of Chiparopai, Curtis took an especially strong stand against current Indian policy. Chiparopai questioned the prevalent assumption that whites, including Curtis, knew what was best for their Native wards and asserted, contrary to most commentators on Indian affairs, that Native Americans must have a voice in decisions about their futures.

Chiparopai's critique of government schools complemented Curtis's view that these institutions unwisely aimed to destroy all elements of tribal cultures, particularly music and folklore. The Indian school system that the two women criticized, although an immediate product of the late nineteenth century, had a long history in U.S.-Indian affairs. From the beginning of white inhabitation of North America the rhetoric of many religious and governmental leaders had urged education as the key to transforming Native Americans. Promises to educate Indian children were included in numerous treaties, and by 1819 Congress, through the Civilization Fund, had offered to finance religious or secular groups willing to labor among the Indians. Following the Civil War interest in educating Native Americans increased. The Peace Policy of President Grant used religious organizations, many deeply involved in educational activities, to manage the affairs of Indian agencies. By the 1870s and 1880s the federal government had become more deeply involved in directly providing education for Indian children. General Richard Henry Pratt set the standard for off-reservation boarding schools when he opened Carlisle Indian School in 1879. After witnessing the progress former Cheyenne, Kiowa, and Comanche prisoners under his command at Fort Marion, Florida, made at the black industrial school Hampton Institute, Pratt decided that bringing Native Americans into direct contact with American society would be the most effective means of assimilation. Carlisle's "outing program" had students live and work with local white families while attending regular public schools. Starting in the late 1880s numerous off-reservation boarding schools tried to imitate Carlisle; however, none of these schools operated in the eastern half of the United States.[31]

By the early twentieth century several types of Indian schools existed. The government supported several off-reservation boarding schools, such as Haskell Institute (Kansas), Chilocco Indian School (Oklahoma), Phoenix Indian School (Arizona), and Sherman Institute (California). Reservation boarding schools provided education from their locations near reservation agencies or other central meeting places, and numerous day schools educated students near their homes. Congress also appropriated money for the operation of Carlisle and Hampton Institute and for some religious schools.[32] It justified the support of sectarian education by arguing that until the government could adequately provide educational facilities for Indian students, any type of education would suffice, and Christian education would especially prepare Indians for assimilation. Other mission schools operated without government assistance by relying instead on private donations.[33]

Schools were designed, at least in theory, to immerse students in American practices and prepare them for citizenship in the United States. Students participated in the "half-day" system, in which they learned the "three Rs" for one half of the day and practiced a trade during the other. In theory this practice was intended to instill a work ethic in students and provide them with a usable trade. In reality student labor often kept schools functioning, while the children suffered from meager appropriations, and their labor often resembled drudgery more than vocational training. In addition to English instruction, rudimentary mathematics, and some vocational training, students learned the ways of "civilized" society, including proper gender roles, Protestant Christianity, and American patriotism. Students lived carefully regimented lives under the watchful eyes of school officials. Newly arrived students, many of whom had never left their homes before, were forced to endure the indignities of public bathing, hair-cutting, delousing, and learning to wear unfamiliar (and often inadequate) clothing. In addition students were forbidden to speak any language but English and had to adopt Americanized (and occasionally ridiculous) names. Students often lived in dormitory-style housing, which was often poorly ventilated, in ill repair, and dangerous. Because most schools were severely underfunded, students often suffered from disease and malnutrition. In addition to the often horrendous living conditions at boarding schools, teachers, matrons, and other school employees regularly assaulted students' cultures and customs. Although conditions varied and students experienced a range of responses to the schools, few could argue that they best met Native American needs.[34]

Critics of the boarding schools varied in the reasons for their opposition. Some humanitarians argued for improvements in basic living conditions, pointing to the high incidence of illness and death.

Others objected to what they perceived as extravagant spending on a group that neither wanted nor deserved special privileges. They noted that graduates often "returned to the blanket" and benefited little from schooling. Many objected to the policy of forced separation of very young children from their parents.[35] Others questioned the rationale behind a course of study that did not seem to prepare students for survival after school. These critics often called for the reduction of off-reservation boarding schools and a heavier focus on vocational training. A few, like Curtis, began questioning the basic assumptions of educational policy, particularly the idea, as Carlisle founder Pratt infamously put it, of "killing the Indian to save the man." Like Curtis, many of these critics shared an appreciation for Native American cultures and feared that schooling would obliterate their musical and artistic treasures.[36]

Curtis's experiences collecting songs within the Indian schools opened her eyes to the problems in educational policy. Curtis initially intended *The Indians' Book* as a text for federal Indian schools. She explained to the anthropologist Franz Boas, "Realizing that the thoughts, the morals, and the lives of the younger Indians are molded in the Government schools, Mrs. Mason and I have felt that the singing of Indians songs in the schools would be one way in which something of the native spirit might be kept alive within the coming generation." *The Indians' Book,* she contended, was undertaken "from the very human standpoint of making possible the use of the songs in government institutions."[37] She later expanded on these themes when she sent a copy of *The Indians' Book* to the anthropologist Aleš Hrdlička in 1912. The volume, she explained, was prompted by a desire to "be of definite help to the Indians themselves and was at first intended for the Indian Schools." As her research developed and more Indians became interested, "the purpose also grew into an endeavor to let the Indians speak through this book to the general public among whom exists so complete a misunderstanding of the mentality of the American natives." *The Indians' Book* did find its way into "all the large Indian schools and in[to] many of their day schools," so Curtis could believe that she had contributed to some reform of the Indian educational system.[38]

In an unpublished introduction to *The Indians' Book* directed at teachers of Native pupils she offered her insights into the problems she had witnessed and suggestions for addressing them. The Indian student struggled, she said, because he had to "suddenly adjust himself from the life and habits of primitive man to those of the American citizen." Teachers needed to assist students in this arduous task by encouraging them to naturally express themselves, rather than forcing them into narrow Anglo-Saxon molds. Curtis suggested that teachers use objects and ideas familiar to their students as starting points for teaching English. Encouraging students to share tribal songs, games, or histories would give them self-confidence and inspire them to learn. Involving older members of the tribe in the educational process, Curtis asserted, was critical to a school's success. *The Indians' Book* could help teachers in their important work. "It is offered," Curtis claimed, "simply as a key to a door in the Indian's nature. The ability to unlock the door lies with the teacher." Her book, she argued, could be used in a variety of ways to improve the education of Native Americans.[39]

Curtis implored teachers of Native students to do more than just learn about their pupils' cultures; she wanted them to collect and encourage Indian songs as well. In an address to the National Education Association at the 1904 fair in St. Louis she argued that "the music of the Indians is beautiful, striking, and unique" and must be preserved. That previous winter, Curtis explained to the assembled teachers, she had shared Native songs with a group of American and European musicians in New York City. The wealth of beauty in the songs astounded them, one exclaiming: "Would that Wagner could have heard these songs. You have a wealth of inspiration in your country." Curtis charged Indian school teachers with the task of preserving and collecting songs from their students and encouraging their pupils to collect songs themselves, "for our own sake as well as for the best development of the Indian." She complained that Americans believed they had no art but refused to recognize Native Americans' "rich gifts of poetry, of art; yea more — gifts of human character rare and noble" that could be "absorbed into our national life." Curtis reassured her audience: "I am not one of those who believe that the Indian should be kept in a glass case like an ethnological specimen. The Indian is a man, not a curiosity." If teachers simply took up this task and "taught that we are glad and eager for his gifts . . . who shall say that this will make him less loyal to his country, less industrious as a citizen?" Now was the time, Curtis declared, for all workers in the field to collect and preserve tribal music.[40]

On several occasions Curtis reiterated the need for preservation of Indian music. There was no good reason "logically, humanely, or in the interest of good government" why the schools could not preserve this remarkable national treasure, she declared. "We cannot afford to lose real spontaneous art, first, because such art is beautiful; secondly, because it furnishes genius with material from which to draw inspiration; thirdly, because it creates an atmosphere which feeds and nourishes genius," she contended. Curtis demanded a system of education that demonstrated the same respect she felt toward Indian art and music and incorporated Native cultures properly into the schools, using studies like her own. She recognized the challenges in overcoming the idea of the necessity of complete assimilation. Government employees, she argued, "feel it is their duty to discourage native Indian art" and to remake their students into white clones as quickly as possible, when instead they could preserve and develop Native American cultural forms.[41]

Curtis believed that respecting the students' cultures and allowing Native Americans a greater role in the educational system would improve federal schools. She pointed out that each school had to respond to its own set of circumstances and needed to adapt its policies according to students' cultures. "For only through tact, sympathy, and understanding can the shaken confidence of the Indian now be won," Curtis insisted. She asserted that "modern educators realize that true education consists not so much in cramming something in as in drawing something out." If teachers encouraged students to sing, if they allowed Indian elders and leaders a role in their classrooms, if they explained to parents the benefits and purpose of education, students would benefit immeasurably. They would recognize the respect being shown other Indians and would be encouraged to strive for a better education themselves.[42] A more culturally sensitive approach, she argued, might do more to help Native Americans adapt to a modern world. "We may provide the undeveloped races with the means of adjustment to the life of modern industry and with the mechanical processes of self-expression," she argued, "but on our side we should at least recognize the inborn racial ideals and inherited art impulses [of Indian students]." Curtis pointed out that "art, particularly among primitive people, is the vehicle for the expression of religious sentiment, poetry, impressions of the outside world and conceptions of life." Schooling that destroyed Native art and music "robs them of their identity" and degrades them, when education should instead encourage and uplift. The nation needed Indian artists to inspire the creation of a new national artistic vision, and this need would in turn provide a commercial outlet for students trained in Native arts in the government schools.[43]

Her urgings gradually fell on receptive ears. In 1913 Secretary of the Interior Franklin Lane appointed Geoffrey O'Hara as supervisor of music in the Department of Indian Education. O'Hara, a composer and lecturer from Canada, received a commission to "preserve and develop the music" of Native Americans and to record and arrange songs for use in government schools. Curtis hoped that his appointment would serve as the basis for continuing change. She recalled her struggles just ten years earlier even to record Native songs and marveled that now "the subject of Indian music is at last not only seriously considered — it has become distinctly popular."[44] She also approved of the inclusion of other forms of Native American arts in classrooms, including pottery, basket weaving, and beadwork. Some schools recognized the practical benefits of "native industries," as they were often termed, for the tourist and art markets and encouraged students to make traditional crafts. Even Pratt's Carlisle opened a shop to develop Native design because of its growing marketability.[45]

Curtis, exhibiting a point of view ahead of her time, pushed for more progressive reforms. She argued that schools become community centers for all tribal members. She foresaw open-air festivals that exhibited student artwork and featured the singing of Indian songs. Outdoor classrooms (suggested and occasionally implemented during the administration of Commissioner of Indian Affairs Francis Leupp, 1905–9) for manual training and choral work were suggested as improvements over the stuffy classrooms of government schools. These would prevent the spread of tuberculosis and encourage Indian students to excel "under natural conditions." Curtis also recommended that "a student of Indian life and habits of thought should be sent to the different reservations to study conditions" and make a full report to suggest practical ways to improve Indian education.[46]

Educational reform was only one among several purposes Curtis envisioned for *The Indians' Book*. She hoped it would establish her as an authority on Indian music and grant her the means to promote her concerns regarding Indian policy. Two magazine articles helped establish her expertise in the public's mind. The *Craftsman*, a journal of the Arts and Crafts movement, presented Curtis as someone who "has probably done more than any one other person to gather together Indian folk songs and put them on record in permanent form." The editors praised her efforts to stop the government from destroying valuable material and for her intimate portrayal of Indian life in her writings. It concluded by stating that Curtis "has been tireless in her efforts to create a sane attitude" toward Indian education by striving to save and develop Native art. The *Outlook*, a liberal Christian reform magazine, maintained that Curtis's "gift in catching the spirit of Indian song and in interpreting it to people who pride themselves on being civilized" was widely acknowledged, as were her efforts to bring out "the artistic riches [of Indian cultures], for generations practically unknown and unrecognized." The *Outlook* expressed its appreciation for Curtis and her efforts to educate the American public.[47]

In the years following the publication of *The Indians' Book* Curtis traveled throughout the Southwest and the East Coast, promoting her book and making contacts with others. Curtis and Peabody sent copies to many important figures in the fields of Native American policy, education, religion, and music. Several of the people who had contributed to *The Indians' Book* received volumes, including James Murie, a Pawnee ethnographer; Bear-Arm-Necklace, a Dakota contributor; H. R. Voth, a missionary and amateur Hopi scholar; and the anthropologists Franz Boas and James Mooney. Theodore Roosevelt, undoubtedly because of his assistance in her research and his potential influence on Indian policy, received a copy, which he found to be "all that I hoped." Peabody and Curtis also gave copies to others involved in Indian policy or education. Frank Mead and the Dakotas Henry Standing Bear and Luther Standing Bear all received the book. Curtis did not forget Hampton and its support, sending copies to Principal Hollis B. Frissell and to Cora Mae Folsom, who worked with the school's Native students. Peabody sent *The Indians' Book* to his colleagues in philanthropic undertakings, notably Dr. Wallace Buttrick, a Baptist minister who worked with Peabody on the General Education Board, administering funds for black education in the South. Perhaps hoping to influence the nation's musicians, the pair sent copies to the conductor Frank Damrosch; the composer Arthur Nevin, who incorporated

Native American themes into his works; and the music educator, writer, and composer Albert Ross Parsons. Peabody sent a
letter to Damrosch, along with a copy of the book. He explained
how Curtis had gained the confidence of her informants by living
among them and treating them with respect. "That a frail woman"
succeeded in this endeavor, Peabody noted, revealed the "power
of gentleness and of the capacity for its appreciation on the part
of those supposed to yield only to force." Americans, both white
and Indian, her patron explained, owed Curtis a debt of gratitude
for recording these songs. People of influence, such as J. P. Morgan
and Neltje de Graff Doubleday (the wife of the publisher Frank
Doubleday and a writer on natural history), also received copies
in the hope that they would spread the book's message through
their particular outlets.[48]

Curtis also sought to influence the public more directly through
numerous lectures on Indian music and culture. She often invited
professional colleagues to these public lectures. In December 1908
she asked Boas to attend a Sunday-afternoon talk in which she
would attempt to "interest people in that side of the Indian which
is so totally unknown to the average white person." She told the
anthropologist that she hoped her lecture would create "even an
indirect pressure of public opinion" and would therefore force the
government to amend its educational methods and make it easier
for those within the service to push for reform. Curtis extended
a similar invitation to Frederick Webb Hodge, encouraging him
to attend a meeting sponsored by the Home Club and the Indian
Office in which she would sing a few Indian songs as part of a larger
program. She informed Hodge that she had also invited Dr. William Henry Holmes, the former head of the Bureau of American
Ethnography (BAE) and currently at the National Museum, and
that she hoped that other BAE members, especially the Indian musicologist Frances Densmore, would attend as well.[49] Clearly Curtis
viewed these lectures as an important way to bring professionals

in anthropology and ethnology together with the general public and as a useful forum for spreading her ideas and goals concerning Native American music.

Curtis lectured in various venues and used several formats, but generally she focused on educating her audiences through Indian music and folklore. Her talk entitled "Lectures on the North American Indians" reveals much about her approach to publicity and reform. The pamphlet that accompanied this talk publicized her work and depicted her as an expert on Indian music and life. The front page contained a quote from a book review to establish her legitimacy: "For the Indian's higher life the niece of George William Curtis has built an enduring legacy." Further endorsements of her book, in the form of favorable reviews of previous lectures and of *The Indians' Book*, were also included, as was a list of prominent supporters such as Hollis B. Frissell, George Foster Peabody, ex–Commissioner of Indian Affairs Robert Valentine, the late Carl Schurz, and Professor Charles Eliot Norton. The pamphlet noted that her travels through Indian country had brought Curtis "into close touch with Indian life and the problem of the future of the Indian" and inspired her to work for the promotion of a "more intelligent understanding of the Indian and his needs."[50]

Her lectures reiterated familiar themes. They began from Curtis's premise that "very little is understood of the real Indian." A lecture pamphlet described her approach: "[Curtis] tries to put the Indian himself before her audience, retelling the legends as she herself has heard them from the lips of tribal leaders; singing the Indian songs as the Indians sing them, with no accompaniment but the drum and rattle; giving examples of the Indian's intellectual ability as shown in his stoic outlook on life, his forceful philosophy, his poetic mythology and his art, which, though primitive, is often of great beauty." She divided her lecture into six parts: myths of "Aboriginal America," "Song-Makers of the Southwest," Indian life and art, the conditions of Indians at the present, the transition from old to new ways of living, and the "Indian's upward struggle on the White Man's Road." Music served as its main focus, and it presented Native American culture as an attractive alternative and a source of inspiration for white Americans. Curtis emphasized that each race, including Indians, had "its own rightful contribution" to make to "the sum of human culture." While training "our dependent peoples" for citizenship and modern industry, educators and policy makers needed to realize the "natural gifts" these groups possessed that were worthy of preservation and development. Curtis used music and its potential value to a national American culture as a way of convincing her audiences of the humanity of Native people and of the need for a more culturally sensitive Indian policy.[51]

Curtis's lectures allowed her to reach out in a personal and probably quite powerful way to a number of people in the Northeastern United States. Reviewers spoke of her charming manner of presentation, earnestness, and sympathy for Native Americans — all deeply felt by the audience. Curtis adapted her talks "to drawing-rooms, clubs, informal meetings, small private gatherings, and to school children." She addressed the International Congress of Americanists; conferences for education in the South; meetings of the National Education Association; and various schools, colleges, and scientific bodies across the United States.[52] The scope of Curtis's lectures shows her belief in the power of public opinion as a means for effecting change on a national level, and it also reveals one of the many often unrecognized ways in which women reformers like Curtis could agitate for change in Indian affairs, both within the prescribed boundaries of the drawing room, informal gatherings, and talks to schoolchildren and in the more public settings of professional and scientific meetings.

She realized that to continue her work she needed to maintain ties with people in the West and draw strength and healing from the region. While caring for her ailing father, who was paralyzed for four years prior to his death, Curtis still managed to make several trips, primarily to the Southwest; to conduct research; to visit friends and family; and to treat her own recurring health problems.[53] She often used her brother George's ranch in southern California as a base from which she could conduct fieldwork and absorb the Western atmosphere. This environment revived her physically and emotionally. She explained to George that a stay in Yuma, with temperatures approaching 110 degrees, had revived her sagging spirits and healed her weary body. The heat, Curtis explained, "starts up the liver and acts like a Turkish bath," and had made her feel better daily. Exposure to the desert sun also benefited her. "I'm black as an Indian, and round and fat," she told George. "You'd be delighted with my tan-coat!" Curtis shared with Hrdlička the need to escape the city and reconnect with the West. She told him: "I hunger and thirst so for a bed on the ground that, once freed, I don't believe I can ever go into New York chains again. What a problem — to have a primeval soul and one's home in New York!" Trips to the region also reinforced her ties to the people who had contributed to *The Indians' Book*. In the spring of 1908, for instance, Curtis traveled to Riverside, California, home of the Indian school Sherman Institute, to visit the Hopi leader Tawakwaptiwa and show him the book he had helped her create. She returned to the Hopi reservation in 1912 and 1913, after her father's death, to observe and comment on ceremonials, and she also spent time in San Diego, Yuma, and Santa Fe.[54]

New York, however, remained Curtis's main residence for most of this period, and from there she cultivated relationships with leading anthropologists and people interested in Indian reform and in Native American music and art. Franz Boas, who taught at Columbia, aided Curtis on professional and personal levels. She began writing him in 1903, seeking advice for articles she was preparing. Over several years she asked Boas for assistance with translations of Hopi phrases, for resources on Native marriage customs, for information on Sioux dances, and even for advice on what price she should charge for transcribing Indian songs from phonographs. Curtis also corresponded with Frederick Webb Hodge, who edited the *American Anthropologist* and worked in the Bureau of American Ethnology, and who was best known for his *Handbook of American Indians North of Mexico.* Hodge had expressed interest in Curtis's work on Indian music, and she asked him for professional advice on topics of concern to the BAE. She also developed a relationship with the Southwest promoter and writer Charles Lummis. Both loved the region and its peoples, and both had collected Indian music in the hopes of preserving and promoting it. Curtis visited Lummis at his home outside Los Angeles and joined the New York branch of his Sequoya League.[55]

One of the most significant contacts Curtis made in this period was with the physical anthropologist Aleš Hrdlička. Hrdlička had arrived in the United States from Bohemia (now the Czech Republic) in the early 1880s and been trained as a physician. Gradually the doctor cultivated an interest in anthropology, particularly in anthropometric methods, and began conducting surveys of Native people in the Americas. When he and Curtis began their correspondence in 1912 Hrdlička headed the Division of Physical Anthropology at the National Museum of Natural History in Washington DC. Curtis first contacted him to discuss issues of Indian reform, particularly her efforts to start her own organization to preserve Native Americans in the Southwest. The two often discussed their concerns about the administration of Indian policy and helped one another establish connections with others in their fields. Curtis occasionally met with the anthropologist in Washington, taking the opportunity to view the collection of skulls and bones he had amassed at the museum. Their relationship was both professional and personal. Curtis referred to him as "Chief Medicine Man" and asked him to grant her a body "equal to my zeal for doing things." Hrdlička wrote several encouraging letters to Curtis during one of her illnesses, including one that did Curtis so much good that she likened it to "one of those Peace-Chants that the Navajos sing after an all-night ceremony." Curtis would later return the favor, penning several letters of condolence to a devastated Hrdlička after the death of his wife. Their friendship and professional relationship helped Curtis both in her research and in her efforts to reform Indian policy.[56]

Commissioner of Indian Affairs Robert Valentine (1909–12) occasionally engaged Curtis in discussions of Indian policy. He sent her a memo entitled "The Present Scope and Limitations of the Government in Dealing with Indian Affairs." Valentine remarked in the margin, "My dear Miss Curtis = a Basis for discussion," demonstrating his intention that they would later meet so Curtis could comment on his proposals. Valentine outlined the Indian Office's duties to Native Americans and the reasons it often fell short of these goals. The commissioner suggested an "Indian Social Service Association" as a possible remedy for the many problems he perceived. Valentine proposed several agencies to deal with health, education, Indian law, and public relations. Although there is no record of Curtis's response to these ideas, she undoubtedly pondered these issues and considered how she could address them herself.[57]

Curtis continued to use her relationship with Roosevelt to forward her vision for Native American music and culture. When the ex-president journeyed to the Hopi reservation in the summer of 1913 to write a series of articles for the *Outlook*, Curtis made sure that she was present at one of his stops. In 1913 she was camped near the Hopi village of Walpi with a group of friends. The "roofless and free" experience made the campers appreciate their escape from "the sordid bargaining of our narrow city lives, the fret and whirl of petty currents that bear us far from our inner goal." She and her friends, who probably included the artist Alice Klauber and the composer Percy Grainger, had grown to appreciate the lifestyles and culture of the Hopi and wondered when someone would put a stop to the "Anglo-Saxon iconoclasm" that sought to change Hopi ways. News of Roosevelt's arrival created quite a stir in the area and forced Curtis to remember that "we too were white people and that our sun-faded garments were no credit to civilization." She decided to remove the dirt and grime accumulated from weeks of desert living with a gasoline bath and was aided in her quest for gas by a "handsome and deep-tanned young cowboy," whom she later learned was none other than Roosevelt's son Archie. Curtis met with the ex-president to renew their ties and to share her ideas about Indian reform.[58]

Curtis tried as forcefully as she could to convince Roosevelt to agree with her belief in the importance of preserving and respecting Native cultures. Roosevelt recalled that as soon as he arrived at Walpi, "I was accosted by Miss Natalie Curtis, who has done so very much to give to Indian culture its proper position." He explained to his *Outlook* readers that she hoped to "preserve and perpetuate all the cultural development to which the Indian has already attained" and to develop and adapt it for modern uses and as "an important element in our National cultural development." During his visit Roosevelt met with the collector of Indian music Geoffrey O'Hara, as well as others involved in Indian affairs, and with Native American leaders, merchants, and artists. Curtis made certain that she guided Roosevelt around the reservation, taking him to schools, showing him the "historic and cultural value of the ancient Indian towns," and explaining to him the advantages of Native styles of architecture. She took him to Hopi ceremonials, including the Flute Ceremony at Walpi and the activities surrounding the Snake Dance at Oraibi. She argued that a study was necessary to understand the actual needs of the reservations and to prepare government employees to educate Hopi youth.[59]

Although Curtis did not convince Roosevelt of all of her opinions on Indian matters, she managed to influence his view of Native cultures and his presentation of Hopi Indians in his *Outlook* article. She recalled a compromise they reached regarding assimilation philosophy: "We agreed with the Colonel that 'there is nothing finer than the Christian religion' but he agreed with us that if we would build true civilization among a people different from ourselves there must first be an interchange of ideas between the two races." In his article Roosevelt defended the preservation of Native cultures: "Many well-informed and well-meaning men are apt to protest against the effort to keep and develop what is best in the Indian's own historic life as incompatible with making him an American citizen, and speak of those of opposite views as wishing to preserve the Indians only as National bric-à-brac." This was not true; civilization remained the overriding goal, but Indians could not be pushed too rapidly and should be allowed to retain the treasures of their heritage. He agreed with Curtis's plan to raise money for a study of the needs of Indian schools and to focus education on "a drawing out of the qualities that are within," rather than foisting a foreign culture upon Native youth. Roosevelt also argued that Indian leaders should play a more important role in the schools; that Native Americans should be allowed to develop according to their own personalities; and that the government ought to interfere less in cultural matters on the reservation, especially the harmless religious dances. Although Roosevelt did not go as far as Curtis may have hoped — he did not argue for the value of Native spiritual beliefs, nor did he call for outright preservation of Indian ways — he certainly upheld many of her opinions.[60]

Although Curtis succeeded in promoting her ideas for Indian reform through her writings, her lectures, and her influence on important figures, she never quite felt comfortable in the larger world of Indian reform. Her attraction to Native forms of spirituality in particular often put her at odds with those people who sought to eradicate them and replace them with Christianity. Curtis pragmatically recognized that Christian missionaries still played a significant role in Indian affairs and avoided direct public criticism of their work. Still, many of her critiques in *The Indians' Book* and other writings challenged their ideas, methods, and goals. Curtis hoped to "help broaden the missionary point of view regarding the Indians" by attending their conferences and speaking about her research. In private she confided to George Foster Peabody that "we have seen so much of the church missionary work among the Indians. We appreciate its purpose, but to be quite honest, we are honestly afraid of it. It is hard for people who have their creed more deeply at heart than anything else to work at any subject without infusing into it their strong belief."[61] Missionaries failed to understand that Indians needed to find the spirituality that best met their needs. Traditional practices, modern Native religious movements, or Christianity could all benefit Native American lives, Curtis believed, but Indians should have the time and space to make these decisions for themselves.

Her distrust of missionaries extended to others in Indian reform, many of whom were guided by Christian zeal, and she occasionally wondered how other reformers perceived her. She confided her concerns to the Hampton principal Hollis Frissell in the fall of 1911. "Excuse me for being a nuisance, but I want to write to you about a matter that has made me a little uncomfortable," she began. Curtis had met the educator and Jewish civic leader Henry Marcus Leipziger on the street in New York City and asked him about the upcoming program at the Lake Mohonk Conference of the Friends of the Indian, the annual meeting of Indian reformers in upstate New York. Leipziger had promised to write Albert Smiley to have Curtis invited. She told Frissell, "I demurred a little at first because I have a vague impression (I don't know where I got it) that Mr. Smiley thinks I am an anarchist and a pagan in Indian matters." Curtis knew that Smiley was aware of her and her work, so when she received no response after Leipziger wrote him, her fears that she was not welcome at Lake Mohonk seemed confirmed. Curtis explained that she had not "the slightest desire to be heard at Mohonk," but she feared that Smiley had a mistaken impression of

her. She asked if Frissell could perhaps write to "assure Mr. Smiley
of my harmless character?" She continued, "It is not that I care personally about being misunderstood, but I feel that misconceptions
from an important person in Indian matters of even so unimportant
a person as myself may injure to some extent my ability to be of
real use in the work I am so anxious to help along."[62]

In some respects Curtis's perceptions about her position as an
outsider within the Indian reform movement were accurate. Her
challenges to the official assimilation policy that had guided both the
government and reform groups since the mid-nineteenth century
certainly set her apart, even if she was not alone in her critiques.
Christian missionary zeal guided many reformers (although this was
slowly changing by the early twentieth century), making Curtis's
calls for not only understanding but learning from Indian spirituality
questionable to some. Although some reformers suggested using
aspects of Indian cultures in the education process or as a means
of employment on reservations, few echoed Curtis's claims that
Americans had a duty to listen to Indian voices or to preserve their
art and music.[63] Curtis did not belong to any of the major reform
organizations, and members may have resented her efforts to work
independently of them.

Perhaps her uncomfortable relations with other Indian reformers
explain her attempt to establish an organization to preserve Native
American music and art. In the spring of 1911 Curtis began formu-
lating ideas for a new type of reform society that would preserve
elements of the cultures of Native Americans in the Southwest.
This undertaking resembled experiments in communal living and
artisanal enterprises promoted by her uncle George's generation at
Brook Farm and by Natalie's contemporaries in the Arts and Crafts
movement. While lecturing at the Brooklyn Academy of Arts and
Sciences she met Franklin W. Hooper, the institution's director,
who expressed interest in Native Americans.[64] Curtis learned of
Hooper's involvement in an organization to preserve the Ameri-

can bison, and the two began planning a similar society in the
Southwest for protecting Pueblo villages and promoting Native
arts and crafts. Apparently buffalo herds and Indian tribes shared
many commonalities in their minds — both were part of nature,
both were physically vanishing, and both were coming to be seen
as national treasures needing to be saved.[65] Hooper had held leadership positions in the American Bison Society, which established a
national bison range in the first decade of the twentieth century.
He had raised funds and generated publicity on the East Coast and
grasped the possibilities for another preservationist group.[66] He
and Curtis both believed that money for Native Americans could
be raised "through lectures and the proper appeal" and that "such
an organization [could] achieve practical results if the efforts are
wisely directed." Hooper suggested that the organization remain
nonsectarian and devote itself to "native industries." Curtis insisted,
"This must be done in the Indian country, among the Indians, in
their homes." Specifically Curtis meant the Pueblos of New Mexico,
whose people had developed distinctive arts and crafts that were
in danger of disappearing.[67]

This preservation plan echoed some of Curtis's earlier ideas.
In 1903 she had asked Boas if an anthropologist could "determine
even hypothetically the lines along which a people like the Moquis
[Hopis] would naturally develop if left to themselves?" She proposed
"an experiment in one village to preserve to some extent — at least
the national character of the town." Drawing on her experiences
as a student in Germany she recalled that the city of Rothenburg
had issued a decree ordering new buildings to be constructed in
keeping with the town's character. Could not the United States,
Curtis asked, do the same with "the ancient towns still extant upon
our native soil?" Such an experimental town, she continued, would
also benefit the Hopis, because they would be "allowed to absorb
only the best and broadest ideas that our culture has to offer, and
under the stimulus of encouragement, permitted to evolve along

their own lines." "I believe in progress," she wrote, "but it seems
to me that the Moqui towns are too rich in ethnological, historic,
and artistic interest to be carelessly entrusted for 'improvement'
to government officials who however conscientious can have but
little appreciation of the real worth of such towns to the world's
history." Curtis had also suggested that the government empower
individuals to enter Hopi towns and work with the people, especially teachers, to change their attitudes regarding the worth of
Native cultures.[68]

When the opportunity arose to develop these ideas, which had
remained latent in her mind for several years, Curtis seized upon
it. In May 1911 Curtis and Hooper announced their ideas for the
Society for the Preservation of the American Indian to others they
believed would share their interests. They aimed "to keep extant
the Indian type, racially, while in no way endeavoring to retard the
Indian's best development." They further hoped to safeguard "worthy
features of the native life, and to encourage practically, and with a
true sense of proper values, the native industries, arts and crafts."
Considering the rapid rate of progress in the United States and
past policies of "crushing out all typically racial traits of character,
thought, industries, and art expression in the Indian," only a few
tribes remained "still sufficiently intact racially and sociologically"
to really benefit from such a movement. Curtis suggested the Pueblos of New Mexico, particularly Acoma, because of its remoteness
from white influence and because "all the Southwestern arts are
practiced in this village." For this undertaking Curtis and Hooper
envisioned a national organization with an executive committee of
six to ten people "who have no religious bias and who are farsighted
in their interest in educational and political questions." This group
would control non-Indian access to the region and encourage Pueblo
people to maintain their traditional arts and crafts. Curtis cited
the German government's efforts to regulate and protect the art
and architecture of historical cities and asked if the United States

could perhaps do the same. She suggested individuals who could
be called upon for help: Frank Mead; Neltje de Graff Doubleday
(who had ties to Eastern Arts and Crafts societies); the Winnebago
artist Angel DeCora; Dr. Felix Adler (the founder of the Society for
Ethical Culture); the conservationist Gifford Pinchot; and Curtis's
patrons and supporters Franz Boas, George Foster Peabody, and
Charlotte Mason.[69]

Once Curtis and Hooper had broadly outlined their society's
goals, they focused on resolving some of the potential problems,
working out details, and garnering additional support. Unsure of
the exact status of the Pueblos, Curtis wrote to better-informed
authorities to determine the extent to which their proposed society
could rely on government support. She tried to arrange meetings
with Commissioner of Indian Affairs Valentine and convinced
others of the need for this organization. Boas offered his support,
suggesting that the group consider economic factors in their plans
for developing "native industries." Felix Adler expressed his interest
and agreed with the ideas behind the movement. By the fall Curtis
had extended her potential supporters to Native American leaders,
including the Cherokee journalist and editor John Oskison, involved
in the newly formed Society of American Indians.[70]

As the society's plans progressed Curtis became more convinced
of its purpose and more determined to see it reach fruition. Upon
learning more about the administration of the Pueblos, for instance,
she believed that government authorities in Santa Fe or Albuquerque
were unable to "carry out such plans as we have in mind, nor that
the reforms that we advocate can be successfully accomplished
except by effort not connected with Government institutions, nor
controlled by such."[71] The society had narrowed its goals to five aims.
The first, to investigate Indians "from the practical standpoint," must
have meant providing studies on Native music and art and finding
ways to develop Indian culture. The second goal was to use "well
established facts" and "approved means" in "harmony with the Indian

authorities" to counteract all things that could lead to "physical or mental deterioration of the Indian." Using those same methods the society also promised to embrace "everything that would tend to sanitary, industrial and cultural improvement of the race" and toward the "preservation and development of whatever inherent talents it possesses." The fourth goal, to aid government officials in this work, would be accomplished by enlightening public opinion on these issues. Finally, the society would endeavor to aid in the preservation "of substantial evidence of the faculties and progress of the Indian in the National Museum of the United States." This last goal may have been the outcome of discussions between Curtis and Aleš Hrdlička, who worked at the museum.[72]

During the winter of 1911–12 the Society for the Preservation of the American Indian called regular meetings for its supporters and officially outlined its agenda. Prominent potential supporters were summoned to lend their influence for this cause. Hooper, for instance, invited Roosevelt to a conference at the Smithsonian Institute on December 29 to help plan for the group's establishment. Hooper explained that the society would focus on isolated portions of Arizona and New Mexico, largely free from white influence, for the purpose of "safe-guarding from destruction the traditions, arts and industries of the Southwest, and the pueblo towns which are historic monuments of an ancient culture." Curtis, acting as temporary secretary, invited Hrdlička to a meeting in January. Stressing the importance of having "the right minds at work on a movement of this kind while the ideas are in a formative state," she expressed her hope that he and others like him would attend. Other invitees included Felix Adler, Frank Doubleday, the conservationist and ethnographer George Bird Grinnell, and members of the educational philanthropy association the Russell Sage Foundation.[73]

Although Curtis evinced a great deal of enthusiasm for this undertaking and seemed to have brought together the kinds of people who would support such an effort, the Society for the Preservation

of the American Indian did not become an established organization, nor did it play an obviously significant role in Indian affairs
at this time. Curtis had trouble raising funds, and support seemed
to lag after the initial burst of enthusiasm in the fall and winter of
1911. One explanation may lie in the rather vague goals outlined by
Curtis and Hooper and the lack of a clearly explicit plan of action.
In many ways too the organization was a decade or more ahead
of its time; its goals and ideals reflect more closely those of John
Collier and other reformers working in the Southwest in the 1920s
and 1930s. Many reformers were simply not ready to relinquish the
goal of complete assimilation. A letter written to Curtis by Shelby
M. Singleton, a Chicagoan identified with many reform organizations, demonstrates this. Singleton responded to Curtis's request
for information regarding Pueblo people's status and the ability of
the government to carry out her preservation scheme, questioning
the very purpose of a preservation society: "Of course it is patent
that these Indians cannot and should not be kept in their present
states, so far as civilization is concerned." "It would be unwise," he
continued, "to try to 'place them in a glass case for anthropologists to look at.'" It was acceptable to preserve some of the ancient
towns, but the government's main duty was to promote the welfare
of Indians by pushing them toward civilization.[74]

Regardless of these setbacks Curtis continued her involvement
in Indian affairs. The West constantly beckoned her, and she spent
much time there trying to continue the reform efforts she had begun
back east. She believed that the reforms she wanted to carry out
needed to originate among Native Americans themselves, and she
had perhaps grown tired of reformers like Singleton and Smiley,
whose opinions on Native cultures seemed so at odds with hers.
Curtis's work in the West could continue as long as she had the
backing of her patrons, but by the fall of 1913 that support had begun
to wane. Her lack of substantive results, as well as the increasing
demands that she turn her attention to African American music,

brought on a stern rebuke from Peabody, which brought Curtis back east and led her to adopt new approaches to her work. Peabody wrote:

> I have thought of you frequently and have been glad, of course, for the interests in the West, which are so much on your heart, that you were there, but I have not been able to believe that it was wise for you to prolong your stay away from this great center [New York City]. You are endowed with a peculiar genius for certain work, and that not narrowly restricted, and in general I feel that your main powers, social and otherwise, have a true field of successful development and accomplishment in and about New York.

He understood and respected her feelings "about the poor Indian and what you might do locally," but Peabody could not believe that her plans would reach a successful conclusion. He had met with Frissell and others involved in Curtis's work to discuss the matter. They all agreed that her "largest and most permanent work will find its central point of efficiency in New York and Washington." He asserted, "You have a rare and forcible personality, which is the greatest of influences and when possible, such an influence should be exerted in the great centers where its reach is widespread." Regarding her ideas for preserving Native cultures in the West, Peabody wrote, "I confess that I can see no basis for the hopes of your Hopi plan being successful." He hoped that she could return east for a conference to discuss these matters and offered to arrange a meeting with Secretary Lane and President Woodrow Wilson so that Curtis could accomplish more for Native Americans than she was currently.[75]

Curtis heeded Peabody's admonition and returned east within a few months to continue her work for Native Americans and to study African American music. Considering her love for the West, her desire to be close to her brother George, and the fulfillment she found working with Native peoples, Peabody's insistence that she return east must have provoked a dilemma. One wonders if she resented the meeting of these powerful men to determine her fate, if she chafed under the financial restrictions they placed on her, if she sensed any irony in being trapped in a patriarchal relationship as her Native subjects often were. Perhaps she appreciated Peabody's assessment of her abilities and potential, but it would have been hard to return east without having fulfilled her own plans for reform and without being able to pursue her own path toward the policy she thought best. In addition Peabody's rebuke struck a personal nerve for Curtis. Her patron had become a father figure to her, and his rejection of her ideas and methods must have stung. Curtis nonetheless dutifully returned to assert her influence in the great centers of the East.

Peabody abided by his promise to arrange meetings between Curtis and the secretary of the interior. She became involved in Lane's efforts to establish competency commissions to amend Indian allotment policy. Lane and his Indian commissioner, Cato Sells, placed a high priority on forcing Native Americans to become self-supporting and free from government control. Many critics of the Indian Office had begun demanding the end of federal responsibility for Indians and placed pressure on Commissioner Sells to accomplish this goal. Both Lane and Sells were obsessed with the idea that land be used productively, and both claimed a desire to "free" competent Indians from their legal ties to the government. The Dawes Act (1887) allotted reservations and assigned plots to individual Indians under a twenty-five-year trust period. Many critics had grown impatient with this protective period, which led to the Burke Act in 1906. This act allowed the issuance of a fee patent title prior to the end of the trust period and, as historian Janet McDonnell argues, led to a "potentially dangerous situation in which an Indian could be released from guardianship" before being truly self-sufficient. Lane and Sells accelerated this process by appointing special commissions to declare Native Americans competent in a more aggressive manner. In the summer of 1915 they assigned

James McLaughlin, an agent and inspector in the Indian Service since 1871, and Frank A. Thackery, a former Pima superintendent, to visit reservations and, with the assistance of local superintendents, decide which Indians were competent, issue them their fee patent titles, and "free" them from federal control.[76]

Curtis met with Lane and McLaughlin to discuss these plans and agreed with the general outlines of the competency commissions until she realized that the trust period would no longer apply and that tribal members risked losing their land after being granted fee simple title. She explained to Hrdlička that a phone call from McLaughlin revealed Lane's plans to allow "the new citizens to sell their land — that is, to annul the usual trust period."[77] It is surprising that Curtis was unaware of Lane's and McLaughlin's views regarding assimilation and Indian land. In his 1910 autobiography McLaughlin had included a chapter entitled "Give the Red Man His Portion," in which he argued for the disbursement of tribal funds to individuals and the end of federal trust protection of Native American land in order to "build up manhood and individual self-reliance, which can never be realized under the present doling-out process." Lane too had written publicly of the need to emancipate Indians from the government's care by ending the trust period sooner. Lane falsely contended that Indians were the richest people in American per capita and that the government really had no need to continue its present obligations. He believed it better "to sever all ties between the Indian and the government, give every man his own and let him go his own way to success or destruction, rather than keep alive in the Indian the belief that he is to remain a ward of the government."[78] Curtis never explained why she had misinterpreted her work with McLaughlin and Lane. Perhaps she was distracted by the research she was beginning on African American and African music. Maybe she refused to see that her associates did not share her concerns for Indian welfare. She may simply have been unaware or kept unaware of what was going on until it was too late.

Curtis had misunderstood the implications of this work, but she sought to rectify the situation through a letter to Lane critiquing the policy and offering her own vision for the administration of Indian affairs. Curtis raised several objections to the proposed policy of relinquishing government protection of Indians declared competent and sought to distance herself from this aspect of the plan. "Had I known, as I have this morning learned from Major McLaughlin," Curtis declared to Lane, "that the present project included complete freedom to the reservation Sioux Indians to get drunk and sell their land, I could not, in conscience have signed the paper." She thought that most Native Americans, "with the exception of some of the educated half-breeds or quarter-breeds who are naturally and justly desirous of their full rights," were not ready for citizenship. Most Native groups had only recently received Western education and lacked the necessary skills to survive in the modern world. "Suddenly to make these people, who a generation ago were hunting buffalo, property owners on a comparatively large scale, is, in my opinion (based on what I have seen) a disastrous procedure," she argued. Curtis recounted her own experience witnessing the "wholesale demoralization and ruin of the people" in Oklahoma when white settlers first moved into the region. She disagreed with the notion that contact with white settlers would uplift Native Americans. Instead of proper values whites brought disease, corruption, greed, and whiskey bottles. Curtis insisted that it was unwise to allow Indians to sell their land, for "without a home he is absolutely without a future and at the mercy of unscrupulous whites." She pleaded with Lane to "use in this policy the utmost discrimination" and to make certain that the competency commissions proceeded slowly and cautiously.[79]

Perhaps, she argued, alternatives could be envisioned that would better meet Indian needs. Curtis promoted an Indian Progress League, to "be run by the Indians themselves," that promised to provide strong local leadership; protect tribes from demoralization; and perpetuate Native social customs "based on cooperation, communism, rather than competition." Native Americans needed leadership and the skills to survive as Indians in the modern world. She argued, "What the Indians need, I think, more than citizenship is strong industrial leadership in their own communities." Pointing to the example of the "pathetic handful of squalid people" among the Mission Indians of California, Curtis asserted that working for whites and being in contact with them did not make Native people self-sufficient or independent. Indians needed to rely on their own talents and characteristics to survive and progress, and an organization run by Indians seemed a far better solution to Curtis than simply declaring Native people competent and cutting them loose.[80]

Curtis urged Lane to consider the social and cultural needs of Native Americans and to adopt an alternative plan for fostering Indian progress toward citizenship and self-reliance. Lane needed to allow the Indian "to live his own life — in other words, he is to be allowed a chance to express himself in his own way." Policy needed to account for and use Native traits, rather than suppress them and foist a foreign way of thinking upon Indians. "When a people have strong sentiments and characteristics, racial art impulses, and definite ideas as to human conduct, — courage, fortitude, loyalty to a friend, truthfulness, trust in a pledge — it is indeed a waste of material not to incorporate such worth individually in all efforts looking toward further development and progress," she contended. Instead of focusing on private land ownership the Indian Office needed to perpetuate tribal village life and allow land to be held communally for grazing, farming, or timber. This land policy would keep Native Americans "strong and intact" and encourage them to develop local industry without the demoralizing influence of greedy whites. White educators had enjoyed success with similar programs in Africa, she maintained, and one need only look to the peoples of the Southwest, "who are still comparatively uncorrupted" because they have been isolated from whites and allowed to retain their own villages. White leaders were now beginning to recognize that "combination and cooperation" were desirable in the industrial world, she continued, and because most tribes already lived communally this plan had a greater chance for success.[81]

Lane of course did not adopt Curtis's suggestions, and it would be another decade or more before other reformers joined her in demanding respect for Native customs and input in government policy. The majority of whites involved in Indian affairs continued to believe that "civilization" should remain their top priority and that allotment, American education, and Christianity could best achieve their goals. Few shared Curtis's ideas that communal living arrangements and respect for Native ideas could solve the "Indian problem." Curtis must have been disheartened as the facts about the competency commissions became known. The historian Frederick Hoxie points out the disastrous effects of this policy: by spring 1918 the competency commissions had patented nearly one million acres of land; 10,956 patents were issued between 1916 and 1919; in the first four years of Sells's administration Indians sold over 155,000 acres of land, and that number doubled between 1917 and 1920.[82] As Curtis and other critics had warned, many of the Indians "freed" by the competency commissions lacked the skills or resources to keep their land. Many Indians objected to being declared competent and were forced to accept their fee patent titles. Whites were only too eager to swarm in and use whatever means necessary to divest Indians of their lands. Lane was fully aware of these problems. He attended one of the special ceremonies held for the newly declared–competent Indians on the Yankton reservation and learned that several Sioux had already contracted to sell their lands before they received titles. Although in this case he withdrew twenty-five people from the list, he made few additional efforts to alter the policy overall. After Lane left office the next secretary of the interior, responding to growing criticism of this policy, abolished the process.[83] Curtis kept in touch with McLaughlin and Lane for a while longer, but realizing her lack of influence and despairing over this course of events, she withdrew from active participation in governmental reform efforts and turned her focus to other issues, especially toward African American music.

THE FIRST TWO DECADES OF THE TWENTIETH CENTURY witnessed a noticeable shift in Indian reform policy. Curtis's reform efforts placed her among the "new" Indian reformers who challenged the assumptions of the assimilationist agenda of the late nineteenth century and moved toward preservation of and respect for Indian cultures, even as many of her beliefs about Indians shared commonalities with those of earlier reformers. Unlike many other collectors of Native American music, Curtis used her research as a means toward reform. Certainly she wanted to preserve Indian music for her own benefit, but she also envisioned preservation as a tool for improving the lives of Indian peoples. She took seriously her sense of moral responsibility as a privileged white American to try to understand and listen to Native Americans, and she firmly believed that the language of music could help her accomplish her goals. She applied these same ideals to her studies of African American folk songs.

6

Folk Songs of a
"Very Musical Race"

Curtis and African American Music

IN THE 1918 INTRODUCTION TO THE SECOND BOOK OF
Negro Folk Songs Natalie Curtis explained her rationale for collecting African American spirituals and other songs. She had begun
this work several years earlier at the request of "a group of earnest
colored men" who asked her to "do for the music of their race what
I had tried to do for that of the Indian: to present it with entire
genuineness and in a form of publication that could readily be
grasped by all people." Curtis undertook this challenge with "the
same uncompromising ideal" that had guided her earlier folk music
research. She endeavored to "put in written form, without addition
or change of any kind, the true folk-song, spirit, and sound, just as
it springs from the hearts and the lips of the folk-singers."[1]

These aspirations led Curtis to collect, preserve, and popularize
African American and African folk songs. As with Native Americans
she viewed blacks as members of "primitive" cultures who could
inspire "overcivilized" Americans and help create a national musical
identity. African American folk music urgently needed preservation, Curtis believed, because as blacks "progressed" they would no

longer be capable of producing such music and would forget their treasured past. Curtis understood the prejudice and oppression blacks faced as a consequence of white misunderstanding of their cultures. She therefore believed that her studies of black musical traditions — using music as a universal language — would increase interracial understanding and lead to improved race relations.

This chapter analyzes Curtis's research into African American and African folk music and her efforts to use black song to establish an interracial dialogue and ease racial tensions. *Negro Folk Songs* and especially *Songs and Tales from the Dark Continent* more clearly reveal Curtis's views on race and her attempts to straddle the evolutionary perspective of her Victorian youth with the burgeoning cultural pluralism of the modern era. This chapter also examines the influence of patronage on her work and how the agenda of Hampton Institute, one of her most significant supporters, shaped her approach to black folk song. Her efforts to preserve and popularize African American music through her research and reform efforts demonstrate that Curtis saw her work as both uplift of a "primitive" group and an attempt to use this group's primitivism as a means to articulate a personal and national identity.

Curtis first became interested in African American music through her contacts with Hampton. As early as 1904 she jotted down spirituals and other songs in the field notebooks she used for collecting Native American music. For instance, in the spring of 1904 she transcribed several songs at the Hampton, Tuskegee, and Calhoun schools.[2] Many of these songs were just fragments or sketches of melodies, but they piqued her interest in the music of "primitive" peoples, as did songs from African groups at the St. Louis World's Fair. Curtis's musical curiosity partly explains her attraction to African American music, but Hampton's influence, particularly its efforts to collect, study, and use black folk songs, clearly had its effect.

Black educational institutions began popularizing Negro spirituals among Northern audiences in the early 1870s. Fisk University's Jubilee Singers first performed these songs on fund-raising tours. School leaders were initially wary of using spirituals because white blackface minstrels often sang them to ridicule African Americans. Educators, and some students, feared that this stigma would tarnish the reputation of the schools and counteract their programs for black progress. The songs the students sang did not exactly resemble renditions by slaves but were "denatured into a form more compatible with Euro-American musical tastes." Spirituals became wildly popular among white audiences, and soon other schools, like Hampton, sent out their own student groups to garner support and raise funds for new buildings and other needs.[3]

Hampton argued that the preservation of black folk songs served several important functions. Studying this music would help teachers better understand their students. A Hampton representative speaking at a typical school performance explained, "It seems well to us to look backward a little and try to find out from what conditions the people have come, and what they have of their own value which they should cherish and preserve for their descendents, together with all this new learning." African Americans needed to respect themselves if they hoped to advance as a race, the speaker continued, and appreciation for "real" Negro songs, not vulgar "coon songs" and ragtime tunes, would facilitate racial pride.[4] Hampton students, many preparing to become teachers in black communities, would learn more about the people they would serve by studying their music. Hampton officials argued that plantation songs were useful because they expressed the range of African American thought during slavery. The school's founder, Samuel Armstrong, and other school officials believed that slavery had served as a positive force on "primitive" Africans by providing them with Christianity and other "civilizing" influences. Therefore blacks should appreciate these songs as reminders of the benefits received in bondage. In *Cabin and Plantation Songs, as Sung by the Hampton Students* a section entitled "The Sunny Side of Slavery" argued that the institution had disciplined blacks and helped the typical African American develop "a strength and stamina, a religious sentiment and character . . . which his weak-natured race could never have gained otherwise." Slave songs served as reminders of what African Americans had endured, but also gained, under slavery. Knowledge of these songs was assumed to improve the instruction of Hampton pupils by providing a foundation upon which students could build.[5]

African Americans may have preferred to forget the painful reminders of slavery or wished to sing these songs on their own terms rather than for white audiences, but Hampton officials dismissed these concerns. In his 1874 preface to *Cabin and Plantation Songs* Thomas Fenner stressed the importance of preserving the songs quickly and in their proper context. He lamented that blacks despised "this wonderful music of bondage" and hoped that his efforts to popularize spirituals would change black attitudes and encourage the further development of these songs. "It may be that this people which has developed such a wonderful musical sense in its degradation will, in its maturity, produce a composer who could bring a music of the future out of this music of the past," he wrote. A writer in the *Southern Workman* lamented the "unfortunate disposition on the part of many of the freed Negroes to despise these songs of bondage." The author contended that the spirituals were a unique cultural expression to be celebrated: "One of the greatest gifts bestowed by God upon mankind is the ability to love and to make music. He showered this blessing upon the Negro people with a lavish hand, for there is probably no race on earth which has given expression to a greater variety of emotions by means of song than did the Negro race in slavery days." Slaves used the "medium of rhythmic and musical sounds" to express "joy or sorrow, love or hatred, pleasure or pain." A Hampton official addressing an audience at Carnegie Hall summed up the school's approach to folk song, stating that the songs were "diligently sought and preserved, and the students are taught to understand the beauty and to treasure them as the unique contribution of the genius of their race to the world of art." The speaker concluded with the assertion, "We wish, not only to preserve this folk lore, but to dignify it in your eye and theirs."[6]

Many of Hampton's folk music presentations compared Native American and African American music. At one such presentation a speaker praised Indians for not despising their music as blacks did. Both groups, the speaker continued, needed to embrace their cultural heritages as a way of understanding themselves and preparing for the future. Both "have a great fund of folk lore which they should take pride in preserving." They should do this not just because the music was interesting or offered possibilities for further development, but because "it will help them to understand themselves better, and to be better understood by other races."[7] In addition African American music could, perhaps more so than Native American song, contribute to a national musical expression. Hampton presented black and Indian music together in its programs and publications, so it is not surprising that Curtis transitioned to the collection of Negro folk music.

Hampton not only strongly influenced Curtis's decision to study African American folk song but also provided Curtis with important resources. In addition to funding and advice from school leaders, she could draw on a student folklore society begun in the 1890s to collect tales, customs, and songs. The society often published its findings in the *Southern Workman*. Hampton also provided Curtis with a readily accessible pool of informants, especially from the many singing groups organized formally and informally on the campus. Ties to other black schools in the South, such as the Penn School on St. Helena Island off the coast of South Carolina, provided her with additional access to black music.

Curtis also found inspiration for collecting and popularizing African American folk music through her work with a New York music school settlement for blacks. An April 1913 *Southern Work-man* article described this undertaking "begun by friends of the race" to provide instruction to students in the community and to promote black music through public concerts. The school hoped to preserve well-known spirituals, the author noted, highlight-ing Curtis's participation and her plans to collect these and other types of folk songs to publish in "a 'Negro Book' on the same plan as her excellent 'Indian Book.'"[8] Curtis first expressed interest in establishing a music school similar to an urban settlement house (she interchangeably referred to this as a school or a settlement) in April 1911. The violinist David Mannes hoped to start a music settlement school in association with the Mary Walton Free Kin-dergarten for Colored Children on West 63rd Street, an institution of which Curtis's mother was vice president. "I think it is a splendid idea to start the music school in the West Side Colored District," Curtis declared, "and Mr. Mannes has a committee or organization to consist in himself, his wife and myself (a close corporation!)." African Americans should "feel that it is *their* school," she explained to the Hampton principal Hollis Frissell. "I think we can expect some good results musically, as well as educationally, from this very musical race."[9] Perceiving this institution as a "partial offshoot of the Hampton purpose," Curtis thanked Frissell for the aid he promised in terms of speakers, singers, and moral support. "I hope that the new school will be bound to succeed having been set on its feet by so many helping hands," Curtis wrote.[10]

Although Hampton was one of these "helping hands," the origins of the settlement went much deeper. Urban reformers and adher-ents of the social settlement movement proposed using music to relieve the poor living conditions of working-class and immigrant communities, to provide youth with wholesome activities, and to help socialize students into American society. Most hoped to instill in students a sense of "culture" and an appreciation for music. The settlement school for New York City blacks grew out of an institu-

tion begun for immigrant children, the Third Street Music School
in New York's East Side. David Mannes, the child of poor Polish
immigrants, had been encouraged in his musical inclinations after a
childhood scalding made him unfit for manual labor. After Mannes
became a professional violinist he volunteered at the Third Street
School and assumed the directorate from 1910 to 1915.[11]

Mannes believed that the Third Street Music School provided
valuable services to the impoverished community beyond lessons
in music. The school instilled students with self-respect, "orderli-
ness, cleanliness, discipline, reverence and generosity." It taught the
attitudes and skills necessary for life in industrial America, while
offering respite from the drudgery of daily existence. "In the midst
of the shambles of a rotting spiritual and physical decay," Mannes
contended, "it is no wonder that the love of music should thrust its
comforting ray of hope into these tenement houses crowded with
people of persecuted background." He did not want to train professionals, but to teach students the benefits of "living *with* music,
instead of by it."[12] Curtis echoed Mannes's ideas. She argued that
modern working conditions separated joy from work but that the
settlement aimed to "put a light into their lives and make work less
crushing." The "goal is to offer to the children of wage-earners an
opportunity for interest in art and that development of the finer
instincts of the child's mind and heart, which music, when rightly
taught, can awaken," Curtis explained. She praised the school because
it brought "culture" into students' lives and mitigated the effects
"of the hand-organ and the moving-picture show." The cultural
implications of the settlement impressed her. "Art is not a luxury for
the cultured few," she contended, but a deeply human need especially vital for the suffering people of the neighborhood. Curtis and
Mannes agreed that such schools were especially important because
they were "leveling barriers of race and creed" and replacing these
with the "common language of the soul — Music."[13] As in her work
with Native American song Curtis perceived music as a universal

form of communication, able to dissolve surface differences and forge links between human beings regardless of race or class.

Mannes sought to break down racial barriers because of a debt he owed his first violin teacher, Charles Douglas, an African American musician whose skin color excluded him from important positions as a professional. Mannes had long harbored the idea of using music to help blacks and repay the debt to his first mentor. Curtis and George Foster Peabody met with Mannes to discuss his idea and invited him to participate in commencement exercises at Hampton. Mannes's performance, in which he played directly to the students seated behind him on the stage, deeply moved those assembled and sparked interest in establishing a school for blacks in New York. Curtis recalled, "The violinist's inspired playing that night seemed a prophecy of that larger act of retribution which has found form in the Music School Settlement for Negroes."[14]

Mannes, Curtis, Peabody, Felix Adler (a religious and social reformer and the founder of the Ethical Culture Society), and others imagined the settlement as a place to develop distinctive and artistic African American music, especially spirituals, in order to promote black racial pride and increase respect for black talents among white Americans. Music, they hoped, would encourage interracial discourse and understanding. "The biggest things have small beginnings," they believed, "and it was the privilege of some of us to witness . . . the inauguration of what promises to be a movement of no little significance in the music education of the negro race in this city and the consequent establishment of a broader sympathy and deeper understanding between the black and white races, based on the cultivation of a latent quality which has been strangely neglected in the past." The settlement could be the answer to the "Negro problem." They articulated the special difficulties African Americans faced in New York. "Unlike the white man, who, no matter how poor, has still a chance to better his condition, the black man, no matter how able, is shut out of most trade unions and may obtain in New York only menial positions whose small salaries oblige the mass of the race to remain in pitiful poverty," settlement leaders claimed. Many black children needed a positive influence in their lives, and the settlement hoped that "the key of music [would] unlock the door to the child's higher nature." They envisioned a social center that would "produce a healthy moral environment for adults and provide instructive recreation" for children as well. It would provide relief from depressing social conditions and improve the way both whites and blacks understood African American culture.[15]

School organizers further believed that African Americans needed to assert racial pride. The settlement would challenge negative black attitudes toward their cultural contributions by developing and preserving elements of their heritage. Robert Moton, a Hampton graduate and administrator (and Booker T. Washington's successor at Tuskegee in 1915), contended that the school should draw "out all that was best in the negro temperament and [link] it with the best of other races." Too often, he noted, white minstrel singers and even black artists derided or mocked African American musical expressions. The settlement would free black musicians from the "demoralizing environment of all-night restaurants and cheap theatrical shows" and bring them "into a world of better effort." Moton argued that any race "that is ashamed of itself, that laughs at itself, that wishes it were anything else but what it is, can never hope to get the respect of other races and can never be a great people." Its founders hoped that the settlement would offer African Americans the opportunity to change attitudes and improve race relations.[16]

African Americans could win a place for themselves in American culture by helping to create a national music for all Americans. Adler believed that the school could cultivate "those qualities and gifts which the colored race is peculiarly fitted to contribute to the common welfare and art" of the United States. He commented: "We should aim at the outset to develop any distinctive and unique talent which the colored people possess. They may have other gifts, but assuredly the musical gift is one. Hence I see in this movement not merely a slight charity added to others but a step fully equal in importance to anything that has ever been consciously undertaken in the way of helping forward the negroes."

David Mannes, in an essay entitled "To the Negro Musicians of America," argued that no one could deny the contributions African Americans would make to the future of a national music. "As the folk-lore of the older nations has been the foundation of their great art-expression, so must the Negro music serve to this country the same high purpose," he asserted.[17]

Because of its broad goals the settlement school could attract the support of philanthropists, community leaders, musicians, and others interested in African American music. The board of directors included Curtis; Mannes; Peabody; W. E. B. DuBois; Lester A. Walton of the *New York Age*; the lawyer Elbridge Adams; the publisher Rudolph Schirmer; several ministers, including Reverend A. Clayton Powell, the pastor of one of the city's largest African American congregations; and other prominent individuals. Noted musicians such as the pianist and composer Percy Grainger, the composer and conductor Kurt Schindler (both close associates of Curtis), the conductor Frank Damrosch, and the African American musician James Reese Europe were honorary members of the settlement.[18]

The Music School Settlement for Colored People opened its doors on November 20, 1911, with seventy pupils, a small staff, and plans for an executive committee. Curtis served as a member of the organization committee. She emphasized the need for African American participation and worked to hire the black violinist David Irwin Martin as the school director. At its initial location on 34th Street the school provided instrument and voice lessons for two years. In the fall of 1914 it moved closer to black populations by relocating to West 131st Street. The new facility boasted several large concert rooms; areas for private instruction; and a new school director, the African American composer and musician J. Rosamond Johnson.[19]

The settlement provided numerous programs and services. It offered instruction in singing, sight reading, theory, and various musical instruments. Students participated in choral societies, a string quartet, glee clubs, and orchestras. More "practical" courses in stenography and typing were offered along with a normal course to train music teachers. Recreational activities included folk dancing, basketball, baseball, track, and tennis. The buildings also provided space for concerts, lectures, social gatherings, and other forms of "wholesome recreation."[20] A weekly lecture series on various topics in music, originally intended for the African American community, began attracting white audiences as well. The lectures featured well-known musicians, writers, and scholars. Many black musicians, such as the composer Harry T. Burleigh, the violinist Clarence Cameron White, the educator E. Azalia Hackley, and the Hampton Quartet, gave performances. Other prominent black lecturers donated their time to the school, including the businesswoman Madame C. J. Walker, the writer and activist James Weldon Johnson, and the politician Charles Anderson. White musicians and speakers also took part. Curtis gave several talks, as did Walter Damrosch; the *New York Tribune* music editor Henry Krehbiel; the singers Kitty Cheatham and David Bispham; Talcott Williams, a sociology professor at Columbia, and others. Curtis's connections in the musical world of New York City helped attract many of these participants. She and other board members hoped that these events would forward the school's aims while providing support for its practical needs.[21]

One of the prominent ways the school worked to garner support was through several benefit concerts of African American music at Carnegie Hall. Curtis drew on her connections to the city's musical world as they planned this event. "Having had some experience with

filling Carnegie Hall (owing to my connection with the Philharmonic, the MacDowell Chorus and other musical organizations),"
Curtis told Frissell, "I feel that the wisdom of taking such a *big*
step as that now must be carefully considered — especially in its
relation to the future appeal of negro music." Mannes meanwhile
found support among African American musicians. He befriended
James Reese Europe, a band leader and organizer of the city's black
musicians. Europe, who hailed from a prominent family from the
Washington DC area, had received extensive musical training as
a youth. In New York he had become well-known as a composer,
arranger, and director of music on the stage. In 1910 Europe established the Clef Club, a sort of trade union for African American
musicians. Europe also encouraged African American musicians to
adapt black song to a national musical culture and therefore offered
his services to the Music School Settlement. Plans for a concert in
May 1912 commenced.[22]

School leaders recognized the importance of the May 1912 Carnegie concert and carefully planned the event. Curtis attended
rehearsals of the Clef Club orchestra. The variety and novelty of the
orchestra's instruments — the ten upright pianos; the more conventional violins, violas, cellos, and basses; and the unique incorporation of mandolins, ukuleles, guitars, and banjos — struck Curtis as
distinctive. She learned that most members lacked formal training
and balanced their musical careers with other jobs. Many of the
musicians, Curtis was shocked to learn, could not read music, and
the entire orchestra rarely attended a rehearsal because so many of
the men worked odd hours. Europe impressed Curtis by his ability to
train his men under such conditions. At a rehearsal she experienced
"the unconscious spirit of creative art that stirred in that humble
group and we felt, with reverence, as though we had been present at
a birth. We had seen the racial soul, denied all opportunity, awake,
nevertheless, and sing; and the song, ephemeral though it was,
seemed a prophecy of the dignity and worth of Negro genius."[23]

Although Curtis saw the promise of these African American musicians, settlement directors worried about the prospects for the benefit concert. The school worked hard promoting the event and promised audiences "all kinds of Negro music," including plantation songs, "pure folk-songs," and sophisticated compositions. Settlement supporters aimed to show New York what African American musicians and composers had achieved and to prove the value of their talent. They solicited official endorsements from Mannes, Frissell, Adler, Washington, and DuBois in an effort to attract as many potential audience members as possible. However, the settlement had sold only one third of the tickets by the end of April. Desperate not to see their dream die, the board of directors penned an editorial appeal in the *New York Evening Journal* on May 1. By the next evening the concert had sold out.[24]

The editorial that won over New York's musical world offered a sympathetic, although somewhat paternalistic, view of African Americans and presented the aims of the settlement in a positive light. It noted that over ninety thousand blacks lived in New York City but that "very little is done for them and very little for their children." "In all directions they are denied, repressed, and kept back," the editorialist wrote. White Americans at the very least owed blacks the opportunity to develop their own gifts. The settlement proposed a solution to the Negro "and the problem he represents for himself and for others in this country" in the distinct music created by the black experience. "Transplanted by force to a country cold and unsympathetic," the editorialist wrote, "the negro from the beginning of the brutal slave days has found his only consolation in melody." This "national, original and real" American music would be featured at the Carnegie concert. The *Evening Journal* encouraged its readers to attend and hoped that "prejudice based on ignorance [would] give place to sympathy and good will."[25]

The concert was a stunning success. It sold out, and it did so with an integrated audience. Curtis believed that the 1912 concert was an important milestone in the history of black music in America. "Music-loving Manhattan felt a thrill down its spine such as only the greatest performances can inspire," she raved. The settlement concerts encouraged both white and black musicians to experiment with themes from spirituals and other folk songs. Many white musicians and musical organizations began performing African American songs, and Europe and other black musicians found their services in increased demand. Curtis credited these developments to the impact of the concert and the "astonishing sight" of the Clef Club orchestra and the irresistible sounds they produced. This "ear-opener" for New York surprised many in the audience and challenged established ideas about African Americans and their music. Curtis recalled reactions she witnessed that night: "'Barbaric,' one college bred Negro called the Clef Club. 'Barbaric' we exclaimed in astonished admiration. That an orchestra of such power, freshness, vitality, and originality could have remained so long undiscovered in novelty-hunting New York, was a silent and reproachful comment on the isolation of the 'Negro quarter.'" This concert confirmed for Curtis her faith that music could improve race relations and bridge the gaps separating whites from blacks.[26]

Inspired by the successful attempt to use music as a language for interracial understanding, Curtis continued to support the Music School Settlement for Colored People while she conducted research for *Negro Folk Songs*. The settlement school staged additional concerts at Carnegie Hall to promote its ideas and raise money. Although many of these concerts were successful, none matched the significance of that first concert in May 1912.[27] Both mainstream and African American newspapers and journals reported on these concerts and evaluated the prospects for the development of African American music. Despite the success of the Carnegie concerts the Music School Settlement struggled to survive and finally shut its doors in 1915. Some have attributed this to a decline in contributions because of the war in Europe. African Americans involved with the settlement desired black control of an institution in their community and asked the white philanthropists to step aside. The school may have lost financial support and ties to other institutions with the philanthropists' departure. Press coverage in the *New York Age* suggests community support for the settlement, but the spirituals and plantation songs may not have been able to compete with other forms of entertainment such as ragtime, blues, and jazz. Mannes explained the school's demise by arguing that it was twenty years ahead of its time. In spite of the closing of the settlement, many of the ideas and goals of the school lived on in the work of Curtis and other white and black musicians who wanted to preserve and develop Negro folk songs.[28]

Curtis began collecting black folk music at the encouragement, even pressure, of her patrons Frissell and Peabody. She had earlier jotted down black folk melodies, but it was not until 1912 that she earnestly began recording songs for publication in a collection. In November Frissell wrote her to schedule a meeting regarding the prospect of collecting songs in the South. He promised that "whatever funds are necessary will be forthcoming." Frissell had spoken with a representative of the publishing firm G. Schirmer, who thought it was "of very great importance that you take up this work." By 1915 Peabody had arranged for payments through Frissell for Curtis "to bring out a book in the name of Hampton dealing as exhaustively as possible with Negro music." Peabody provided a monthly stipend and additional money for travel expenses and assistants (which Curtis occasionally hesitated to accept when the research was not progressing as she hoped). Peabody explained that both he and Frissell believed Curtis was "qualified for this work as no one else in the country is."[29]

The two men expressed great confidence in her abilities as a musicologist, and they both believed that her work would have a significant influence on public perceptions of African Americans, their education, and Hampton's agenda. Frissell worked under the legacy of Hampton's founder, Samuel Armstrong, and his "Hampton model." The Hampton model did not stress social or political equality for blacks in the South. Armstrong and other white educators believed African Americans had the intellectual capacity to participate in American society but that they lacked the necessary moral and cultural tools. The school taught that blacks had not evolved as far as whites and needed time to progress as a race. School leaders accepted black subordination and urged students to acquiesce to present limitations. Hampton recognized the important role African American labor played in the Southern economy and encouraged its students to remain in the South. This ideology coincided with the views of Southern whites who wanted to exploit black labor without granting them full social or political equality. William Watkins comments that Armstrong "marketed his racial accommodation as progress. He sold evolution as revolution." The Hampton model united North and South and promised to solve the "Negro problem" through the idea of economic development and the maintenance of white superiority. The historian James D. Anderson adds that although the majority of blacks in the South desired the same educational opportunities as whites, Armstrong's ideas about the cultural and moral deficiencies of blacks severely limited their schooling at Hampton.[30]

Frissell, who served as Hampton's vice principal under Armstrong, supported the founder's ideals and sought to extend them under his tenure. Like Armstrong he wanted to maintain support for Hampton by portraying its students in a positive light but without appealing for full equality. So although a book extolling the value of African American music might at first seem at odds with these goals, it could actually do much to foster the school's principles. By presenting aspects of black culture as worthy, it helped to justify Hampton's purpose of educating blacks in the first place. But by finding value in the "primitive" nature of African American music, it also helped reinforce the racial hierarchy. Curtis often parroted

Hampton's ideas about African Americans. At a celebration of the school's fiftieth anniversary she praised Armstrong's "Great Idea, the training of selected youth as teachers and leaders of their own people on the conception of racial *self-help* and on the dignity and worth of work." In *Negro Folk Songs* Curtis dedicated "O Ride on, Jesus" to Armstrong and praised his work to educate the "ignorant and helpless" races at Hampton. She described the "sense of reverence" one felt at the school "for the heroic genius of Armstrong." In her dedication to Frissell she paid tribute to the "Doctor of Human Kindness" and his efforts to spread the Hampton ideal across the United States and around the world.[31]

Although Frissell and Hampton exerted an important influence on Curtis, her relationship with Peabody, who had strong ties to the school and to Southern education in general, had a far greater impact. Peabody numbered among a group of Northern white philanthropists who, according to Anderson, expected that their support of limited education for African Americans in the South would strengthen ties between the regions and facilitate economic growth and harmonious labor relations. Peabody, involved with Hampton since the late 1870s, believed that the school's model provided a solution for race problems in the South. He used his banking skills to assist Hampton and similar educational organizations, earning the informal title of "the investment banker of the southern education movement." Peabody served on the Southern Education Board and the General Education Board, groups that promoted universal schooling for Southern whites and blacks and especially upheld the Hampton model. Peabody used his business connections to sell the Hampton idea to Northern leaders. Curtis praised the role Northerners like Peabody played in Southern education, contending that they "sought the nation's good by the uplift of the individual through education" and fostered "the growth of better understanding between South and North."[32]

Philanthropists like Peabody promoted the Hampton model by

promising Northern business leaders that it insured a docile and subordinate labor force in the South and therefore a stable region for investments and markets. Northern businessmen, in exchange, supported the ideology of white supremacy, which viewed blacks as childlike inferiors with no legitimate claims to political participation in American society. In the racist context of early twentieth-century America, however, their support for any type of black education was often met with accusations of "worshipping Negroes" from the popular press and Southern whites. Peabody's support of Curtis's career further complicates this issue. Peabody viewed African Americans as "primitives" and probably believed that the majority would and should remain in subordinate roles in the modern economy, but he did want to promote black self-respect and racial pride. He expressed interest in aiding individual African American musicians, and he agreed with Curtis that black folk music could make a definite contribution to American national culture.[33] Curtis, describing Peabody as a "champion of racial political democracy and of that democracy of the spirit that cannot rest at ease while those less fortunate must suffer for lack of opportunity," believed that Peabody had the best interests of African Americans at heart and wanted *Negro Folk Songs* to promote racial understanding and black pride."[34]

Peabody and Frissell encouraged Curtis to collect music for *Negro Folk Songs* because they hoped that her work would advance their goals and promote the type of race relations they desired, but other influences prevented Curtis's work from becoming mere propaganda for Hampton. The anthropologist Franz Boas and Curtis's wealthy benefactor Charlotte Mason both assisted Curtis in collecting black songs, although for different reasons. Boas and Curtis had begun corresponding when she first started collecting Indian music in the Southwest. Curtis told Boas in 1913 that she was finally beginning the "work that you have long ago suggested my undertaking." She asked the anthropologist for advice as her project progressed and kept him apprised of her findings.[35] Boas encouraged her because he respected her skills as a musician but also because of his own belief that social scientists needed to use their scholarship to improve race relations.

Boas became a more vocal critic of American race relations as he solidified his place in U.S. anthropology. Influenced by his liberal political views and his belief that scientists had an obligation to express their opinions on issues they studied, Boas challenged conventional racist views among scientists and the general public. He encouraged the use of research to refute ideologies that supported racism. Vernon Williams argues that Boas carried out a three-pronged approach — he used anthropometry to gather more data to support his antiracist views, he used scientific reasoning to question racist assumptions, and he conducted research to show that alleged racial traits were actually universal human ones. The anthropologist proposed several projects to study the "Negro problem" with scientific methods, and he encouraged his students to do the same.[36]

Considering Boas's desire to eradicate the underlying ideas behind American racism, it is understandable that he would encourage Curtis to collect black music as a means of refuting ideas of cultural inferiority. Boas was wary of her predilection to view African Americans as "primitive" and "child-like" people, but he believed that she was "doing something that is very promising." He often challenged ideas of black inferiority by pointing to the cultural achievements of Africans and arguing that this legacy was evidence for black potential. He encouraged African Americans to take pride in their history and to use it as inspiration for the future. At a commencement address at Atlanta University in 1906 Boas told the graduates to learn about the "capabilities of your own race." He pointed out African achievements in ironwork, agriculture, political and military organization, trade, law, and art. This noble past could help students recover "the strength that was their own before they set foot on the shores of this continent." Similarly Boas expressed hope that Curtis's collection of African American songs would demonstrate to European Americans the contributions blacks promised to American culture. Boas, writing to Peabody about *Negro Folk Songs*, expressed his desire that the book would create "some means of bringing home to the negroes the great achievements of their race" and foster the kind of racial pride he had hoped to generate by his address in Atlanta.[37]

Although Boas supported Curtis's research he was often uneasy about the primitivistic streak in her work. The influence of Charlotte Osgood Mason helps explain Curtis's attraction to and insistence on viewing blacks as "primitives." Mason was an enigmatic figure, infatuated with alternative spiritualities among so-called primitive peoples. Eventually known as the "Godmother" for her patronage of the Harlem Renaissance, Mason was a wealthy, powerful, generous, manipulative, and influential patron who reigned over her protégés from her Fifth Avenue penthouse. Her wealth and knowledge of literature, theater, politics, and world affairs made her a powerful figure who exerted a great deal of control over her "subjects," although none were to publicly credit her support. Many of her protégés found themselves dependent on the "Godmother" for research and publishing support and had to abide by her expectations to live up to her ideas about art, spirituality, and race.[38]

Mason believed that nonwhite cultures possessed a spirituality absent from white modern societies. The modern world, she feared, was destroying the sacred, and only a return to primitive belief could save a dying American culture. "'Primitives' had always enchanted" her, as David L. Lewis asserts, and this enchantment began with her support for *The Indians' Book*. For her, Curtis's book served as a kind of bible, preaching the superiority of primitive spirituality. African Americans, like Native people in *The Indians' Book*, could embody her primitive fantasies. Langston Hughes, who endured Mason's patronage, recalled that Mason "felt that [blacks] were

America's great link with the primitive, and that they had something very precious to give to the Western world. She felt that there was mystery and mysticism and spontaneous harmony in their souls, but that many of them had let the white world pollute and contaminate that mystery and harmony and make of it something drab and ugly, commercial and, as she said, 'white.'" Mason demanded that her protégés embrace her notions of primitiveness. Although she could not ask Curtis to "'slough off white culture' and be [her] 'savage sel[f],'" as she did her African American protégés, she certainly expected Curtis's research to reflect her primitivism.[39]

Curtis, however, brought her own ideas and strong personality into her relationship with each of her patrons. All four of them left their mark on Curtis's work — they encouraged and supported her efforts to record black folk music, they shared their ideas about how she should present and interpret the songs, and they helped to promote her work after its completion — but in spite of all this Curtis was the one who did the fieldwork and produced *Negro Folk Songs*. The book represents the variety of influences in her life, but it also reveals Curtis's own ideas about African Americans and their music.

Curtis solidified these ideas as she collected music from Hampton's formal and informal quartets, as well as other Southern black singers. She aimed to capture the part-singing that she viewed as among the most unique talents black singers possessed. Curtis relied on "the little Edison phonograph that had accompanied me to many an Indian reservation" and supplemented the recordings by transcribing songs line by line from the "live voice of the singer." Many of the pieces in *Negro Folk Songs* came from two all-male quartets, whose songs Curtis often compared. One was a "self-organized quartet of Hampton boys, who had formed for Hampton meetings in the North during the summer of 1915." The other group, the "Big Quartet," consisted of older graduates who sang for Hampton for several years. Newly arrived students from more distant parts of the South also shared regional songs with her on campus.[40]

Curtis wanted to uncover additional "primitive" songs from African Americans isolated from mainstream society. In 1915 she drew on the support of Frissell and Peabody to conduct research on St. Helena Island, South Carolina, at the Penn Industrial School, another institution based on the "Hampton model." The school had originated as part of the Port Royal Experiment in 1862 but had declined as white support dissipated. Around 1900 white educators espousing the Hampton ideal arrived and revitalized the school. Many figures involved with Hampton, including Peabody and Frissell, served on Penn's board of directors or in other leadership positions.[41]

St. Helena offered Curtis insights into the more "primitive" music of African Americans in the South and conjured in her a sense of romanticism and mysticism. Rural black song impressed Curtis with its spontaneity and communal ethos — what historian Lawrence Levine describes as "communal re-creation."[42] She later described her research among uneducated and spontaneous black singers: "The white musician in the South stumbles upon experiences that may be counted as among the most awakening of his life for there the spirit of the Negro is often loosed in music that makes one wonder at the possibilities of the race." Curtis traveled to the "black belt" of Alabama in search of folk songs and found "nothing less than the primitive essence of untaught and unteachable creative art." She described waiting for a meeting of African Americans to begin when "suddenly a rhythmic tenor seemed to sway over the ground as a sweep of wind stirs grasses," and a hum rose up and formed itself into a song from this "floating embryo of music." On another occasion, at a "ramshackle meeting-house" in Virginia, she witnessed a similar event. "The mutterings, the ejaculations, grew louder, more dramatic, till suddenly I felt the creative thrill dart through the people like an electric vibration," she exclaimed.

From "crude and primitive" tobacco workers Curtis heard such sweet and penetrating music that it seemed as if nature was singing through the people. She thought: "Yes, — that is the Negro. So he has done always. With song he has colored his shadowed life, evoking hope, joy, beauty even, from within himself."[43] It was this essence of African American music that so intrigued Curtis, this ability to express the range of life's emotions in song and to do so with such apparent ease. For someone who labored as an adolescent to master the piano and who struggled to find meaning in an increasingly "overcivilized" world, the folk expressions of the black congregations and workers were amazing and inspiring.

She shared the meanings, personal and nationalistic, with other Americans when she published *Negro Folk Songs* as four separate books between 1918 and 1919. The first two books contained a typical collection of spirituals, and the last two featured less commonly collected work and dance songs. Each book in the series contained four to six songs recorded in four-part harmony and dialect. Curtis dedicated many of the songs to prominent figures at Hampton, in black education, or in the musical world. In each book she explained how she had collected the songs and the context in which they were sung. She often provided instructions for a white audience unfamiliar with Southern black music on how to properly sing the songs. Curtis also explained the symbolism African American composers employed in their work so that the songs made sense to her readers. She first presented the lyrics without music, as poems of a sort, and then provided the songs in their entirety. The four books that make up *Negro Folk Songs* dealt with several important themes. Curtis explained the recording process, emphasizing how her collection differed from others. Describing and explaining the unique qualities she had discovered in black folk music was another dominant strain in this work. Related to that was Curtis's focus on what she perceived as innate racial gifts, musical and spiritual, that African Americans possessed. Finally, *Negro Folk Songs* focused on how the special traits of blacks and their music could rejuvenate American music and life.

The recording and collecting process for *Negro Folk Songs*, Curtis contended, separated it from other collections of black music. She explained to Boas, "My collection differs from many others in that instead of collecting the melody merely and harmonizing that with a piano accompaniment of my own (and after the manner of most white musicians), I have recorded the Negro's own spontaneous harmonies, for, as you know, the Negro songs are usually sung by the Negroes in parts, the people themselves making up alto, tenor, or bass as they go along." Curtis tried to record on paper the nuances of black music in the hopes of capturing "a musical photograph" of a song's performance. One reviewer of *Negro Folk Songs* remarked on this distinctiveness, claiming that this was a collection "quite different from anything that has previously been done in this field" because of her presentation of songs in their harmonic parts and because of the careful recording process she employed.[44] Many of her contemporaries ignored part-singing in their collections or, as in the popular *Slave Songs of the United States* (1867), denied that it truly existed. Other collections presented only simplistic recordings of folk songs or provided very little musical information about the songs. A few, such as Henry Krehbiel's *Afro-American Folk Songs* (1914), did try to approach African American music from a sophisticated and scholarly standpoint. Curtis believed that by capturing the singers' harmonization, the communal nature of black folk song production and performance, she was adding something distinctive to the field.[45]

In the introduction to *Negro Folk Songs* Curtis explained her desire to record the music as accurately as possible. She intended the songs to be "faithful efforts to place on paper an exact record of the old traditional plantation songs *as sung by Negroes*." She assured readers that she had neither added nor omitted anything from the originals. Because her black informants seemed to harmonize the old songs naturally, Curtis believed she had discovered a talent innate to African Americans. "It seemed to me an obvious artistic duty," she intoned, "to set down these intuitive harmonies and to note, in so far as possible, the emotional and dynamic qualities of Negro singing." The ability to harmonize impressed Curtis greatly, and she strove to record these parts by using the phonograph and her own ear as a guide.[46]

She took seriously her duties as a collector and recorder of African American folk song. "In music there can be scarcely a task more reverent than that of a scribe to the unlettered song of a people," she wrote. "A folk-song, expressing as it does the soul of a race, is in that sense a holy thing, for through it sings the voice of humanity." This enormous task called for "humility, for selfless dedication, and for warm human sympathy as well as artistic training." She asserted that "one must love the People as well as their music, and one must feel *with them* in order first to understand and then to write what has risen from the depths of racial experience." To do this Curtis spent hours with her collaborators learning about their lives and finding ways to "drink in the atmosphere" that produced folk music. This resulted in the folk song becoming "a part of the recorder's own being, so that he thinks and feels musically in the same rhythms and accents with the singers, till at last there grows up within him an almost intuitive conception of an adequate written form."[47]

Curtis recognized the challenges of this task, especially of reproducing a musical form in a very different format than originally intended. She had also experienced this problem during the research and writing of *The Indians' Book* and thus drew on many of the same skills and methods in this project. As with Indian songs she believed that she was late to the "harvesting" and feared that the songs would die out as the older generation passed away, a fear shared by many collectors of black folk music. She further realized "how approximate only is any notation of music that was never conceived by the singers as a written thing." She related the written form to the "peep of a caged canary," as compared to the "free caroling of a bird on open wing." Many white recorders of African American music, she argued, missed the special qualities of the songs and instead provided "a musical translation" that reflected white views of what music should sound like. Curtis hoped to avoid that pitfall by capturing the harmonic, rhythmic, and emotional qualities that appealed to her in black folk song.[48]

A second theme of *Negro Folk Songs* was extolling the unique qualities of the music in the collection. Curtis attributed these traits to the special experiences of blacks in the United States, to the influence of African traditions, and to the racial attributes of African Americans. Differences between African American folk music and the European traditions she had grown up with intrigued Curtis. She wrote in *Negro Folk Songs* that the biggest difference between these two forms was rhythm. The "usually even and symmetrical" rhythms of European music strongly contrasted with the "uneven, jagged, and at first hearing, eccentric" beats of syncopated black music. Curtis remarked, "Rhythmically the Negro folk-song has far more variety of accent than the European" composition. She also commented on the prevalence of the pentatonic, or five-note, scale in the folk songs she recorded. "The archaic simplicity of the five-tone scale," she suggested, "seems almost a basic human art-instinct," as it also appeared in other types of "primitive" music. A final distinction of African American music that Curtis identified was "a harmonic sense indicating musical intuition of a high order." Black singers, she argued, naturally sang four-part harmony. This characteristic of black music, this seemingly innate ability to harmonize songs in group settings, fascinated Curtis and shaped her research agenda.[49]

The special experiences of African Americans in the United States accounted for the distinctive traits in their folk music, according to Curtis. She attributed the origins of spirituals and work songs to slavery and argued that the limited opportunities blacks had under bondage produced the imagery and symbolism that she found so appealing. As primitive people living close to nature, Curtis hypothesized, slaves, like their African ancestors, sang "at all times." Their songs therefore represented their entire range of feelings. The folk songs of her collection were the "prayer-songs of slavery," which provided inspiration, hope, comfort, and "the realm wherein the soul, at least, soared free." She noted that many of the distinct traits and seemingly quaint or simplistic phrasing in these songs resulted from difficulties their composers faced with a foreign language. Whites might poke fun at this imagery, but, Curtis countered, it was the limitations under slavery that kept blacks from "the highest reaches of poetic imagination." In her explanation of "God's A-gwine Ter Move All de Troubles Away" she speculated that slaves had limited access to the Bible and adapted its heroes to their own circumstances. Rather than mocking the imagery in slave songs, Curtis found the prevalence of symbolism "sheer poetry." She marveled at the adaptability and resilience she found in these songs, seeing the range of human emotions this music expressed.[50]

Other collectors of black music ignored or dismissed work songs, but Curtis found them as interesting, revealing, and inspiring as spirituals. She devoted two of her four books to these songs because they revealed much about life under slavery and because their focus on work could inspire modern musicians as well. She collected a "Corn-shuckin' Song" at Hampton and quoted Booker T. Washington to explain that "the simple, natural joy of the Negro in little things converted every change in dull routine of this life into an event." Some tunes shed light on relations between slaves and the "Big House," such as the "Peanut-Pickin' Song," with its imagery about the promise of gifts from the slave's owner after the work was completed. Curtis perceived the "Big House" stretching "forth a kindly and affectionate hand to the simple black man." Other work songs demonstrated how slaves had "molded the monotonous toil into a form of rhythmic life." Curtis repeatedly pointed out that the songs in her collection, both spirituals and work songs, were distinctive because of the black experience under slavery and because they demonstrated an integration of art and daily life.[51]

Although she was correct that slave work songs served an important function in the lives of their singers, her tendency to romanticize life under "the peculiar institution" undermined her understanding of the spirituals. Curtis resembled mid-nineteenth-century romantics, described by George Fredrickson, who believed that African Americans possessed special gifts that should be viewed as positive virtues. This "romantic racialism" predominated in the North and was probably shared by many in the Curtis family. Romantics viewed the African American as a "symbol of something that seemed tragically lacking in white American civilization." Childlike traits, often embodied in the image of the good, docile slave, made blacks spiritually and emotionally superior. Curtis romanticized black culture and, to some extent, the experience of slavery. In addition to her depictions of "a kindly and affectionate" plantation owner, her presentation of contemporary black singers recalled this romanticism. Hearing Hampton students sing evoked these feelings: "On me, these evenings made a never to be forgotten impression — the soft twilight, the stillness over the lawns that sloped to the water's edge, and the voices of these young men of to-day who sang the songs of their fathers' yesterdays against the background of a far distant African past." For Curtis being among blacks fostered feelings of tranquility, of being in touch with nature, and of escape from the troubles of her modern world.[52]

These images of a romanticized South and a largely imagined past were not just vestiges of an earlier romanticism that Curtis inherited from her family. They also represented the accommodationist ideology of Hampton, whose influence Curtis certainly felt. African Americans deserved decent treatment because of their crucial role in the Southern economy, but they also warranted some kindness because many had retained the traits of loyalty and faithfulness, a stereotypical image of the "good slave." Fredrickson notes that accommodationists pointed to the "fidelity, gratitude, and a peculiar aptitude for music and religion" when discussing the positive virtues of African Americans. Curtis borrowed from this view when describing the music in *Negro Folk Songs*. For example, "Cott'n-Pickin' Song," she said, evoked images of the "wide plantations under the hot sun, the tall rows of cotton-plants, the bending Negroes, with here and there a wide-brimmed battered straw hat shading the face of some old man, the black and white contrasts of the fluffy cotton bolls and the dark hands and arms." This image of slaves at work seemed more like a picturesque glimpse of plantation life than the brutal reality of forced labor and also reinforced accommodationist views of the worth of black labor. Many accommodationists, especially in the South, drew on fond memories of their black "mammies" to justify fair treatment for African Americans. Curtis found a way to incorporate this powerful image into her commentary on black music. "In fact, as they [black students at Hampton] sing, I dream again of my old Negro 'Uncle,' my grandmother's cook, who used to carry me high on his shoulders," Curtis recalled. "My childhood held no greater luxury than when tired out with play, I was sung to sleep by the tender, wistful voice of 'Uncle Hen'ry.'" Memories of those special songs of her "Uncle" allowed Curtis to imaginatively participate in the romantic black world she believed existed. It helped legitimate collecting black folk songs by giving her a personal attachment to African Americans while still allowing for enough distance to make their music appear distinctive.[53]

An additional explanation for the unique traits of Negro folk songs, Curtis also argued, lay in their African origins. Some of Curtis's contemporaries doubted that any vestiges of the African heritage survived in the spirituals; many argued that slaves had just mimicked the music they heard whites sing at camp meetings and churches. Spirituals, in other words, were poorly rendered versions of white hymns, not original creations by African Americans. Some music critics, like Henry Krehbiel, asserted that African musical characteristics predominated in black spirituals and other folk songs. Curtis weighed in on this debate. "The Negro," she wrote, "transplanted to other lands, absorbed much musically from a surrounding civilization, yet the characteristics which give to his music an interest worthy of particular study are precisely those which differentiate Negro song." Scholars have identified several traits that support Curtis's claim that African traits exist in African American music. Arnold Shaw points to the call-and-response pattern, complex rhythms, and the pentatonic scale as defining characteristics of African music in black spirituals. He further notes that a religious outlook on daily struggle, the use of abstractions that take concrete form in the songs, a lack of distance between the deity and the singers, and a focus on emotion over meaning also derive from African influences. Levine adds that the slave-song style, "with its overriding antiphony, its group nature, its pervasive functionality, its improvisational character, its strong relationship in performance to dance and bodily movement and expression, remained closer to the musical styles and performances of West Africa . . . than to the musical style of Western Europe." Curtis's comparison of African and African American music confirmed her belief in the prevalence of African influence in the shaping of black folk song.[54]

Curtis might have concluded, as many scholars have, that slaves retained African elements as they forged an African American culture.[55] Instead of focusing on cultural continuity she determined that innate racial talents explained the unique sounds of black music and the special talents of black singers. This third theme of *Negro Folk Songs* — that African Americans possessed racial gifts for music making, harmonization, and emotional expression — reappeared throughout Curtis's writings. Although one might argue that Curtis was simply expressing a common anthropological view of racial traits, her insistence on this racialist viewpoint detracts from her more noteworthy accomplishments in collecting black folk song.

To illustrate this notion of innate African American musical characteristics Curtis often recounted an incident in which a European visitor expressed astonishment at the ability of the Hampton chorus to sing harmony:

> "Who trains the chorus? It is marvelous!"
>
> The question was eagerly put by a young German musician who was visiting Hampton Institute in Virginia and for the first time heard the great chorus of nine hundred colored students sing the "Plantations," as the Negroes call the old melodies that had their birth in days of slavery. . . . From a technical as well as purely musical standpoint the extraordinary unity, the precision in "attack" and the faultless pitch of the Negro singers impelled the musician's query.
>
> And my answer baffled him: "Why, no one trains these Negro boys and girls, their singing is natural."

Curtis assured the foreign musician that the singers invented the parts extemporaneously and always sang together in a spontaneous manner. She further asserted that any additional "chorus-drilling" would mean "certain death to the inspirational spirit of these superbly simple old Negro songs." Hampton students confirmed Curtis's ideas about how they sang together. Robert Moton, then the commandant at the school, exclaimed, "Why, *nobody* ever taught us to sing. . . . We *just sing* — that's all!" Other black singers responded similarly to the question of how they sang their "parts" so well: "We don't know just how we sing till you ask us. We just sing the way we *feel!*"[56]

Curtis concluded from these experiences that the students at Hampton, as well as other people of African descent, were blessed with racial gifts for music. "Surely a people who can 'just sing' in extemporaneous four- and six- and eight-part harmonies," she argued, "are gifted not only with rare melodic and rhythmic sense, but also with a natural talent for harmony that distinguishes the black race as among the most musically endowed of peoples." She believed not only that African Americans possessed the innate ability to sing harmonies but that they approached life in a fundamentally different manner than whites. For instance, in her explanation for a song entitled "Hyah Rattler!" she stated that the "song-loving black man" will sing about everything and anything. The song, composed after a snake bit a man, led her to conclude that "it is probably a fact that the Negro *thinks* tunefully." An emphasis on biological, inherited racial traits, rather than on culture or experience, explained for Curtis the distinctiveness of black harmonization and musical imagery.[57]

Curtis saw African Americans as primitive people who, like Native Americans, risked losing their "primitive" nature, and therefore their splendid music, as they evolved. As in her writings on Indians Curtis emphasized many positive traits in the "primitiveness" of black cultures. She valued black music because it expressed something that the more evolved white races could no longer naturally create. Curtis described an afternoon recording session at Hampton after the young men had just finished a day of school and work. As the quartet sang "unconcernedly as though they were simply resting from labor," she "sat with pencil and paper astounded at the untaught facility and the unfaltering harmonic instinct of these natural singers." What struck Curtis most was the manner in which the students sang. "It is perhaps this inherent losing of self in a song that gives to primitive Negro part-singing such amazing unity — emotional as well as musical," she wrote. While collecting in the Deep South, Curtis found these features even more apparent and the musical ability more striking: "With the Negro, it would seem that the further back one traces the current of musical inspiration that runs through the race (that is, the more primitive the people and thus the more instinctive the gift), the nearer does one come to the divine sources of song — intuition, which is in turn the wellspring of all genius." The more primitive the singer, the closer to nature and the source of creativity the music would be.[58]

The primitivism she found so appealing could rejuvenate her modern world. This fourth theme of *Negro Folk Songs* — that black folk music could revitalize American music and culture — echoed Curtis's arguments about Native Americans. African Americans furthermore could contribute more to American culture because they were better integrated into mainstream American life than Indians. Their abilities to sing in harmony, to create intoxicating rhythms, and to find song in everyday life combined with their African heritage and experiences on American soil to produce wonderful gifts from which all Americans could benefit. Curtis's research sought to reintegrate art and work. In *Negro Folk Songs* she complained, "To have lost art out of the life of the worker is one of the most deadening blights of commercial civilization." In the music of African Americans she found an answer to this dilemma. She contrasted the work songs she heard in the South with those of the Northern factory. "With us Anglo-Saxons, song as a labor invigorator seems to have died away with the invention of machinery," but blacks in America still drew on songs from their African heritage to lighten their labor. Blacks could do this, Curtis believed, because they had not evolved so far as to lose touch with nature and their bodies. "Is it not, after all, a most vital and priceless thing," Curtis asked regarding black work songs, "this art which is part of a man's own pulse-beat, his own muscle, his own will? What a contrast to the silent, deadening toil of the modern factory." She continued, "The primitive race — child-races, clasping the mother-hand of Nature — still have a vigorous gladness in life itself and in the proud strength of the human body; while we, already weary in our maturity, feel little but the strain of forced marching on the road to progress, and the fever for the goal."[59]

African Americans had more to offer the nation than just a new attitude toward work; their primitiveness could infuse modern life and revitalize whites. Whites needed "the nature-people to call us back to that youth of natural poetry and song." Curtis recognized that African Americans had always influenced American life, but that whites refused to acknowledge or accept what they offered. "We of the white race are at last awakening to the fact that the Negro in our midst stands at the gates of human culture with full hands, laden with gifts," Curtis wrote. "Too long in this county have we barred the door." The recent world war meant that "we no longer merely tolerate the presence of the black race, and with anxiety at that — we need the Negro, and he is here to stay." This meant more than just recognizing the contributions blacks had made to the Southern economy or as soldiers in the war. Curtis demanded that her fellow white Americans "unlock the gate to see that he [the Negro] can be equally important to cultural evolution in the 'melting pot' of the United States, and that his presence among us may be a powerful stimulus to the art, music, letters, and drama of the American Continent."[60] White Americans could no longer afford to ignore the musical gifts of blacks.

Curtis recognized that African Americans influenced the sound of popular music, but she hoped that the spirituals and work songs that she had collected would have a greater, more artistic influence on national culture. Ragtime, "whose melodies are on all lips, and whose rhythms impel our marching feet in a 'war for democracy,'" was the most popular and widely copied African American musical expression at the time. Curtis critiqued this genre: "'Ragtime' is not unjustly condemned by many for the vulgarity of its first associates that cannot be too deeply deplored, but which is fortunately fast slipping out of the march and dance songs of to-day." The real appeal of this music, she argued, was its infectious syncopated rhythms. The same syncopation could be found in spirituals, which lacked the objectionable themes and origins of ragtime. Spirituals, dealing with religion and the serious nature of human emotion, provided a far superior alternative. Other white musicians shared Curtis's opinion of ragtime and spirituals. Historians of black music note that many collections "validated the spirituals as an exalted and noble art form — in the eyes of many the best America had to offer — and consequently made them a more palatable resource for concert treatment than any other black idiom."[61] In fact a movement grew among white musicians to develop African American, along with Native American, music and to use these "folk" cultures to create a distinctive American style of music.

While Curtis generally supported white musicians using works like *Negro Folk Songs* to generate a new national music, more significantly she wanted African American musicians to undertake this work. Blacks needed to collect this folk music. At Hampton Curtis helped establish a branch of the American Folklore Society. "The Negro has an inestimately rich gift to make to the culture and to the distinctive civilization of America," she argued. "In asking the students at Negro schools to take definite and active part in the saving of this folk-lore to our country, it seems to me that we would help to dignify in the eyes of the Negroes themselves, the value of their own race-gifts." In the 1890s a white teacher, Alice Mabel Bacon, had established a similar society. Like Curtis, Bacon insisted that black students do the majority of the collecting. The society gathered folk tales, customs, superstitions, proverbs, and songs and presented its findings at conferences and in the *Southern Workman* and the *Journal of American Folklore*.[62] Curtis wished to build from this foundation and added the hope that by collecting and sharing folklore African Americans could "stimulate a certain race solidarity" between the North and the South and cement bonds between black schools. She wanted to see an infusion of "young blood" into the folklore group that met at Hampton. Curtis envisioned branches of the folklore society at black schools that would periodically meet at conferences to share their findings and promote racial pride.[63]

Additionally Curtis praised black musicians who encouraged the performance and perpetuation of spirituals and plantation songs. Hampton's Robert Moton received special recognition from Curtis for promoting these songs at Hampton. Curtis also dedicated a song to Harry T. Burleigh, an African American composer who had introduced Antonín Dvořák to African American music and helped inspire his *From the New World*. Curtis explained that to Burleigh "the Spirituals were not to be looked down on and willfully ignored as reminders of a condition of servitude, but rather to be revered as living proof of a race's spiritual ascendancy over oppression and humiliation." In her publications and through the Music School Settlement for Colored People Curtis encouraged other black musicians, such as R. Nathaniel Dett, J. Rosamond Johnson, and Will Marion Cook. She also used her connections to Hampton, her patrons, and the New York City music world to promote and assist African American composers.[64]

Curtis also continued to use musical performances as a means to advance her goals for African American music. For example, in the spring of 1921 she offered to assist a group planning a concert of black music. She wrote Peabody to ask for permission to use part of the Palmer Fund, money she had received to promote Hampton, to assist a woman identified only as Mrs. Marshall to "make this public Negro affair a real success." Curtis justified her intervention by arguing that "the whole sake of Negro prestige in which Hampton's name is involved" depended on a successful outcome. Somewhat condescendingly, Curtis explained that she would have to "superintend rehearsals and *train* Simango in his recitations" and prepare an address in case James Weldon Johnson could not speak. She believed that her past experience organizing concerts would salvage the group's efforts. She asked Peabody to keep her assistance discreet, "as the Negroes would not understand and it would hurt my influence with them for the right thing."[65] This statement reveals a certain patronizing attitude that she and other whites involved in "uplifting" African Americans often expressed. Despite much of Curtis's rhetoric about equality among people of all races and promoting self-help and respect among African Americans, she still often treated blacks as children in need of her expert care. As she planned the concert that spring she complained to Peabody about the many problems she faced. Curtis described how Marshall had sent out incomplete letters "before I took hold" that wasted money in additional printing costs. She confided to Peabody that Marshall "did some killingly funny naïve things" that she could not wait to share with him. Although Curtis admired Marshall's "characteristic Negro optimism," she declared that for the concert to be successful "someone *who knows how*, had got to *work* it out all right."[66] Even though Curtis obviously respected African Americans and admired their "racial gifts," she could not fully overcome her society's insistence on Negro inferiority.

In spite of Curtis's condescending attitude toward the African Americans she tried to help, she did have insights into many of the problems blacks faced. She believed that progress, though limited, had been made toward increasing black pride and self-respect. She wrote to Peabody, "When I look back and remember how, a few years ago, the colored people were *ashamed* of their own music and their own skins, and wanted to forget their own melodies and be like white people, the fact that they are now agitating [for] a '*National* school of *Negro* music,' and are calling themselves 'Negro' instead of 'a school for *Colored People*' which they insisted on before — well, I thank *you* for making it possible for me to do a little bit toward helping to stimulate that self-respect without which no people can progress." Curtis viewed racial pride as an important step forward for blacks, and although she often understood this in primitivistic terms, she believed that any positive views of black music and culture could benefit African Americans. While arranging publicity for the concert Curtis complained to Peabody, "It is terrible hard, as Booker Washington once said, to get any notice of the *good* things Negroes do; but let a black man steal a pocket-book and he gets head-lined on the front page!" Despite all the struggles and setbacks the concert took place at the end of April. It received a favorable review in the *New York Times*. Curtis hoped that her strategy of building racial pride among blacks and showcasing their musical talents to whites would lead to interracial dialogue and improved race relations.[67]

Curtis's approach to racial cooperation based on music raises questions about the possibilities of interracial musical dialogue, especially a dialogue tied to white notions of black "uplift." The historian Susan Curtis, in her study of black and white interaction in New York City theater in this period, argues for the difficulties of interracial communication: "The crosscurrents, inequality, and ambiguity of cultural hybrids emerge as clearly as the beautiful image of black and white artists joining hands across the color line."[68] Many blacks, particularly of the small but growing middle class, agreed with Curtis's strategy of using the more "dignified" spirituals as a tool to promote racial pride and gain white acceptance. The historian Kevin Gaines, in *Uplifting the Race*, examines the ways the African American elite responded to white supremacy in the first half of the twentieth century. He asserts that elite blacks shared with Curtis the notion that improving the image of all African Americans would decrease racism. Middle-class blacks, far more so than Curtis, were fully aware of the negative images of African Americans in popular culture and traced this in part to minstrels and their songs. By attacking stereotypes perpetuated by minstrelsy they hoped to improve their own status in society. Elite African Americans therefore snubbed the "low-life" association of ragtime in favor of more dignified and acceptable forms of music. They demanded "a universalizing fusion of black and European forms, in a manner that nonetheless privileged nonblack aesthetic criteria," Gaines argues. Several African American elites attempted to use spirituals as a form of uplift. Gaines points to W. E. B. DuBois's conception of the black "folk" and his hopes that their music would earn blacks a place in American society as a prominent example. "By equating spirituals with the Volkslied of German romantics," Gaines writes, "DuBois departed from minstrelsy, creating an international context for his definition of black high culture." Curtis and DuBois shared many of the same motivations and inspirations in their support for the use of spirituals, particularly because European composers who drew upon folk themes in their work influenced them both. Curtis's goals for the development of the spirituals therefore coincided with the views of many black leaders.[69]

Many African American musicians brought out folk song collections during this period. From Hampton, R. Nathaniel Dett, the school's music director, published *Religious Folk-Songs of the Negro*. Dett too hoped that his collection of songs would dispel negative views of African Americans — the "darky" image so prevalent in popular culture — and reveal the true nature of black people. Dett stressed that African American spirituals demonstrated more than a musical contribution to American culture. Blacks possessed a spiritual nature, "a religious faith almost past understanding," that served as just one example of the worth of the race. These songs, unlike more popular music, captured black spirituality and offered this as a gift to all Americans. In a "country given over to enterprise," Dett asserted, "there should be at least one wellspring of spiritual issue." Dett, like Curtis, believed that blacks had "inadvertently voiced the cry of the world" and that out of this emotional expression all Americans could find spiritual comfort.[70]

Other African American musicians tried to use spirituals, at least in part, as a tool for racial uplift. The composer Harry Burleigh also stressed the "deep religious feeling" of his collection of spirituals. Burleigh further noted the important gifts of rhythm that black music had to offer the world. The brothers James Weldon Johnson and J. Rosamond Johnson, the former director of the Music School Settlement for Colored People, published two books of Negro spirituals as well. They stressed the sincerity of the songs' meanings and tried to separate this music from representations by minstrels. The Johnson brothers agreed with Curtis on the African origins of the music and the uniqueness of black harmonization of these folk songs. They approved of the recent popularity of spirituals because the songs exposed all Americans to the beauty and dignity of black culture and helped advance African Americans.[71]

Although many African American musicians and educators valued this approach to racial uplift endorsed by Curtis and other white sympathizers, other African Americans, often the very ones they sought to help, disagreed. Many working-class blacks preferred the more popular ragtime, blues, and jazz. They often disliked spirituals as a reminder of slavery or resented the moralizing that accompanied discussion of the songs. Some African Americans displayed increased self-consciousness about traditional folk culture. The "new models, the new standards, the new possibilities" presented to them by educators and white society in general generated real tensions over plantations songs, as Lawrence Levine points out. Some probably preferred more popular African American music for precisely the reasons middle-class blacks and whites found it distasteful. Some black musicians, as Ann Douglas argues, resented "the charge that they were untutored talents whose musical gifts were 'natural ones.'"[72] Students at Hampton occasionally complained about the school's policy regarding spirituals. When Robert Moton first entered the school he refused to sing spirituals because he came there to "learn something better" and "objected to exhibiting the religious and emotional side of our people to white folks." Only after several years, and the persuasion of Armstrong, did he come to see the spirituals as a "priceless legacy." Dett, as the school's director of music, labored to create a music department — "a MUSIC TRADE SCHOOL" — that trained students to be professional musicians and did more than simply perpetuate plantation songs. Students, he argued, desired to expand the scope of their training through exposure to a wider variety of music. He noted that the emphasis on folk songs was "only a partial success" and pointed out that other black institutions had "put the taboo on folk-songs." He also

contended that students believed they sang folk songs as part of
a show for white visitors. They feared that Hampton "was trying
to give white people the impression that Negroes haven't learned
anything in music since the days of slavery." Dett strongly supported
the preservation and development of spirituals, for many of the
same reasons other middle-class African Americans and whites
like Curtis did. Working with his students, however, Dett realized
that more was needed to bring about a distinctive black song and
contribute to an American school of music.[73] And perhaps he also
realized that more than an appreciation for black folk music was
necessary to bring about increased civil rights.

CURTIS'S WORK PROMOTING BLACK MUSIC AND THE PUB-
lication of *Negro Folk Songs* established her as a recognized voice
on African American folk music. She continued this work with
the 1921 publication of *Songs and Tales from the Dark Continent*.
This publication further reveals the ambiguities of Curtis and her
career. On the one hand, she again offered a misunderstood and
oppressed group a voice and demanded that they be respected
because of their potential contributions to the nation. But once
more she premised this on her understanding of blacks as "primitive" people who, because of their less evolved nature, offered gifts
that "overcivilized" whites had lost in the modern world.

Songs and Tales originated from research for *Negro Folk Songs*.
Hoping to prove African origins for African American music, Cur-
tis studied the folk songs of two Hampton students — Columbus
Ka'mba Sima'ngo, of the Ndau (or Vandau) tribe of Portuguese East
Africa (today, Mozambique), and Madika'ne Quande'yana Ce'le, a
Zulu from South Africa. *Songs and Tales*, like Curtis's other major
collections of "primitive" music, contained folk songs, proverbs,
and stories as told to her by tribal members. In the introduction
Curtis explained her purpose and elaborated on her methodology.
She divided the book into sections for each tribe. Her collaborators

introduced the material, and Curtis added details on their lives in their native countries and in the United States. A mix of folk tales and ceremonial, religious, dance, game, and love songs followed, interspersed with Curtis's commentary on the music and its overall significance.

Curtis's patrons encouraged this foray into non-American music because it contributed to the same goals that had led them to support *Negro Folk Songs*. Frissell believed that her research would advance Hampton's long-standing interest in African cultures and its desire to spread the "Hampton model" across the Atlantic. The *Southern Workman* published many articles on African life and culture, and the school aligned itself with several missionaries, many of them Hampton graduates, working and teaching in various African nations. The school hoped that studying African cultures would also shed light on the students' heritages. Collections of African art and other items of material culture were housed on campus to facilitate this study. In addition to aid from Hampton, Peabody financially supported one of the collaborators while he worked with Curtis, and Boas helped her with revisions and advice on African history, culture, and language.[74]

Her methodology in part resembled the strategies she had used in her other collections. Curtis relied on native informants who spoke enough English to allow for some communication. She again used both a phonograph and her own ear to record songs and often asked informants to sing repeatedly to capture all the nuances of the music. She admitted to the difficulty of the work but claimed that she had tried to "be true to both spirit and letter" of the songs and poems by painstakingly reviewing each word of the translation to be certain it met her goal of accuracy. The principal difference between this collection and her other works was Curtis's lack of firsthand experience with the cultures she described. Curtis realized this shortcoming. "Could the work have been done *in Africa*," she exclaimed, "how much less difficult and how much more satisfac-

tory would have been the result!" Even though she never made it
to the "Dark Continent," she believed strongly enough in her two
native informants to base her entire research project around their
recollections of tribal songs and stories.[75]

Madika'ne Q. Ce'le, a native of South Africa and a man of "royal
Zulu blood," shared material on tribal dance, the military, courtship,
and creation songs. Ce'le's father had held a high-ranking government position but had converted to Christianity and become a
missionary to other Zulus. He wanted his son to get a Western
education in the United States. Ce'le eventually found his way to
Hampton, where he developed a talent for public speaking and
became very active in school events. Curtis commented that the
"tall and powerful, quiet and unassuming" young man possessed a
"low, melodious African voice" through which "the silent millions
of Black Africa seemed to speak." Ce'le became a minor celebrity
at Hampton. Students selected him to be the president of the class
of 1911 and to deliver the commencement address. His graduation
even drew attention from the *Chicago Defender,* which reported
that a "Zulu Crown Prince Graduates at Hampton."[76]

Throughout his years at the school Ce'le gave addresses on Zulu
culture and the need for the civilizing influence of Christianity. The
most dramatic example of his public appeal for missionary aid to
Africa was a Hampton-sponsored play entitled *For Unkulunkulu's
Sake.* Ce'le starred as an African king who falls prey to dishonest
European traders and their "spirit water" and is enslaved by the
superstitious beliefs of his village witch doctor. Only the arrival
of missionaries saves the king and his village. Out of gratitude and
respect for his new religion the king sends his son to get a Hampton-
style education and to return and establish a little Hampton in
Africa. Within a few years of graduation Ce'le fulfilled the goals
of this play and returned to his country of birth. He struggled to
establish an industrial school and to spread the Hampton creed. He
and his American wife, who died within a few years of her arrival in

Africa, suffered greatly during World War I and sent many desperate pleas for aid back to Hampton. Prior to his departure Ce'le met with Curtis to contribute Zulu music and folklore to her collection, as well as an autobiographical sketch.[77]

The other African student, Columbus Ka'mba Sima'ngo (or Simango, as he was most commonly called), also attended Hampton in order to become a missionary. This "full-blooded native" from Portuguese East Africa had grown up "in a pagan village where life was guided by belief in the all-pervading presence of the spirits of the dead." He left his village at around the age of fifteen to work for Portuguese merchants in the port city of Beira. He labored at a variety of jobs until he met another young worker who introduced him to a missionary schoolteacher. The Portuguese tried to prevent Simango from receiving an education, but he finally managed to escape to a school in Rhodesia. Simango eventually found his way to the Mount Silinda Mission in Natal, where teachers encouraged him to pursue an industrial education at Hampton. Simango spent over five years at the Virginia school, where, according to Curtis, he "won the respect and good-will of his companions and instructors."[78]

Like Ce'le, Simango became an active participant in school events and in efforts to raise awareness about the needs of Africans. He contributed numerous articles to the *Southern Workman* and the *Hampton Student* on African beliefs and his people's need for missionary aid. Simango also delivered addresses on these topics to a variety of missionary and art organizations on the East Coast.[79] His hectic schedule made it difficult for him to work closely with Curtis, despite his enthusiasm for the project. Curtis devised a solution. She hired Simango through Hampton's "outing program" to work for her at the family home at Wave Crest for the summer. Every morning the young man would cut grass, rake, sweep, and do other chores until his nine o'clock meeting with Curtis. She described Simango as "smilingly ready for our musical and ethnographical research" and completely devoted to the task. Curtis expressed thanks that "in spite of missionary training he had retained the balanced judgment and the keenness of vision to realize that all was not bad in the native life simply because it was pagan." Simango shared her hope that the book would enlighten readers about Africa and provide an accurate portrayal of its peoples. Curtis asserted that "he was working for the recognition of his race."[80]

Curtis fondly recalled Simango's stay with her and her family. She praised the African for his intelligence, patience, hard work, enthusiasm for her research, and commitment to serve other Africans. She noted his "keen sense of humor, and his strong teeth, filed in African fashion," that "often flashed in a ready smile," as well as his constant possession of a copy of the New Testament. Simango entertained the entire Curtis clan in the evenings by telling stories of African life and customs. Curtis explained that Simango's "powerful dramatic sense" was common in "people who have lived as part of the elemental drama of Mother Nature." His descriptions of witchcraft "made one's flesh creep", while his stories of "the deliberate demoralizations" from Europeans outraged the family. Simango complained that even whites "who want to be just and kind still like us to feel the weight of their hand upon our head. They wish us to know that we may not rise higher than they allow." The African youth also entertained the Curtises with music. He played a small native instrument called a "mbi'la" that sounded to Curtis like "the tuneful drip of raindrops twinkling down in different pitch." Her nephews especially enjoyed his playing and followed this "benign Pied Piper" endlessly about the house. On occasion he performed traditional dances and amazed Curtis with his highly developed sense of rhythm. The "dignity of many of the native dances and . . . Sima'ngo's unconscious nobility of mien" deeply impressed the Curtis family.[81]

Simango's hard work and dedication to the project so moved Curtis that she asked him to make a direct address to the readers of *Songs and Tales*. Like High Chief in his introduction to *The Indians' Book*, Simango began by asserting, "These are genuine African songs, untouched by European music." He explained that he had not only been born in Africa but that he had actively participated in the songs, dances, and games described in the text and that he played the drums and several other traditional instruments. Simango praised Curtis's devotion to capturing the songs exactly as he sang them. "Miss Curtis and I were not satisfied by 'almost like it' but by 'just like it,'" he explained. Curtis impressed him with her ability to re-create "the real African song" in this collection. Simango concluded, "It is a noble work of bringing the weak and unnoticed race to the enlightened people of the civilized world, and I was willing to give every *minute* that I could spare." He expressed his gratitude for the larger purpose of her undertaking — that whites would hear real African music that others had misrepresented in the past.[82]

Although Simango and Curtis seemed satisfied with the results of their collaboration, some critics questioned their methodology. In his review of *Songs and Tales* in the *New York Tribune* Henry Krehbiel, the music critic and author of *Afro-American Folk Songs*, challenged Curtis's use of the two African students as the basis for her entire book. He identified Curtis as "an indefatigable and enthusiastic worker in the field of primitive folkmusic" and noted that, as with her other books, she here exhibited "that warm sympathy with the thoughts and feelings of primitive peoples." He noted that he found her method "more scientific and convincing" than in her earlier works but then asserted that "she does not always leave us free from doubt as to the strict authenticity of her musical records." He especially questioned the information Curtis had received from Simango. Although he recognized the lengths to which she had gone to prove his familiarity with native culture, Krehbiel remarked, "It is something of a strain on our credulity to believe that after many years of dissociation from his people he could still chant seventeen 'Spirit Songs,' 'Rain Songs,' and 'Dance Songs' of the savages of Portuguese East Africa" and still correctly add the harmony and rhythmic accompaniments. He reiterated that he was not questioning Curtis's methods themselves but contended that "we can not help marveling at so retentive a memory as that of a man who had practically severed all connections with his people" at the age of fifteen. Krehbiel concluded his review on a positive note, saying that *Songs and Tales* "makes much for pleasure and more for profit" and that it would be a definite contribution to the study of folklore in general and folk music in particular.[83]

Curtis's supporters instantly rallied to her defense by responding to Krehbiel's remarks in letters to the editor in the *Tribune*. Peabody assured readers of Simango's authenticity. He pointed out that even when the African was away from his village "he was not separated from the life of native Africa, but was in touch with it until he came to America." Simango had begun his work with Curtis shortly after he arrived, before he had time to forget it. Furthermore, Peabody asserted, the remarkable memory that Krehbiel questioned was "not uncommon among unlettered races who have cultivated memory as the sole repository" of their cultures. Other researchers, including Boas, found Simango a reliable informant, Peabody concluded. Boas himself penned an editorial in Curtis's defense. Perhaps to justify his use of Simango in his own investigations (research supported in part by Peabody's generosity), Boas contended that Krehbiel's concerns about Simango's authenticity were not "justified by the facts." The anthropologist argued that Simango possessed a "keen interest in the primitive life of his people" and "a remarkably clear memory" of his childhood and native customs. The African also displayed "a very critical mind in regard to his own knowledge." Boas concluded that readers "may be assured of the genuineness of the material sung by Mr. Simango and of the painstaking accuracy of rendition" claimed in the volume."[84]

Curtis had known Krehbiel from her adolescence, had respected his opinions, and had even cited his work on African American folk music in her own writings. His critique of her work deeply upset her. She had hoped that Krehbiel would respond to the editorials written in her defense. Curtis complained to Peabody that "Mr. Krehbiel (Mr. 'Crab-bile' somebody well called him) maintains a discreet and dignified silence. No comment: he doesn't so much as squeak!" The music critic had telephoned Curtis "and really quite irritated me with his silly questions and his sillier assumptions that because I am interested in Negroes and Indians, I am 'unscientific,' 'unreliable,' and color every statement with my own 'enthusiasms.'" She countered that his criticisms of her work were even more "unscientific," because she believed they were based on "personal speculation, and personal prejudice instead of an examination of facts." Getting personal herself, Curtis remarked that she should not have been so upset, because Krehbiel was "an old man, ill and worn, but still in harness because he can't afford to retire. Such people should *be retired*, however, on pensions in the interest of public welfare." In Krehbiel's defense he did print Peabody's and Boas's letters, and for that Curtis and Simango were grateful.[85]

Although Krehbiel questioned her research, he and many other reviewers found much they deemed useful and worthwhile in *Songs and Tales from the Dark Continent*. Krehbiel may have criticized Curtis for her "enthusiasms" regarding Africans and other people of color, but even Curtis had to admit that her advocacy shaped the content and purpose of her books. Her desire to help these groups made her work stand out to reviewers and readers alike and separated her from more serious, "objective" anthropologists. In *Songs and Tales* Curtis used an approach similar to that of *The Indians' Book*. She provided a space for actual Africans (although far fewer in number) to voice their ideas about their cultures; to dispel harmful myths and stereotypes; and to offer their own contributions to the worlds of art, literature, and music. Unlike in *The Indians' Book* Curtis here claimed credit as the author of *Songs and*

Tales, but both works shared the goal of improving race relations by pointing to the contributions "primitive" peoples could make to the modern world and arguing for mutual understanding between them and whites. Curtis told readers that she hoped they would "see that the human family is near of kin and that basic emotions of love, of sorrow, or rejoicing and of prayer, whether men be primitive or advanced, white, yellow, red, or black, are the same root-feeling planted in us all."[86]

Curtis also offered more specific, and much more pragmatic, reasons for shifting her research to the peoples of the "Dark Continent." Whites needed to know more about Africans and people of African descent because of recent events in the world that brought these groups into closer contact with one another. The recent world war loomed largest in Curtis's mind. She began *Songs and Tales* by linking her study to the disruptions caused by the war. "The future of the black African, whether on the Dark Continent or in the Americas, is to-day sharply silhouetted against that red which still burns in the sky although the fires of war are quenched," she stated. Curtis suggested that European colonialism had contributed to the war but argued that the important issue was that Africans had fought alongside whites and that both had learned they depended on one another. Curtis proposed that "when the dust shall clear, we shall find that men of diverse colors and creeds, men high and low, have been brought to know one another as never before." Curtis painted a far rosier picture of the war's impact for people of African descent than most actually experienced. After reading a draft of this introduction Boas responded angrily: "It seems to my mind that the introduction praising the Negroes' participation in the war misrepresents actual conditions, because all that has happened was that the people were compelled by superior force to participate in the wars that were entirely without any interest to them, except as in so far as they helped their own exploitation. To make of that a representation of brotherhood, seems to me almost a ghastly joke."

Boas did not change Curtis's view of the war or lessen her hopes that the loyalty of black soldiers would be rewarded in some way. She sincerely believed that if whites only understood what blacks had accomplished, harmony between all people would prevail.[87]

Curtis, hoping to facilitate better understanding, devoted a portion of *Songs and Tales* to describing contemporary Africa and its historical, anthropological, and ethnological features. She traced the origins of blacks in Africa and highlighted major groups that had traditionally lived there. Nonblack peoples, including several "yellowish" races (the "Bushmen" and the "Hottentots"), Arabs and other Muslims, and Jews, were described in relation to their interactions with black Africans. Curtis expressed great interest in the types of cross-cultural contacts that existed among these various groups. She also traced the history of the Zulu and Ndau tribes of her informants, both of which belonged to the Bantu linguistic family. She noted that many whites perceived Zulus as "fiercely militant" but assured readers that not all Bantu speakers shared the Zulu's characteristics. The Ndau, for example, "were particularly peaceful, agricultural and pastoral." When Europeans first arrived these peoples had already developed many of the traits of "civilized" societies.[88]

She recognized the impact of European colonization. "This child of the Dark Continent has indeed a curious status in his own land," Curtis remarked. "Black Man's Africa" consisted of only two small states, Abyssinia and Liberia, while the remainder of the continent was divided among the colonizing nations. Europeans had brought slavery, exploitation, disease, and alcohol abuse, but under white domination blacks had still made progress. Intertribal warfare had ended, and black numbers had increased. Curtis cited population figures to demonstrate the sheer numbers of Africans and people of African descent throughout the world and asked if these should not "evoke serious consideration" among whites. They certainly evoked questions from Boas, who once again questioned Curtis's representation of Africans in the modern world. He questioned how "black" Abyssinia really was and found Curtis's statistics questionably high. Curtis, however, wanted to retain this information to impel her readers to ask, "Should we not indeed do well to know more of these dark neighbors who now form a part of the future civilization of so many nations?" She ignored Boas's advice.[89]

She did adopt Boas's approach to racial uplift, one also employed by W. E. B. DuBois, by pointing to major achievements of the African past as a way to argue for respect, fair treatment, and optimism for modern blacks. Citing both of these scholars, Curtis noted the accomplishments of African civilizations prior to European conquest. First on her list of notable achievements was the use of iron, which, as Boas had argued, originated in Africa, not in Europe. She further pointed to the logical organization of Bantu villages, impressed by their lack of private property. African law, with its basis in reparation, not retribution, seemed even more praiseworthy. "In fact, the principle of a life for a life, rather than of death for death, and reparation instead of vengeance, shows a constructive logic," she insisted. Africans had developed complex systems of governance as well. Curtis asked, in light of all these African attainments, "Why has the Black race, as a whole, remained primitive in Africa?" Using DuBois as a guide, Curtis explained that topography, warfare, the slave trade, the climate, and European exploitation had all hampered progress. That blacks had survived these many tribulations seemed to Curtis a testimony of their potential. "But the Black race seems destined for a future," she exclaimed, and that future would develop from the unique traits residing in their "racial soul."[90]

Because of the conditions of contemporary Africa, the impact of the recent war, and the potential for black achievement in the future, Curtis asserted that whites had a dire need, even a duty, to understand the people of the "Dark Continent." Whites knew little about Africans except "from the outside" as laborers and had "known little of the soul of the black man." Curtis hoped that her collection would alleviate this problem. She explained that she had collected the songs not just for "their intrinsic interest" but also "for what they reveal of the mind and heart of the black man and of his life and customs." Drawing from her experiences with Native American and African American music, Curtis contended that a folklorist could discover the "racial soul" in a people's music. Music was such an intrinsic part of "primitive" life that it revealed much more about "primitive" people than one could learn of "civilized" people through their songs. "In the folk-music of a people is imaged the racial soul; to simple or primitive men who are close to nature and are impelled by her creative spirit, song is a vital part of existence itself," she explained. Music was more than an amusing accompaniment to daily living, but "the voice of tribal, even of racial prayer; the moulding, in art-form, of communal group sentiment; and the living fluent utterance of a people's inspiration." Her study of African music, she claimed, had taught her much about African culture and the contributions it could make in the modern world.[91]

Curtis repeatedly asserted that Africans were still climbing up the evolutionary ladder and that whites needed to remember this before judging them too harshly. Africans retained superstitions and believed in witchcraft, but that did not mean, as some whites had concluded, that "the native is a being of definitely limited intelligence, incapable of higher development." Curtis instead urged readers to realize that "the African is only passing through a period of development wherein he holds beliefs common to mankind at large at certain stages of mental evolution." She suggested that white tendencies to denounce primitive society, a stage that "we have ourselves barely outgrown," reflected "our own primitive manner of thinking." Further, anthropologists had demonstrated that blacks were not inferior and were quite capable of participating in modern life. Perhaps they lacked the intellectual attainments of more advanced races, she postulated, but surely mental achievement was not the only measure of a person's worth: "Granting that it may be years before the black race as a whole attains the intellectual development of the white, must we not concede that there are qualities other than those of the intellect alone that may also aid in the progress of human beings?"[92]

Blacks had many traits and talents that Curtis believed modern white Americans lacked. She hoped that whites would come to not only respect these characteristics but learn from them as well. She believed, for example, that blacks were more emotional than whites. African Americans, she argued, had been "segregated, discriminated against, mobbed, and murdered" but had managed to face these horrors with "a long-suffering patience, an absence of resentment, a sunny good temper that would seem heroic were it not so simple and childlike." Curtis obviously misread the actual attitudes of African Americans in the United States who were speaking out against such treatment (a surprising fact, considering she cited DuBois throughout her introduction). Perhaps she needed to see blacks as patient, good-natured, and optimistic in order to use their cultures to enrich her own.[93]

Curtis believed that blacks had innate talents for music and art that they could share with the rest of the world, if only given the chance. She defined art as "the imperishable legacy of a people" whose influence could be "transmitted to other generations and different lands" like an "unending vibration." "As a creator of beauty the black man is capable of contributing to the greatest art of the world," declared Curtis. Many people recognized the musical gifts of people of African descent. Spirituals in the United States were widely appreciated. Her research into African song, "the parent stem" of African American music, proved that a "genuine art-sense" existed in Africans. She believed the songs in this book could "offer to modern music a new silhouette." African rhythms, melodies, and sense of form in songs could present modern musicians with new inspiration. The "song-poems" she had collected stood as potential contributions to the world of literature.[94]

Most important, Curtis believed that Africans' primitive under-standing of life had much to teach whites like herself who felt "over-civilized" and out of touch with natural forces. Primitive people understood the important things in life. All people sought answers to the questions of life. Primitives accepted that "life is" and asked "who gave it to me?" Native Americans answered "the Earth-Mother," because their "concepts have always a poetic and cosmic scope." The "literal, logical, and personal" Africans answered, "a mother bore me." To Curtis this seemed a revolutionary approach to understanding the meaning of life. She wrote, "If we could strip from humanity the complexities and artificialities with which civilization so often overlays the real, pulsing, naked form of life, there might be found in all of us the same instinctive and overpowering sense of rever-ence for the *creation of life* that fills the mind of primitive man, for whom the great essentials of existence stand out, unblurred by smaller outlines, on the bas-relief of Time." Curtis believed that this approach to creating art and music could rejuvenate the mod-ern world. An instinctual appreciation for the process of creation inspired her with hope for the future of art and music, as well as for the future of Africans around the world. She hoped that this collection of songs would be appreciated "not as an achievement, but as a prophecy."[95]

CURTIS'S STUDY OF AFRICAN AND AFRICAN AMERICAN MUSIC continued the work she had begun with the music of Native Ameri-cans. She discovered much in the songs and tales from which she could draw personal and musical inspiration. Throughout her career she had argued that American musicians needed to learn from primitive peoples if they hoped to create a distinctively American musical identity. Many musicians followed her advice and created works they believed manifested a genuine national sound. Even Curtis could not resist the urge to participate in this movement. Inspired by her research on "primitive" music, her advocacy for these groups, and her affiliation with other artists, particularly her painter husband, Paul Burlin, Curtis spent the last part of her life trying to incorporate the music and art of African Americans and Native Americans into her own expression of American identity.

7

"The Spirit of the Real America"

Curtis's Search for an American Identity

ON FEBRUARY 19, 1915, NATALIE CURTIS SAT IN THE ACADEMY in Philadelphia listening to the rehearsal of Ferruccio Busoni's *Indian Fantasy*. Having once taken lessons with the great pianist, Curtis had supplied Busoni with a "few Indian melodies" that she thought appropriate for "greater development and expansion" in a larger work. Busoni's *Indian Fantasy*, the outcome of this collaboration, thrilled her. It reinforced her argument that Native American music could represent the essential themes of the nation. Listening to the performance Curtis sensed that "the walls melted away, and I was in the West, filled again with that awing sense of vastness, of solitude, of immensity. The boundless horizon, the endless stretch of plains and deserts, the might of the Mississippi, the towering grandeur of the Rocky Mountains — all this, the spirit of the real America."[1]

Curtis believed that Busoni's work epitomized this spirit and did justice to the Indian songs upon which he had based his composition. She praised Busoni for allowing the Indian tunes, with their "own sharp rhythmic and melodic outline," to maintain their distinctiveness. She further commended his use of Native music, arguing that he treated the songs like "musical seeds" to be "sown in the soil of a receptive, re-creative mind" and that he had developed Indian songs "according to their own nature and character." Others shared her opinion. The audience "seemed also to have felt that a new and really important art-work had been born in music through the stimulus of American life — not the life of our cosmopolitan cities but the open life of the great expanse beyond the Mississippi."[2]

Curtis's career centered on her search for a personal and national identity. She shared with other Americans, particularly white, middle-class ones, a sense of cultural malaise and feelings of unease with the modern world they inhabited. She searched for real meaning in her own life and for the cultural identity of the nation. Music provided her with a language to explore these questions of identity and became her answer as well. The search for an American identity, for a personal and meaningful way of understanding her changing world, for authenticity, and for a viable spirituality coalesced in her attempts to use Native American and African American folk songs to create an American music.

Although the West often beckoned Curtis she repeatedly returned to New York City. Her hometown not only offered the comforts of family and friends but had become, by the early decades of the twentieth century, a "magnet attracting and concentrating the talents of a nation," in Ann Douglas's words. The city served as the country's cultural capital, as the center for the creation and consumption of art, literature, and music. Because of its position at the center of American cultural production, as Matthew Guterl notes, New York had also become the focal point for discussions of race and American culture in the 1910s and 1920s. Like other young artists Curtis continually returned to New York for the intellectual and artistic stimulation it offered.[3]

One attractive New York outlet for Curtis was the *Craftsman Magazine*, the organ of the Arts and Crafts movement. She wrote a number of articles for the magazine, much of her work reflecting the Arts and Crafts ideals upon which this periodical was based. She shared with other Americans the anxieties and concerns that attracted people to this movement and found within it many of the same answers. She distinguished herself from many fellow Arts and Crafts adherents, however, by incorporating her ideas about the music and art of Native Americans and African Americans into this vision for society.

The *Craftsman Magazine* (1901–16), one of the major periodicals of the American Arts and Crafts movement, was founded by the furniture manufacturer Gustav Stickley (1858–1942) to promote his products and spread his ideas. The periodical moved from Syracuse to New York City in 1905. Stickley had introduced an Arts and Crafts–style furniture line at his factory and wanted to promote it through a magazine devoted to "better art and a more human society." Benefiting from a boom in the magazine subscription industry, especially among "house organs" used by manufacturers like Stickley, he developed his ideas with little knowledge or experience in publishing. The periodical grew in size and scope through its move to Manhattan in 1905, incorporating a variety of topics within its pages.[4]

The *Craftsman* promoted handcrafted goods and upheld the "dignity of labor" and the value of simplicity. Stickley provided readers with plans for houses, furniture, and craft projects, along with ads for his own line of household goods. He also espoused the notion of simplicity in decorative design and lifestyle, stressing a return to nature and strenuous living. The magazine sought to develop higher tastes in art among its readers, particularly for handcrafted goods. The journal often featured American Western themes. The regular contributions of George Wharton James, a popular speaker on Indian topics and the author of *What the White Man May Learn from the Indian*, along with reports and studies on Western Native Americans, shaped the magazine. Other contributors, like Frederick Monsen and Curtis, admired and sympathized with Southwestern Indians and argued that whites in the Arts and Crafts movement could learn much from Native American artistic production and design.[5]

The *Craftsman* grew out of and represented a broader Arts and Crafts movement that had its origins in the social and cultural transformations of the late nineteenth and early twentieth centuries. The historian Eileen Boris examines the development of this movement in the United States from its British origins, based on the ideas of John Ruskin and William Morris. She argues that the "craftsman ideal" was a reaction to industrialization, urbanization, and modernization — against the growth of "bureaucratized corporate structure in the context of capitalist social relations." Between 1880 and 1920 Americans witnessed the creation of a new world, one that was more centralized, urban, and heterogeneous. The decline of the family farm, the artisan's workshop, and the small town, along with increases in the numbers of wage laborers, white-collar workers, and mass-produced consumer goods, concerned growing numbers of Americans, particularly the educated middle classes. In this context Arts and Crafts ideas that criticized the new corporate structure and offered solutions in the familiar guise of handicrafts and simplicity appealed to many. Adherents sought a "new wholism" by uniting art and labor, as a means of counteracting the fragmentations that had "destroyed beauty in the process of degrading work." These notions were expressed through Arts and Crafts societies; through efforts to revive traditional folk art, particularly among immigrant and Appalachian women; and through attempts to organize commercial enterprises along craftsman ideals. Magazines like the *Craftsman* spread these ideas to a diverse group of people in search of alternatives to those offered by the modern industrial world.[6]

The Arts and Crafts movement served as just one outlet for Americans disillusioned with the modern world and in search of ways to express their disenchantment. In *No Place of Grace: Antimodernism and the Transformation of American Culture* T. J. Jackson Lears examines the social and cultural conditions that made journals like the *Craftsman* attractive. Lears sees antimodernism as an ambiguous movement of a diverse group of educated upper- and middle-class Americans who questioned the basis of their modern industrial society and sought alternatives in medieval, Oriental, and artisanal traditions. Many believed that America had become "overcivilized" and sought more "authentic experiences" that promised to rejuvenate them and their society. In many ways antimodernists responded to the anxieties of their class — they feared labor unrest and the threat of radicalism, and they expressed uneasiness with Americans' growing racial and ethnic diversity. By controlling these groups many adherents sought to quell these fears. Further, antimodernists feared that modernization came at the price of individual autonomy and worried that personal identities had fragmented. They turned to movements like Arts and Crafts because they promised, Lears contends, "to reintegrate selfhood by resurrecting the authentic experience of manual labor."[7]

Although in many ways antimodernist ideas began as a challenge to and critique of American culture and society, Lears argues that "antimodernists unwittingly allowed modern culture to absorb and defuse their dissent." Their turn to premodern and artisanal traditions, for example, often showed little concern for laborers or for the "primitive" people they supposedly admired. Rather than pursue their challenge to the corporate system by offering a viable alternative for themselves, as well as working-class and minority groups, most antimodernists chose to pursue their own social, cultural, and especially economic interests. Antimodernist undertakings, like the Arts and Crafts movement, often degenerated into nothing more than a therapeutic means of coping with life in an urban, industrial, modern world, not a means for changing it. In their quest for "real life" antimodernists came to focus only on the self, with the unintended result, as Lears asserts, of easing the "transition to secular and corporate modes of modern culture."[8]

Throughout her career Curtis partook of many of the activities and ideas that Lears terms "antimodernism," but her story adds an additional dimension to this search for understanding and identity. The influence of race on her thinking, particularly a romanticized and essentialized image of blacks and Indians, suggests that not all Americans regarded Native Americans and African Americans with fear, contempt, or pity. Curtis, and others like her, struggled with the same cultural dilemmas as other Americans but chose to look to the nation's "folk" for answers to their longings. She found answers in the "American" soil, which had produced the most "American"-sounding music and the most representatively "American" art. Like the writers Sherry Smith examines in *Reimagining Indians,* Curtis represents "a western corollary to earlier views of antimodernism which focused too myopically on the Northeast and Europe."[9] Her search for identity involved a blending of desires for a preindustrial American past with hopes for a future in which Americans benefited from a national culture derived from its most authentic roots.

Curtis had been reacting to many of the same concerns and anxieties that fueled the antimodernist movement since her initial trip to the Southwest. The appeal she found in Zuni corn-grinding or black work songs reflected her idealization of art and work; even the very design of *The Indians' Book,* with its stylized "Indian" lettering, clearly reflected Arts and Crafts ideals. Historians of the movement have acknowledged the attraction of "primitive" cultures, but most have given only passing reference to the role Native American and African American cultures played in the movement or to the ties between craftsman ideals and concerns for Native Americans. Scholars have portrayed antimodernists as unconcerned with alleviating the social conditions of "primitive" peoples, but Curtis's example reveals that not every proponent of these ideas disregarded the rights or the needs of Native Americans.[10] Even so Curtis also promoted Indian artisans as alternative models for overcivilized Americans. Leah Dilworth argues that some adherents of the Arts and Crafts movement, in their revival of "a republican myth of artisanal labor," viewed Native American craftwork as an "antidote to the alienated labor of industrial production." This image of Native people, built upon "claims that authenticity resided in the primitive mind and in primitive culture," led to the notion that white middle-class Americans could revitalize their own culture by "playing Indian."[11] Curtis's work on music further demonstrates the Arts and Crafts fascination with primitive lifestyles and the willingness of the movement's proponents to appropriate aspects of these cultures for their personal identities and for national cultural regeneration.

Many antimodernists idealized the female Native American artist as the embodiment of art integrating with daily life. The *Craftsman* served as one of the few spaces in which Curtis explicitly discussed women. Although her gender certainly affected how (and even why) she collected Native American and African American music, Curtis rarely discussed this topic in her public or private writing. In her *Craftsman* pieces she collected music and folklore from women informants and placed her discussion of art and work within a female context. Surprisingly for someone who had identified as a New Woman from adolescence, Curtis focused on domesticity and motherhood rather than on the more liberating aspects of Native American women's lives that, as Margaret Jacobs discusses, attracted feminists to Southwestern Indians in the 1920s.[12]

Curtis focused on how the lives of Pueblo women reflected the benefits of living close to nature and blending work and art in daily life. In "The Pueblo Singer" Curtis described an early-morning walk in the New Mexican pueblo of Laguna during which she heard a "strange and lovely" melody from women grinding corn. One singer explained that they had songs for different times of the day and for different types of work. Curtis was struck by the way "this brown-skin child of nature" lived "all her life in harmony with the cosmic world around her." These women in Laguna possessed the key to meaningful living, integrating beauty into their work and living in tune with nature. Native American women's connection to nature deepened in motherhood. In "The Song of the Indian Mother" Curtis declared, "To the American Indian woman, herself a part of nature, motherhood is the natural flowering of life, as natural as that the blossom should follow the bud." From the squash-blossom hair whorls of Hopi maidens to the lullabies sung to their children, Native American women expressed their intimacy with nature. Curtis's analysis of several lullabies explained how one could hear the sea in the "low-toned monotonous song of the waves" in Kwakiutl lullabies, or the "song of the bee in sunshine" in the lullabies of Plains mothers. Indians so integrated themselves in nature that they unwittingly expressed it in their most intimate forms of music, songs sung to their beloved children.[13]

Following a now-familiar strategy Curtis urged *Craftsman* readers to translate their appreciation for the lessons Native Americans could teach them into increased respect and expanded rights for Indians. She wanted readers to recognize Native Americans' humanity and to support efforts to preserve and respect their cultures. "If the Indian's sense of justice, his fortitude, and his religious spirit compel our respect," she argued, "so his truth in human relations, his loyalty in friendship, and his devoted parenthood should win our sympathy."[14] In an article on Northwestern Indian mythology she insisted that European Americans "must put ourselves in the Indian's place, for the elements, the animals and the natural world are so close to the Indian that all are endowed with personality." Once outsiders understood the beauty of these traditions, once the power and beauty of Northwestern art became apparent, they would have no other choice but to preserve and develop these art forms. Curtis asked, "Why not, in civilizing these crude and natural artists, wood-carvers, and singers, — why not train a few of them to occupations, crafts, and industries in which use could be made of native gifts?"[15] By providing Native American youth with a similar educational program to that proposed for European American proponents of the Arts and Crafts movement, Curtis demonstrated that she sought more than the appropriation of Native American cultures for European American use; she desired to make Indians beneficiaries of this movement as well.

The application of Arts and Crafts ideas to the education of European American children in the East also attracted Curtis's interest. She completed a series of essays on Stickley and his proposal for a country school for boys founded on craftsman principles near his home in Morris Plains, New Jersey.[16] Curtis explained the goals and benefits of Stickley's Morris Plains farm and the ideas of its founder to *Craftsman* readers and made explicit connections between this endeavor and her research into Native American cultures.

Visiting Craftsman Farms on a hot June day in 1910 to learn more about the educational ideals of Stickley and his proposed school, Curtis remembered the words of an elderly Native American man who asked, "Of what avails the wisdom of the 'talking leaves' if when a man must stand alone he is helpless as a babe?" As Stickley escorted her through the cottages, gardens, and orchards, he remarked that life in the country taught people lessons they could never learn in books or in the city. He hoped to create an environment that upheld the values of simple living, provided opportunities for "higher needs," brought people in touch with the natural world, and fostered beauty in everyday life. By combining instruction with the practice "of *doing something useful* with brains and hands" on the farms, he believed students would learn to seek out the knowledge they needed for real life. Students alternating work on the farm and studies in the classroom would learn "independence of thought and creative initiative." Most important, they would learn to live meaningful lives in the real world because of their close contact with nature and the practical aspects of their education. Curtis drew comparisons between Stickley's goals and her idealization of Native American life. She again quoted the wise Indian man: "It seems to us Indians that you white people know nothing of the real world. You do not understand the animals, the trees and flowers, the wind and streams. To the Indian, all these things speak; from them and from the mountains and the stars come to man the messages of Tirawa, the One above."[17]

Curtis saw much similarity between Stickley's approach to education and her experiences among Native Americans. Indians had taught her the benefits of connecting mental and physical labor. These "superb types of physical humanity" possessed sharper senses and more endurance than whites while still being intellectually alert. "Nature has taught them all they know," she argued, but "they are the people of yesterday." White Americans now needed to combine their intellectual capacity with the Indians' ability to learn from nature. If whites could find a "true balance between the physical life and the intellectual," then "each may serve the other toward a common end — progress."[18] Indians, however, could teach European Americans even more.

Craftsman ideals about adapting architecture to the natural environment and the practical needs of a house's inhabitants also appealed to Curtis and reminded her of the Native American homes she had often admired. The log house on Craftsman Farms attracted her because it combined the primitivism of the rustic cabin with the needs of modern living. The house used local materials and blended in with its surroundings, thereby connecting its occupants more fully with the natural world and providing an ideal haven for family life. The same results could be achieved in other parts of America as well. Curtis visited such a home in southern California during a family vacation in 1913. The "Hilerô" in La Jolla possessed "unusual individuality and charm" because it blended in with its environment and evoked the romantic past of the Spanish missions. The architect, Curtis's longtime friend Frank Mead, explained that a "house should be an absolute expression of the soil. It should be an intrinsic part of the landscape, a harmonious note in the whole geographical song." This structure, inspired by local material and design, allowed the natural world inside and combined an appreciation for the artistic with awareness of the practical needs of its inhabitants. This architecture showed Curtis the possibilities of extending these ideals to other areas of American life and culture. The designers, by drawing from indigenous resources, had succeeded in creating a unique work of art that expressed American ideals.[19]

This concern for an art that reflected an American identity became a personal one for Curtis in her marriage to the modernist painter Paul Burlin. Somewhat unexpectedly, considering her dedication to her work and her determination to be an independent woman, Curtis decided to wed. Less surprising was the manner in which she described their relationship — as one of shared commitments to art, intellectual and spiritual compatibility, and mutual support for the other's career. Interestingly, love and attraction were seldom cited by Curtis as she shared her good news with family and friends. Burlin and Curtis's marriage, however, reflected newfound modernist ideas about love and relationships, which stressed that "shared artistic or political labor became a requirement of love," according to Christine Stansell.[20] "I have at last found the 'Great Happiness,'" Curtis exclaimed to her aunt Natalie Stacey, in the "well-known New York painter whom I met in New Mexico last summer and who was a member of our camping-party for many months." The "intimacies" of camp life had brought the two together in the spring of 1916, and although they had known each other for less than a year, "a great certainty" convinced Curtis that they were meant for each other. She confided that, despite appearances to the contrary, she had waited a long time for a relationship like this, one based on "sound friendship, mutual aims, and absolute intellectual and spiritual rapport." Curtis understood that the family would have preferred a marriage to a "rich banker! or some version of the well-to-do and 'tired businessman,'" but she admitted, "I could never have been really happy with anyone but an artist of some kind, because my whole make-up demands that kind of understanding and rapport since I myself am built that way!" Even better, "my people as well as my friends *like* Paul," especially her brother George.[21]

Burlin, born in New York City in 1886, had spent part of his youth in England. He returned to New York and worked as a commercial artist for the *Delineator* magazine, referring to this work as "the usual drudgery" and a "period of doing stinkweed decorations." Burlin attended the National Academy of Design briefly and then studied in Paris, Brittany, and parts of Italy in 1910. Later describing this as a "period of incoherence and drifting," the young artist returned to New York. Friends encouraged him to submit some of his paintings to the Armory Show in 1913. Burlin sought something deeper, something more "primitive," and upon the advice of some romantically inclined friends he traveled to the Southwest to find it. There the "first glimmerings of an esthetic vision" struck the painter, and he began incorporating Native design into "a modern expression." Burlin deliberately avoided Taos, disliking its "commercial picture-making," and settled in Santa Fe, "with its unspoiled peace and quiet." Traveling on horseback he took in "the primeval, erosive, forbidding character of the landscape" and tried to learn more about local Native Americans, who both fascinated and frightened him. Burlin claimed he listened to their chants, saw "strange ceremonial rites," and was "entranced by his [Native American] witchdoctor and the whole aspect of the metaphysical propitiation of the forces of nature." He wanted to capture the "configurations that were indigenous to the character of the land," discover a way to translate what he saw in Native design into modern forms, and bring his study of Fauvism and Expressionist styles to the picturesque landscape and people of the Southwest.[22]

Curtis's good news of her marriage to this artist met with mixed responses from her family and friends. Although all shared in her joy and excitement, the wedding surprised some people who had never expected Curtis to embrace matrimony. The Southwest promoter and writer Charles Lummis replied to Curtis's announcement, "I had not prevision of any such news as I have just received," but he expressed his pleasure at her new happiness and invited the couple for a visit. Lummis, however, confided in his diary: "Yesterday brought the astonishing announcement that N.C. has married with a young man in Santa Fe. I don't know whether he is young or not. But he Draws a Good Girl — and I would little have suspected her of such freaks at her age [she was forty-one]." The anthropologist Aleš Hrdlička was more understanding. He extended to Curtis's mother, Augusta, his hope that the marriage "will lead to that calm happiness which she is in need of and which she so much deserves."[23]

After announcing their engagement and obtaining the blessings of Curtis's family and patrons, the couple planned a Southwestern wedding for the summer of 1916. They wanted to marry immediately, but health and financial circumstances postponed their nuptials. Burlin struggled financially and also suffered from tuberculosis (which later excused him from military service). Curtis's health also faltered that fall and forced Burlin to place her under George Curtis's care in San Diego. After regaining their health that winter the couple returned east and obtained in person the family's consent to wed. Curtis explained that because of "the uncertainty of these war times" they followed "my little Mother's level-headed advice" and planned to marry quietly in Santa Fe in the summer of 1917. Wedding announcements, designed by the couple and featuring a Southwestern scene of mountains and pueblos, informed friends and family of their marriage on the twenty-fifth of July.[24]

Curtis's family may have outwardly approved of the marriage, for Natalie's sake, but they harbored reservations about Paul Burlin. After the wedding Augusta Curtis wrote to her son George, hinting that more than the war and finances had led Curtis to opt for a quiet wedding in Santa Fe rather than in New York. Augusta told George that she had sent out about a thousand announcements and that "Paul's list included many Goldbergs, Frybergs ... — not in the Social Register." She was relieved that Curtis had foreseen the potential awkwardness of the situation and "out of the generosity of her heart [had the wedding in Santa Fe] ... instead of at home knowing that the Montagues and Capulets would not blend in a NY wedding." A bit of elitism and perhaps anti-Semitism clouded the Curtis family's relationship with Burlin. His inability to fully support Curtis and the ten-year age difference added to their misgivings. Augusta also concealed a low opinion of her son-in-law's paintings from her daughter. She wrote to George's wife, Lora, about an exhibition of Burlin's work in New York in 1918. She expressed her hope that "people will like [it] better than I do" and pronounced, "His picture of George was the worst thing I have ever seen bar none." But even Augusta admitted, "They seem to be very congenial, and I hope they may have many years of happiness together."[25]

Curtis and Burlin's happiness seemed quite genuine; their shared commitment to art as a revitalizing force and their common interest in primitivism in the Southwest seem to have been the foundation of their relationship. Curtis explained this bond to Hollis Frissell just before the wedding. Reassuring the Hampton principal that marriage would not interfere with her collection of African American folk music, she suggested that their relationship would actually enhance her research. She believed in the compatibility of their work: "it is one of my dearest wishes that Mr. Burlin and I go South together where he could put the American Negro into American art" while she preserved their songs for American national music. "It would be ideal," she declared, "if I could work at the music while he paints!" Curtis sent along clippings about her fiancé's work, explaining that "as Mr. Burlin and his work are *one*, I enclose some of the critiques of his paintings of Indians made last summer." Curtis was proud of her husband, believing him to be among "the strongest figure[s] in modern American art today," and had the utmost enthusiasm for their work together.[26]

The clippings that Curtis enclosed described Burlin as "one of the few important painters of the country." Many of the critics, writing for the *New York Times,* the *New York Evening Post,* and the *Christian Science Monitor,* praised his ability to paint Native Americans, to capture the "primitive nature" of Southwestern Indians, and to give "the impression of seeing through Indian eyes." It requires little imagination to understand Curtis's attraction to Burlin and his art. Both of them were drawn to New Mexico for similar reasons. He first arrived in Santa Fe in 1913, right after exhibiting at the famous Armory Show in New York City that introduced Americans to the radically new ideas of European modernist art and served, in one historian's words, as "shock treatment that transported them to the plane of the avant-garde present." Burlin's familiarity with modernist trends in the art world prepared him "to interpret the landscape and people of the Southwest very differently from the traditional renderings of his contemporaries." Like Curtis and many other artists and writers who found their way to this region, Burlin was captivated by the stunning scenery and by the even more fascinating people who inhabited the land.[27]

Curtis and Burlin planned an active, artistic life living and working together in the Santa Fe community. Many other artists and writers joined them in this northern New Mexico artists' haven. The Santa Fe and Taos art colonies, along with the Eastern colonies of Woodstock, Provincetown, and MacDowell, were part of a broader movement of people rejecting city life in favor of living close to nature. Although part of this tradition, the two Southwestern communities, according to the historian Arrell M. Gibson, were unique in the length of their existence, the size of their populations, and their efforts to function as viable communities. In addition to the special appeal they held for women like Curtis, the landscape and people of New Mexico attracted those who desired an escape from European influences and other traditions that prevented the creation of a new American art form. Both Santa Fe and Taos were small, isolated towns at the beginning of the twentieth century, when writers and artists first began arriving. This isolation itself was part of their initial appeal. Changes in the art world, particularly the decline of commercial outlets for painters, brought to the region more people who were attracted by the cheaper cost of living. Santa Fe and Taos drew artists who hoped to create American art apart from the rigid demands of the National Academy; who shared the communities' openness and celebration of pluralism; and who expressed alienation and "bitter contempt for progress, and a glowering impatience with society." The relatively low cost of living and the invigorating climate, both important factors for Curtis and Burlin, coupled with the breathtaking scenery, multiethnic population, acceptance of artists, and atmosphere of timelessness, made this region quite popular with those who sought artistic and spiritual renewal.[28]

Curtis and Burlin evinced a strong commitment to the Santa Fe artistic community. Upon her marriage to Burlin, Natalie Curtis, who had a much longer history in the region, decided to live and work in Santa Fe on a more permanent basis. During the winter of 1919 she purchased a home with some of the proceeds from an inheritance. She told George Foster Peabody that she could buy a house for around eight hundred dollars and that, because the town was "booming as a summer tourist resort," she expected to make a profit on her purchase. By May 1920 the couple had purchased "a tiny Mexican house" to which they began inviting friends and colleagues. "My slice of land," she explained to her brother George, held a house with a studio, a bath, running water, a phone, and electric lights. Although their home was a bit drafty (they slept outdoors all summer anyway), she assured George that if he came to live with her that summer they would have a "jolly time" together in Santa Fe.[29]

Paul Burlin thrived in their Southwest community. He traveled around New Mexico painting and periodically exhibited his works locally and in New York City. Generally his paintings, Augusta's opinions to the contrary, were well received by critics. The art historian Sharyn Udall contends that Burlin was well aware of his position as the leading modernist in the region. His sense of responsibility in this role led him to participate in many local artistic events and to take part in activities at Santa Fe's art museum. He also maintained his ties with trends in modern art and the New York City art world, exhibiting his Southwestern work, for example, at the 1917 exhibition of the Society of Independent Artists. Burlin later wrote that Curtis had helped him improve his insights into Native culture. Curtis brought him with her when she collected Indian ceremonies, chants, and rituals and offered her own insights into Native American artistic design.[30]

Curtis supported Burlin's work and shared his desire to create a distinctive American art form from Native American and Western material. She publicized his art and elucidated his goals to the public. In 1917 she introduced him to the readers of *International Studio* as a "painter whom the war kept at home" but who had discovered in his own country inspiration "directly in line with the whole trend of modern art." In New Mexico and Arizona Burlin had become "an interpreter who brings to his task the reverence of the thinker as well as the talent of the artist." His work expressed the feeling and power of the land and gave personality to the grandeur of the Southwest. Curtis especially highlighted Burlin's Native American pieces, claiming he provided "worthy utterance" for the "primitive soul of the brown-skinned native race" as no other artist could. "Here are not stage Indians," Curtis asserted, "no melodramatic poses, no sentimental conventions about the 'Noble Savage.'" Instead Burlin captured the "real Indian, strong and silent," "stoic, reserved, self-contained, baffling and impenetrable." Although this description reminds one of a stereotypical "Indian," Curtis seemed to be insisting that Burlin refused to romanticize his Indian subjects, that he tried to capture their human essences. Curtis argued that Burlin portrayed those qualities that made the region such a promising source of inspiration.[31]

Burlin's work impressed Curtis because they shared the notion that American art and music needed to draw inspiration from the American environment. Curtis argued that when American artists went abroad to develop their art it became stagnant. Before the war "art, like all our civilization, was growing so sophisticated, patterned and platitudinous," she contended, that artists like Burlin hungered for simplification. The "primitive" peoples of the Southwest inspired him. In the Southwest Burlin discovered the "vital stimulus of a land and people still at the dawn period, still close to the roots of things, and *alive* — not belonging to an alien soil, nor to a vanished past." The war may have kept painters in the United States, but Burlin viewed this as a new opportunity. "In the West," Burlin explained, "a *new kind of painting might arise.*" By turning inward Americans could even surpass Europe in the development of modern art. Curtis continued this theme in a 1919 *Southern Workman* piece in which she complained that long contact with Native Americans had still not inspired whites to see their art as an asset to a national culture. "We echo Europe," she lamented, "whereas we might develop a decorative art truly American." Native American artists needed encouragement, not oppression or ridicule, to develop their talents and contribute to a national school of American art and design. Artists like Burlin raised questions about the perils of ignoring the contributions of Indian artistry.[32]

The Burlins saw their work as part of a larger, communal undertaking, along with other artists and writers living in northern New Mexico. Other New Yorkers joined them in the region in search of real experience, authenticity, and inspiration. One of the most significant figures who epitomized this trend was Mabel Dodge, who arrived in the Southwest prepared to discover "unique inspi-

ration." As her biographer Lois Rudnick notes, Dodge found "a
world of individuals rooted in communities whose traditions were
life-enhancing and, therefore, worth protecting and learning from."
Then newly married to the artist Maurice Sterne, who encouraged
her to make the move, Dodge arrived in New Mexico in December
1917 in search of relief from the boredom she had felt living in New
York City. In New Mexico she discovered what she believed to be
an almost utopian society; like the Burlins, she argued that the
region provided solutions to the problems of the modern world.
Her husband had befriended the Burlins and admired their role in
the community. "They're more like pioneers," Sterne told Dodge.
"Paul really *sees* the material here. And Natalie Curtis collects Indian
music, you know." Dodge's first impression of Curtis and Burlin
was far less positive. She described their initial meeting as among
"the first really tiresome things that happened" to her upon arrival
in Santa Fe. She provided a meanspirited depiction of Curtis as "a
little old doll that had been left out in the sun and the rain. She had
faded yellow hair, cut in Buster Brown bob, and faded blue eyes."
Although Dodge found Burlin "fresher" and thoughtful, her initial
dislike of the Burlins might have stemmed from the fact that they
were all fleeing New York for similar reasons, all trying to escape
people just like themselves, and all anxious to lay claim to the land
and its people.[33]

Although they shared many of the same attitudes toward Native
art and life, Dodge's disdain for the couple grew from disagreements
over the use of Native American cultures by European Americans.
At a dance at the pueblo of Santo Domingo, Dodge, struck by the
beauty of the landscape and intrigued by the music and dancing,
underwent an epiphany in which she "heard the voice of the One
coming from the Many." After the dance she exclaimed that she
hoped no one else would ever know about the scene she had just
witnessed. Burlin disagreed and claimed, "I think an Art Form like
this should be known to the world, so people could enjoy it." "This

isn't an Art Form," Dodge snapped. "It's much more than that. It's a living religion." Popularization by people like the Burlins would commercialize and cheapen the spirituality of Indian art, Dodge feared, even as she sought to appropriate Pueblo religion for her personal spiritual edification.[34]

Their disagreement also extended to Curtis's collection of Native American music. Dodge, in a description riddled with inaccuracies, recounted a trip with Curtis to an Indian home to collect a song.[35] Curtis arrived at the house and asked for a song. In a "manner that was slightly condescending, as to children," an Indian man whom Dodge referred to as Geronimo repeatedly sang in a gentle voice. "Natalie was listening intently — humming it along with him," Dodge recalled. She described the scene when Geronimo asked Curtis to sing: "She started to sing. She had caught the simple phrase, she had the time and the tune: but not the feeling! She injected something into it that did not belong there. It became sweet, and had a willful virtue in it. Indian music is not sweet, and neither is it moral. She made it sound virtuous, even sentimental — Protestant!" Dodge recalled that the elder Indian smiled kindly while the younger men at his home knowingly smirked at one another. Geronimo replied, "You make a white man's song." He sang it once more for her, a song "strong and gentle, full of life, but quite impersonal." Curtis repeated it once more, but she "couldn't reproduce the sounds the Indian psyche used to utter its meaning of life." Dodge further commented on Curtis: "She *had* to be sweet, resigned, and good, or whatever it was that was coming out of her. What a gulf opened between us in that room! Between the Indians and us." Curtis, Dodge claimed, remained blissfully unaware of this disconnect with her informants and concluded: "I think she never knew the Indians laughed kindly at her way of singing Indian music. She never knew she was unequal to the transcription."[36]

Curtis of course believed herself capable of understanding and translating Indian music. Unlike Dodge, who had met her first Native

Americans just a few weeks before she made the above observations, Curtis strongly believed that other Americans needed to learn Indian songs and use these art forms to create a national cultural identity. Indian songs, for example, could inspire modern poets with their spiritual themes, rhythms, and structure. In *The Path on the Rainbow* Curtis and other European American writers and musicians advanced Indian song as distinctly American poetry.[37] More significant, though, was the potential Native music held for the creation of a national song. She joined with other musicians in what scholars have since dubbed the "Indianist" movement. Beginning in the early 1900s and expanding rapidly in the 1910s, adherents of this movement contended that Native Americans constituted a real "folk" that America had seemed to lack and that the nation needed to look to this "folk" for inspiration.

The "Indianist" movement, largely an Eastern phenomenon, had to draw heavily from the work of ethnomusicologists and folklorists. The collections of Curtis, Alice Fletcher, Frances Densmore, and Frederick Burton inspired the interest of classical composers searching for ways to express American identity and free the United States from the tyranny of European tradition. Many musicians clamored for the use of Indian folk songs as a solution to America's musical backwardness and as a way for composers to make their mark on the musical world. Some of these musicians, including Curtis, also incorporated African American, Appalachian, and "cowboy" songs and motifs into their "American" musical expressions. Much of the focus of this effort, however, remained on the use of Native American music. Composers participating in this movement tended to come from the white upper middle classes, believed in the uplifting power of music, and fought to gain acceptance as professional American musicians. Some voiced concerns over the growing heterogeneity of urban America. Many resented the domineering control the New England elite exerted over the shape and scope of American music. They accused this group of perpetuating musical traditions that represented a very limited vision of the nation and its peoples.[38] Indianist composers and supporters, like Curtis, advanced an image of the United States that found national character in the West, in the spirituality found in nature and by extension in Native Americans, and in the beneficial influences of non-European elements in American culture.

A long-lived concern over a national music in the United States took on special import at the beginning of the twentieth century as the country gained ascendancy as a world power in commerce and industry and flexed its imperialist muscles in places like Cuba and the Philippines. Observers nervously noted that America lagged behind in cultural and artistic pursuits, and many openly wondered if the United States was even capable of developing its own musical idiom. Many pointed to the lack of educational facilities in the United States, which meant that most musicians were trained in Europe and consequently developed a prejudice against American forms of cultural expression. Others noted the lack of a viable folk culture from which Americans, as European composers had done, could draw. It seemed that American composers lacked the experience, training, or desire to develop a national music.[39]

Antonín Dvořák, during his visit to the United States in the 1890s, offered a proposition to musicians seeking a national music in his famous composition *From the New World*. He called for American musicians to make greater use of the music of its distinct peoples, primarily African Americans and Indians. His own experiences with black musicians such as Harry Burleigh and Will Marion Cook — both individuals with whom Curtis later worked — helped inspire Dvořák to use these "folk" themes in his work. Having incorporated folk music into his own compositions and perhaps unaware of the intricacies of American race relations, Dvořák perceived few problems in calling on Americans to do the same.[40]

One of the most significant figures in the Indianist movement, Arthur Farwell, called for American musicians to heed Dvořák's call. In "A Letter to American Composers" in 1903 Farwell foretold of a "new era in American music" that would draw on past traditions and "derive its convincing qualities of color, form, and spirit from our nature-world and our humanity." To develop distinctive American qualities in its music the nation needed to forget about Europe and turn instead to its own traditions and unique qualities. Farwell founded the Wa-Wan Press in 1901 to publish music by American composers, particularly those incorporating melodies and themes of American Indians. The press offered "a broader range of context and an expansion of the expressional vehicle" for American composers finding it difficult to get a hearing elsewhere. Curtis's 1902 publication of *Songs from a Child's Garden of Verses* with Wa-Wan reflected her desire to create an American work. Composers such as Henry Gilbert, Harvey Washington Loomis, and Carlos Troyer, experimenting with Indian or African American themes, published with Farwell's press.[41]

Curtis shared with *Craftsman* readers her thoughts about how American folk songs could form the basis of an American identity and satisfy the antimodernist yearnings of many white middle- and upper-class Americans. The country had its share of musical organizations, "but it is not alone by the established art of the cities that we can judge of the musical impulse of a nation." One must look, Curtis declared, to "the people" as well. Four groups of "folk" existed — Native Americans, African Americans, Appalachian whites, and Western cowboys — whose music was "rich in suggestions and offer[ed] opportunity for valuable research and fascinating study." Curtis asserted that these four types served an important function for a nation struggling to become musical itself. She pointed to the social conditions that limited musical production — the changes in the nature of work, the rise of cities, and the increasingly rapid and harried pace of modern life — but offered hope for the future. "When the seething stress of our young life is over and continuity shall replace the restless and constant change incident to our rapid growth today," she argued, a genius may rise up to reveal the American nature in art and music. This person will be the "true product of all that has gone before him in the making of the nation," and, if a musician, the "flower of his genius . . . may be rooted deeply, though unconsciously, in the folk-music of his native country."[42]

As interest in this musical movement grew, Curtis must have felt gratified to see the fruits of her many years of labor. Her long experiences collecting Indian music, however, forewarned her of the potential criticisms of Indianist music, especially claims that it was too "primitive" or not truly representative of America. Indianist composers realized that they needed to refashion Native Americans as a true American "folk" to justify their use of Indian song. Curtis often argued that Native Americans, because of their proximity to nature, created true folk music. Others justified its use as an American folk music by arguing that Native song was "indigenous and is on that account the only true folk music that America is entitled to claim." Composers trying to craft a national song, they argued, needed to express the character of the land and the impact that the American soil exerted on its inhabitants regardless of race or ethnicity.[43] Charles Wakefield Cadman, an opera composer who used Indian songs and themes, asserted that "the folk-song that we *have* attempted to idealize has sprung into existence on the American continent." Not only did this music spring up from the land, but it also expressed the history and natural distinctiveness of the United States. Cadman wrote that the "inconquerable spirit of the Redman" could still be felt in the "awesome canyons, the majestic snow-capped peaks and the voiceless and beautiful solitude of the desert." In *The Indians' Book* Curtis implored her readers to "pause in the stress of our modern life and listen to the ancient lore of our own land." This ability of Indian music to connect listeners to the history and landscape of America offered one of the strongest attractions for Indianist composers. It also provided a

drastic contrast to modern American life. Native peoples offered
cultural and spiritual authority rooted in the past and could stand
in as the nation's ancestors. This allowed Americans like Curtis to
address their growing perceptions of moral stagnation and lack of
spirituality in a society that increasingly seemed to have less and
less in common with its past traditions.[44]

Although Curtis encouraged other musicians to develop and use
Native American music, she remained wary of those who lacked
sufficient knowledge or concern for the groups from which they
borrowed. Many Indianists believed Native American music to
be inferior to their own and thought it needed "idealization" to
be acceptable. Frederick Burton, for example, argued that whites
failed to understand Indian music, not because they lacked adequate
knowledge of Indian life, but because Indian music had not fully
developed. Until composers harmonized Indian tunes, Burton
argued, few listeners would ever comprehend Indian music. He
even suggested that musicians forgo their reliance on original Indian
songs and instead develop their own styles based on themes inspired
by Indian song and legend. Charles Wakefield Cadman, in "The
'Idealization' of Indian Music," asserted that composers needed to
complete or "idealize" original Indian songs before placing them
into art music. He agreed that knowledge of Indian traditions and
legends served the composer well, but he did not value actual contact with American Indians, and he even suggested that it was not
necessary to hear the actual singing of an Indian song before using
it. Even he cautioned, though, against thoughtless and incomplete
use of Indian melodies. He rejected the premise that "taking an
Indian melody and pasting some chords to it and calling the stuff
'Sitting Bull's last Glimpse of his Squaw' constituted an American
work of art."[45]

Curtis agreed with Cadman's warning and made a further
distinction between the Indian music that she collected and the
"Indian" music she believed many composers tried to pass off on an

uninformed public. "Using an Indian theme as the suggestion for a musical composition is a very different thing," she contended, "from harmonizing Indian melodies and calling that 'Indian music.'" If a musician collected a song from a tribal member, she expected the composition to reproduce exactly what the informant had sung. Curtis strenuously objected to the harmonization of Native songs, particularly because "these inevitably distorted versions" were often portrayed as authentic Indian renderings. No matter the intended use of an Indian song or theme, the white musician had certain obligations to the music and its original creators. Curtis further cautioned composers to recognize that music remained a vital force among Native Americans. Many songs had sacred meanings or should be sung only at certain times and places. Others belonged to individuals or special groups and could not be sung by other people. Composers, Curtis warned, should take no Indian song lightly.[46]

Some Indianist composers agreed with Curtis's calls for more responsible use of Native American melodies and themes in their works. Some musicians insisted on living among Native peoples to truly understand their music and legends. For instance, Arthur Nevin, the composer of several English-language operas based on Indian themes, argued that "to have the real awakening that Indian music is capable of producing one should actually live with and take part in the everyday life." Nevin found Indian music thrilling in its possibilities for creating an American music and rejuvenating the nation. The "weird charm" of Blackfeet melodies connected him with nature, and his experiences during his stay made him feel more alive than ever before. Nevin incorporated this authentic experience into his compositions as a sort of antimodernist reaction to his society.[47]

Farwell too lamented misuse of Indian music by white artists. He joined Curtis in the contention that musicians needed to break "through the barriers of traditional secrecy, native reticence, and long justified suspicion." "It is difficult for us," he continued, "surrounded and protected as we are on every hand by every species of artifice known to civilized man, to understand, or rather to feel that native and enveloping sense of intimacy with the elements in which the Indian lives." Curtis agreed with Farwell's assertion, but her solution to this quandary differed greatly from those offered by Farwell and other Indianists. She contended that musicians should allow Native Americans to express themselves and encourage them to develop their own music. As an illustration of how to do this Curtis described the participation of Pueblo Indians from San Ildefonso in the dedication of the New Mexico Museum of Art in Santa Fe. Curtis served as the spokesperson for a group that wanted to "show the white man what Indian dances really are, and what Indian songs express." The audience, she reported, responded enthusiastically to the performance. The goal of finding "in the art of the red man as keen an inspiration as any offered by the dance and song of the Old World" was met by allowing Native people to perform their songs and dances in their own way.[48]

Curtis also believed that composers, folklorists, and ethnomusicologists needed better training and more concern for their informants so that the original melodies and meanings would not become distorted in Indianist compositions. In "Recording for Posterity the Music of Primitive Humanity" she defined the ideal collector of folk music: "If there is one in whom love of art and love of science should unite in the quest of truth that being should be the humble folk-lorist." Curtis believed that her many years of experience had taught her to bridge the gap between the artistic inclinations of Indianist composers and the scientific motives of anthropologists. Curtis also stressed "a sensitive musical intuition" as a useful attribute for musicians who worked with non-Western musical forms. She noted that science had taught her to evaluate music based on a realization of what the singers hoped to achieve, not on adherence to white standards. A student of primitive song should approach "naïve humanity . . . not with a flourish of the dissecting knife but with the warm hand of ready and understanding friendship." Indians and African Americans, or any other group from which one hoped to collect material, had to be treated like human beings, not data.[49]

Technical skills, determination, "resourcefulness, tact, and the patience that smiles on disappointment," as well as a willingness to work with little immediate reward — all were attributes a folk music collector needed. Folklorists must also realize their rather insignificant role in the lives of these people. "They are not," Curtis argued, "looking for any Messianic coming of the folk-lorist to save their tradition." Unless a collector approached them with sympathy and understanding, "primitive" peoples would never share their music, art, or stories. Working with people she considered her friends made the process feel collaborative for Curtis. "To all of us," she recalled of a group of Hopi singers, "folk-lore recording was a cooperative effort to save on paper a fast-vanishing bit of native art." Curtis argued that "primitive" people were well aware of the intentions of outside recorders. Many collectors claimed no folk music existed because few Native people trusted them enough to share their songs. She had recently noticed among potential informants "an up-to-date suspicion that the singers will be exploited for some vast money-making enterprise." Curtis believed it all the more critical then that composers, anthropologists, and folklorists approach these groups with sincerity and sympathy, not just to fulfill their own selfish needs.[50]

Although Curtis primarily collected and preserved Native American songs as sung to her by her informants, she too produced compositions based on Native themes. These works shared the Indianists' goals of expressing "American" music, but Curtis tried to use her compositions and their performances as a means to improve the lives of Native peoples. With her husband she created a play entitled *American Indian Dance Pageant* that brought together her research into Native American cultures with their desire for shared creative expression. In the spring of 1919 Curtis pitched this plan to the anthropologist Francis LaFlesche. She explained that she hoped to gather a group of Pueblos for "an artistic mission to the white man, to show Washington and the public at large what the Indian poetic and musical rituals really are." Having secured the "financial guarantee of several of our most public spirited American citizens," including her patron George Foster Peabody, Curtis and Burlin planned to bring eight Pueblos from San Ildefonso — the same dancers who had performed at the Santa Fe museum dedication the previous year — east for a series of performances. They planned for initial shows in New York and Boston and hoped for more in Chicago, Detroit, St. Paul, Kansas City, and Denver on the trip home. Curtis also proposed a private performance for the president, his cabinet, and other high-ranking officials. She was optimistic about receiving favorable press coverage and expected the performance to easily draw audiences because it showcased "the worth and dignity of this Indian offering."[51]

To exert the influence she sought, Curtis recognized the need for careful planning. She explained to LaFlesche that she hoped to form committees of patrons in each city to insure support and guarantee the performances. Museums, art galleries, and prominent citizens could lend financial and structural assistance. Curtis vowed that the high aims of the performances would not be forgotten in the quest to fill seats. Native American music and dance would retain all its dignity, and Native art "will be placed in the position which it should occupy in this country." To fulfill this goal Curtis wanted to select patrons carefully. She asked LaFlesche and the ethnomusicologist Alice Fletcher, who worked closely with him, if they would serve on an advance committee along with Peabody, Curtis, and the banker and art patron Otto Kahn. Curtis expected to hire a professional manager to estimate the costs and help with the initial planning. One manager had already promised her this would be a "tremendous awakening to the American people and would do a great deal of good." Curtis had other reasons for optimism as well. Her husband would paint the scene settings, which would provide "that spirit of reverence which would lift it entirely out of the domain of any theatrical exploitation." The dancers from San Ildefonso, personal friends of Curtis, clearly understood the purpose of this undertaking and fully supported it, Curtis assured LaFlesche. The current vogue for Indianist music and art would help draw audiences and support.[52]

She anticipated that her Indian music and dance drama would speak to larger concerns about the nation's musical and artistic culture and identity. Americans, she claimed, had grown accustomed to hearing "there is no Art in America." "Nothing is further from the truth," Curtis countered. She claimed that among those "who sprang from the soil of this great continent there is an Art complete, beautiful, and unlike any other in the world." Past policies of assimilation and destruction threatened these art forms. "Pictorially, musically, and dramatically this Art summons those who recognize it to utter a plea for its salvation," she stated, especially Indians of the Southwest. Curtis expected other Americans to join in preserving "this priceless artistic legacy" and to recognize in Native dance the same appeal Americans currently celebrated in Russian and Japanese expressions. Once people witnessed these rarely seen "dance-dramas of such solemn beauty and poetry," they would recognize the contributions of Native Americans to the nation's cultural identity.[53]

Curtis planned a performance she alternately entitled *American Indian Dance Pageant* or *The Deer Dance*. In many ways this work was far more complex than previous undertakings. The score called for an assortment of instrumentation, particularly by percussion pieces. It also contained very detailed instructions for the dancers, who were to represent hunters, maidens, deer, buffalo, and elemental forces of nature, including one dancer who would symbolize "a dramatized cloud-burst" at the climax of the dance. To keep the drama "truly Indian in character" Curtis planned elaborate staging and costuming. Burlin would employ his painting skills and experience with Native people to create authentic scenery and costumes. Both Curtis and Burlin hoped to present "an electrifying glimpse into the life and spirit of native America" that would speak to larger desires to create an American art form without losing the "strongly original racial quality which must permeate the production."[54]

Curtis placed herself in the familiar role of interpreter of Native American music and art to a white audience. As in her other writing Curtis missed the irony in the fact that she, a non-Indian, was composing an authentically "Indian" play or that this "dance-drama" did not reflect actual Pueblo practices. Because few Americans knew anything about Pueblo culture, Curtis would lecture on Southwestern history, archaeology, and art. As the dance began she would interpret the symbolism and comment on the "song-life" of Pueblo people. Curtis planned to showcase the "striking examples of ancient communal forms of civic and tribal organization" and the "high degree of culture" these groups had retained from before white contact. *The Deer Dance* would confirm that Native culture "offers inspiration almost fantastic in its wealth of interest and color" and that Indian songs were "unequaled for splendor of rhythm and for inspiring and barbaric music." She hoped to "transmit this extraordinary native American pageantry into art-form, condensing the most striking features of these dance-dramas into a short one-act dance-pageant, to be performed upon the white man's stage."[55]

This "dance-pageant" drew from Pueblo myth and attempted to use Native ideas to express themes with which all Americans could identify. As the audience waited for the curtain to rise, Curtis would relate the legend of a drought- and famine-stricken community desperate for food and water in which a Pueblo spiritual leader dreams of "two of the fairest maidens" journeying to nearby mountains to entice deer and buffalo to their village. Then the

curtain would rise upon a group of dancers in a kiva, an underground ceremonial chamber. Village elders would anxiously discuss
sending two young women to fulfill the prophecy. The pair would
leave the village, and the next scene would reveal the triumphant
return of the "Deer Maidens," followed by herds of dancing animals
and greeted with joyful dancing by the grateful villagers. The next
scene, a reenactment of the hunt through "pantomimic gestures,"
would symbolize forces of nature and the Rain-Spirits or Katzinas.
A glorious celebration of dance would close the pageant as the
much-needed rain fell from the sky.[56]

The Deer Dance in many ways reflected the Indianist operas
popularized by Charles Wakefield Cadman, Arthur Nevin, and
Victor Herbert. These works also symbolized spiritual and emotional themes in stylized music and dance and drew their plots
from romantic, "Indianized" myths and legends. They made similar
claims to authenticity but rarely included Native American participants in their efforts to provide "peculiar character and 'color'" to
American theater.[57] However, Curtis wanted this pageant to do
more than simply entertain Eastern audiences; she hoped it would
change Indian policy and give Native Americans a voice in their
representations, even if one mediated through her.[58]

The pageant Curtis proposed to LaFlesche in 1919 probably never
occurred on the grand scale Curtis proposed. She did take additional
steps to bring this work to fruition and quite probably would have
staged it had she not died in the fall of 1921. Curtis had *American
Indian Dance Pageant* copyrighted in 1921 and deposited a copy of
the score in the Library of Congress. She contracted with the ballet
dancer and choreographer Adolph Bolm in February 1921. Bolm
had watched Native American dances with Curtis and had danced
for the Indians in return. He hoped to produce Curtis's "ballet" in
the United States, Canada, and Europe, and she agreed to lease it
to him under certain conditions. Bolm promised to "observe as
far as possible the American Indian racial character of the work"

and to allow Curtis to be present at rehearsals. Burlin received the rights to paint backdrops for the productions, and both he and Curtis would advise Bolm on costuming and other details. No records of any such performance have been discovered. Although *The Deer Dance* probably never made it to the stage, it still speaks to the cultural significance of the use of pageantry to give Native Americans a voice and of incorporating Native American music into a national artistic expression.[59]

Curtis composed less grandiose musical works based on Native American themes whose performances she did witness. Besides directly contributing to Busoni's *Indian Fantasy* in 1915, which she enthusiastically endorsed, Curtis composed small pieces that were performed in New York City. The Musical Art Society of New York featured among its April 13, 1920, offerings *Three Songs of North America*, by Curtis. It included two pieces based on Native American tunes and a "Cowboy Song." In the latter song Curtis hoped to capture the image of the American cowboy — the "strong, bronzed and a little uncouth, but graceful [figure] with the poise of perfect muscular development and daringly self-reliant through the freedom of life under the open heavens." Her own friendships with "cowpunchers" and "bull-whackers," made during her many trips to the West, especially with her brother George in Arizona, prepared her specifically for this musical task. "Cowboy Song" featured the "typical" refrain of "Ti yippy yippy yah" and tried to re-create the distinctive drawl of Westerners. Curtis recalled her time among cowboys: "It was a grim, monotonous existence, but somehow it was especially big." This sense of space, a distinctive trait of the American experience, inspired her composition. She had earlier suggested that cowboy music (as well as Appalachian) could influence national culture. Cowboy songs, with their "certain wild freedom, characteristic of the singers," expressed the grandeur of the American environment."[60]

Like "Cowboy Song" her two Indian-themed pieces, Curtis

believed, expressed ties between people and nature. "Dawn Song," based on a Cheyenne melody Curtis had collected from Wolf Robe for *The Indians' Book,* was not simply an arrangement of the song taken from her book. Instead she considered it "an effort to reproduce the spirit and the elemental atmosphere of that half-barbaric music that belongs essentially to the great nature-world." She explained to the New York audience that because primitive people lived so intimately with nature, it became the "unconscious background to the voice of the Red Man." Nature provided harmony to Indian songs. Curtis hoped her song re-created this natural world in which humans blended so effortlessly into their environment. She employed "typical Indian song phrases" and "rhythmic ejacula-tions," as well as instrumentation by the flute and oboe, to mimic the sounds she heard on the open prairies. She realized that "no transplanted version" of an Indian song could totally capture this experience but maintained that her "years spent among the Indians studying Indian music" allowed her to "echo . . . that racial voice which should be part of the heritage of American art."[61]

Curtis emphasized that her experience among Native Americans allowed her to create the proper context as other musicians simply could not. "Victory Song," she explained, was originally sung by warriors returning triumphantly to their village at dawn. Although the words may have seemed straightforward to New Yorkers, Curtis revealed that the song contained an "inner meaning" in the choral setting concerning the "triumph of the sun, of whose conquering rays man is a human symbol." Curtis aspired to "keep wholly true to the racial idiom" by focusing on the rhythm, melody, and dynamics of Indian music. She further encouraged performers to grasp the Native understanding of the music, which required playing with the "highest sense of dramatic import." Drummers, for example, should recognize that the beat was "not a mere thumping, but the very life-pulse of the music." Only by treating "Indian music from an Indian standpoint" could composers truly develop an authentic American music.[62]

These same songs appeared on a folk song program at the People's Music League of the People's Institute a few weeks later. *Songs of North American Indians* revealed a distinct racial music that was "a constant singularly important expression of existence itself" and comprised "a rich and almost untouched field of inspiration" for the United States. For this performance Curtis adapted a "Corn-Grinding song" from women at Zuni, with a rhythm section that reproduced the sounds of the women at work. She also modified a butterfly song intended for a dance that she had collected from Koianimptiwa (Hopi). The folk music concert also featured African American spirituals arranged by Curtis. Two pieces from *Negro Folk Songs* were included on the program. The Clef Club Male Quartette sang "Go Down Moses," a song full of the "elemental drama that underlies primitive music," and "Couldn't Hear Nobody Pray." Curtis claimed that these "prayer songs" expressed the "aspirations, the emotions and the religious faith of the race." She presented the songs as she did Native American music, as among the most precious treasures of the country's heritage and suitable for all Americans because of their origin in the American environment.[63]

Other musicians sought to create a national music by drawing from the "folk" songs of African Americans. As with the Indianist movement proponents argued that because black music derived from experiences on American soil, it constituted a folk tradition from which composers could find inspiration. Furthermore this music offered a broad range of musical expressions. Curtis argued that, from the "childlike and submissive pathos" of slave songs to the "good-humored charm" and "irresistible pulse in the rhythm" of social and work songs, this music could leave an indelible mark on American culture. Black music moreover was already influential. "Our children dance, our people sing, even our soldiers march to 'rag-time,'" Curtis argued, "which is fast becoming a national 'Pied Piper' to whose rhythm the whole country moves." Already popular among the musical masses and expressing distinct aspects of life in America, Negro folk songs could easily be developed by composers into more cultured forms of expression.[64]

White and black musicians responded to impulses similar to those that drove Curtis's work with African American folk music. They used poems, arranged spirituals and other folk songs, or borrowed the rhythmic sounds of black music to create a distinctive American sound. Some argued that African American song was better suited for a national music than Indian melodies because more white Americans lived in contact with blacks and were much more familiar with the themes and symbolism of spirituals. In addition, African American folk song had incorporated Western musical forms in ways that Native American music had not. Unlike most Indians, African Americans had become professional composers and consciously attempted to arrange and develop their folk traditions in order to express their "American" nature.[65]

Most of these black composers of the early twentieth century, according to Eileen Southern, "may be regarded as nationalists in the sense that they consciously turned to the folk music of their people as an inspiration for their compositions." Many of those who gained distinction were well trained, could compose in European styles, but "reserved much of their creative energy for Negro-inspired composition." Harry Burleigh, who was active in the Music School Settlement for Colored People, composed *Six Plantation Melodies* (1901), *From the Southland* (1914), *Southland Sketches* (1916), *Saracen Songs* (1914), and *Five Songs* (1919) as attempts to transform folk melodies into art songs. Will Marion Cook, another participant in the concerts of the Music School Settlement, arranged African American folk songs for choral groups and for musicals such as *The Southerners* (1904), *The Traitor* (1913), *In Darkeydom* (1914, with James Reese Europe), and *The Cannibal King* (1914). Many of Cook's popular songs were published in *A Collection of Negro Songs* in 1912. Other black composers, notably J. Rosamond Johnson, who served as the director of the settlement school, his brother James, and their cowriter Bob Cole, adapted traditional African American songs for popular audiences. These composers were "surprisingly successful" on the stage, according to Southern. Popular journals published their writings, and white musicians performed their works. Southern argues that this group was important because they were the "first composers to truly assimilate the characteristic idioms of Negro folksong into a body of composed music."[66]

R. Nathaniel Dett, one of the most prolific writers and composers of nationalist music based on black folk songs and a close associate of Curtis, especially encouraged composers to use spirituals in the creation of American national song. As the director of the Hampton choir and a composer of numerous works, including his choral work *Listen to the Lambs* (which won a prize at the Music School Settlement in 1912), *Magnolia* (1912), and *In the Bottoms* (1913), Dett argued for the development of popular spirituals. He emphatically stated that these songs constituted an American folk tradition well suited for development by composers. He warned that serious composers had to combat the legacy of white minstrels with their "farcical 'coon songs'" of the vaudeville stage but believed proper treatment would lead to a positive reception. The music "will be of no value unless we utilize it, unless we treat it in such manner that it can be presented in choral form, in lyric and operatic works, in concertos and suites and salon music." In 1918 he wrote in *Musical America* about his gratification in seeing that many composers were joining "those of us who believe with Dvořák that 'the future music of this country must be founded on what is called Negro melodies.'" In another piece he contended, "There is hardly any folk music which so poignantly touches all the fundamentals of life as that of the American Negro." He believed the United States fortunate, "with her great heterogeneous population," to possess "this one vital thing, truly indigenous to the soil," and that this allowed American composers to escape the "almost slavish devotion" to European styles and standards.[67]

Dett often worked closely with Curtis, and each admired and supported the other. Curtis had impressed him while collecting music at Hampton for *Negro Folk Songs*, particularly by her ability to capture harmonization. In a 1919 article in *Musical America* Dett asserted that ethnologists, with their "superior knowledge of the great fundamentals of life, as peculiarly expressed in the folk idioms of various races," could show composers "how to climb higher up, by stooping down a little." Composers, informed by this "light of truth," could create a vibrant national music. The "true ethnologist" did more than collect folk traditions; he or she labored to generate better understandings and appreciation of the "common people." Dett reserved special praise for Curtis: "One of the foremost figures in contemporary music history is that of Mrs. Natalie Curtis-Burlin. She has done more, perhaps, than any other in showing what real beauty lies in the simple undecorated tunes of the primitive people of the United States." *Negro Folk Songs*, he promised, would aid composers using African American music because Curtis had captured the harmonies and the intrinsic charm of these rapidly vanishing songs.[68]

Curtis did more than simply preserve folk songs for other musicians to use. She also participated alongside African American composers in efforts to create American music based on spirituals. She had pieces from *Negro Folk Songs* included in several music concerts in New York City. For instance, three songs — "Go Down Moses," "Couldn't Hear Nobody Pray," and "Good News, Chariot's Comin'!" — were featured in a concert by the Choral Art Club alongside traditional concert pieces by Haydn, Mendelssohn, Brahms, and Saint-Säens. The program praised Curtis's work on *Negro Folk Songs* and regretted that her "voluminous notes . . . which are of such value and absorbing interest" could not be sufficiently condensed for the program. Curtis's friend Kurt Schindler, the conductor of the Schola Cantorum, used "God's a gwine ter move all de troubles away" in a July 1918 performance. An editorial in the

Southern Workman claimed that the white singers sang "exactly as the untaught Negroes sing in the South — as nearly as a white chorus [could]." The editorialist commented that the "intuitive, warm, rich Negro harmonies, which were sung at Mr. Schindler's concert, held their own amid the more elaborate art-settings of folk-songs from other lands." One reviewer was so impressed by these works that he exulted, "Surely the music of the black race is now to be accepted as *one of the most precious artistic treasures of America*."[69]

Curtis believed that African American spirituals could contribute to the American musical climate unedited and unadorned, but she also encouraged composers, as Dett had done, to develop these songs into "higher" forms. She undertook this task by producing songs closely based on black spirituals for the concert stage. In 1919 Curtis published *Two Old Negro Christmas Songs*. She had arranged these tunes from music collected in Virginia and South Carolina. Frank Damrosch, the director of the Musical Art Society of New York, included them on a Christmas program that December. "Dar's a Star in de East," based on themes sung to Curtis by J. E. Blanton, an African American musician and superintendent at Penn Industrial School, tried to maintain the harmony and "unconscious simplicity" of the original songs. Curtis explained that in the song the response of the shepherds to the tidings from heaven demonstrated "a vivid reality that proves anew the strong dramatic instinct of the black man." The second song, "Mary's Baby," preserved the "quaint speech" of African American women, who, romantically enough, "still wore bandana turbans and carried baskets on their heads" on St. Helena Island. Curtis hoped to use this song to show white audiences how the most isolated and untouched black music really sounded.[70]

Curtis's attempts to develop concert compositions based on African American folk songs were lauded by the music critic Henry Krehbiel. Her "experiment in adapting folksong to an artistic use," he argued, deserved more attention on concert programs. He further commented, "It was a new experiment, for we had 'spirituals' at a concert of the society two years ago, beautifully and reconditely arranged by Mr. Burleigh, but Miss Curtis made a good and convincing demonstration of the proper treatment of folk songs of this character." The audience, so moved by the "impressive, even electrifying" performance, refused to leave until it was played again. Another reviewer of this concert, calling Curtis the "most inspired folklorist in America," praised her "unfailing zeal for the recognition of Negro art."[71]

Curtis used concerts as platforms from which to express her ideas about African American music's role in national cultural life and about the place of blacks in the nation. As she had argued throughout her life, music could be a universal human language, drawing diverse people together in common sympathy and appreciation. She wrote, "If anything can bring harmony from this present clashing of the two races during this difficult period of problems and adjustment, it might well be the peace-giver — music!"[72] She would repeat this theme — that acceptance of African American songs would be "a prophecy of true democracy" and help white Americans appreciate black contributions to American life — in the promotion of her "Hymn of Freedom," a tune also included on Damrosch's program. A concert reviewer hailed Curtis's vision for the new role of African Americans in the United States, a position they deserved because of both black contributions to American cultural development and their participation in the war. The reviewer believed that the inclusion of the songs in the first of the society's concerts since the war began had "more than an artistic significance." It also suggested that "we are injecting into our national life something of the spirit of Democracy for which we fought in Europe."[73]

The "Hymn of Freedom" represented Curtis's contribution to the war effort, an attempt to use her musical skills to help African Americans. Influenced by her patron Peabody, who strongly supported the peace movement, Curtis hoped to use African

American involvement in the war as a way to demonstrate the gifts blacks brought to American culture. Some black leaders, including W. E. B. DuBois in his "Close Ranks" editorial in the Crisis, had advanced similar arguments that supporting the war would lead to civil rights and full citizenship. Curtis and Peabody also saw the war as a chance for blacks to prove their patriotism and claim their rightful place in American society, but they (paternalistically) feared that blacks, particularly those from isolated regions of the South, would not comprehend the larger meanings of the war effort.[74]

Curtis composed the "Hymn" based on the melody of an old spiritual, "O Ride On, Jesus!," and devised words that would explain the cause for which black men fought. The resulting "Hymn of Freedom" proclaimed:

> O march on, Freedom,
>> March on, Freedom,
>> March on, conquering hosts,
>>> Liberty is calling.
>
> To martyred Belgium,
>> Freedom!
> To wounded France,
>> Freedom!
> 'Tis God who summons our advance,
>> Liberty is calling.

The song also hoped for freedom for "struggling Russia," the "starving Pole," "bowed Roumainia [sic]," and "the stricken Serb." Curtis included two verses linking the "war for democracy" with her concerns about racial and religious equality at home:

> To Jew and Christian,
>> Freedom!
> To white man and black,
>> Freedom!

Democracy can not turn back,
      Liberty is calling.

and,

    To each religion,
      Freedom!
    And to every race,
      Freedom!
    March with the dawn of light in our face,
      Liberty is calling.

The song concluded with the promise that "Victory is calling."[75]

Curtis explained her motivations for the hymn in a letter she sent to several of her supporters, including the anthropologists Aleš Hrdlička and Franz Boas. While visiting St. Helena Island in April of 1917 she "became convinced that her own 'war bit' lay right here in America in working for that Democracy which is the end and the aim of the war." She wanted to create a song to help African Americans understand the larger aims of the war and to serve as a call for equality at home and for increased respect for the contributions of blacks. Basing the song on the melody of a spiritual, Curtis expected African Americans to easily and quickly take up the hymn. The lyrics, however, which were not written in a "black" dialect, would appeal as well to white soldiers and even white choruses.[76]

Because "Hymn of Freedom" was initially intended to explain the war to isolated blacks on St. Helena Island, its first performance took place at the community center at the Penn Industrial School. The principal Grace Bigelow House described the scene and the effect of the song in a letter to Peabody, which was later published in part in the *Southern Workman*. Eighteen men from the island were drafted, including two from the school. House called a meeting for the draftees before they left. This "most picturesque" and carefully orchestrated affair took place in a hall patriotically festooned with American flags. The draftees, with "their dark, troubled faces, solemn and pathetic," listened to talks on the history of African American participation in past wars, on YMCA work in military camps, on the causes of the war, and on why they were called to "fight for freedom." J. E. Blanton, the superintendent of Penn School Farm and Industries, along with other black teachers, then led the singing of the hymn for the first time. "It was stirring," House proclaimed. "There can be no doubt of its appeal to all our Negro soldiers." The allure of the spiritual, she continued, was immediately felt by the audience in the dimly lit hall. House recalled the "rows of anxious, troubled faces listening so patiently to get an understanding of what their 'call' meant," who experienced an "easing of their burdens" after hearing Curtis's song. "'We feel all right about going now!' was the expression of the men after the meeting," claimed House. She concluded, "This song, which expresses so simply and clearly the ideals for which the American soldiers are willing and eager to fight, must undoubtedly give help and inspiration to our soldiers, both white and black, in the testing times ahead of them."[77]

Curtis wanted her "Hymn of Freedom" to do exactly that, and she began promoting it to an audience broader than the confused and fearful draftees on St. Helena Island. In a letter sent to her supporters Curtis shared her idea that "in the music of the Negro lay a possible bond between the races." If her song became widely sung in military camps she anticipated a "better feeling of comradeship between white and colored troops." Curtis further explained that the War Department had expressed interest in spreading the song and arranged for Blanton to visit African Americans in the camps to encourage them to sing the hymn and more traditional black folk songs. Curtis believed that Blanton had "met with great success" and attested that his letters to her "are deeply touching and most enthusiastic." In a *Southern Workman* article Curtis explained her rationale for introducing the hymn to soldiers in the camps:

"Since, with unhesitating alacrity, we have paraphrased lighter forms of Negro music in the popular songs sung by the troops — the all prevalent 'ragtime,' which the war has spread far and wide — is it not equally appropriate that the nobler music of the Negro, the prayerful spirituals, should form the basis of a battle hymn in this war, wherein the freed black man, side by side with the white man, fights for the larger liberty of humanity?" Blanton, the article reported, had met with success in the camps. Officers welcomed any effort to make better soldiers, and African Americans in the camps purportedly responded well to the "racial" music that had helped past generations survive hardships.[78]

Curtis obviously painted too rosy a picture of the situation African Americans in the armed forces faced during the war. Her very suggestion that "the freed black man, side by side with the white man, fights for the larger liberty of humanity" was absurd in light of the tightly segregated military of the time. Incidents of discrimination and prejudice against African Americans in uniform abounded, and few white Americans believed that the war would or should lead to better treatment of blacks. Curtis was not completely unaware of these problems. She joined with other concerned whites and many black leaders who encouraged African Americans to fully support the war effort in the hopes that their loyalty and service would reap their just rewards. She complained bitterly in a letter to her brother George about white nurses in the Red Cross who refused to serve with black nurses because they feared "social equality!" "'War for democracy,' mind you!" Curtis exclaimed. "Isn't is up to us to make that slogan come true at home, too?" Although she outwardly wore a hopeful disposition regarding the war, Curtis knew that many blacks did not "really see why they have any reason to fight for America," as one soldier told Blanton, but she hoped as always that the powerful influence of music would help whites recognize the many contributions African Americans had made to the country and bring democracy home as well.[79]

The war also brought Spanish-speaking Americans in the Southwest out of their relative isolation, and Curtis again believed music could provide a coping mechanism for them and ease their transition into mainstream society. She described to her brother an address she delivered in Taos at a benefit for the Salvation Army. "You picture the audience!" she exclaimed. Curtis described "cultured artists [and] American residents" (including the blacksmith as the ticket taker and "the Jewish shop-keeper the master of ceremonies!") joining the crowd with "quantities of Mexicans or Spanish Americans as they prefer to be called; cow-punchers; campers; ranchmen; and a handful of Pueblo ('Peeablo') Indians!" She spoke on the war and her hopes for its domestic impact. The Taos audience "raised the roof," she cried, "when I offered a resolution to wipe out race-prejudice." Inspired by this experience, she composed "Cowboy War-Song," which she sent to George but never published. Curtis was also moved by the response of a Mexican American who thanked her for her talk and for her interest in their songs, especially in light of the "race feeling" she had noticed between them and whites in the area, "perfectly unreasonable" tensions in Curtis's mind.[80]

Perhaps hoping to improve relations between Anglos and Hispanics in the region, Curtis penned an article on how Spanish American music helped these communities cope with the war experience at home. As with the blacks of St. Helena the war had brought residents of the Far West out of isolation. The draft had forced them to consider the aims of the war and the consequences of their participation. The entire Southwest had been "abruptly seized by the collar and jerked out of its isolation," and now these longtime residents of the region anguished over the fate of their loved ones fighting an "unseen enemy" far away. Curtis applied her romantic and essentialist ideas about music and race to her study of this music. "Of course an emotional Latin people must reflect this great new experience in song," she asserted. One song, "Adelita," became popular among young men as they left for military camps and could often be heard on the lips of "some dark-eyed girl in the village to whose heart the love-sick words of the soldier's farewell strike deep." Curtis described this "typical" song as "impassioned, sentimental, dramatic," but it expressed the level of devotion that Hispanics were now giving to the war effort. Importantly, the spirit embodied in this song provided the people with hope for the future — for the spread of democracy abroad and at home. As with African American music it also demonstrated the contributions Hispanics could make to a national American culture.[81]

Curtis maintained her optimism about the democratic goals of the war even after the conflict ended and it became apparent to many that the war had done little to improve the conditions of the groups she championed. She kept busy after the war promoting her books on African and African American music and her Indianist compositions. Paul Burlin, however, had grown increasingly frustrated with life in the United States. His biographer explains the decision to leave America: "In 1921, as a result of the bitter reaction against modern art in the years immediately following the first World War, Burlin went to Paris as one of the Expatriates." Burlin's attitude towards postwar America had soured considerably after a "violent attack" by the critic of the *Philadelphia Morning Telegraph* on one of his paintings at the Pennsylvania Academy of Fine Arts. He accused his reviewers of a "palsy of the spirit," which had infected many other Americans in the "return to normalcy": increased chauvinism, provincialism, and hostility toward the creative arts. The move to Paris became for Burlin "as much a pilgrimage to the center of modern art as an escape from America."[82]

Although Curtis supported her husband's decision and probably shared some of his attitudes, her actions suggest she did not fully share his desire to leave the United States at that time. For one thing, *Songs and Tales from the Dark Continent* had been recently published, and Curtis wanted to promote this work. She shared a detailed strategy with Peabody for garnering attention for the book and its message. She employed several assistants to canvas New York City bookstores (the "good shops," not the "second-raters") to get them to carry *Songs and Tales* and place it in prominent display areas. Increased postwar American interest in black-white relations at home and in a global context may have allowed her assistants to successfully place her work. Curtis made certain that copies were sent to leading papers for literary and musical reviews, and she ensured that prominent figures knew about her latest work. She felt driven by a sense of purpose. "I wake up everyday with a new thrill when I think of the near approach of the great day of fulfillment," she shared with Peabody. Curtis confessed, "I shall feel so gratefully glad if the sale of this book really can help toward a better understanding of our black brethren." All her hard work writing and promoting this book would be rewarded if people read it and acted on its messages.[83]

Her efforts to promote *Songs and Tales* in the United States ended when she and Burlin sailed for Europe in May. Although Curtis acknowledged to friends and family that this trip was to further her husband's career and to provide her with a well-deserved break, she found it difficult not to work on board the ship, which she called a "floating sea-side resort." In letters to Peabody she described the variety of people she met on board, including a group of Zionists heading to Palestine and some Peruvian passengers (the "Incas" she and Burlin called them), and her success in collecting their songs. In spite of her claims of relaxation Curtis tried to maintain contact with people and the news back home.[84]

Curtis and Burlin arrived in London in mid-June and stayed with friends she described to her mother as "sympathetic, kind and full of 'live-[and]-let-live.'" "We are very, very happy here," especially Burlin, she confirmed. In England Curtis felt unable to work and instead visited the usual tourist attractions. Although she had opportunities to further her career, Curtis confessed, "I feel too relaxed and sleepy all the time to attempt any public effort." She met Mary

Austin, the Southwestern promoter and writer, at a gallery where Austin was promoting a book of Indian legends. Curtis experienced some pangs of guilt: "I know I have been rather spineless here, but I can't seem to get up steam. It's climate, they say — Rockaway heaviness multiplied by North East West and South!" Hoping to escape these doldrums Curtis made plans to leave for Paris before Burlin had finished with his business.[85]

She arrived in the city to find it "full of artists, musicians, all bustling with ideas and new expression; the atmosphere is quick, encouragingly purposeful." She secured a "quiet but up-to-date" hotel and visited some of the places she remembered from her teenage trip to France. She also sought out evidence of the war's impact on the country and its people. After visiting trenches and noticing wheat growing on the battlefields, she remarked, "I thought it astonishing how swiftly nature had passed an obliterating hand over man's outrages." Even so, she later observed that the war still affected people deeply. "The culture-hunger of Europe is almost tragic," Curtis commented. "Nations accustomed to a rich cultural life were as spiritually starved during the four years of war as they were materially." People sought to relieve this hunger in many ways, leading many to flock to Paris. "Everybody in the art-world is here," Curtis noted, "and it is a great source of inspiration and development to us both to be in touch with all these creative people."[86]

When Burlin joined his wife in Paris he immediately took advantage of this artistic and creative atmosphere. He established a close relationship with Albert Gleizes, a French painter and writer on the principles of Cubism, who had known Burlin in New York. Gleizes arranged a membership for Burlin at an artists' club, which provided him with discounted supplies and, more important, contacts with other artists. Curtis relished conversations that she and Burlin had with Gleizes and his wife on the philosophy of modern art. The Burlins also took time to visit the Champs Élysées to observe Parisian crowds and to attend the many modern art exhibits in the city. After seeing works by Picasso and Braques, Curtis enthused to her mother, "[This school] has broken away from representation *completely* and *entirely* and are doing purely abstract things with forms and color and line — nothing in the pictures to recall a visual object, any more than designs on Indian pottery look like visual rain-storms, or real corn-fields." Curtis admitted her preference for "the purely abstract things to the intermediate stage when there was a certain amount of objectivity." This abstract art, which seemed to echo in some ways her ideas about primitivism, appealed to her greatly and might have reignited her passion for her work, which had noticeably dimmed since she arrived in Europe.[87]

Experiments in modern art inspired Curtis to seek out new ideas in music as well. In an article in the *Freeman* she described a musical movement in a city "where new ideas in art meet in gladiatorial combat with the accepted order." A performance at the "Theatre des Champs Elysees" by musicians using "futurist" instruments, was "meant to make possible a new kind of music unfettered by the present orchestral limitations, which to futurists, seem to hinder an adequate expression of the spirit of this age." Curtis connected the new music with the efforts of painters "to reflect in art the forces which have been brought to bear upon modern life through the invention of machinery which has enlarged man's possibilities of achievement and dwarfed the importance of the individual." The idea of "noise-maker" instruments appealed to Curtis more than the actual sounds of the performance. This group felt oppressed by the traditions of the past, Curtis explained, but she distrusted their valorization of the machine. "We need to humanize machinery, not further to mechanize humanity," she countered. Curtis instead suggested that new movements in music, like those she had advocated at home, should embrace the spiritual and emotive aspects of the individual. She asserted, "There is a cosmic music — if one may call it so — all about us, full of beauty to which we are only half awake." The universal emotional and spiritual elements of music, rather than the sterility of the machine, should pave the way to the future.[88]

Inspired by the creative and intellectual life so abundant in Paris, Curtis threw herself back into her work. The French "are most enthusiastic about the blacks," she observed, and she planned to capitalize on this new market for her books. The French interest in African American music stemmed from the increased presence of black soldiers and musicians in the country during the war. It also drew from social and cultural anxieties concerning French identity in the interwar years, which produced a more general fascination with *"l'art nègre* — especially African art and sculpture."[89] Curtis's book therefore found an eager audience. In mid-July she exclaimed to Peabody, "The African book seems to have taken fire in France." She explained how Gleizes, who was familiar with her writings, had shown her books to Alexandre Mercereau, a French writer involved with Cubism and interested in the peace movement. Mercereau hoped to translate her African book into French and had asked Curtis to discuss this project with his publisher, Jacques Povolozky. Povolozky also "took fire" over *The Indians' Book* and her two volumes on black music. Both men "seemed to understand at once the *Spirit* of the work," Curtis rejoiced.[90]

Her enthusiasm for this undertaking was dampened, however, once they began discussing the logistics of translating and publishing her three books in France. Curtis and Povolozky devised a plan by which an American investor or group of investors would furnish funds up front to start the process. They would be reimbursed for this once Povolozky published the volumes. Curtis immediately turned to Peabody for assistance. He shared her enthusiasm for this opportunity but warned her to act with caution. He advised Curtis on the technical details of attracting investors, dealing with her American publishers, and making financial arrangements with the French publisher. Curtis sent him long letters asking about the particulars of the publishing deal. She was unsure of who had the rights to each of her books or how to get permission to use them as she wanted. She sent him lists of figures, detailing the approximate costs of publication with Povolozky. She worried too about her personal finances and admitted to writing magazine articles again "to be on the safe-side financially." The appeal of translating her ideas about Native American and African American music to a far more receptive audience in France overrode whatever financial worries she faced, and Curtis pursued these plans to the tragic end of her life.[91]

Curtis believed that this opportunity to have her works published in France was in a sense fated. Before Curtis left for Europe, Charlotte Mason had predicted great things for her: "Don't, in your interest in Paul's work, forget your own, for you have something to give that Europe will be anxious for. Don't forget the consecration with which the Indian's Book was made. Every step of its path was persued [*sic*] with a high ideal, and it's very material life was made possible through a believing friend (Foster). The vibrations of that work have already gone further than you know." Curtis believed that this prophecy was coming true in France. She had received several offers to give talks on Native American, African American, and African music and folklore. She and Mercereau had discussed the possibility of organizing a society of "Friends of Dark Races" to give conferences, exhibits, concerts, and readings on the cultures of "primitive" peoples. Offers for Curtis to do translations of her Native American songs for poetry anthologies had also arrived.[92]

Curtis's opportunity to express her ideas about the role of the "folk" in American cultural life finally arrived. An International Congress of Art History met at the Sorbonne that fall. Curtis told her brother George how impressed she was with the "broad-mindedness of all the French intellectuals," who, unlike most Americans at home, held so little animosity toward Germans that they were already willing to discuss art with them. Delegates from around the world converged in Paris for this event. Although "thousands and thousands" of Americans currently lived in Paris, Curtis lamented, "Belgium sent 78 delegates, America 4!" She served on the American delegation along with Cecilia Beaux, a painter; Edward Burlingame Hill, a music professor from Harvard and a follower of the French music school, who served as the music representative; and her artist friend Alice Klauber, the secretary of the delegation. Klauber "*insisted* that I speak because America was making so slim a showing," Curtis reported.[93]

At the conference European musicians greeted the Native American songs Curtis sang with "much enthusiasm"; many "were astonished to find [the songs] so beautiful." Delighting as always in the positive reception newcomers gave to Indian music, Curtis was prepared to demonstrate how this folk music of her country could become its national contribution to the world. Curtis was deeply troubled then when an "American Professor of music at one of our big eastern universities [Hill]" read a paper "in which he said that the reason our American composers had not done anything characteristic in music was because American hadn't any folk music." Curtis immediately challenged Hill's assertion, and he smugly replied that Native American and African American song could never be classified as "American."[94]

Curtis prepared for a public confrontation with Hill to debate the possibilities for an American music and the existence of "folk music" in America. Some tutoring in French from Gleizes's wife helped prepare her for what she saw as a crucial showdown. At stake was the basis of her entire career — her efforts to use Indian and black music to create a distinctive American music, her desire to eclipse the elitism of the Eastern establishment Hill represented, and most important, her faith that music would unite the diversity of her country and pave the way for a more complete democracy. At stake in this debate was her formulation of what it meant to be an American, what the "spirit of the real America" would be.

Realizing that she may have offended members of the official

American delegation by her assertions, Curtis offered to withdraw from the conference. The presiding officer, finding the topic of American folk music "new and interesting," refused to allow Curtis to leave. Curtis confessed that she did not want to embarrass Hill, but "*he knew my viewpoint* and my subject." Hill had earlier warned Curtis, "I intend to say that the reason we haven't any great music in American is because we have no folk music — I intend to say we haven't any, and I suppose you'll say we *have*?" Curtis had replied, "I most certainly will." Hill came first on the program, so Curtis felt compelled to challenge his representation of American music. "I couldn't help speaking out for my Dark Brother," she claimed, "no matter if I offended the whole of Harvard College!"[95]

Curtis gave her address on American folk music and its potential for a national, even universal, cultural expression: "When I sang those songs about the American maize, about the big, hot American sun that rides his turquoise horse across our Rocky [M]ountains; those chants that have come out of *America* itself — the audience was literally electrified!" Curtis refuted Hill's dismissal of blacks as not true Americans. The nation's twelve million blacks — "who are good enough 'Americans' to die for American ideals in our wars [and are] completely loyal and unhyphenated Americans, whose blood and brawn have gone into the upbuilding of our whole great South" — were more than qualified to be "American." "If those songs that are the very voice of our South are not American, what is!" she exclaimed. Curtis especially resented "Mr. Hill's everlasting monopoly of the white race, and I resented the notion that only New England with Harvard College as its 'hub' can be 'American'!" Curtis's America "is an agglomeration of races that have given us a folk-lore almost as rich and diverse as that other agglomeration of races that we call Russia. And *all* the music of America is not found in universities and schools but out in the great expanse of territory that stretches from the Atlantic to the Pacific Oceans and from Canada to Mexico." Her America included all of the land and all of the people, and its cultural expressions should represent this blending of traditions.[96]

The audience's enthusiastic response overwhelmed Curtis and assured her that her views had real merit, no matter Hill's challenges. Curtis recalled, "People said they had *no idea* that there was anything like this in America." They asked, "*Why* didn't Americans realize what was in their own country instead of copying Europe in music!" Curtis reflected on the day's events. "I feel so proud of the wonder and force of the American background — the big hinter-land of our Country that is so striking in character, so forceful, so dynamic, so red-blooded," she wrote. It was not what European-trained composers did that mattered to American music, she declared, but "the thing that's of the land itself, the thing that's in the soil."[97]

Her triumphant reception at the Sorbonne as the defender of Native Americans and African Americans and their musical traditions became a fitting climax for Curtis's career. Tragically this was probably her last public presentation on the music to which she had devoted her life's work. Here once again the universal language of music allowed her to bridge the divides that separated people from understanding and sympathy for one another. Music had provided Curtis with a language to express herself, a crucial and powerful tool for the construction of a personal identity. The music of Native Americans and African Americans — rising, as she believed, from the very soil of her native land — became as well the key to her identity as an American.

Conclusion

Remembering Natalie Curtis

ON OCTOBER 23, 1921, AN AUTOMOBILE STRUCK NATALIE Curtis Burlin as she descended from a streetcar in Paris. She died two hours after the accident, without having regained consciousness. This tragedy shocked her family, friends, and patrons. At the time of her death Paul Burlin was painting in Marseilles at his studio and failed to join his wife before she expired. He later confided to his mother-in-law, Augusta, that while on the train to Paris, "I called upon your image and hers so that our strength and *prayers* would 'keep' Natalie." The artist Alice Klauber sat with her close friend until the end. She comforted the Curtis family that she died without "knowing anything of the pain and distress of it all." Klauber painted an image of her final moments: "She looked in death serene and beautiful; her slight smile, the great tranquility of the room in which she rested, the beauty of the flowers banked around her would have meant much to you, as they did to me." Just being in the same room with her, she remarked, had brought Klauber great peace. She insisted that in recent months "Natalie was happier than I have ever before seen her" and that her marriage had "enriched her life." When Burlin arrived he made the necessary arrangements for his departed wife.[1]

Curtis's death devastated her family. George was "knocked all of a heap" when he first learned of his sister's death. He lamented: "What a brilliant mind, what character, what driving force, with the tender sympathy and understanding that found the best in everyone, and gave her power to help people to help themselves. The world seems to me dingy and mean, without her. What a blind, brutally stupid waste there is in her taking-off. . . . How few who could not have been better spared. It's enough to make the human race hold an indignation meeting and pass resolutions of censure." He grieved as well for the loss of her inspiring influence. "Seems to me," he confided to his brother Bridgham, "she kept us all better and cleaner, morally[,] than we otherwise have been." Her sister Marian expressed her grief by searching for some meaning in this tragedy. "It *could not* have been simply a blind, stupid accident," she despaired. Marian believed that Natalie surely had a "higher duty" to fulfill in the next world, that she was "alive and happy" there, and that "the veil that separates us is a very thin one." Thankfully, she wrote, Natalie "never feared death and said that she hoped that the end would come quickly." Their mother concurred. "She never had the slightest feeling about death," Augusta told George, "and would be perfectly willing to go at any moment — except to leave Paul. I never met a person so sure of the circumstance of the soul."[2]

Curtis's death crushed her husband, who reached out to his wife's family for support and comfort. Knowing that they could not come to Paris soon, Burlin kept them apprised of events and shared his feelings about Curtis as a wife and fellow artist. "Before my marriage [I] never knew happiness in any abundance," he confessed to Augusta. Hard times and isolation from his family had built "a crust of suspicion, of cynicism," that threatened to destroy him before he met Curtis. She was "a saint, a symbol, who could give to the world . . . her love, whose whole life has been consecrated to 'others.'" Unlike other artists Curtis never demanded "worship." Instead her "flood gates were always open for ideals and . . . [her] love and pity for humanit[y's] struggles was [*sic*] felt in every book she wrote." Burlin worried that "too many years of an inheritance of irritability" had made him unfit to "have been the noblest man for Natalie," but he was confident that as artists and companions their lives complemented one another in significant and important ways. Curtis had given Burlin something no one else ever could. He concluded that it would be "a blasphemy to deny that our shared married life was not a *very* rich one!"[3]

Burlin arranged services in Paris while the Curtis family arranged their own memorial in the United States. A simple family gathering sufficed until Augusta and her daughter Connie traveled to Paris to retrieve Curtis's remains. The pair returned home with Burlin and joined Marian, Bridgham, Canon Winfred Douglas, and childhood friend Bessie Day at the family cemetery in Providence, Rhode Island. Paul lowered his wife's ashes into her father's grave. All that was left, Augusta claimed, was to realize that Natalie was truly gone.[4]

Burlin returned to Europe to continue the artistic pursuits he had begun there. He continued to paint until his death in 1969 at the age of eighty-two. Burlin "described himself as 'a man who uses his darts in all directions,'" referring to the many styles of painting from which he drew. He worked in Cubist and abstract-expressionist styles and experimented with color and space in his later works. Burlin returned to America ten years later and continued to promote American art. He lectured and taught at several major universities and art centers. He won some important awards for his paintings, including one from the Chicago Art Institute and a National Council of Arts award for his lifetime of service to the field. Burlin remarried within a few years but never returned to the Southwest to paint, claiming that without Curtis he could find no further inspiration there.[5]

Curtis's family came to terms with her death by ensuring that her work lived on. Burlin pursued the French translations of her major works with her publisher Jacques Povolozky. He even hoped to travel to Germany, where he might exhibit some work, to discuss the chances for German editions of his wife's books. He told Bridgham, "It would have given Natalie the greatest satisfaction to have *The Indians' Book* published in French and German." Burlin continued negotiations with her French publisher and received investment promises from Charlotte Mason and possibly the Carnegie Foundation. He believed that Curtis's success at the Sorbonne had created a new audience for her work and lamented that she did not live to see the fruits of her labor in Europe.[6]

Bridgham too wanted to ensure that his sister's work would have the influence it might have had if she had not died. He explained to Charles Lummis, "I am trying to make a collection of my sister's magazine articles." He inquired if she had published anything in *Out West* and if Lummis could send him copies. Bridgham also allowed others to reprint her work to advance agendas that Curtis would have supported. Aleš Hrdlička received a copy of "Pueblo Poetry" in 1923, for instance, because Bridgham hoped it would shed light on the current state of Indian affairs in the Southwest. George Foster Peabody asked the *Outlook* editor Lawrence Abbott if he would reprint an article on Pueblo culture to counter Commissioner of Indian Affairs Charles Burke's order prohibiting Native dances on reservations. Peabody also proposed sending copies of her article to every member of Congress to reveal to them the "true relation of dance to the Indians' fundamental religious instincts." Her friends and family believed that Curtis's opinions on Native American cultures remained valid and could influence Indian policy.[7]

Others believed that her contributions to the world of music comprised her legacy. Curtis's collections of Native American and African American song, her own compositions based on this music, and her inspiration to folklorists and composers were not soon

forgotten. Percy Grainger in particular strove to keep Curtis's musical works before concert audiences and to explain the significance
of her folk music research. He often corresponded with Curtis's
mother, Augusta, sharing with her his views of Curtis's music and
his efforts to promote it.[8] Augusta greatly appreciated his work
on her daughter's behalf. She saved several of the programs from
"Grainger's Room — Music Concerts." A program given in the spring
of 1925, for instance, featured *Memories of New Mexico*, three songs
Curtis had composed based on Spanish American pieces. Grainger
commented that Curtis should be remembered for her "gift of penetrating into the inner soul of the art of alien people" and because of
her sympathetic nature and musical acumen. In another concert he
featured music from *Negro Folk Songs* and praised the collector for
her "unsurpassable prerequisites for the supremely difficult task"
of recording harmonized folk tunes, as well as for her "penetrating
human sympathy with all primitive art." Curtis's skills as a musical
folklorist and her ability to understand and sympathize with "primitive" peoples made her work important and worth remembering
to her contemporaries.[9]

NATALIE CURTIS'S WORK IS CERTAINLY WORTH REMEMBERING,
in part for her efforts to understand America's musical heritage and
in part because of the ways her life revealed the struggles, challenges,
and possibilities inherent in her search for an American identity.
Through the language of music Curtis successfully fashioned a spiritual and artistic personal identity. From her childhood passion for
the piano, to that moment in the early twentieth century when she
first heard an Indian song, to her efforts to promote Native American
and African American songs as a national musical expression, Curtis
found personal meaning in music. Furthermore her passion for music
and the research she conducted provided her with an identity as a
New Woman. She created a life of independence and meaningful
work that eluded many of her New York City contemporaries. The

study of Native American and African American music fulfilled the many longings she expressed as an adolescent, and Curtis hoped that the personal identity she had acquired through her love of music could be experienced by other Americans.

Curtis could find identity through music in part because she believed that music could overcome the barriers that separated Americans from one another — that music promoted understanding and a shared sense of humanness. Curtis discovered the beauty and spirituality of Native American and African American music, and through this appreciation she came to see these often disparaged groups as fellow Americans. This led her to take action to improve the conditions of her informants. She believed that her experiences would translate to other Americans — that once white Americans recognized the value and worth of this music, the treatment of these groups would improve.

She strongly believed that the United States needed a shared national identity and that music could unite all Americans. She devoted her career to creating a national musical expression based on the spiritual and artistic beauty she found in Native American and African American songs. Her sincerity in using this music to create a national cultural expression is undeniable. The search for an American identity, however, proved an impossible task for Natalie Curtis, as it did for her uncle George Curtis's Transcendentalist friends and as it continues to elude Americans today. Her formula of adding the flavor of the country's newly discovered "folk" to the European heritage she hoped to eclipse proved unworkable. It ignored or whitewashed decades of violence and conflict, and it sought to impose a "proper" art form on the popular music of these peoples. Curtis ultimately failed to take into account the aspirations and beliefs of the many people who also claimed an American identity or those who believed the nation could have multiple "American" identities.

This inability to fully listen to these other voices stemmed from her inability to divorce herself from the racialist thinking that underlay her work. Despite her obvious sympathy for "primitive" people, as she continually insisted on calling the groups with whom she worked, they always remained "child races" to her, always occupying a lower rung on an evolutionary ladder that Curtis could never topple in her mind, even when challenged to do so. Operating from this premise she could never truly engage in an honest dialogue with the Native Americans and African Americans whom she called friends. In addition she could not fully allow these groups to speak for themselves. Although her work opened spaces for these voices to be heard, she tried to control and manipulate their words to ensure they remained authentically "primitive" and suited her personal desires. Her assumption that she could "feel Indian inside," or understand the hardships black Americans faced by singing spirituals or learning Hopi rain songs, speaks volumes about her inability to use music as a language for interracial discourse.

NATALIE CURTIS'S SEARCH FOR AN AMERICAN IDENTITY, despite its racialist or racist overtones, or perhaps because of these, remains significant because of her willingness to grapple with these issues of race and identity. For all the shortcomings of her racialist thinking, she strove to understand and sympathize with Americans whose voices were often disparaged by her contemporaries. What began for Curtis as a search for a personal identity — an effort to make sense of her life and career in tumultuous times — became much larger. She presented through her writing and her own example a new vision for the country she loved. Curtis's America encompassed the entire nation — it included the West and the South as well as the Northeast; it included women, Indians, and blacks too. Curtis, for all her flaws and misguided ideas, struggled to articulate a different, more inclusive, more just, more beautiful America than the one that she inhabited, and for that she should be remembered.

NOTES

ABBREVIATIONS

AAA   Archives of American Art, Washington DC

ARCIA   *Annual Report of the Commissioner of Indian Affairs* (Washington DC: Government Printing Office, various years)

DAMA   Denver Art Museum Archives, Denver CO

PCFB   *The Professional Correspondence of Franz Boas* (Wilmington DE: Scholarly Resources, 1972)

GDCD   George DeClyver Curtis Diaries, 1904, George DeClyver Curtis Papers (collection 1247), Department of Special Collections, University Research Library, University of California, Los Angeles

HUA   Hampton University Archives, Hampton VA

LOC   Library of Congress, Washington DC

NAA   National Anthropological Archives, Smithsonian Institution, Washington DC

NCBA   Natalie Curtis Burlin Archives, Raleigh NC

INTRODUCTION

1. "Discours d'Alexandre Mercereau a la memoire de Natalie Curtis Burlin," NCBA (see http://www.nataliecurtis.org).

2. For more on these women see Mullin, *Culture in the Marketplace*, especially for Sergeant. See also Henderson, *Turquoise Trail*.

3. Carol Stanley to Elbridge Adams, Dec. 16, 1921 (copied by Augusta Curtis), NCBA.

4. Augusta Curtis to Percy Grainger, May 11, 1923, Percy Grainger Collection, LOC.

5. "Natalie Curtis," 127–40.

6. "Natalie Curtis," 127–29.

7. "Natalie Curtis," 133.

8. "Natalie Curtis," 135–38.

9. "Natalie Curtis," 139–40.

10. Clements, *Native American Verbal Art*; Babcock and Parezo, *Daughters of the Desert*; Parezo, *Hidden Scholars*.

11. Wood, "Women and Music."

12. Jacobs, *Engendered Encounters*; Mullin, *Culture in the Marketplace*; Packer and Frankiel, "Natural Sympathies"; Babcock and Parezo, *Daughters of the Desert*; Parezo, *Hidden Scholars*; Jameson, "Toward a Multicultural History of Women."

13. Prucha, *Great Father*; Hoxie, *Final Promise*.

14. D. W. Adams, *Education for Extinction*; Lindsey, *Indians at Hampton Institute*; Mihesuah, *Cultivating the Rosebuds*; Ellis, *To Change Them Forever*; Lomawaima, *They Called It Prairie Light*; Trennert, *Phoenix Indian School*.

15. N. Curtis, *Indians' Book*, xxi.

16. Mark, "Francis LaFlesche"; Gidley, "Cultural Broker."

17. Said, *Orientalism*; Torgovnick, *Gone Primitive*; Dilworth, *Imagining Indians in the Southwest*; Carr, *Inventing the American Primitive*.

18. Berkhofer, *White Man's Indian*; Deloria, *Playing Indian*; Huhndorf, *Going Native*.

19. Southern, *Music of Black Americans*; Stewart, *African American Music*; L. Levine, *Black Culture and Black Consciousness*; William Clements, "'Offshoot' and the 'Root.'"

20. Lears, in *No Place of Grace*, examines a number of themes of antimodernism. I agree with Sherry L. Smith, who argues in *Reimagining Indians* that some antimodernists who worked with Native Americans did more than just appropriate Native cultures.

1. AN "ATMOSPHERE OF CULTURE AND HIGH PURPOSE"

1. George De Clyver Curtis, unpublished biography of Natalie Curtis, 1957, NCBA.

2. Henry and May's son Ephraim (1642–1734) was best known for his development of Worcester and for his dealings with Native Americans in the region. One of his sons, John (1707–1797), was "a prominent citizen" of Worcester as a military commander and leader. His son David (1763–1813), a blacksmith and leading citizen, fathered Natalie's grandfather George. Henry H. Chamberlin, "George William Curtis and His Antecedents," 3–4; Shrady, *College of Physicians and Surgeons*, 410; Milne, *George William Curtis*, 3.

3. Chamberlin, "George William Curtis and His Antecedents," 12.

4. Kennedy, "Crisis and Progress," 18.

5. Milne, *George William Curtis*, 5.

6. Folpe, *It Happened on Washington Square*, 70–82; Harris, *Around Washington Square*, 34–37, 97.

7. Willis, "George Curtis," 62.

8. "George William Curtis" (*American*), 895; Kennedy, "Crisis and Progress," 26–28; Cooke, *Early Letters*, 104.

9. Milne, *George William Curtis*, 48–49.

10. Kennedy, "Crisis and Progress," iii.

11. Milne, *George William Curtis*, 118–21, 174–75.

12. N. Curtis to Elizabeth Day, Oct. 5, 1892, NCBA.

13. Milne, *George William Curtis*, 10–17, 28; Kennedy, "Crisis and Progress," 26–30.

14. "George William Curtis" (*Dictionary*), 615.

15. Milne, *George William Curtis*, 90–93, 99, 104.

16. Natalie Curtis, "Life of a Gifted Woman: Elizabeth Burrill Curtis," *Springfield Daily Republican*, Apr. 15, 1914. See also Milne, *George William Curtis*, 104.

17. Kennedy, "Crisis and Progress," 74, 90–101.

18. McPherson, *Abolitionist Legacy*, 343.

19. McPherson, *Abolitionist Legacy*, 40–50, 79.

20. G. W. Curtis, quoted in McPherson, *Abolitionist Legacy*, 323; see also 318–23.

21. Milne, *George William Curtis*, 183–84; Kennedy, "Crisis and Progress," 144–76.

22. N. Curtis, "Life of a Gifted Woman," 17.

23. N. Curtis, "Life of a Gifted Woman," 17.

24. N. Curtis, "Life of a Gifted Woman," 17.

25. Shrady, *College of Physicians and Surgeons*, 410.

26. Beckert, *Monied Metropolis*, 36.

27. Shrady, *College of Physicians and Surgeons*, 411–12.

28. King, *King's Handbook of New York City*, 47; McCabe, *Lights and Shadows of New York Life*, 54.

29. Hammack, *Power and Society*, xv, 33–43.

30. Hammack, *Power and Society*, 59; Beckert, *Monied Metropolis*, 2–3.

31. Rothstein, *American Physicians in the Nineteenth Century*, 198–206. See also Schlereth, *Victorian America*, 286–87.

32. Edward served as a clinical assistant at the New York Eye and Ear Infirmary and as a microscopist at the Manhattan Eye and Ear Infirmary. He taught *material medica* at the medical school. For more on Edward's tenure at the college and his reception there see Shrady, *College of Physicians and Surgeons*, 122–24; Rothstein, *American Physicians in the Nineteenth Century*, 201–3.

33. The Equitable had assets of $57,548,716 in 1884; $279,353,157 in 1899; and $412,438,381 in 1904. See Alexander, *Seventy-Five Years of Progress and Public*

Service, 25–26. For additional descriptions of Hyde's company and the remarkable building he erected for it see *Sun's Guide to New York City,* 138.

34. Shrady, *College of Physicians and Surgeons,* 412; McCabe, *Lights and Shadows of New York Life,* 520, 710. Edward made roughly $15,000 each year. McCabe notes that only a select few doctors made more than $20,000 and that a salary of $5,000–10,000 constituted a good income.

35. Shrady, *College of Physicians and Surgeons,* 412; Browne, *Great Metropolis.*

36. Beckert, *Monied Metropolis,* 254, 260–64.

37. *Sun's Guide to New York City,* 91–105; King, *King's Handbook of New York City,* 556–57.

38. Beckert, *Monied Metropolis,* 56.

39. Henry James, *Washington Square,* quoted in Harris, *Around Washington Square,* 30.

40. King, *King's Handbook of New York City,* 167.

41. Rydell, *All the World's a Fair,* 11.

42. Rydell, *All the World's a Fair,* 13–19, 32–33.

43. Rydell, *All the World's a Fair,* 23–27. For more on representations of Native Americans at fairs and expositions see Hoxie, *Final Promise.*

44. Rydell, *All the World's a Fair,* 27–29.

45. Logan, *Negro in American Life and Thought.*

46. Higham, "Reorientation of American Culture in the 1890's." See also Lears, *No Place of Grace;* Trachtenberg, *Incorporation of America.*

47. For more on this generation's rebellion against its parents, particularly its mothers, see Douglas, *Terrible Honesty;* Stansell, *American Moderns.*

48. Katherine Chapin to N. Curtis, Dec. 13, 1912, NCBA.

49. Augusta's great-grandfather was Davis Bevan. His daughter Anna Bevan married George Stacey (1764–1808), a Harvard-educated lawyer and merchant in Chester who had once served as the U.S. consul to the Isle of France. Their son David Stacey married Sara Van Dycke, and Augusta was one of the daughters of this union.

2. "THEY DON'T KNOW WHAT BLISS IS!"

1. H. L. Horowitz, "'Nous Autres.'"

2. G. Curtis, unpublished biography of Natalie Curtis, NCBA.

3. Smith-Rosenberg, "Female World of Love and Ritual."

4. Lavignac, *Musical Education.* Although this was originally a French work, it still held validity in the United States. The author was a professor at the Paris Conservatory, an institution emulated by most music educators in the United States.

5. Block and Neuls-Bates, "Historical Introduction"; Roell, *Piano in America*, 3–5.

6. Roell, *Piano in America*, 8–9.

7. Block and Neuls-Bates, "Historical Introduction," xx; Block and Steward, "Women in American Music," 142–45.

8. N. Curtis to Day, June 3, 10, 1890, Dec. 5, 1892, all NCBA.

9. W. S. B. Matthews, "Young Woman Pianist and Her Business Prospects," 64. See also Bauer, "Young Woman in Music," 42.

10. Fay, *Music-Study in Germany*. See also Daniels, *American Girl in Munich*. Daniels recounts her experiences as a composition student: she spent all morning in study, followed by afternoon lessons in composition, piano, and voice with private instructors and in seminary classrooms. Daniels also confirms that serious female piano students often spent five to six hours in practice each day.

11. N. Curtis to Day, June 29, 1890, NCBA.

12. N. Curtis to Day, Feb. 24, 1982, Jan. 7, 1891, Dec. 5, 1892, Mar. 17, 1893, all NCBA.

13. "William M. Semnacher."

14. N. Curtis to Day, Feb. 21, 1891, NCBA.

15. MacKay, "Long Island Country Houses and Their Architects." For more on Long Island's development see Weigold, *American Mediterranean*.

16. N. Curtis to Day, May–June 1892, NCBA.

17. N. Curtis to Day, Aug. 25, 1892, n.d., 1892, June 29, 1890, May–June, June 12, 1892, all NCBA.

18. N. Curtis to Day, Aug. 25, 1892, n.d., 1892, both NCBA.

19. Roberge, "Ferruccio Busoni in the United States."

20. Stuckenschmidt, *Ferruccio Busoni*, 178–83. For more on Busoni's view of pedagogy see the essays in his *The Essence of Music and Other Papers*.

21. J. Matthews, "Busoni's Contributions to Piano Pedagogy," 21.

22. N. Curtis to Day, Jan. 25, 1891, NCBA.

23. Raynor, *Music and Society since 1815*, 164–67.

24. N. Curtis to Day, Mar. 13, 1892, NCBA.

25. N. Curtis to Day, June 3, 1890, NCBA.

26. N. Curtis to Day, June 29, 10, 1890, both NCBA.

27. N. Curtis to Day, Dec. 2, 1890, NCBA; Krehbiel quoted in Kolodin, *Story of the Metropolitan Opera*, 112–13.

28. N. Curtis to Day, Feb. 15, 17, Jan. 16, 15, 1891, all NCBA.

29. J. Horowitz, *Wagner Nights*, 5.

30. N. Curtis to Day, Feb. 21, 1891, NCBA.

31. N. Curtis to Day, Nov. 27, 1891, NCBA.

32. Landau, *Ignace Paderewski*, 23, 70–79.

33. N. Curtis to Day, Nov. 27, 1891, NCBA.

34. N. Curtis to Day, Nov. 30, Dec. 17, 1891, both NCBA.

35. Dizikes, *Opera in America*, 214–17, 231–33; Lahee, *Grand Opera in America*, 225–30, 240–50.

36. J. Horowitz, *Wagner Nights*, 200–206; Dizikes, *Opera in America*, 239–42.

37. Dizikes, *Opera in America*, 236, 237.

38. J. Horowitz, *Wagner Nights*, 1, 8.

39. J. Horowitz, *Wagner Nights*, 90, 216, 224–25.

40. Damrosch, *My Musical Life*, 64.

41. J. Horowitz, *Wagner Nights*, 80–81. George Martin, in *The Damrosch Dynasty*, argues that Walter Damrosch was constantly hindered by undeserved criticism from the media, particularly the *Musical Courier*. He presents a far more favorable account of Damrosch's career.

42. Quoted in J. Horowitz, *Wagner Nights*, 101; Martin, *Damrosch Dynasty*, 197.

43. N. Curtis to Day, Feb. 24, 1892, NCBA.

44. N. Curtis to Day, Sept. 8, 1890, NCBA.

45. For more on Lilli Lehmann see Wagnalls, *Stars of the Opera*; J. Horowitz, *Wagner Nights*, 115–17.

46. N. Curtis to Day, June 8, 1890, NCBA.

47. N. Curtis to Day, May 7, 1891, NCBA.

48. N. Curtis to Day, Jan. 7, Feb. 17, Jan. 16, 1891, all NCBA.

49. N. Curtis to Day, Apr. 28, 1891, NCBA.

50. N. Curtis to Day, Nov. 30, 1891, NCBA. Despite this harsh assessment Edward also encouraged his daughter's interests. He and Natalie composed a song together that Edward based on Longfellow's "A Rainy Day." Natalie helped him harmonize this song, which she believed was "really his *chef-d'oeuvre.*" The pair considered joining the Manuscript Society, a group established in 1889 to promote the interests of American amateur composers.

51. N. Curtis to Day, Sept. 1, 1893, NCBA.

52. N. Curtis to Day, Sept. 5, 1893, NCBA.

53. Mason, "Passing of a Prophet."

54. Campbell, *Ancient Wisdom Revived*, 8–10.

55. Tweed, *American Encounter with Buddhism*, 50–70.

56. American Section of the Theosophical Society, *Primer of Theosophy*, 86, 113. Other publications by the society include Leadbeater, *Textbook of Theosophy*,

and Blavatsky, *Key to Theosophy*. Other scholarly accounts of the Theosophical Society include Burfield, "Theosophy and Feminism"; Cranston, HPB; Taylor, *Shadow Culture*.

57. Braude, *Radical Spirits*, 3. For another look at the intersections between gender and Spiritualism see Goldsmith, *Other Powers*.

58. N. Curtis to Day, Sept. 15, 1893, NCBA.

59. N. Curtis to Day, Sept. 15, 1893, NCBA.

60. N. Curtis to Day, Sept. 15, 1893, NCBA.

61. Versluis, *American Transcendentalism and Asian Religions*, 3–8.

62. Fay, *Music-Study in Germany*, 159. See Daniels, *American Girl in Munich*, for another, less rosy, account of music study in Germany. Davis, unlike the pianist Fay, studied composition and met with considerable opposition from the male-dominated music academies.

63. N. Curtis to Natalie Stacey, May 1, 1891, NCBA. For the article Curtis cites see "Flickers," 407.

64. N. Curtis to Day, May 1893, NCBA.

65. N. Curtis to Day, May 1893, NCBA.

66. G. Curtis, unpublished biography of Natalie Curtis, NCBA.

67. Augusta Curtis, "Reminiscences of Bayreuth," unpublished manuscript, NCBA.

68. Spotts, *Bayreuth*, 114; A. Curtis, "Reminiscences of Bayreuth," NCBA.

69. A. Curtis, "Reminiscences of Bayreuth," NCBA.

70. A. Curtis, "Reminiscences of Bayreuth," NCBA; Spotts, *Bayreuth*, 6.

71. A. Curtis, "Reminiscences of Bayreuth," NCBA.

72. Finck, "Musical Outlook for Women," 151.

73. Winn, "Woman Musician," 335.

74. Block and Neuls-Bates, "Historical Introduction," xix.

75. G. Curtis, unpublished biography of Natalie Curtis, NCBA.

76. Tick, "Women as Professional Musicians in the United States."

77. Ammer, *Unsung*, 72–74.

78. Levy, "Double-Bars and Double Standards"; Tick, "Women as Professional Musicians in the United States," 115.

79. Plantinga, *Romantic Music*, 107; Hallmard, *German Lieder in the Nineteenth Century*, x–xii.

80. For more on Farwell and the Wa-Wan Press see Culbertson, *He Heard America Singing*; Culbertson, "Arthur Farwell's Early Efforts on Behalf of American Music."

81. Plantinga, *Romantic Music*, 341–42; N. Curtis, "Franz Liszt."

3. "I AM FULL OF PLANS"

1. N. Curtis to Theodore Roosevelt, July 29, 1903, Theodore Roosevelt Papers, LOC.

2. White, *Eastern Establishment and the Western Experience*. For more on late-nineteenth- and early-twentieth-century perceptions of manliness and ties to Western adventure see Bederman, *Manliness and Civilization*.

3. Dilworth, *Imagining Indians in the Southwest*, 2–3, 78. For more on the role of women and gender in creating Southwest tourism see Wiegle, "Exposition and Mediation."

4. Babcock and Parezo, *Daughters of the Desert*, 1–7; Mullin, *Culture in the Marketplace*, 47–49.

5. Georgi-Findlay, *Frontiers of Women's Writing*, x; Mills, *Discourses of Difference*, 1–2. Recently historians and other scholars have examined the travel writing of women, locating their work within a larger body of colonialist discourse and feminist (or proto-feminist) writing. See Mills, *Discourses of Difference*, for Mills's discussion of these trends and her proposed methodology for understanding these texts (a feminist, Foucaultian analysis).

6. Natalie Curtis, "An Arizona Penitentiary," *New York Evening Post* (Saturday supplement), Oct. 10, 1903.

7. Natalie Curtis, "Where Man's Art Availeth Not," *New York Evening Post* (Saturday supplement), Oct. 24, 1903. For more on this type of posturing in imperial travel texts see Pratt, *Imperial Eyes*.

8. N. Curtis, "Bit of American Folk Music"; Babcock, "'New Mexican Rebecca.'"

9. N. Curtis, "American Indian Composer."

10. Natalie Curtis, "Navajo Indians at Pasadena," *New York Evening Post* (Saturday supplement) Nov. 28, 1903.

11. G. Curtis, unpublished biography of Natalie Curtis, NCBA. Further analysis of her ability to capture Native American music can be found in chapter 4.

12. Lurie, *Women and the Invention of American Anthropology*, 1–9. See also Parezo, "Anthropology"; Parezo, *Daughters of the Desert*. Some scholars disagree that white women possessed special talents for relating to Native Americans. See, e.g., Kamala Visweswaran, who in "'Wild West' Anthropology and the Disciplining of Gender," argues for the "inseparability of gender from racial positioning" (95–96). She contends that white women could not identify with Indian women as women and used their research as a means to challenge their own subordination. She also argues for the possibility of "womanist frontier machismo" (97) among female anthropologists. For more on the relationship between white women and Native Americans see Packer and Frankeil, "Natural Sympathies"; Riley, *Women and Indians on the Frontier*.

13. Lurie, *Women and the Invention of American Anthropology*, 4–6; Parezo, "Matilda Coxe Stevenson."

14. Parezo, "Anthropology," 5; Babcock and Parezo, "Introduction," 4.

15. Basson, "History of Ethnological Research." For more on the beginnings of interest in Zuni see McFeely, *Zuni and the American Imagination*.

16. V. L. Levine, "Reading American Indian Music as Social History," xix.

17. Little comprehensive work on Densmore has been done. For more on her work see Hofmann, *Frances Densmore and American Indian Music*; Peterson, "On the Trail of Red Sky Lady"; Archabal, "Frances Densmore."

18. Mark, *Stranger in Her Native Land*, 216–19. Curtis corresponded with Fletcher briefly regarding her studies of Indian music.

19. V. L. Levine, "Reading American Indian Music as Social History," xix–xxix; Keeling, "Beginnings of Musicological Research."

20. The Hopi reservation encompasses three mesas that jut out into the desert from east to west. Third Mesa is the farthest to the west.

21. Fewkes, "On the Use of the Phonograph"; Fewkes, "Additional Studies of Zuni Songs and Rituals."

22. See Curtis's field notebooks in the Natalie Curtis Collection, DAMA. Curtis also wrote down the songs of birds she encountered in the Southwest. Kachina dances consisted of rituals using elaborate masks to portray a variety of supernatural beings. Kachina dances were often associated with rain and fertility, among other things.

23. Natalie Curtis, "United States, Arizona, Hopi, Navajo and Zuni Indians," 1903 (sound recording), accession number 54-027-f, Archives of Traditional Music, Indiana University.

24. Charles Burton, "Report of School at Keams Canyon, Arizona," ARCIA 1900, 474–75.

25. Whiteley, *Deliberate Acts*, 91–95; Charles Burton, "Report of the School Superintendent in Charge of Moqui," ARCIA 1902, 153. *Moqui*, a term applied to the Hopi by government officials, was later dismissed upon realization of its negative connotations to tribal members. H. C. James, *Pages from Hopi History*, 123–29; M. Thompson, *American Character*, 244–55. See also Lummis, *Bullying the Moqui*.

26. N. Curtis, "Mr. Roosevelt and Indian Music."

27. Roosevelt to N. Curtis, July 2, 1903, Roosevelt Papers, LOC; N. Curtis, "Mr. Roosevelt and Indian Music," 399.

28. Roosevelt to Ethan Allen Hitchcock, July 22, 1903, in Roosevelt, *Letters*, 503. For more on this "Indian cabinet" see Hagan, *Theodore Roosevelt and Six Friends of the Indian*. Hagan notes that this letter "disturbed that curmudgeon,

who did not appreciate private citizens' intruding on his bailiwick," but Hitchcock evidently complied with Roosevelt's requests. Hagan, *Theodore Roosevelt
and Six Friends of the Indian*, 149.

29. N. Curtis to Roosevelt, July 29, 1903, Roosevelt Papers, LOC.

30. N. Curtis, "American Indian Composer." *Pahana* or sometimes *bahana*
could refer to an American or any white person and was used because of its
connection to a Hopi prophecy that a white brother (the *pahana* or *bahana*)
would return to the Hopi to teach and help them.

31. N. Curtis, "Shepherd Poet."

32. Natalie Curtis, "The Story of an Indian Song," *New York Evening Post*,
Dec. 19, 1903.

33. N. Curtis, "Bit of American Folk Music."

34. N. Curtis, "Perpetuating of Indian Art."

35. Although Fletcher later returned to unharmonized recordings of Native
song because of critiques of this approach, her most famous work, *Indian Story
and Song*, presented music in a harmonized format.

36. N. Curtis, "American Indian Composer," 626. Dwight Moody, a Christian
evangelist, and the musician Ira Sankey composed a number of popular gospel
hymns in the late nineteenth century.

37. N. Curtis, "American Indian Composer," 628–29; Huhndorf, *Going Native*,
especially introduction and chapter 1; Deloria, *Playing Indian*.

38. N. Curtis, "American Indian Composer," 628, 632.

39. Carr, *Inventing the American Primitive*, 21, 148–49.

40. She prepared manuscript versions of songs she had collected in 1903,
some of which reappeared in *The Indians' Book*. For example, she transcribed
a Navajo dance song from the Nightway ceremony in the handwritten appearance she later employed in her book. This and other songs can be found in the
Native American Song Manuscript Collection, LOC.

41. N. Curtis, "Winning of an Indian Reservation." Charlotte Mason is perhaps
better known as the "godmother" of the Harlem Renaissance. She became a
patron of Langston Hughes and Zora Neale Hurston, among other African
American writers and artists. Mason preferred anonymity — Curtis never publicly acknowledged Mason's assistance with *The Indians' Book* until the 1921
edition — and was known for her domineering ways with her protégées. See
Hughes, *Big Sea*, and Hurston, *Dust Tracks on a Road*, for more on Mason's
relationships with her protégées.

42. N. Curtis to George Foster Peabody, Oct. 24, 1904, George Foster Peabody
Papers, LOC. For more on Peabody see Ware, *George Foster Peabody*.

43. Lindsey, *Indians at Hampton Institute*, 182. Lindsey remarks on Hampton's

policy of cultural preservation: "The great paradox of the Hampton position on the worth of indigenous cultures is that honoring the cultural histories and artifacts of racial minorities seemed perfectly compatible with white supremacy and paternalism."

44. N. Curtis, "Value of Indian Art"; N. Curtis, "Hampton's Double-Mission."

45. See, e.g., N. Curtis, "Shepherd Poet"; N. Curtis, "Indian Song on a Desert Path"; N. Curtis, "Indian Song" (Dec. 1905); N. Curtis, "Indian Song" (Apr. 1906).

46. "Indian Music at Hampton's Anniversary"; "Virginia Day."

47. N. Curtis to Hollis B. Frissell, Dec. 7, 1905, Dr. H. B. Frissell Collection — Correspondence, HUA.

48. N. Curtis to Frissell, Dec. 7, 1905, HUA; "Indian Music at Hampton's Anniversary."

49. See Native American Song Manuscript Collection, LOC.

50. N. Curtis to Matilda Coxe Stevenson, Feb. 12, 1906, Curtis Collection, DAMA. See her notebooks in this collection as well.

51. Rydell, Findling, and Pelle, *Fair America*, 52–53.

52. Rydell, Findling, and Pelle, *Fair America*, 54–57.

53. Magnaghi, "America Views Her Indians."

54. N. Curtis to Day, Oct. 19, 1893, NCBA. Curtis sent Day a letter from the Grand Pacific Hotel in Chicago, saying, "I have realized all my wildest hopes" by visiting the fair. Curtis had visited with "Papa" and could not begin to describe everything that she saw to Day. "Nothing I could say would give you any idea of the surpassing beauty of the buildings and grounds," she gushed to her friend.

55. Many attendees, "armed with notebooks," arrived at the fair hoping for a similar educational experience. Frederick Starr, of the University of Chicago, even offered a course entitled "The Louisiana Purchase Exposition Class in Ethnology" at the fair. According to Rydell, "society co-eds" from Chicago and St. Louis schoolteachers attended lectures and gained hands-on experience with several of the Native groups brought to the fair. See Rydell, *All the World's a Fair*, 166.

56. In his diary George noted material from the fair that his sister included in *The Indians' Book*. For example, returning to his diary in 1930, he wrote in the margins, next to an explanation of Geronimo's song, that the material appeared on p. 324 of *The Indians' Book*.

57. G. Curtis diaries, NCBA; Natalie Curtis, field notebook, ca. 1904, Curtis Collection, DAMA. For more on Jacob Morgan see Parman, "J. C. Morgan."

58. In his memoirs — *Geronimo: His Own Story* — Geronimo does not mention Curtis, although he shared her assessment of Igorote music. He wrote: "I am glad I went to the fair. I saw many interesting things and learned much of the white people. They are a very kind and peaceful people" (165).

59. George DeClyver Curtis, diary from St. Louis World's Fair, 1904, NCBA.

60. Rydell, *All the World's a Fair*, 155–57; Kramer, "Making Concessions"; F. Hoxie, *Final Promise*, 88–92.

61. Natalie Curtis, "The Music of Many Lands," *New York Times*, Sept. 25, 1904.

62. Fair historian Martha Clevenger urges scholars to examine the ways individuals responded to the spectacle and impermanence of the exposition, rather than focus only on the fair planners' intentions. See Clevenger's introduction to *"Indescribably Grand."*

63. Hoxie, *Final Promise*, 84–99; Trennert, "Resurrection of Native Arts and Crafts"; Trennert, "Fairs, Expositions, and the Changing Image."

64. See, generally, GDCD.

65. Entry for Nov. 25, 1904, GDCD.

66. Entry for Nov. 28, 1904, GDCD.

67. Entries for Feb. 8, 15, 1905, GDCD.

68. Entry for Dec. 1, 1904, GDCD.

69. See, e.g., entries for Dec. 11, 16, 19, 31, 1904, GDCD.

70. N. Curtis, field notebook, 1904, Curtis Collection, DAMA.

4. "THE PENCIL IN THE HAND OF THE INDIAN"

1. N. Curtis, *Indians' Book*, ix–x.

2. Tisdale, "Women on the Periphery of the Ivory Tower."

3. N. Curtis, *Songs of Ancient America*, iii–v.

4. This collection contained a Southern Cheyenne Sun Dance song and a Zuni corn-grinding tune, along with a French translation and explanations of the music from Curtis. It lacked the art and photographs of *The Indians' Book*, and it did not contain musical transcriptions. "Chansons Indiennes" may have been intended to introduce French audiences to Curtis's work, or it could have been part of a lecture Curtis planned to promote her work overseas. She had to publish this work herself, which, along with the lack of musical notation and visual imagery, suggests that it did not receive a wide reception. It may have made Curtis and her work known to some French scholars, as Curtis later returned to France to lecture on Native American music after *The Indians' Book* became successful in the United States.

5. The 1907 edition was the only one to use color. The 1923 edition and the 1963 Dover edition, the most widely available today, only contain black and white images.

6. Several copies of High Chief's signature can be found among the artwork at the Natalie Curtis Burlin Archives. Curtis chose one of the more "primitive"-looking ones for her book.

7. Roosevelt to N. Curtis, May 3, 24, 1906, both Roosevelt Papers, LOC. Curtis was originally unhappy with part of Roosevelt's letter and asked him to rewrite his supporting statement.

8. N. Curtis, *Indians' Book*, 535.

9. Dippie, *Vanishing American*, xii; Berkhofer, *White Man's Indian*, 49–59; Smith, *Reimagining Indians*, 7. For more on this shift in views toward Native Americans see Hoxie, *Final Promise*.

10. Trachtenberg, *Shades of Hiawatha*, xxiv, 10–20; Dippie, *Vanishing American*, 199. See also Huhndorf, *Going Native*, 53–56; Deloria, *Playing Indian*, 96–101. Torgovnick discusses how certain groups have identified the "primitive" with their own origins, creating a "home" in which they can seek comfort and find identity. See *Gone Primitive*, 185–88.

11. N. Curtis, *Indians' Book*, xxx, 11, 47, 425.

12. N. Curtis, *Indians' Book*, xxi.

13. N. Curtis, *Indians' Book*, xxi–xxii.

14. N. Curtis, *Indians' Book*, 350.

15. N. Curtis, *Indians' Book*, 313–14.

16. N. Curtis, *Indians' Book*, 475–77.

17. N. Curtis, *Indians' Book*, xxix, 533. Curtis used "barbaric" here in terms consistent with the "scientific" usage at the time, as indicating a distinct stage of human evolution. See Fiske, *Discovery of America*, vol. 1.

18. Fletcher, *Indian Story and Song from North America*, viii; Fillmore, "Scientific Importance"; Fillmore, "Forms Spontaneously Assumed by Folk-Songs"; N. Curtis, *Indians' Book*, xxv–xxvi.

19. Torgovnick, *Gone Primitive*, 8–11; Dilworth, *Imagining Indians in the Southwest*, 3–5.

20. Vickers, *Native American Identities*, 40–42. See also Berkhofer, *White Man's Indian*, 71–78. For more on this notion of nostalgia for the past see Rosaldo, *Culture and Truth*. In his chapter entitled "Imperialist Nostalgia" Rosaldo describes this notion as a longing "for the very forms of life they [agents of imperialism] intentionally altered or destroyed." He sees this "innocent yearning" as a means to draw attention to one's subject and to hide one's complicity in forms of domination. See especially pp. 69–70.

21. Berkhofer, *White Man's Indian*, 28. See also W. Matthews, "Songs of the Navajos"; Cushing, "Outlines of Zuni Creation Myths." For Boas see Jonaitis and Inglis, "Power, History, and Authenticity." Jonaitis and Inglis comment on Boas's efforts to re-create an "authentic" replica of a Native shrine in a museum. For more on authenticity see Hinsley, "Authoring Authenticity"; Orvell, *Real Thing*.

22. See Lyman, *Vanishing American and Other Illusions*, for more on the staging of Edward S. Curtis's photographs. See also Gidley, *Edward S. Curtis and the North American Indian*, for his critique of Lyman's analysis and his discussion of Edward S. Curtis's inclusion of modern objects and themes in his photographs. Natalie Curtis, as discussed below, occasionally discussed Indians in modern society.

23. N. Curtis, *Indians' Book*, 298–99, 348. Evidence of Curtis's role in shaping the presentation of photographs can be seen in a collection of material at the Natalie Curtis Burlin Archives and in several photographs by Curtis at the National Anthropological Archives. A collection of artwork is housed in the NCBA that contains Curtis's notes on reproduction and display. The Kwakiutl photographs can be found opposite p. 300 in *The Indians' Book*. The NAA holds several of Curtis's photographs from St. Louis. Backgrounds were painted blue so that the viewer could not tell what was originally in the picture. A few photographs, though, show buildings from the fairgrounds, and one contains an editing note instructing that the offending background be removed. Another photograph reveals modern clothes beneath a man's ceremonial costume. This photograph of course was not used in Curtis's book. See Breitbart, *World on Display*, for a discussion of the use of photography in the representation of "primitive" peoples at the fair.

24. N. Curtis, *Indians' Book*, 147–60.

25. N. Curtis, *Indians' Book*, 425.

26. Dilworth, *Imagining Indians in the Southwest*, 125–26.

27. N. Curtis, "Story of an Indian Song."

28. See Clements, *Native American Verbal Art*. See especially pp. 164–66 for Clements's critique of Curtis's portrayal of Lololomai and Tawakwaptiwa. For more on this factionalism in Oraibi see Titiev, *Old Oraibi*; H. James, *Pages from Hopi History*; Rushforth and Upham, *Hopi Social History*; Whiteley, *Deliberate Acts*.

29. N. Curtis, *Indians' Book*, 480. See above sources for more details on this split. Tensions between the two factions had reached a head by early Sept. 1906. Leaders of each faction agreed to settle their differences through a shoving match between the two groups. The losing side, the "Hostiles," were forced to

leave Oraibi and eventually settled in a new village on the mesa. Leaders on both sides were jailed, including Tawakwaptiwa, who was forced to attend a government boarding school in Riverside CA. Curtis later visited him there to present him with a copy of *The Indians' Book*.

30. N. Curtis, *Indians' Book*, xxviii.

31. N. Curtis, *Indians' Book*, xxx.

32. W. Matthews, *Navaho Legends*, 59–60; F. Burton, *American Primitive Music*, 177–87.

33. N. Curtis, "American Indian Artist."

34. DeCora, "Native Indian Art"; McAnulty, "Angel DeCora." Often white women like Curtis were the ones controlling Indian artists and the market for their art in the 1920s, especially in the Southwest. See Mullin, *Culture in the Marketplace*; Jacobs, *Engendered Encounters*.

35. N. Curtis, *Indians' Book*, xxix.

36. N. Curtis, *Indians' Book*, 426.

37. Douglas, *Terrible Honesty*, 282; Watson, *Harlem Renaissance*, 144–46; Hurston, *Dust Tracks on a Road*, 184.

38. See, e.g., A. E., "Snake Dance." The author argued that Indians sought the "same spirit of divine truth" as Theosophists did. Perhaps Curtis's earlier involvement with the group encouraged her to take a similar viewpoint. See also Jackman, "Price the Hopi Indians Are Paying."

39. G. W. James, *What the White Race May Learn from the Indian*; Smith, *Reimagining Indians*, 146; Troyer, *Zuni Indians and Their Music*, 12–14. For more on ways white women in the Southwest used positive evaluations of Native cultures to critique their society and advance their own agendas in the 1920s see Jacobs, *Engendered Encounters*; Mullin, *Culture in the Marketplace*.

40. For more on the use of Indians as symbols for white Americans see Berkhofer, *White Man's Indian*, xiv–xv; Carr, *Inventing the American Primitive*, 8.

41. N. Curtis, *Indians' Book*, 58–59.

42. N. Curtis, *Indians' Book*, 244. See also items in Cheyenne folder, Curtis Collection, DAMA.

43. People who had not even met with the informants contributed to the editing process. For example, Curtis often sent home handwritten pages while she conducted fieldwork. Her father, Edward, helped with the editing process and occasionally commented on his daughter's work. See various items in the Curtis Collection, DAMA.

44. W. Matthews, *Navajo Legends*, 53; Fletcher, *Indian Story and Song from North America*, 49.

45. N. Curtis to James Mooney, Apr. 18, 1905, James Mooney Papers, NAA.

46. N. Curtis, *Indians' Book*, xxiv–xxv.

47. N. Curtis, *Indians' Book*, 104–6.

48. Bevis, "American Indian Verse Translations"; Sands and Sekaquaptewa, "Four Hopi Lullabies."

49. Krupat, "On the Translation of Native American Song and Story."

50. Smith, *Reimagining Indians*, 5–13.

51. N. Curtis, "Indian Song on a Desert Path."

52. N. Curtis, "Old Town of the New World."

53. See Curtis's notebooks in the Curtis Collection, DAMA.

54. N. Curtis, *Indians' Book*, xxii, 477; N. Curtis, "American Indian Composer," 632; Nettl, *Study of Ethnomusicology*, 74–77.

55. Mark, *Stranger in Her Native Land*, 146–52.

56. N. Curtis, *Indians' Book*, xxii.

57. N. Curtis, "Perpetuating of Indian Art"; Kurt Schindler to Eldridge Adams, read by George Foster Peabody at the Hampton memorial service for Natalie Curtis; reprinted in *Southern Workman* 55 (Mar. 1926): 127–40.

58. Szasz, *Between Indian and White Worlds*, 137–38.

59. For more on Cheyenne affairs in the period see Berthrong, *Cheyenne and Arapaho Ordeal*.

60. N. Curtis, *Indians' Book*, 486.

61. N. Curtis, *Indians' Book*, 9–10, 57, 160, 480.

62. N. Curtis, "American Indian Cradle Songs."

63. N. Curtis, *Indians' Book*, 38, 154, 324.

64. Archambault, "Sun Dance."

65. N. Curtis, *Indians' Book*, 151–52.

66. N. Curtis, *Indians' Book*, 480–94. See, e.g., Voth and Dorsey, *Oraibi Soyal Ceremony; Mishongnovi Ceremonies of the Snake and Antelope Fraternities.*

67. W. Matthews, "Songs of the Navajo," 197; N. Curtis, *Indians' Book*, 349–73.

68. See Mooney, "Ghost Dance Religion."

69. N. Curtis, *Indians' Book*, 41–47.

70. See LaBarre, *Peyote Cult*, for the differences between peyote and mescal.

71. N. Curtis, *Indians' Book*, 162–64.

72. N. Curtis, *Indians' Book*, 164–65, 223.

73. N. Curtis, *Indians' Book*, 98.

74. N. Curtis, *Indians' Book*, 57–58, 463.

75. N. Curtis, *Indians' Book*, 47, 222, 244.

76. N. Curtis, untitled introduction to *Indians' Book*, n.d., Curtis Collection, DAMA.

5. "THE WHITE FRIEND"

1. Joan Mark writes about Fletcher's efforts to allot the Omahas and Winnebagos: "The tragedy of Alice Fletcher's life is that she was a benevolent, well-intentioned person who ended up hurting the people she tried to help." See *Stranger in Her Native Land*, 201.

2. Parezo, "Matilda Coxe Stevenson." For more on Stevenson see McFeely, *Zuni and the American Imagination*, especially chapter 3.

3. See Smith, *Reimagining Indians*, for discussions of several of these writers, including George Bird Grinnell, Charles Lummis, George Wharton James, Mary Austin, and Mabel Dodge Luhan.

4. Hoxie, *Final Promise*, 6–10.

5. Prucha, *Great Father*, 626–28. Sioban Senier, in *Voices of American Indian Assimilation and Resistance*, questions the extent to which Jackson supported complete assimilation and provides an alternative interpretation of her writings. For more on Jackson see Mathes, *Helen Hunt Jackson*.

6. Holm, "Indians and Progressives," 21–22; Ahern, "Assimilationist Racism," 25–26. See also Bolt, *American Indian Policy and American Reform*, 93; Berens, "Old Campaigners, New Realities"; G. Thompson, "Origins and Implementation of the American Indian Reform Movement." ,

7. Bolt, *American Indian Policy and American Reform*, 90–92; Prucha, *Great Father*, 615–17. For descriptions of the early development of Indian reform organizations see also Mardock, *Reformers and the American Indian*; Prucha, *Americanizing the First Americans*. For an account of the IRA see Hagan, *Indian Rights Association*. For more on the Lake Mohonk Conferences see Burgess, "Lake Mohonk Conference on the Indian." This and additional material on Indian reformers and educational policy are drawn from Wick, "'Practical Education.'"

8. Prucha, *Great Father*, 772–74; Bolt, *American Indian Policy and American Reform*, 94; Berens, "Old Campaigners, New Realities," 59. The Burke Act upset reformers because it altered the terms of the Dawes Act, ending the automatic granting of citizenship to Indian allottees following the twenty-five-year trust period. Reformers believed this delay to be antithetical to their goal of quickly incorporating Indians into American society. The Lacey Act originally intended to allot tribal funds to individual members of tribes, but Representative Charles Burke added a clause that allowed a division of funds only if an individual requested it, thereby overturning the intentions of the reformers.

9. Bolt, *American Indian Policy and American Reform*, 101; Berens, "Old Campaigners, New Realities," 59.

10. Prucha, *Great Father*, 763–89; Dippie, *Vanishing American*, 183–85. Kenneth

O'Reilly argues that the problems reformers faced did not differ greatly from those of earlier periods, and he insists that the policy of the government and that of the reform groups remained essentially similar. Past methods continued to be used to bring Indians to civilization, especially the emphasis on education. See O'Reilly, "Progressive Era and New Era American Indian Policy."

11. Hoxie, *Final Promise*, xii–xiv, 241–43. Prucha responds to Hoxie's arguments by contending that Hoxie "stresses a radical change in policy after 1900 that does not take account of significant evidence of continuity in policy" (*Great Father*, nn759–60).

12. Hoxie, *Final Promise*, 103–6. Many historians view the reformers of the Progressive Era as well-intentioned humanitarians struggling to do what seemed best for Native Americans. Altschuler explains the push for assimilation as the only way reformers could envision any preservation of Indian peoples. In short, assimilation was the Indians' "last best hope." O'Reilly comments on the tragic outcome of these beliefs, noting that the reformers really believed that their ideas were "benevolent and scientifically correct," as they drew from Social Darwinian thought. See Altschuler, *Race, Ethnicity and Class in American Social Thought*, 30–32; O'Reilly, "Progressive Era and New Era American Indian Policy," 47–48.

Other historians of Indian policy view the intentions of reformers and government officials more critically. Wilber Ahern argues that reformers' endorsement of American expansion conflicted with their defense of Indian rights. Their solution to this dilemma, reflecting their low valuation of Indian cultures, "denied self-determination to the Native American" and only allowed for the complete adoption of white values. The educational policy based on these views "comforted America," as it let most Americans "avoid either admitting that they were involved in blatant conquest or confront[ing] the complex task of recognizing the legitimate demands of Native Americans." Thomas Holm also notes the racist biases of reform groups whose members felt that inherited traits and Indian lifestyles prevented Native Americans from evolving as white people had, but he does note that the growing popularity of "Indianness" created ambiguities for reformers. Holm identifies two types of reformers: the "old" reformers supported the individualization of Indians and their resources and expressed cultural bigotry; the "new" reformers expressed more tolerance of Indian cultures but also espoused racial biases. See Ahern, "Assimilationist Racism," 26–29; Holm, "Indian and Progressives," 127–64.

13. N. Curtis, "Winning of an Indian Reservation," 327; Hagan, *Theodore Roosevelt and Six Friends of the Indian*, 148–49.

14. Hagan, *Theodore Roosevelt and Six Friends of the Indian*, 151; Khera and

Mariella, "Yavapai"; Mariella, "Political Economy of Federal Resettlement Policies"; Frances Leupp, "Report of the Commissioner of Indian Affairs — Camp McDowell Reservation, Arizona," ARCIA 1905, 98–103. Other accounts of this event, however, suggest that the chief sent by the Yavapais was actually named Yuma Frank or Kapalwa.

15. F. Leupp, "Report of the Commissioner of Indian Affairs," 98–99; Khera and Mariella, "Yavapai," 42.

16. N. Curtis, "Winning of an Indian Reservation," 328–29; Khera and Mariella, "Yavapai," 42; Hagan, *Theodore Roosevelt and Six Friends of the Indians*, 148.

17. N. Curtis to Roosevelt, Aug. 31, 1903, and Roosevelt to N. Curtis, Sept. 3, 1903, both Roosevelt Papers, LOC.

18. Quoted in Hagan, *Theodore Roosevelt and Six Friends of the Indian*, 151. The Indian Rights Association even investigated Mead's private life, especially accusations that he had an affair with a married woman while working on an architectural project in Philadelphia, but made no public charges against him.

19. N. Curtis, "Winning of an Indian Reservation," 330.

20. Khera and Mariella, "Yavapai," 42. See C. W. Goodman, "Report of the Superintendent in Charge of Phoenix School and Camp McDowell Reservation," and William H. Gill, "Report of Farmer in Charge of Camp McDowell Reservation," both ARCIA 1905, for accounts of the immediate struggles the Yavapai faced after the establishment of the reservation.

21. N. Curtis, "Plight of the Mojave Apache Indians," 630–31.

22. N. Curtis to Peabody, May 25, 17, 1905, both Peabody Papers, LOC.

23. N. Curtis, "Shepherd Poet," 148.

24. N. Curtis, "Bit of American Folk Music"; N. Curtis, "Navajo Indians at Pasadena."

25. N. Curtis, *Indians' Book*, xxiii, xxxii.

26. Review of N. Curtis, *Indians' Book* (*Review of Reviews*); F. F. Kelly, "Indian Legends, Art and Songs," *New York Times*, Oct. 19, 1907.

27. N. Curtis, *Indians' Book*, 313–14, 424, 475–76.

28. Government officials dealt with two groups of Winnebagos separately — one group stayed in Wisconsin, and the other moved to Minnesota (they briefly held lands at Blue Earth). In the late 1870s this group was removed to Nebraska. See Lurie, "Winnebago," 690–707.

29. N. Curtis, *Indians' Book*, 94, 222, 243–44.

30. N. Curtis, *Indians' Book*, 339–40, 568–70.

31. Good general works on Indian education and related topics include D. W. Adams, *Education for Extinction*; E. C. Adams, *American Indian Education*;

Berkhofer, *Salvation and the Savage*; DeJong, *Promises of the Past*; Szasz, *Indian Education in the American Colonies*.

32. Support for religiously affiliated schools did not continue into the twentieth century. Because Catholic-sponsored schools outnumbered Protestant ones, the mainly Protestant reform organizations pushed for the end of government support of religious schools. In the *Quick Bear v. Leupp* (1907) decision the courts ruled against the Protestant reformers, deciding that tribal funds could support sectarian schools. See Prucha, *Churches and the Indian Schools*.

33. A multitude of works on specific Indian schools exists. The following is a brief list of these works: Mihesuah, *Cultivating the Rosebuds*; Ellis, *To Change Them Forever*; Lomawaima, *They Called It Prairie Light*; Trennert, *Phoenix Indian School*.

34. For a useful overview of boarding schools see D. W. Adams, *Education for Extinction*, as well as chapters in Prucha, *Great Father*, and Hoxie, *Final Promise*. Previously cited studies of individual boarding schools demonstrate both the shared characteristics of the schools and the variations among them. Fruitful research on the boarding school experience notes that students had a variety of responses to the schools, not all of them negative, and that boarding schools may have helped foster pan-Indian reform movements that developed in the twentieth century.

35. See work by Margaret Jacobs on protests over the removal of Native children from their mothers, which she generously shared with me: "Maternal Colonialism" and "Great White Mother."

36. Scholars of Native American education acknowledge practical concerns that drove these criticisms and relate them to the perceived overall shift in Indian policy. D. W. Adams, in *Education for Extinction*, acknowledges that government policy during the Progressive Era became more gradualist in scope, but he argues that the movement toward industrial education did not alter the main goals of education because industrial training had long been a part of Indian schooling. He also attributes changes in education policy to perceived cruelty in an education process that forcibly separated children from their parents. Margaret Szasz, in *Education and the American Indian*, attributes the declining support for off-reservation boarding schools to a response to the high cost and limited outcomes of such schools. In *American Indian Education* E. C. Adams remarks that education following the Dawes Act "was being carried on with little reference to what was happening to the Indian's land, his chief economic asset." Hoxie characterizes post-1900 education policy as "a more modest approach" toward Indian education and characterizes the educational system of Estelle Reel as a "curriculum of low expectations and practical lessons." He argues

that educational policies came to reflect the diminished perception of Indian potential. See *Final Promise*, 103–6, 189–200.

Studies of individual boarding schools, such as Trennert's *Phoenix Indian School* and Ellis's *To Change Them Forever*, affirm that after 1900 schools emphasized vocational training more and reflected diminished goals for graduates. As Ellis notes, the official policy "became clouded by increasingly loud complaints about what the government could reasonably expect from a backward race" (135–49).

37. N. Curtis to Franz Boas, Mar. 3, 1907, PFCB.

38. N. Curtis to Aleš Hrdlička, Mar. 6, 1912, Aleš Hrdlička (1869–1943) Papers, NAA.

39. N. Curtis, untitled introduction to *Indians' Book*.

40. N. Curtis, "Indian Music and Indian Education." Curtis spoke at the NEA convention on a similar topic the following year. Educators, she argued, needed to "know the Indian" and could do so through study of the "unwritten literature" of Indian music. N. Curtis, "Music of the American Indian."

41. N. Curtis, "Perpetuating of Indian Art"; Natalie Curtis, untitled essay, Apr. 1911, Music Collection — Natalie Curtis Burlin, HUA.

42. N. Curtis, "Perpetuating of Indian Art," 627–28; N. Curtis, untitled essay, Music Collection — Natalie Curtis Burlin, HUA.

43. N. Curtis, "Perpetuating of Indian Art," 625; N. Curtis, untitled essay, Music Collection — Natalie Curtis Burlin, HUA.

44. "To Preserve Indian Music," *New York Times*, Mar. 20, 1913; N. Curtis, "Perpetuating of Indian Art," 621–31. See also "Recording the Indian's Music."

45. "Back to Nature for the Indian"; Coffin, "On the Education of Backward Races"; Flynn, "Preservation of Aboriginal Arts"; Garland, "Red Man's Present Needs"; Monson, "Destruction of Our Indians"; United States Bureau of Indian Affairs, *Course of Study*.

46. N. Curtis, untitled essay, Music Collection — Natalie Curtis Burlin, HUA. It would be another decade or more before these reforms would take place. See Szasz's work in general for developments in educational policy in the twentieth century. No full-scale study of Indian education took place until the 1920s. "The Indian Problem: Resolutions of the Committee of 100" provided a positive assessment of government schools in 1924. *The Problem of Indian Administration* (better known as the Meriam Report) gave a far grimmer view of Indian education. See Prucha, *Great Father*, 835–40.

47. "People Who Interest Us: Natalie Curtis"; "Indian Music."

48. Peabody to Frank Damrosch, May 1, 1907, Board of Trustees Collection — George F. Peabody, HUA. A copy of this itemized list for disbursement

of *The Indians' Book* from 1907 can be found in the Peabody Papers, LOC. In all, Curtis and Peabody gave away over one hundred copies of her book. See also Roosevelt to N. Curtis, Oct. 24, 1907, Roosevelt Papers, LOC.

49. N. Curtis to Boas, Dec. 17, 1908, PCFB; N. Curtis to Frederick Webb Hodge, Feb. 28, 1914, Frederick Webb Hodge Papers, Braun Research Library.

50. "Lectures on the North American Indian," NCBA.

51. "Lectures on the North American Indian," NCBA.

52. "Lectures on the North American Indian," NCBA.

53. Curtis confided to Frissell and later Hrdlička that she understood nursing her father as her duty as a woman and as an unmarried daughter in the Curtis household. She gave music lessons to help pay for a nurse but devoted large portions of these four years to personally caring for Bogey. See N. Curtis to Frissell, Oct. 2, 1911, Dr. H. B. Frissell Collection — Correspondence, HUA; N. Curtis to Hrdlička, ca. May 1919 (n.d.), Hrdlička Papers, NAA.

54. N. Curtis to G. Curtis, June 15, 1908, NCBA; N. Curtis to Hrdlička, Mar. 30, 1916, Hrdlička Papers, NAA. The Natalie Curtis Burlin Archives contains wonderful photographs from this visit of Curtis and Tawakwaptiwa singing from a copy of *The Indians' Book*. That Curtis visited the exiled Hopi leader at Sherman demonstrates her awareness of the political situation at the reservation even though she neglected to comment on these problems in any of her writings on the Hopi.

55. See correspondence in PCFB under the following dates for more on their relationship: Mar. 11, 18, Nov. 24, 1908, Jan. 23, 1914, Oct. 17, 23, 1916; N. Curtis to Hodge, Dec. 15, 1907, Correspondence 1907, MS.7.BAE.1.49, Hodge Papers, Braun Research Library; N. Curtis to Charles Fletcher Lummis, Dec. 20, 1913, Correspondence, MS.1.1.979, Charles Lummis Papers, Braun Research Library; N. Curtis to Hodge, Feb. 28, 1914, Stamped F.W.H. MAR 1, 1915, Correspondence 1915, MS.7.EIC.1.45, Hodge Papers, Braun Research Library.

56. N. Curtis to Hrdlička, Nov. 29, Dec. 25, 1915, both Hrdlička Papers, NAA. For more on Hrdlička and his work as a physical anthropologist see F. Spencer, "Aleš Hrdlička, MD."

57. Robert Valentine, "The Present Scope and Limitations of the Government in Dealing with Indian Affairs," unpublished memo, n.d., Curtis Collection, DAMA.

58. N. Curtis, "Theodore Roosevelt in Hopi Land." For more on Roosevelt's trip see Hagan, *Theodore Roosevelt and Six Friends of the Indian*, 231.

59. Roosevelt, "Hopi Snake Dance"; N. Curtis, "Theodore Roosevelt in Hopi Land," 90–91.

60. N. Curtis, "Theodore Roosevelt in Hopi Land," 90; Roosevelt, "Hopi Snake Dance," 367–68.

61. N. Curtis to Peabody, May 17, 1905, Peabody Papers, LOC.

62. N. Curtis to Frissell, Oct. 15, 1911, Dr. H. B. Frissell Collection — Correspondence, HUA.

63. See Smith, *Reimagining Indians*, for a discussion of other reformers or regional popularizers who began to challenge assimilationist policy in the period. Jacobs, in *Engendered Encounters*, discusses the way that proassimilation reformers in the 1920s tried to use arts and crafts as a means to bring Indians into mainstream American society.

64. For more on Hooper see "Professor Hooper Dies in New Hampshire," *New York Times*, Aug. 2, 1914; Macmahon, "Franklin W. Hooper."

65. In fact, in 1913 the first Indian head/buffalo nickels were minted.

66. Coder, "National Movement to Preserve the American Buffalo," 118–30, 252–96; Senate Committee on Indian Affairs, *To Establish a Permanent National Bison Range*, 60th Cong., 1st sess., 1908, Report no. 467.

67. N. Curtis to Frissell, Mar. 31, 1911, Dr. H. B. Frissell Collection — Correspondence, HUA.

68. N. Curtis to Boas, Aug. 15, 1903, PCFB.

69. N. Curtis to Frissell, May 7, 1911, Dr. H. B. Frissell Collection — Correspondence, HUA.

70. N. Curtis to Frissell, June 2, Oct. 25, 1911, both Dr. H. B. Frissell Collection — Correspondence, HUA.

71. N. Curtis to Frissell, June 2, 30, 1911, both Dr. H. B. Frissell Collection — Correspondence, HUA.

72. N. Curtis to Hrdlička, Jan. 4, 1912, Hrdlička Papers, NAA.

73. Franklin Hooper to Roosevelt, Dec. 16, 1911, Roosevelt Papers, LOC; N. Curtis to Hrdlička, Jan. 4, 1912, Hrdlička Papers, NAA.

74. Shelby M. Singleton to N. Curtis, July 26, 1911, Music Collection — Natalie Curtis Burlin, HUA.

75. Peabody to N. Curtis, Oct. 13, 1913, Music Collection — Natalie Curtis Burlin, HUA.

76. McDonnell, "Competency Commissions and Indian Land Policy"; Prucha, *Great Father*, 879–85.

77. N. Curtis to Hrdlička, Mar. 14, 1915, Hrdlička Papers, NAA.

78. McLaughlin, *My Friend, the Indian*, 388–404; Lane, "From the War-Path to the Plow." This article was reprinted in part as "The Future of the Indian."

79. N. Curtis to Franklin Lane, Mar. 14, 1915, Hrdlička Papers, NAA.

80. N. Curtis to Lane, Mar. 14, 1915, Hrdlička Papers, NAA.

81. N. Curtis to Lane, Mar. 14, 1915, Hrdlička Papers, NAA.

82. Hoxie, *Final Promise*, 182–83.

83. Prucha, *Great Father*, 881–85; McDonnell, "Competency Commissions and Indian Land Policy," 24–34.

6. FOLK SONGS OF A "VERY MUSICAL RACE"

1. Curtis-Burlin, *Negro Folk Songs*, Book 2, 3.
2. N. Curtis, field notebooks, "Negro Melodies," 1904, Curtis Collection, DAMA.
3. Southern, *Music of Black Americans*, 224–31; L. Levine, *Black Culture and Black Consciousness*, 158–59.
4. Untitled, unsigned speech intended for a folk music presentation, n.d. [ca.1900–1915], Folklore Society Collection, HUA.
5. Armstrong and Ludlow, *Hampton and Its Students*, 73–74, 95–97, 127–28.
6. Fenner, *Cabin and Plantation Songs*, 172; Barrett, "Negro Folk Songs"; program for "Folksongs of the American Negro and Indian," Carnegie Hall, Jan. 29, 1907, Music Collection — Misc., HUA.
7. Untitled speech for a folk music presentation, Folklore Society Collection, HUA.
8. "Negro Music."
9. N. Curtis to Frissell, Apr. 30, 1911, Dr. H. B. Frissell Collection — Correspondence, HUA.
10. N. Curtis to Frissell, May 1911, Dr. H. B. Frissell Collection — Correspondence, HUA.
11. S. L. Green, "'Art for Life's Sake'"; Martin, *Damrosch Dynasty*, 137–40; Howard, "Music School Settlement Idea"; C. D. Leupp, "Climbing Out through Music." See also Egan, *Music and the Arts in the Community*.
12. Mannes, *Music Is My Faith*, 166–67, 171, 188.
13. N. Curtis, "Value of Music School Settlements in Cities."
14. N. Curtis, "Value of Music School Settlements in Cities," 288.
15. "The New Musical Settlement Work and Its Bearing on the Evolution of the Negro Race in America," n.d., and "Music School Settlement for Negroes," n.d., both Music Collection — Misc., HUA.
16. "New Musical Settlement Work," HUA; N. Curtis, "Negro's Contribution to the Music of America."
17. "Music School Settlement for Negroes"; David Mannes, "To the Negro Musicians of America," May 28, 1912, Mannes-Damrosch Collection, LOC. It is unclear whether Mannes published this essay or delivered it at an address to black musicians.
18. From programs for the Music School Settlement for Colored People, 1915–16, 1916–17, Mannes-Damrosch Collection, LOC.

19. N. Curtis to Frissell, Nov. 8, 1911, Jan. 1, 1912, both Dr. H. B. Frissell Collection — Correspondence, HUA; E. Adams, "Negro Music School Settlement." See also Clements, "'Offshoot' and the 'Root.'" Curtis drew on Frissell's support to help free Martin from his job at the postal service.

20. From programs for the Music School Settlement for Colored People, 1915–16, 1916–17, Mannes-Damrosch Collection, LOC.

21. See programs for the Music School Settlement for Colored People, 1915–16, 1916–17, Mannes-Damrosch Collection, LOC. See also Music School Settlement for Colored People, "Sunday Afternoon Music-Lecture Recitals" in the Mannes-Damrosch Collection, LOC, for a sample schedule and list of topics.

22. N. Curtis to Frissell, Jan. 22, 1912, Dr. H. B. Frissell Collection — Correspondence, HUA; Mannes, *Music Is My Faith*, 217–18; Badger, *Life in Ragtime*; "Negro's Place in Music," 60–61.

23. N. Curtis Burlin, "Black Singers and Players."

24. Letter and program from Music School Settlement for Colored People announcing concert on May 2, 1912, n.d., Mannes-Damrosch Collection, LOC; Martin, *Damrosch Dynasty*, 212.

25. "A Concert of Negro Music," *New York Evening Journal*, May 1, 1912.

26. N. Curtis, "Black Singers and Players," 501–3; Natalie Curtis, "Negro Musicians and Music," *New York Evening Post*, Sept. 7, 1912; N. Curtis, "Negro's Contribution to the Music of America," 663–65.

27. For reviews of these concerts see "Black Music Concerts in Carnegie Hall."

28. Mannes, *Music Is My Faith*, 219–20; Badger, *Life in Ragtime*, 124–26. George Martin, describing the turnover of control at the settlement, argues that "the ousting of the white philanthropists was done hastily and arrogantly" (*Damrosch Dynasty*, 215). Badger's and Mannes's accounts do not suggest that the white directors resisted this move or that the types of ill feelings that Martin describes existed.

29. Frissell to N. Curtis, Nov. 1, 1912, Dr. H. B. Frissell Collection — Correspondence, HUA; Peabody to Frank K. Rogers, June 12, 1915, F. K. Rogers to Peabody, June 15, 1915, Peabody to F. K. Rogers, June 17, 1915, all Board of Trustees Collection — George F. Peabody, HUA.

30. Anderson, *Education of Blacks in the South*, 44–54; Watkins, *White Architects of Black Education*, 33–55. For more on Armstrong and Hampton see Engs, *Educating the Disenfranchised and Disinherited*.

31. N. Curtis, "Significance of Hampton's Fifty Years"; Curtis-Burlin, *Negro Folk Songs*, Book 1, 7, 26.

32. Anderson, *Education of Blacks in the South*, 80–88; Curtis-Burlin, *Negro Folk Songs*, Book 2, 12.

33. Anderson, *Education of Blacks in the South*, 88–94; Watkins, *White Architects of Black Education*, 127–29, 136.

34. Curtis-Burlin, *Negro Folk Songs*, Book 2, 20.

35. N. Curtis to Boas, Dec. 2, 1913, Oct. 17, 1916, both PCFB.

36. Hyatt, *Franz Boas*; Williams, *Rethinking Race*. Hyatt contends that Boas's experiences with anti-Semitism led him to combat racism. Williams portrays Boas more ambivalently, arguing that the anthropologist was torn between his liberal outlook and his anthropometric studies that suggested black inferiority.

37. Boas, "Outlook for the American Negro"; Boas to Peabody, June 13, 1918, PCFB.

38. Lewis, *When Harlem Was in Vogue*, 151; Douglas, *Terrible Honesty*, 282; Hemenway, *Zora Neale Hurston*, 104; Hughes, *Big Sea*, 312–15; Watson, *Harlem Renaissance*, 146–47.

39. Lewis, *When Harlem Was in Vogue*, 152; Hughes, *Big Sea*, 316; Douglas, *Terrible Honesty*, 282.

40. Curtis-Burlin, *Negro Folk Songs*, Book 1, 7–8, Book 2, 3, 13. The Hampton University Archives contains folders for each member of the "Big Quartet" with information on their schooling, careers, and singing abilities.

41. N. Curtis to Frissell, Feb. 28, Mar. 8, 1915, both Dr. H. B. Frissell Collection—Correspondence, HUA; Jacoway, *Yankee Missionaries in the South*, xii, 121–24.

42. L. Levine, *Black Culture and Black Consciousness*, 26–27.

43. N. Curtis, "Negro Music at Birth."

44. N. Curtis to Boas, Mar. 20, 1917, PCFB; "Negro Folk Songs Recorded," 26.

45. Allen, Ware, and Garrison, *Slave Songs of the United States*. Scholars have viewed Curtis's efforts to express this aspect of black folk music in a positive light. L. Levine comments that her account is "musically the most accurate one we have" and praises her attempt to show the spirituals as a "product of an improvisational communal consciousness" ("Slave Songs and Slave Consciousness," 159–60). Lovell depicts her as "another bright star in the spiritual firmament" for her attempts to capture the songs and their meanings (*Black Song*, 417).

46. Curtis-Burlin, *Negro Folk Songs*, Book 1, 3.

47. Curtis-Burlin, *Negro Folk Songs*, Book 2, 3–4.

48. Curtis-Burlin, *Negro Folk Songs*, Book 2, 10, 21.

49. Curtis-Burlin, *Negro Folk Songs*, Book 2, 5–7. Other scholars have recognized similar distinctive traits in African American music. See Shaw, *Black Popular Music in America*; Stewart, *African American Music*.

50. Curtis-Burlin, *Negro Folk Songs*, Book 1, 4–5, Book 2, 8, 22, 26.

51. Curtis-Burlin, *Negro Folk Songs*, Book 3, 28, 32, Book 4, 10.

52. Fredrickson, *Black Image in the White Mind*, 97–102; Curtis-Burlin, *Negro Folk Songs*, Book 3, 8.

53. Fredrickson, *Black Image in the White Mind*, 284–89; Curtis-Burlin, *Negro Folk Songs*, Book 3, 10, Book 4, 31.

54. Curtis-Burlin, *Negro Folk Songs*, Book 2, 4–5; Shaw, *Black Popular Music in America*, 9; L. Levine, *Black Culture and Black Consciousness*, 6.

55. See L. Levine's discussion of the origins of the spirituals in *Black Culture and Black Consciousness*.

56. Curtis-Burlin, *Negro Folk Songs*, Book 3, 5, Book 2, 21.

57. Curtis-Burlin, *Negro Folk Songs*, Book 3, 5, Book 4, 38. In his review of *Negro Folk Songs* musician Percy Grainger supported Curtis's assertions. He claimed that she had successfully captured the "unconscious harmony" of primitive music and praised the songs for their "unconscious" creation by a people with no formal training. He shared her fears that this music would soon die out. See Grainger, "Mrs. Burlin's Study of Negro Folk-Music," *New York Times*, Apr. 14, 1918.

58. Curtis-Burlin, *Negro Folk Songs*, Book 1, 8–9.

59. Curtis-Burlin, *Negro Folk Songs*, Book 4, 24, Book 3, 8.

60. Curtis-Burlin, *Negro Folk Songs*, Book 2, 10.

61. Curtis-Burlin, *Negro Folk Songs*, Book 3, 5–6; Stewart, *African American Music*, 28–29.

62. Waters, *Strange Ways and Sweet Dreams*. See also "Folk Lore and Ethnology" (July 1894); "Folk Lore and Ethnology" (Feb. 1895).

63. N. Curtis to unnamed Hampton official [possibly Cora Mae Folsom], June 18, 1919, and N. Curtis to James Gregg, July 31, 1919, both Music Collection — Natalie Curtis Burlin, HUA.

64. Curtis-Burlin, *Negro Folk Songs*, Book 1, 36, Book 4, 8–9.

65. N. Curtis to Peabody, n.d. (ca. Apr. 1921), Peabody Papers, LOC.

66. N. Curtis to Peabody, n.d. (a second letter from ca. Apr. 1921), Peabody Papers, LOC.

67. N. Curtis to Peabody, n.d. (second letter from ca. Apr. 1921), May 5, 1921, both Peabody Papers, LOC; "Negro Music Benefit," *New York Times*, Apr. 25, 1921.

68. S. Curtis, *First Black Actors along the Great White Way*, 14.

69. Gaines, *Uplifting the Race*, xiii–xiv, 67–76, 184–85.

70. Dett, *Religious Folksongs of the Negro*, xi–xiv.

71. Burleigh, *Negro Spirituals*; Johnson and Johnson, *Books of American Negro Spirituals*.

72. L. Levine, *Black Culture and Black Consciousness*, 143; Douglas, *Terrible Honesty*, 431.

73. R. Nathaniel Dett, "Report to Dr. Frissell, Principal," 1914, 5, and "Report of the Department of Music," 1919, 29, both Music Collection — R. Nathaniel Dett — Biographies — Family — Reports #7, HUA. See also R. N. Dett, "Report of the Director of Music at Hampton Institute" (1915), Music Collection — R. Nathaniel Dett — Biographies — Family — Reports #7, HUA; Robert Moton, *Finding a Way Out: An Autobiography*, quoted in L. Levine, *Black Culture and Black Consciousness*, 162.

74. For more on Hampton's collection of African art see Holtgreen and Zeider, *Taste for the Beautiful*; Peabody to Boas, Nov. 18, 1915, N. Curtis to Boas, Jan. 23, Oct. 5, 1914, and Boas to N. Curtis, Nov. 6, 1914, all PCFB.

75. N. Curtis, *Songs and Tales from the Dark Continent*, xxiv.

76. N. Curtis, *Songs and Tales from the Dark Continent*, 57–61; "Class President's Address," *Hampton Student*, May 1, 1911, and "Zulu Crown Prince Graduates at Hampton," May 6, 1911, both African Collection — Madikane Q. Cele, HUA.

77. "For Unkulunkulu's Sake," *Hampton Student*, May 1, 1913, program for "For Unkulunkulu's Sake," Mar. 22, 1913, and C. K. Simango, "Cele's Work in Africa," *Hampton Student*, Apr. 1, 1917, all African Collection — Madikane Q. Cele, HUA.

78. N. Curtis, *Songs and Tales from the Dark Continent*, 1–5; Simango, "South African's Story." Curtis also shared Simango's biography with the readers of the *Outlook* in the Sept. 14, 1921, volume.

79. See, e.g., Simango, "African and Civilization"; C. K. Simango, "Halley's Comet and Some Africans," *Hampton Student*, Apr. 15, 1915, and C. K. Simango, "Why the Africans Do Not Believe in the Resurrection: An African Story," *Hampton Student*, July 1, 1915, both African Collection — Columbus Kemba Simango, HUA.

80. N. Curtis, *Songs and Tales from the Dark Continent*, 5–6.

81. N. Curtis, *Songs and Tales from the Dark Continent*, 6–10.

82. N. Curtis, *Songs and Tales from the Dark Continent*, 12.

83. H. E. Krehbiel, "A New Book on Primitive Folkmusic by Mrs. Burlin," *New York Tribune*, Jan. 16, 1921, Music Collection — Natalie Curtis Burlin, HUA.

84. George Foster Peabody, editorial, *New York Tribune*, Jan. 20, 1921, and Franz Boas, editorial, *New York Tribune*, Jan. 18, 1921, both Music Collection — Natalie Curtis Burlin, HUA. Peabody had provided financial support and other assistance to Simango to free him to collaborate with Boas beginning in the summer of 1920. See correspondence in PCFB: May 5, 8, 12, 14, July 30, Aug. 31, Sept. 7, 1920. The result of Boas and Simango's labor was entitled "Tales and Proverbs of the Vandau of Portuguese South Africa."

85. N. Curtis to Peabody, Jan. 30, 1921, Peabody Papers, LOC.

86. N. Curtis, *Songs and Tales from the Dark Continent*, xii.

87. N. Curtis, *Songs and Tales from the Dark Continent*, xi; Boas to N. Curtis, Sept. 30. 1919, PCFB.

88. N. Curtis, *Songs and Tales from the Dark Continent*, xiv–xv.

89. N. Curtis, *Songs and Tales from the Dark Continent*, xiii; Boas to N. Curtis, Sept. 30, 1919, PCFB.

90. N. Curtis, *Songs and Tales from the Dark Continent*, xv–xvii.

91. N. Curtis, *Songs and Tales from the Dark Continent*, xi–xii.

92. N. Curtis, *Songs and Tales from the Dark Continent*, xvii–xviii.

93. N. Curtis, *Songs and Tales from the Dark Continent*, xix.

94. N. Curtis, *Songs and Tales from the Dark Continent*, xix–xxi.

95. N. Curtis, *Songs and Tales from the Dark Continent*, xxiii–xxv.

7. "THE SPIRIT OF THE REAL AMERICA"

1. N. Curtis, "Busoni's Indian Fantasy."

2. N. Curtis, "Busoni's Indian Fantasy."

3. Douglas, *Terrible Honesty*, 10–15, 25; Guterl, *Color of Race in America*, 10–12.

4. Fish, *New Craftsman Index*, 9–18.

5. Fish, *New Craftsman Index*, 11–20; Boris, "'Dreams of Brotherhood and Beauty,'" 216–18. See also *Frederick Monsen at Hopi*.

6. Boris, *Art and Labor*, xi–xiv. For more on the British origins of the American Arts and Crafts movement see Kaplan, "Lamp of British Precedent." Historians have also argued that changes in work patterns challenged traditional notions of the work ethic, leading some to adopt the ideas of the Arts and Crafts movement. See Gilbert, *Work without Salvation*.

7. Lears, *No Place of Grace*, 4–43, 60–61.

8. Lears, *No Place of Grace*, 57–58.

9. Smith, *Reimagining Indians*, 8–9.

10. An important exception is Sherry Smith, who argues that several of the writers she examines, "in pushing for Indian policy reform, however bumpily, . . . take on additional national significance and diverge from other antimodernists" (*Reimagining Indians*, 17).

11. Dilworth, *Imagining Indians in the Southwest*, 125–26, 151–58.

12. Jacobs, *Engendered Encounters*. For more on European American women and their uses of Native American culture in the Southwest see Mullin, *Culture in the Marketplace*.

13. N. Curtis, "Pueblo Singer"; N. Curtis, "Song of the Indian Mother."

14. N. Curtis, "Song of the Indian Mother." Curtis repeated many of the same arguments (and much of the same material) in a 1921 article in *Musical Quarterly* in which she shared Indian lullabies to show the "human, intimate side of Indian parentage" and to contend that whites could learn to live in the same type of harmony with nature — "And yet the heritance of Nature is ours for the outstretched hand and the voice that asks" ("American Indian Cradle Songs," 429, 558).

15. N. Curtis, "People of the Totem-Poles." For assistance with these articles Curtis asked Boas about Native American beliefs regarding an afterlife. He shared his knowledge with her and even corrected proofs for Curtis. See N. Curtis to Boas, June 26, 30, 1909, both PCFB.

16. Beginning in 1908 Stickley laid out plans for a home, cottages, and farm buildings for his proposed school, which was to open in June 1913. The school never opened, but a sizeable log house and other outbuildings were completed. For more on the Craftsman Farms see Cathers, *Gustav Stickley's Craftsman Farms*.

17. N. Curtis, "Visit to Craftsman Farm."

18. N. Curtis, "Value of a Country Education."

19. N. Curtis, "New Log House of Craftsman Farms"; N. Curtis, "New Type of Architecture in the Southwest." The house in La Jolla belonged to Wheeler Bailey, who may have been her relative, although she makes no comment on their relationship in the article. The NCBA contains several photographs of the Curtis family and their friends visiting his home. Some contain the label "Uncle Wheeler Bailey."

20. Stansell, *American Moderns*, 249–51.

21. N. Curtis to Aunt Natalie [Stacey], May 27, 1917, NCBA.

22. Udall, *Modernist Painting in New Mexico*, 19; Paul Burlin, "Paul Burlin: Autobiographical Sketch," unpublished manuscript, summer 1947, Paul Burlin Papers, AAA; Rushing, *Native American Art and the New York Avant-Garde*, 49–55.

23. Lummis to N. Curtis, Correspondence, Aug. 2, 1917, MS.1.1.979, and Charles Fletcher Lummis, Typed Journal Series, July 30–Aug. 5, 1917, Thursday, Aug. 2, 1917, p. 7, MS.1.2.278, all Lummis Papers, Braun Research Library; Hrdlička to A. Curtis, July 28, 1917, Hrdlička Papers, NAA.

24. Statements by Charlotte Mason, Ruth Townsend, and Paul Burlin, Burlin Papers, AAA; N. Curtis to Frissell, June 15, 1917, Dr. H. B. Frissell Collection — Correspondence, HUA; wedding announcement for Natalie Curtis and Paul Burlin, NCBA.

25. A. Curtis to G. Curtis, Aug. 18, 1917, and A. Curtis to Lora Curtis, Feb. 12, 1918, both NCBA.

26. N. Curtis to Frissell, June 5, 1917, Dr. H. B. Frissell Collection — Correspondence, HUA. Burlin did a painting in 1921 entitled *The Negro* that must have resulted from his wife's influence.

27. "Some Press Comments on Recent Paintings by Paul Burlin," Dr. H. B. Frissell Collection — Correspondence, HUA; Udall, *Modernist Painting in New Mexico*, 19.

28. Udall, *Modernist Painting in New Mexico*, 2–10; Gibson, *Santa Fe and Taos Colonies*, xi–xii, 3–22.

29. N. Curtis to Peabody, Nov. 20, 1919, Peabody Papers, LOC; N. Curtis to Hrdlička, May 4, 1920, Hrdlička Papers, NAA; N. Curtis to G. Curtis, Mar. 9, 1921, NCBA. Curtis also purchased a horse, Buck, at this time. He was worth ten dollars, the bridle and saddle valued at fifteen dollars. See statement by Ralph Pearson, Burlin Papers, AAA.

30. Udall, *Modernist Painting in New Mexico*, 26–28; Rushing, *Native American Art and the New York Avant-Garde*, 53.

31. N. Curtis, "New Art in the West."

32. N. Curtis, "New Art in the West"; N. Curtis, "Our Native Craftsman."

33. Rudnick, *Mabel Dodge Luhan*, 143–45; Luhan, *Edge of Taos Desert*, 21–22.

34. Luhan, *Edge of Taos Desert*, 59–68.

35. Among the inaccuracies of Dodge's account are the statements that they collected the song from Geronimo in Santo Domingo — the Apache leader died in 1909 — and that Curtis published her book of Indian music in 1917 rather than 1907.

36. Luhan, *Edge of Taos Desert*, 68–69.

37. Cronyn, *Path on the Rainbow.*

38. For more on this group see Moore, *Yankee Blues.*

39. Useful histories of the development of and debate over national music are Kingman, *American Music*, 411–46; Levy, "Search for Identity in American Music"; Tischler, *American Music*; Zuck, *History of Musical Americanism.*

40. Hamm, "Dvořák, Stephen Foster."

41. Farwell, "Letter to American Composers," 73; W. S. B. Matthews, "Publications of the Wa-Wan Press"; Gilman, "New American Music." See also "Is There a Distinctive Note in American Music." For more on Farwell and his work see Culbertson, *He Heard America Singing*; Culbertson, "Arthur Farwell's Early Efforts on Behalf of American Music."

42. N. Curtis, "Folk-Music of America."

43. Farwell, "Toward American Music"; Geddes, "Recorder of the Red Man's Music."

44. Cadman, "'Idealization' of Indian Music"; Cadman, "American Indian's Music Idealized"; N. Curtis, *Indians' Book*, xxix–xxx.

For more on this late nineteenth- and early twentieth-century desire to reimagine Indians as white Americans' spiritual and cultural ancestors through appropriation of cultural forms or Native identities see Huhndorf, *Going Native*; Deloria, *Playing Indian*; Trachtenberg, *Shades of Hiawatha*. For more on the creation of American tradition in general see Kammen, *Mystic Chords of Memory*.

45. F. Burton, *American Primitive Music*, 177–87; F. Burton, "Music from the Ojibway's Point of View"; Cadman, "American Indian's Music Idealized," 659; Cadman, "'Idealization' of Indian Music," 389–96.

46. N. Curtis, "Perpetuating of Indian Art."

47. Nevin, "Impressions of Indian Music"; Nevin, "Two Summers with the Blackfeet Indians of Montana."

48. Farwell, "Artistic Possibilities of Indian Myth"; N. Curtis Burlin, "Indians' Part in the Dedication of the New Museum." Curtis also participated in a 1920 presentation with the School of American Research in New York City entitled "The Resurrection of the Red Man." Along with other researchers on Indian art and music Curtis presented her personal collection of Southwestern art and led the congregation in the singing of Native American songs. See "Resurrection of the Red Man."

49. Curtis-Burlin, "Recording for Posterity the Music of Primitive Humanity."

50. Curtis-Burlin, "Recording for Posterity the Music of Primitive Humanity."

51. N. Curtis to Francis LaFlesche, Apr. 16, 1919, Alice Fletcher (1838–1923) Papers, NAA.

52. N. Curtis to LaFlesche, Apr. 16, 1919, Fletcher Papers, NAA.

53. Enclosure in N. Curtis to LaFlesche, Apr. 16, 1919, Fletcher Papers, NAA.

54. Enclosure in N. Curtis to LaFlesche, Apr. 16, 1919.

55. Enclosure in N. Curtis to LaFlesche, Apr. 16, 1919; Natalie Curtis, "The Deer Dance: A Pueblo Indian Legend-Dance," unpublished manuscript, NCBA.

56. N. Curtis, "Deer Dance"; Natalie Curtis, "American Indian Dance Pageant," unpublished manuscript, 1921, Performing Arts Reading Room, LOC.

57. Finck, "American Operas," 412; "American Indian in Opera"; Farwell, "American Opera on American Themes."

58. In this regard *The Deer Dance* resembled the pageants, especially the 1913 Paterson Strike Pageant, that bohemian New Yorkers had applauded enthusiasti-

cally for their admixture of politics and art. See M. B. Green, *New York 1913*.

59. A. Curtis to Grainger, June 20, 1924, Grainger Collection, LOC; Adolph Bolm to Bridgham Curtis, Nov. 6, 1924, NCBA. Bolm did not produce *The Deer Dance* within the agreed-upon time frame of three years. Augusta Curtis believed it would not happen without Natalie Curtis's "inspiring presence." Bolm contacted Natalie Curtis's brother Bridgham late in 1924, expressing interest in renewing the contract. Memorandum of Agreement between N. Curtis and Bolm, Feb. 28, 1921, NCBA.

60. Program from the Musical Art Society of New York, Apr. 13, 1920, NCBA; N. Curtis, "Folk-Music of America," 419.

61. Program from the Musical Art Society of New York, Apr. 13, 1920, NCBA. See also Natalie Curtis Burlin, "Dawn Song," Native American Song Manuscript Collection, LOC.

62. Curtis Burlin, "Dawn Song," LOC. See also "Victory Song (Pawnee)," Native American Song Manuscript Collection, LOC.

63. Program from People's Music League of the People's Institute, "Six Centuries of Folk Songs of Europe and North America," Apr. 29, ca. 1920, NCBA.

64. N. Curtis, "Folk-Music of America," 417–18; N. Curtis, "Negro's Contribution to the Music of America."

65. Some more acculturated Native Americans did try to use Native song outside of traditional tribal settings. Tsianina Redfeather, e.g., worked closely with Charles Cadman on Indianist compositions and in performances. The Society of American Indians also used Native songs at the group's public functions as a way of attracting white interest in their reform agenda. Overall, however, Native Americans had only a minor impact on the Indianist movement and lacked the much stronger presence of African American composers.

66. Southern, *Music of Black Americans*, 267–80.

67. Dett, "Helping to Lay Foundation"; Dett, "Negro Music at the Present." See also Simpson, *Follow Me*.

68. Dett, "Ethnologist Aids Composer."

69. Program for the Choral Art Club, n.d., Music Collection — Music Department Programs, 1907–1946, HUA; "Negro Music."

70. Program for the Musical Art Society of New York, Dec. 16, 1919, Music Collection — Music Department Programs, 1907–1946, HUA.

71. H. E. Krehbiel, "Aristocratic Music Offered by Art Society," *New York Tribune*, Dec. 18, 1919, Music Collection — Natalie Curtis Burlin, HUA; Grant, "Recognizing Our Debt to Negro Music."

72. N. Curtis, "Folk-Music in America," 668–69.

73. "Recognition of Negro Music"; Grant, "Recognizing Our Debt to Negro Music."

74. Jacoway, *Yankee Missionaries in the South*, 125–28. Curtis supported efforts for peace herself. For example, she wrote a very favorable review of an antiwar play by Peabody's wife, Katrina Trask. See N. Curtis, "'In the Vanguard.'"

75. Curtis-Burlin, "Hymn of Freedom."

76. N. Curtis to Boas, Nov. 23, 1918, PCFB.

77. Grace Bigelow House to Peabody, July 18, 1918, Peabody Papers, LOC; House, "Origin of the Hymn."

78. N. Curtis to Boas, Nov. 23, 1918; House, "Origin of the Hymn," 476–77. See also Natalie Curtis Burlin, "To Soldiers, Sailors, and Singers," unpublished essay, June 1918, Music Collection — Natalie Curtis Burlin, HUA.

79. N. Curtis to G. Curtis, Aug. 12, 1918, NCBA; House, "Origin of the Hymn," 477.

80. N. Curtis to G. Curtis, Aug. 12, 1918.

81. N. Curtis, "War Song of the Far West."

82. Sandler, *Paul Burlin*, 6–7.

83. Guterl, *Color of Race in America*, 55; N. Curtis to Peabody, Jan. 30, 1921, Peabody Papers, LOC.

84. N. Curtis to Peabody, n.d. (ca. June 1921), and June 10, 1921, both Peabody Papers, LOC.

85. N. Curtis to "Birdy-Mouse" [Augusta Curtis], June 18, 1921, and N. Curtis to "Dearest Darling Mimsey Mouse" [Augusta Curtis], June 20, 1921, both NCBA.

86. N. Curtis to Peabody, July 1, 1921, and N. Curtis to "Friends," July 27, 1921, both Peabody Papers, LOC.

87. N. Curtis to "Mimsey" [Augusta Curtis], July 4, 1921, NCBA.

88. N. Curtis, "Futurist Experiment."

89. Jackson, *Making Jazz French*, 1–6, 17–19, 26–27.

90. N. Curtis to "Friends," July 13, 1921, Peabody Papers, LOC.

91. N. Curtis to "Friends," July 13, 1921; Peabody to N. Curtis, July 27, 1921, N. Curtis to "Friends," July 27, 1921, and N. Curtis to Peabody, n.d. (ca. early Aug. 1921), all Peabody Papers, LOC.

92. N. Curtis to "Friends," July 27, 13, 1921, both Peabody Papers, LOC.

93. N. Curtis to G. Curtis, Sept. 28, 1921, NCBA; N. Curtis to "Dearest Friends," Oct. 16, 1921, Music Collection — Natalie Curtis Burlin, HUA.

94. N. Curtis to Boas, Oct. 6, 1921, PCFB.

95. N. Curtis to "Dearest Friends," Oct. 16, 1921, HUA.

96. N. Curtis to "Dearest Friends," Oct. 16, 1921.

97. N. Curtis to "Dearest Friends," Oct. 16, 1921.

CONCLUSION

1. A. Curtis to G. Curtis, Oct. 27, 1921, Marion Curtis Rogers to G. Curtis, Nov. 7, 1921 (copy of Alice Klauber to A. Curtis, Oct. 24, 1921), and Paul Burlin to A. Curtis, Nov. 2, 1921, all NCBA.

2. G. Curtis to B. Curtis, Oct. 29, 1921, M. Curtis to G. Curtis, Nov. 7, 1921, and A. Curtis to G. Curtis, Oct. 27, 1921, all NCBA.

3. Burlin to A. Curtis, Nov. 2, 1921, NCBA.

4. Burlin to A. Curtis, Nov. 2, 1921, and A. Curtis to G. Curtis, Jan. 11, 1921, both NCBA.

5. "Paul Burlin, 82, Artist, Teacher," *New York Times*, Mar. 15, 1969.

6. Burlin to A. Curtis, Nov. 2, 1921, and Burlin to B. Curtis, Nov. 10, 1921, both NCBA.

7. B. Curtis to Lummis, Correspondence, June 14, 1922, MS.1.1.977, Lummis Papers, Braun Research Library; Hrdlička to B. Curtis, Apr. 4, 1923, Hrdlička Papers, NAA; Peabody to Lawrence Abbott, Apr. 4, 1923, Board of Trustees Collection — George F. Peabody, HUA.

8. Augusta and Grainger corresponded until June 1933, when Augusta died at the age of ninety-two.

9. A. Curtis to Grainger, Feb. 26, 1924, and Apr. 18, 1925, both Grainger Collection, LOC; programs from "Grainger's Room — Music Concerts," Spring 1925, and "Grainger's Orchestral and Choral Concert," n.d., both NCBA.

BIBLIOGRAPHY

UNPUBLISHED SOURCES

Archives of American Art, Washington DC
   Paul Burlin Papers
Archives of Traditional Music, Indiana University, Bloomington
Braun Research Library, Autry National Center of the American West, Los
      Angeles CA
   Frederick Webb Hodge Papers
   Charles Lummis Papers
Denver Art Museum Archives, Denver CO
   Natalie Curtis Collection
Hampton University Archives, Hampton VA
   African Collection
   Caroline Andrus Collection
   Annual Reports and Catalogue
   Board of Trustees Collection
   Dr. H. B. Frissell Collection
   Folklore Society Collection
   James Edgar Gregg Collection
   Music Collection
   Outgrowths of Hampton Collection
Library of Congress, Washington DC
   Natalie Curtis Manuscripts, Performing Arts Reading Room
   Percy Grainger Collection (microfilm), Performing Arts Reading Room
   Mannes-Damrosch Collection, Performing Arts Reading Room
   Native American Song Manuscript Collection (AFC 1957/001), American
      Folklife Center Reading Room
   George Foster Peabody Papers, Manuscript Reading Room
   Theodore Roosevelt Papers (microfilm ed., 485 reels), Manuscript
      Reading Room
Natalie Curtis Burlin Archives, in possession of Alfred and Virginia
      Bredenberg, Raleigh NC

National Anthropological Archives, Smithsonian Institution, Washington DC
    Natalie Curtis photograph collection
    Alice Cunningham Fletcher (1838–1923) and Frances LaFlesche (1859–
        1932) Papers
    Aleš Hrdlička (1869–1943) Papers
    James Mooney (1861–1921) Collection
University Research Library, Department of Special Collections, University
    of California, Los Angeles
    George DeClyver Curtis Papers (collection 1247)
    George DeClyver Curtis Diaries

PUBLISHED SOURCES

Adams, David Wallace. *Education for Extinction: American Indians and the
    Boarding School Experience, 1875–1928.* Lawrence: University of Kansas
    Press, 1995.
Adams, Elbridge. "The Negro Music School Settlement." *Southern Workman*
    44 (March 1915): 161–65.
Adams, Evelyn C. *American Indian Education: Government Schools and
    Economic Progress.* New York: King's Crown Press, 1946.
A. E. "The Snake Dance. A Religious Ceremonial." *Theosophical Quarterly* 9
    (1912): 308–15.
Ahern, Wilbert. "Assimilationist Racism: The Case of the 'Friends of the
    Indian.'" *Journal of Ethnic Studies* 4 (Summer 1976): 23–32.
Alexander, William. *Seventy-Five Years of Progress and Public Service: A Brief
    History of the Equitable Life Assurance Society of the United States.* New
    York: Newcomb Printing, 1934.
Allen, William Francis, Charles Pickard Ware, and Lucy McKim Garrison,
    eds. *Slave Songs of the United States.* New York: A. Simpson and
    Company, 1867. Reprint, New York: Dover Publications, 1995.
Altschuler, Glen C. *Race, Ethnicity and Class in American Social Thought,
    1865–1919.* Arlington Heights IL: Harlan Davidson, 1982.
"American Indian Opera." *Hampton's Magazine* 24 (February 1910): 284.
American Section of the Theosophical Society. *A Primer of Theosophy.*
    Chicago: Rajput Press, 1909.
Ammer, Christine. *Unsung: A History of Women in American Music.*
    Contributions in Women's Studies Series, no. 14. Westport CT:
    Greenwood Press, 1980.
Anderson, James D. *The Education of Blacks in the South, 1860–1935.* Chapel
    Hill: University of North Carolina Press, 1988.

Annual Report of the Commissioner of Indian Affairs. Washington DC: Government Printing Office.

Archabal, Nina M. "Frances Densmore, Pioneer in the Study of American Indian Music." In *Women of Minnesota: Selected Biographical Essays*, ed. Barbara Stuhler and Gretchen Kreuter, 94–115. Minneapolis: Minnesota Historical Society, 1977.

Archambault, JoAllyn. "Sun Dance." In *The Plains*, ed. Raymond J. DeMallie, vol. 13 of Sturtevant, *Handbook of North American Indians*, 983–95.

Armstrong, Mrs. M. F., and Helen W. Ludlow. *Hampton and Its Students*. New York: G. P. Putnam's Sons, 1874. Reprint, Freeport NY: Books for Libraries Press, 1971.

Babcock, Barbara. "'A New Mexican Rebecca': Imagining Pueblo Women." *Journal of the Southwest* 32 (Winter 1990): 400–437.

Babcock, Barbara, and Nancy J. Parezo. *Daughters of the Desert: Women Anthropologists and the Native American Southwest, 1880–1980*. Albuquerque: University of New Mexico Press, 1988.

"Back to Nature for the Indian." *Charities and Commons* 20 (June 6, 1908): 336–40.

Badger, Reid. *The Great American Fair: The World's Columbian Expositions and American Culture*. Chicago: Nelson Hall, 1979.

———. *A Life in Ragtime: A Biography of James Reese Europe*. Oxford: Oxford University Press, 1995.

Barrett, Harris. "Negro Folk Songs." *Southern Workman* 41 (April 1912): 238–45.

Basson, Keith H. "History of Ethnological Research." In *The Southwest*, ed. Alfonso Ortiz, vol. 9 of Sturtevant, *Handbook of North American Indians*, 14–21.

Bauer, Emile. "The Young Woman in Music." *Musician* 11 (January 1906): 42.

Beckert, Sven. *The Monied Metropolis: New York City and the Consolidation of the American Bourgeoisie, 1850–1896*. Cambridge: Cambridge University Press, 2001.

Bederman, Gail. *Manliness and Civilization: A Cultural History of Gender and Race in the United States, 1880–1917*. Chicago: University of Chicago Press, 1995.

Berens, John. "Old Campaigners, New Realities: Indian Policy Reform in the Progressive Era." *Mid-America* 59 (January 1977): 51–64.

Berkhofer, Robert. *Salvation and the Savage: An Analysis of Protestant Missions and American Indian Response, 1787–1862*. New York: Atheneum Press, 1972.

————. *The White Man's Indian: Images of the American Indian from Columbus to the Present.* New York: Alfred A. Knopf, 1978.

Berthrong, Donald. *The Cheyenne and Arapaho Ordeal: Reservation and Agency Life in the Indian Territory, 1875–1907.* Norman: University of Oklahoma Press, 1992.

Bevis, William. "American Indian Verse Translations." *College English* 35 (March 1974): 693–703.

"Black Music Concerts in Carnegie Hall." *Black Perspectives in Music* 6 (Spring 1978): 71–88.

Blavatsky, H. P. *The Key to Theosophy.* First Simplified Adyad ed., by Clara M. Codd. Adyar, Madras, India: Theosophical Publishing House, 1953.

Block, Adrienne Fried, and Carol Neuls-Bates. "Historical Introduction." In *Women in American Music: A Bibliography of Music and Literature,* ed. Adrienne Fried Block and Carol Neuls-Bates, xviii–xxiii. Westport CT: Greenwood Press, 1979.

————, eds. *Women in American Music: A Bibliography of Music and Literature.* Westport CT: Greenwood Press, 1979.

Block, Adrienne Fried, assisted by Nancy Steward. "Women in American Music, 1800–1918." In *Women and Music: A History,* ed. Karin Pendle, 142–60. Bloomington: Indiana University Press, 1991.

Boas, Franz. "The Outlook for the American Negro." Commencement Address at Atlanta University, May 31, 1906. Atlanta Leaflet, no. 19. In *The Shaping of American Anthropology, 1883–1911: A Franz Boas Reader,* ed. George W. Stocking Jr., 310–15. New York: Basic Books, 1974.

————. *The Professional Correspondence of Franz Boas.* Wilmington DE: Scholarly Resources, 1972.

Boas, Franz, and Columbus Kamba Simango. "Tales and Proverbs of the Vandau of Portuguese South Africa." *Journal of American Folklore* 35 (April–June 1922): 151–204.

Bolt, Christine. *American Indian Policy and American Reform: Case Studies of the Campaign to Assimilate the American Indians.* London: Allen and Unwin, 1987.

Boris, Eileen. *Art and Labor: Ruskin, Morris and the Craftsman Ideal in America.* Philadelphia: Temple University Press, 1986.

————. "'Dreams of Brotherhood and Beauty': The Social Ideas of the Arts and Crafts Movement." In Kaplan, *"Art That Is Life,"* 208–18.

Braude, Ann. *Radical Spirits: Spiritualism and Women's Rights in Nineteenth*

Century America. 2nd ed. Bloomington: Indiana University Press, 2001.

Breitbart, Eric. *A World on Display: Photographs from the St. Louis World's Fair, 1904.* Albuquerque: University of New Mexico Press, 1997.

Browne, Junius Henri. *The Great Metropolis: A Mirror of New York.* Hartford NJ: American Publishing, 1896. Reprint, New York: Arno Press, 1975.

Buley, R. Carlyle. *The Equitable Life Assurance Society of the United States, 1859–1964.* New York: Appleton-Century-Crofts, 1967.

Burfield, Diana. "Theosophy and Feminism: Some Explorations in Nineteenth Century Biography." In *Women's Religious Experience,* ed. Pat Holden, 27–56. London: Croom Helm Press, 1983.

Burgess, Larry E. "The Lake Mohonk Conferences on the Indian, 1883–1916." Ph.D. dissertation, Claremont Graduate School, 1972.

Burleigh, Harry T. *Negro Spirituals.* London: B. Ricordi, 1921.

Burton, Frederick. *American Primitive Music: With Especial Attention to the Songs of the Ojibways.* New York: Moffat, Yard, 1909.

———. "Music from the Ojibway's Point of View: Art an Unknown Word to These Primitive People, and Song a Part of Everyday Living." *Craftsman* 12 (July 1907): 375–81.

Busoni, Ferruccio. *The Essence of Music and Other Papers.* Trans. Rosamond Levy. New York: Dover Publications, 1957.

Cadman, Charles Wakefield. "The American Indian's Music Idealized." *Etude* 38 (October 1920): 659–60.

———. "The 'Idealization' of Indian Music." *Music Quarterly* 1 (July 1915): 387–96.

Campbell, Bruce F. *Ancient Wisdom Revived: A History of the Theosophical Movement.* Berkeley: University of California Press, 1980.

Carr, Helen. *Inventing the American Primitive: Politics, Gender and the Representation of Native American Literary Traditions, 1789–1936.* New York: New York University Press, 1996.

Cathers, David, ed. *Gustav Stickley's Craftsman Farms: A Pictorial History.* Morris Plains NJ: Craftsman Farms Press, 1999.

Chamberlin, Henry H. "George William Curtis and His Antecedents." Paper read before the Worcester Society of Antiquity, Wooster MA, 1893. Privately printed.

Clements, William. *Native American Verbal Art: Texts and Contexts.* Tucson: University of Arizona Pres, 1988.

———. "The 'Offshoot' and the 'Root': Natalie Curtis and Black Expressive Culture in Africa and America." *Western Folklore* 54 (October 1995): 277–301.

Clevenger, Martha, ed. *"Indescribably Grand": Diaries and Letters from the 1904 World's Fair*. St. Louis: Missouri Historical Society Press, 1996.

Coder, George D. "The National Movement to Preserve the American Buffalo in the United States and Canada between 1880 and 1920." Ph.D. dissertation, Ohio State University, 1975.

Coffin, Ernest W. "On the Education of Backward Races." *Pedagogical Seminary* 15 (March 1908): 1–60.

Cooke, George Willis, ed. *Early Letters of George William Curtis to John S. Dwight: Brook Farm and Concord*. Port Washington NY: Kennikat Press, 1971.

Cranston, S. L. *HPB: The Extraordinary Life and Influence of Helena Blavatsky, Founder of the Modern Theosophy Movement*. New York: G. P. Putnam's Sons, 1993.

Cronyn, George W., ed. *The Path on the Rainbow: An Anthology of Songs and Chants from the Indians of North America*. New York: Boni and Liveright, 1918.

Culbertson, Evelyn Davis. "Arthur Farwell's Early Efforts on Behalf of American Music, 1889–1921." *American Music* 5 (Summer 1987): 156–75.

———. *He Heard America Singing: Arthur Farwell, Composer and Crusading Music Editor*. Metuchen NJ: Scarecrow Press, 1992.

Curtis, Natalie. "An American Indian Artist." *Outlook* 124 (January 14, 1920): 64–66.

———. "An American Indian Composer." *Harper's Magazine* 107 (September 1903): 626–32.

———. "American Indian Cradle Songs." *Musical Quarterly* 7 (October 1921): 549–58.

———. "Another Talk with the Host of Craftsman Farms: The Country and Long Life." *Craftsman* 19 (February 1911): 485–88.

———. "A Bit of American Folk Music: Two Pueblo Indian Grinding Songs." *Craftsman* 7 (October 1904): 35–41.

———. "Busoni's Indian Fantasy." *Southern Workman* 44 (October 1915): 538–44.

———. "A Country Home for the Businessman: A Second Visit to Craftsman Farms." *Craftsman* 19 (October 1910): 55–62.

———. "Creation Myths of the Cochans (Yuma Indians)." *Craftsman* 16 (August 1909): 559–67.

———. "Folk-Music of America: Four Types in the United States Alone." *Craftsman* 21 (November 1911): 180–89.

———. "Franz Liszt, His Greatness as a Musician and Man: An Appreciation on the Occasion of the Liszt Centenary." *Craftsman* 21 (November 1911): 180–89.

———. "A Futurist Experiment." *Freeman* 5 (July 5, 1922): 400–402.

———. "Hampton's Double-Mission." *Southern Workman* 34 (October 1905): 543–45.

———. "An Historic House on the Hudson: The Silent Witness of the Growth of American Freedom." *Craftsman* 17 (October 1909): 3–11.

———. "The Hudson-Fulton Memorial Exhibit in New York." *Craftsman* 17 (November 1909): 124–41.

———. "Indian Music and Indian Education." *Addresses and Proceedings of the National Education Association* (1904): 979–81.

———. *The Indians' Book: An Offering by the American Indians of Indian Lore, Musical and Narrative, to Form a Record of the Songs and Legends of their Race.* New York: Harper Brothers, 1907. Reprint of the 1923 edition, New York: Dover Press, 1968.

———. "Indian Song." *Southern Workman* 34 (December 1905): 675.

———. "Indian Song." *Southern Workman* 35 (April 1906): 206.

———. "An Indian Song on a Desert Path." *Southern Workman* 33 (June 1904): 344–45.

———. "'In the Vanguard': Katrina Trask and Her Work." *Out West* 8 (May–June 1914): 258–66.

———. "Mr. Roosevelt and Indian Music: A Personal Reminiscence." *Outlook* 121 (March 5, 1919): 399–400.

———. "The Music America Buys: What the New York Season Offers in Many Fields." *Craftsman* 23 (January 1913): 390–400.

———. "Music of the American Indian." *Addresses and Proceedings of the National Education Association* (1905): 933–34.

———. "Negro Music at Birth." *Musical Quarterly* 5 (January 1919): 86–89.

———. "The Negro's Contribution to the Music of America: The Larger Opportunity of the Colored Man of Today." *Craftsman* 23 (March 1913): 660–69.

———. "A New Art in the West." *International Studio* (November 1917): xiv–xvii.

———. "The New Log House of Craftsman Farms: An Architectural Development of the Log Cabin." *Craftsman* 21 (November 1911): 196–203.

———. "A New Type of Architecture in the Southwest." *Craftsman* 25 (January 1914): 330–35.

———. "The Oldest Orchestral Organization in America: What the Philharmonic Society Has Done for Music in this Country." *Craftsman* 19 (February 1911): 492–97.

———. "An Old Town of the New World." *Four-Track News* (May 1905): 314–15.

———. "Our Native Craftsman." *Southern Workman* 48 (August 1919): 389–96.

———. "The People of the Totem-Poles: Their Arts and Legends." *Craftsman* 16 (September 1909): 612–21.

———. "The Perpetuating of Indian Art." *Outlook* 105 (November 22, 1913): 621–31.

———. "The Plight of the Mojave Apache Indians." *Outlook* 129 (September 7, 1921): 621–31.

———. "The Pueblo Singer: A Bit of Native American History." *Craftsman* 24 (July 1913): 400–401.

———. "The Shepherd Poet." *Southern Workman* 33 (March 1904): 145–48.

———. "The Significance of Hampton's Fifty Years." *Outlook* 122 (June 4, 1919): 197–98.

———. "The Song of the Indian Mother." *Craftsman* 15 (October 1908): 57–63.

———. *Songs and Tales from the Dark Continent.* New York: G. Schirmer, 1921.

———. *Songs of Ancient America.* New York: G. Schirmer, 1905.

———. "Theodore Roosevelt in Hopi Land. Another Personal Reminiscence." *Outlook* 105 (September 17, 1919): 87–93.

———. "The Value of a Country Education to Every Boy: A Talk with the Host of Craftsman Farms." *Craftsman* 19 (January 1911): 389–94.

———. "The Value of Indian Art." *Southern Workman* 33 (August 1904): 448–50.

———. "Value of Music School Settlements in Cities." *Craftsman* 21 (December 1911): 283–89.

———. "A Visit to Craftsman Farm: The Study of an Educational Ideal." *Craftsman* 18 (September 1910): 638–46.

———. "A War Song of the Far West." *Dial* 65 (December 1918): 589–90.

———. "The Winning of an Indian Reservation." *Outlook* 122 (June 25, 1919): 327–30.

———. "The Words of Hiaropai: A Leaf from a Traveler's Diary, Showing the Indian's Outlook upon the Transitional Period." *Craftsman* 13 (December 1907): 293–99.

———. *See also* Curtis-Burlin, Natalie, *and* Curtis Burlin, Natalie.

Curtis, Susan. *The First Black Actors along the Great White Way*. Columbia: University of Missouri Press, 1998.

Curtis Burlin, Natalie. "Black Singers and Players." *Musical Quarterly* 5 (October 1919): 499–504.

———. "The Indians' Part in the Dedication of the New Museum." *Art and Archaeology* 7 (January 1918): 30–32.

———. *See also* Curtis, Natalie, *and* Curtis-Burlin, Natalie.

Curtis-Burlin, Natalie. "The Hymn of Freedom." *Southern Workman* 47 (October 1918): 475–78.

———. *Negro Folk Songs*. 4 vols. New York: G. Schirmer, 1918–19.

———. "Recording for Posterity the Music of Primitive Humanity." *Musical America* 35 (March 18, 1922): 3, 38.

———. *See also* Curtis, Natalie, *and* Curtis Burlin, Natalie.

Cushing, Frank Hamilton. "Outlines of Zuni Creation Myths." *13th Annual Report of the Bureau of Ethnology 1891–1892*. Washington DC: Government Printing Office, 1896.

Damrosch, Walter. *My Musical Life*. New York: Charles Scribner Sons, 1923. Reprint, Westport CT: Greenwood Press, 1972.

Daniels, Mabel Wheeler. *An American Girl in Munich: Impressions of a Music Student*. Boston: Little, Brown, 1905.

Decora, Angel. "Native Indian Art." *Southern Workman* 36 (October 1907): 527–28.

DeJong, David H. *Promises of the Past: A History of Indian Education in the United States*. Golden CO: North American Press, 1993.

Deloria, Philip J. *Playing Indian*. New Haven: Yale University Press, 1998.

Dett, R. Nathaniel. "Ethnologist Aids Composer to Draw Inspiration from Heart of People." *Musical America* 30 (May 31, 1919): 36.

———. "Helping to Lay Foundation." In Spencer, *R. Nathaniel Dett Reader*, 21–22.

———. "Negro Music at the Present." In Spencer, *R. Nathaniel Dett Reader*, 42–47.

———. *Religious Folksongs of the Negro: As Sung at Hampton Institute*. Hampton VA: Hampton Institute Press, 1927.

Dilworth, Leah. *Imagining Indians in the Southwest: Persistent Visions of a Primitive Past*. Washington DC: Smithsonian Institute Press, 1996.

Dippie, Brian. *The Vanishing American: White Attitudes and U.S. Indian Policy*. Middletown CT: Wesleyan University Press, 1982.

Dizikes, John. *Opera in America: A Cultural History*. New Haven: Yale University Press, 1993.

Douglas, Ann. *Terrible Honesty: Mongrel Manhattan in the 1920s.* New York: Noonday Press, 1995.

Egan, Robert F. *Music and Arts in the Community: The Community Music School Settlement in America.* Metuchen NJ: Scarecrow Press, 1989.

Ellis, Clyde. *To Change Them Forever: Indian Education at Rainy Mountain Boarding School, 1893–1920.* Norman: University of Oklahoma Press, 1996.

Engs, Robert. *Educating the Disenfranchised and the Disinherited: Samuel C. Armstrong and Hampton Institute, 1839–1893.* Knoxville: University of Tennessee Press, 1999.

Farwell, Arthur. "American Opera on American Themes." *Review of Reviews* 43 (April 1911): 441–48.

———. "The Artistic Possibilities of Indian Myth." *Poet-Lore* 15 (1904): 46–61.

———. "A Letter to American Composers." In *A Guide to the Music of Arthur Farwell and to the Microfilm Collection of his Work,* ed. Brice Farwell. Briarcliff Manor NJ: Brice Farwell, 1972.

———. "Toward American Music." *Out West* 20 (May 1904): 454–58.

Fay, Amy. *Music-Study in Germany.* Ed. Mrs. Fay Peirce. New York: Macmillan, 1897.

Fenner, Thomas, ed. *Cabin and Plantation Songs, as Sung by the Hampton Students.* In *Hampton and Its Students,* ed. Mrs. M. F. Armstrong and Helen W. Ludlow. New York: G. P. Putnam's Songs, 1874. Reprint, Freeport NY: Books for Libraries Press, 1971.

Fewkes, Jesse Walter. "Additional Studies of Zuni Songs and Rituals with the Phonograph." *American Naturalist* 24 (November 1890): 1094–98.

———. "On the Use of the Phonograph among the Zuni Indians." *American Naturalist* 24 (July 1890): 687–91.

Fillmore, John Comfort. "The Forms Spontaneously Assumed by Folk-Songs." *Music* 12 (1897): 289–94.

———. "The Scientific Importance of the Folk-Music of Our Aborigines." *Land of Sunshine* 7 (1898): 22–25.

Finck, Henry T. "American Operas." *Nation* 106 (April 14, 1918): 412.

———. "The Musical Outlook for Women." *Etude* 17 (May 1899): 151.

Fish, Marilyn. *The New Craftsman Index.* Lambertville NJ: Arts and Crafts Quarterly Press, 1997.

Fiske, John. *The Discovery of America.* Boston: Houghton Mifflin, 1892.

Frederick Monsen at Hopi. Reprint Series, no. 2. Santa Fe: Museum of New Mexico Press, 1979.

Fletcher, Alice. *Indian Story and Song from North America*. Boston: Small Maynard, 1900. Reprint, New York: Johnson Reprint Co., 1970.

"Flickers." *American Art Journal* 56 (April 11, 1891): 407.

Flynn, A. J. "The Preservation of Aboriginal Arts." *NEA Journal of Proceedings and Addresses* (1909): 947–50.

"Folk Lore and Ethnology." *Southern Workman* 23 (July 1894): 131–33.

"Folk Lore and Ethnology." *Southern Workman* 24 (February 1895): 30–32.

Folpe, Emily Kies. *It Happened on Washington Square*. Baltimore: Johns Hopkins Press, 2002.

Frederickson, George M. *The Black Image in the White Mind: The Debate on Afro-American Character and Destiny, 1817–1915*. New York: Harper and Row, 1971.

Gaines, Kevin K. *Uplifting the Race: Black Leadership, Politics, and Cultures in the Twentieth Century*. Chapel Hill: University of North Carolina Press, 1996.

Garland, Hamlin. "The Red Man's Present Needs." *Outlook* 66 (September 1, 1900): 476–88.

Geddes, Alice Spencer. "Recorder of the Red Man's Music." *Sunset* 32 (January 1914): 165–66.

"George William Curtis." In *American National Biography*, 6:845–96. New York: Oxford University Press, 1999.

"George William Curtis." In *Dictionary of American Biography*, 2:614–15. New York: Charles Scribner's Sons, 1958.

Georgi-Findlay, Brigitte. *The Frontiers of Women's Writing: Women's Narratives and the Rhetoric of Westward Expansion*. Tucson: University of Arizona, 1996.

Geronimo. *Geronimo: His Own Story*. Ed. S. M. Barret. New York: E. P. Dutton, 1942.

Gibson, Arrell Morgan. *The Santa Fe and Taos Colonies: Age of the Muses, 1900–1942*. Norman: University of Oklahoma Press, 1983.

Gidley, Mick. "The Cultural Broker in the Context of Edward S. Curtis' *The North American Indian*." In *Between Indian and White Worlds: The Cultural Broker*, ed. Margaret Szasz, 197–215. Norman: University of Oklahoma Press, 1994.

———. *Edward S. Curtis and the North American Indian, Incorporated*. Cambridge: Cambridge University Press, 1998.

Gilbert, James B. *Work without Salvation: America's Intellectuals and Industrial America, 1880–1910*. Baltimore: Johns Hopkins Press, 1977.

Gilman, Lawrence. "The New American Music." *North American Review* 179 (December 1904): 288–94.

Goldsmith, Barbara. *Other Powers: The Age of Suffrage, Spiritualism, and the Scandalous Victoria Woodhall.* New York: A. A. Knopf, 1998. Reprint, New York: Harper Collins, 1999.

Grant, Frances R. "Recognizing Our Debt to Negro Music." *Musical America* 31 (December 13, 1919): 36.

Green, Martin Burgess. *New York 1913: The Armory Show and the Paterson Strike Pageant.* New York: Scribner, 1988.

Green, Shannon Louise. "'Art for Life's Sake': Music Schools and Activities in United States Social Settlement Houses, 1892–1942." Ph.D. dissertation, University of Wisconsin, 1998.

Guterl, Matthew Pratt. *The Color of Race in America, 1900–1940.* Cambridge: Harvard University Press, 2001.

Hagan, William T. *The Indian Rights Association: The Herbert Welsh Years, 1882–1904.* Tucson: University of Arizona Press, 1985.

———. *Theodore Roosevelt and Six Friends of the Indian.* Norman: University of Oklahoma Press, 1997.

Hallmard, Rufus, ed. *German Lieder in the Nineteenth Century.* New York: Schirmer Books, 1996.

Hamm, Charles. "Dvořák, Stephen Foster, and American National Song." In *Dvořák in America, 1892–1895,* ed. John C. Tibbetts, 149–55. Portland OR: Amadeus Press, 1993.

Hammack, David. *Power and Society: Greater New York at the Turn of the Century.* New York: Russell Sage Foundation, 1982.

Harris, Luther S. *Around Washington Square: An Illustrated History of Greenwich Village.* Baltimore: Johns Hopkins University Press, 2003.

Hemenway, Robert E. *Zora Neale Hurston: A Literary Biography.* Urbana: University of Illinois Press, 1977.

Henderson, Alice Corbin. *The Turquoise Trail: An Anthology of New Mexico Poetry.* Boston: Houghton Mifflin, 1928.

Higham, John. "The Reorientation of American Culture in the 1890's." In *Writing American History: Essays on Modern Scholarship,* 73–102. Bloomington: Indiana University Press, 1970.

Hinsley, Curtis M., Jr. "Authoring Authenticity." *Journal of the Southwest* 32 (Winter 1990): 462–78.

Hofmann, Charles. *Frances Densmore and American Indian Music.* New York: Museum of the American Indian, 1968.

Holm, Thomas. "Indians and Progressives, From Vanishing Policy to the Indian New Deal." Ph.D. dissertation, University of Oklahoma, 1978.

Holtgreen, Mary Lou, and Jeanna Zeider. *A Taste for the Beautiful: Zairian*

Art from Hampton University Museum. Hampton VA: Hampton University Press, 1993.

Horowitz, Helen Lefkowitz. "'Nous Autres': Reading, Passion, and the Creation of M. Carey Thomas." *Journal of American History* 79 (1992): 68–95.

Horowitz, Joseph. *Wagner Nights: An American History*. Berkeley: University of California Press, 1994.

House, Grace Bigelow. "Origin of the Hymn." *Southern Workman* 47 (October 1918): 475–78.

Howard, John Trasker, Jr. "The Music School Settlement Idea." *Musician* 24 (June 1919): 8.

Hoxie, Frederick. *A Final Promise: The Campaign to Assimilate the Indians, 1880–1920*. Lincoln: University of Nebraska Press, 1984.

Hughes, Langston. *The Big Sea*. New York: Alfred A. Knopf Press, 1940.

Huhndorf, Shari M. *Going Native: Indians in the American Cultural Imagination*. Ithaca: Cornell University Press, 2001.

Hurston, Zora Neale. *Dust Tracks on a Road*. Philadelphia: J. B. Lippincott, 1942.

Hyatt, Marshall. *Franz Boas: Social Activist*. Westport CT: Greenwood Press, 1990.

"Indian Music." *Outlook* 103 (March 29, 1913): 969–97.

"Indian Music at Hampton's Anniversary." *Southern Workman* 33 (June 1904): 327–28.

"Is There a Distinctive Note in American Music?" *Current Literature* 40 (June 1906): 635–37.

Jackman, O. S. "The Price the Hopi Indians Are Paying for Civilization." *Harper's Weekly* 51 (November 30, 1907): 1760–61.

Jackson, Jeffrey H. *Making Jazz French: Music and Modern Life in Inter-war Paris*. Durham: Duke University Press, 2003.

Jacobs, Margaret. *Engendered Encounters: Feminism and Pueblo Cultures, 1879–1934*. Lincoln: University of Nebraska Press, 1999.

————. "The Great White Mother: Maternalism and American Indian Child Removal in the American West, 1880–1940." In *One Step Over the Line: Toward a History of Women in the North American Wests*, ed. Elizabeth Jameson and Shelia McManus. Edmonton AB: Athabasca University Press, 2008.

————. "Maternal Colonialism: White Women and Indigenous Child Removal in the American West and Australia, 1880–1940." *Western Historical Quarterly* 36 (Winter 2005): 453–76.

————. *White Mother to a Dark Race: Settler Colonialism, Maternalism, and the Removal of Indigenous Children in the American West and Australia, 1880–1940*. Lincoln: University of Nebraska Press, 2009.

Jacoway, Elizabeth. *Yankee Missionaries in the South: The Penn School Experiment*. Baton Rouge: Louisiana State University Press, 1980.

James, George Wharton. *What the White Race May Learn from the Indian*. Chicago: Forbes, 1908.

James, Henry. *Pages from Hopi History*. Tucson: University of Arizona Press, 1974.

Jameson, Elizabeth. "Toward a Multicultural History of Women in the Western United States." *Signs* 13 (Summer 1988): 761–91.

Johnson, James Weldon, and J. Rosamond Johnson. *The Books of American Negro Spirituals* (*The Book of American Negro Spirituals*, 1925 and *The Second Book of Negro Spirituals*, 1926). New York: Viking Press, 1940.

Jonaitis, Aldona, and Richard Inglis. "Power, History and Authenticity: The Mowachaht Whalers' Shrine." In *Eloquent Obsessions: Writing Cultural Criticism*, ed. Marianna Torgovnick, 157–84. Durham: Duke University Press, 1994.

Kammen, Michael. *Mystic Chords of Memory: The Transformation of Tradition in American Culture*. New York: Alfred A. Knopf, 1991.

Kaplan, Wendy, ed. *"The Art That Is Life": The Arts and Crafts Movement in America, 1875–1920*. Boston: Museum of Fine Arts, 1987.

————. "The Lamp of British Precedent: An Introduction to the Arts and Crafts Movement." In Kaplan, *"Art That Is Life,"* 52–60.

Keeling, Richard. "The Beginnings of Musicological Research, 1880–1920." In *North American Indian Music: A Guide to Published Sources and Selected Recordings*, xiii–xviii. New York: Garland Publishers, 1997.

Kennedy, Robert. "Crisis and Progress: The Rhetoric and Ideals of a Nineteenth Century Reformer, George William Curtis (1824–1892)." Ph.D. dissertation, University of Illinois, 1993.

Khera, Sigrid, and Patricia S. Mariela. "Yavapai." In *The Southwest*, ed. Alfred Ortiz, vol. 10 of Sturtevant, *Handbook of North American Indians*, 38–54.

King, Moses, ed. *King's Handbook of New York City*. Boston: Moses King, 1893.

Kingman, Daniel. *American Music: A Panorama*. 2nd ed. New York: Schirmer Books, 1990.

Kolodin, Irving. *The Story of the Metropolitan Opera 1883–1950: A Candid History*. New York: Alfred A. Knopf, 1953.

Kramer, Paul. "Making Concessions: Race and Empire Revisited at the Philippine Exposition, St. Louis, 1901–1905." *Radical History Review* 73 (Winter 1999): 74–114.

Krehbiel, Henry Edward. *Afro-American Folksongs.* New York: G. Schirmer, 1914.

Krupat, Arnold. "On the Translation of Native American Song and Story: A Theorized History." In *On the Translation of Native American Literatures,* ed. Brian Swann, 3–32. Washington DC: Smithsonian Institute Press, 1992.

LaBarre, Weston. *The Peyote Cult.* 5th ed., enlarged. Norman: University of Oklahoma Press, 1989.

Lahee, Henry C. *Grand Opera in America.* Boston: L. C. Page, 1902.

Landau, Rom. *Ignace Paderewski: Musician and Statesman.* New York: Thomas Y. Crowell, 1934.

Lane, Franklin. "From the War-Path to the Plow." *National Geographic* 27 (January 1915): 73–87.

———. "The Future of the Indian." *LaFollette's Magazine* 7 (March 1915): 12–13.

Lavignac, Albert. *Musical Education.* Trans. Esther Singleton. New York: D. Appleton, 1903.

Leadbeater, C. W. *A Textbook of Theosophy.* Wheaton IL: Theosophical Publishing House, 1912.

Lears, T. J. Jackson. *No Place of Grace: Antimodernism and the Transformation of American Culture, 1880–1920.* New York: Pantheon Press, 1981.

Lee, Frederic S. "John Green Curtis." In *Dictionary of American Biography,* vol. 2. New York: C. Scribner's Sons, 1958.

Leupp, Constance D. "Climbing Out through Music." *Outlook* 102 (October 26, 1912): 403–9.

Levine, Lawrence. *Black Culture and Black Consciousness: Afro-American Folk Thought from Slavery to Freedom.* Oxford: Oxford University Press, 1977.

———. "Slave Songs and Slave Consciousness." In *American Negro Slavery,* ed. Allen Weinstein and Frank Otto Gatell, 153–82. Oxford: Oxford University Press, 1973.

Levine, Victoria Lindsay. "Reading American Indian Music as Social History." In *Writing American Indian Music: Historic Transcription, Notations, and Arrangements,* ed. Victoria Lindsay Levine, xix–xxxvi. Middleton WI: A–R Editions, 2002.

Levy, A. H. "Double-Bars and Double Standards: Female Composers

in America, 1880–1920." *International Journal of Women's Studies* 6
    (March–April 1983): 162–75.

———. "The Search for Identity in America Music, 1890–1920." *American
    Music* 2 (Summer 1984): 70–78.

Lewis, David Levering. *When Harlem Was in Vogue.* New York: Alfred A.
    Knopf, 1981.

Lindsey, Donal F. *Indians at Hampton Institute, 1877–1923.* Urbana:
    University of Illinois Press, 1995.

Logan, Rayford. *The Negro in American Life and Thought: The Nadir, 1877–
    1901.* New York: Dial Press, 1954.

Lomawaima, K. Tsianina. *They Called It Prairie Light: The Story of Chilocco
    Indian School.* Lincoln: University of Nebraska Press, 1994.

Lovell, John, Jr. *Black Song: The Forge and the Flame.* New York: MacMillan
    Company, 1972.

Luhan, Mabel Dodge. *Edge of Taos Desert: An Escape to Reality.* Vol. 4 of
    Intimate Memories. New York: Harcourt, Brace, 1937.

Lummis, Charles. *Bullying the Moqui.* Flagstaff AZ: Prescott College Press,
    1968.

Lurie, Nancy Oestrich. "Winnebago." In *The Northeast,* ed. Bruce G. Trigger,
    vol. 15 of Sturtevant, *Handbook of North American Indians,* 690–707.

———. *Women and the Invention of American Anthropology.* Prospect
    Heights IL: Waveland Press, 1999.

Lyman, Christopher M. *The Vanishing American and Other Illusions:
    Photographs of Indians by Edward S. Curtis.* Washington DC:
    Smithsonian Institute Press, 1982.

MacKay, Robert B. "Long Island Country Houses and Their Architects:
    1860–1940." *Long Island Historical Journal* 6 (1994): 168–90.

Macmahon, Henry. "Franklin W. Hooper: The Director of the Brooklyn
    Institute." *World Today* 10 (February 1906): 194–97.

Magnaghi, Russell M. "America Views Her Indians at the 1904 World's Fair
    in Saint Louis." *Gateway Heritage* 4 (1983–84): 20–29.

Mannes, David. *Music Is My Faith.* New York: W. W. Norton, 1938.

Mardock, Robert W. *The Reformers and the American Indian.* Columbia:
    University of Missouri Press, 1971.

Mariella, Patricia. "The Political Economy of Federal Resettlement Policies
    Affecting Native American Communities: The Fort McDowel Yavapai
    Case." Ph.D. dissertation, Arizona State University, 1983.

Mark, Joan. "Francis LaFlesche: The American Indian as Anthropologist."
    Isis 73 (1982): 497–510.

———. *A Stranger in Her Native Land: Alice Fletcher and the American Indians.* Lincoln: University of Nebraska Press, 1988.

Martin, George. *The Damrosch Dynasty: America's First Family of Music.* Boston: Houghton Mifflin, 1985.

Mason, Charlotte Osgood. "The Passing of a Prophet: A True Narrative of Death and Life." *North American Review* 185 (August 16, 1907): 896–70.

Mathes, Valerie Sherer. *Helen Hunt Jackson and Her Indian Reform Legacy.* Austin: University of Texas Press, 1990.

Matthews, Joseph. "Busoni's Contributions to Piano Pedagogy." Ph.D. dissertation, Indiana University, 1977.

Matthews, Washington. *Navajo Legends.* Boston: Houghton Mifflin for the American Folklore Society, 1897. Reprint, New York: Kraus Reprint Co., 1969.

———. "Publications of the Wa-Wan Press." *Music* 22 (December 1902): 288–94.

———. "Songs of the Navajo." *Land of Sunshine* 5 (1896): 197–201.

———. "The Young Woman Pianist and Her Business Prospects." *Etude* 24 (February 1906): 64.

McCabe, James D. *Lights and Shadows of New York Life; or, The Sights and Sounds of the Great City.* Philadelphia: National Publishing, 1872.

McDonnell, Janet. "Competency Commissions and Indian Land Policy, 1913–1920." *South Dakota History* 11 (Winter 1980): 21–34.

McFeely, Eliza. *Zuni and the American Imagination.* New York: Hill and Wang, 2001.

McLaughlin, James. *My Friend, the Indian.* Boston: Houghton Mifflin, 1910.

McNulty, Sarah. "Angel DeCora: American Indian Artist and Educator." *Nebraska History* 57 (1976): 143–99.

McPherson, James. *The Abolitionist Legacy: From Reconstruction to the* NAACP. Princeton: Princeton University Press, 1975.

Mihesuah, Devon. *Cultivating the Rosebuds: The Education of Women at the Cherokee Female Seminary, 1851–1909.* Urbana-Champaign: University of Illinois Press, 1993.

Mills, Sarah. *Discourses of Difference: An Analysis of Women's Travel Writing and Colonialism.* London and New York: Routledge, 1991.

Milne, Gordon. *George William Curtis and the Genteel Tradition.* Bloomington: Indiana University Press, 1956.

The Mishongnovi Ceremonies of the Snake and Antelope Fraternities. Anthropological Series, vol. 3, no. 3. Chicago: Field Columbian Museum, 1901.

Monson, Frederick. "The Destruction of Our Indians: What Civilization Is Doing to Extinguish an Ancient and Highly Intelligent Race by Taking Away Its Arts, Crafts, Industries, and Religion." *Craftsman* 11 (March 1901): 683–91.

Mooney, James. "The Ghost Dance Religion and the Sioux Outbreak of 1890." In *14th Annual Report of the Bureau of Ethnology (1892–1893)*. Washington DC: Government Printing Office, 1896.

Moore, MacDonald Smith. *Yankee Blues: Musical Culture and American Identity*. Bloomington: Indiana University Press, 1985.

Mullin, Molly H. *Culture in the Marketplace: Gender, Art and Value in the American Southwest*. Durham: Duke University Press, 2001.

"Natalie Curtis." *Southern Workman* 55 (March 1926): 127–40.

"Natalie Curtis Burlin." *Southern Workman* 50 (December 1921): 528–29.

"Negro Folk Songs Recorded." *Talking Machine World* (March 1926) 127–40.

"Negro Music." *Southern Workman* 42 (April 1913): 195–97.

"Negro's Place in Music." *New York Evening Post*, March 13, 1914. In *Reminiscing with Sissle and Blake*, ed. Robert Kimball and William Bolcom, 60–61. New York: Viking Press, 1973.

Nettl, Bruno. *The Study of Ethnomusicology: Thirty-One Issues and Concepts*. New ed. Urbana: University of Illinois Press, 1982, 2005.

———. "Two Summers with the Blackfeet Indians of Montana." *Musical Quarterly* 2 (April 1916): 257–70.

Nevin, Arthur. "Impressions of Indian Music as Heard in the Woods, Prairies, Mountains, and Wigwams." *Etude* 38 (October 1920): 663–44.

———. "Two Summers with the Blackfeet Indians of Montana." *Musical Quarterly* 2 (April 1916): 257–70.

O'Reilly, Kenneth. "Progressive Era and New Era American Indian Policy: The Gospel of Self-Support." *Journal of Historical Studies* 5 (Fall 1981): 36–40.

Orvell, Miles. *The Real Thing: Imitation and Authenticity in American Culture, 1880–1940*. Chapel Hill: University of North Carolina Press, 1989.

Packer, Rhonda, and Tamar Frankiel. "Natural Sympathies: Anglo Women and Indians in the West, 1895–1920." *International Social Science Review* 70 (1995): 68–75.

Parezo, Nancy. "Anthropology: The Welcoming Science." In Parezo, *Hidden Scholars*, 3–37.

———, ed. *Hidden Scholars: Women Anthropologists and the Native American Southwest*. Albuquerque: University of New Mexico Press, 1993.

————. "Matilda Coxe Stevenson: Pioneer Ethnologist." In Parezo, *Hidden Scholars*.

Parman, Donald L. "J. C. Morgan: Navajo Apostle of Assimilation." *Prologue* 4 (Summer 1972): 83–98.

Pendle, Karin, ed. *Women and Music: A History*. Bloomington: Indiana University Press, 1991.

"People Who Interest Us: Natalie Curtis, the 'Friend of the Indians.'" *Craftsman* 18 (September 1910): 678–79.

Peterson, Elsa. "On the Trail of Red Sky Lady and Other Scholars." *Triangle of MuPhi Epsilon* 75 (1981): 8–10.

Plantinga, Leon. *Romantic Music: A History of Musical Style in Nineteenth Century Europe*. New York: W. W. Norton, 1984.

Pratt, Mary Louise. *Imperial Eyes: Travel Writing and Transculturation*. London: Routledge Press, 1992.

Prucha, Francis Paul, ed. *Americanizing the First Americans: Writings by the "Friends of the Indian," 1880–1900*. Cambridge: Harvard University Press, 1973.

————. *The Churches and the Indian Schools: 1888–1912*. Lincoln: University of Nebraska Press, 1980.

————. *The Great Father: The United States Government and the American Indians*. Lincoln: University of Nebraska Press, 1984.

Raynor, Harold. *Music and Society since 1815*. New York: Taplinger Publishing, 1978.

"Recognition of Negro Music." *Southern Workman* 49 (January 1920): 6–7.

"Recording the Indian's Music." *Literary Digest* 46 (April 26, 1913): 951.

"The Resurrection of the Red Man." *El Palacio* 8 (July 1920): 196.

Review of *The Indians' Book*, by Natalie Curtis. *Dial* 43 (October 1907): 383.

Review of *The Indians' Book*, by Natalie Curtis. *Outlook* 87 (October 19, 1907): 358.

Review of *The Indians' Book*, by Natalie Curtis. *Review of Reviews* 36 (November 1907): 637–38.

Riley, Glenda. *Women and Indians on the Frontier, 1825–1915*. Albuquerque: University of New Mexico Press, 1984.

Roberge, Marc-André. "Ferruccio Busoni in the United States." *American Music* 13 (Fall 1995): 295–332.

Roell, Craig H. *The Piano in America, 1890–1918*. Chapel Hill: University of North Carolina Press, 1989.

Roosevelt, Theodore. "The Hopi Snake Dance." *Outlook* 105 (October 13, 1913): 365–73.

———. *The Letters of Theodore Roosevelt.* Sel. and ed. Elting E. Morison.
  Cambridge: Harvard University Press, 1951.

Rosaldo, Renato. *Culture and Truth: The Remaking of Social Analysis.* Boston:
  Beacon Press, 1993.

Rothstein, William G. *American Physicians in the Nineteenth Century.*
  Baltimore: Johns Hopkins University Press, 1989.

Rousmeiere, John. *The Life and Times of the Equitable.* New York: Equitable
  Companies, 1995.

Rudnick, Lois Palken. *Mabel Dodge Luhan, New Woman, New Worlds.*
  Albuquerque: University of New Mexico Press, 1984.

Rushforth, Scott, and Steadman Upham. *A Hopi Social History:
  Anthropological Perspectives on Sociocultural Persistence and Change.*
  Austin: University of Texas Press, 1992.

Rushing, W. Jackson. *Native American Art and the New York Avant-Garde: A
  History of Cultural Pluralism.* Austin: University of Texas Press, 1995.

Rydell, Robert. *All the World's a Fair. Visions of Empire at American
  International Expositions, 1876–1916.* Chicago: University of Chicago
  Press, 1984.

Rydell, Robert, John E. Findling, and Kimberly D. Pelle. *Fair America:
  World's Fairs in the United States.* Washington DC: Smithsonian
  Institute Press, 1984.

Said, Edward W. *Orientalism.* New York: Vintage Books, 1979.

Sandler, Irving. *Paul Burlin.* New York: American Federation of Arts, 1963.

Sands, Kathleen M., and Emory Sekaquaptewa. "Four Hopi Lullabies: A
  Study in Method and Meaning." *American Indian Quarterly* 4, no. 3
  (1978): 195–210.

Schlereth, Thomas J. *Victorian America: Transformations in Everyday Life,
  1876–1915.* New York: Harper Collins, 1991.

Senate Committee on Indian Affairs. *To Establish a Permanent National
  Bison Range.* 60th Cong., 1st sess., 1908, Report no. 467.

Senier, Sioban. *Voices of American Indian Assimilation and Resistance: Helen
  Hunt Jackson, Sarah Winnemucca, and Victoria Howard.* Norman:
  University of Oklahoma Press, 2001.

Shaw, Arnold. *Black Popular Music in America.* New York: Schirmer Books,
  1986.

Shrady, John, ed. *The College of Physicians and Surgeons of New York and
  Its Founders, Officers, Instructors, Benefactors and Alumni.* New York:
  Lewis Publishing, 1907.

Simango, Columbus Kamaba. "The African and Civilization." *Southern
  Workman* 46 (October 1917): 552–55

―――. "A South African's Story." *Southern Workman* 48 (May 1919): 268–70.

Simpson, Anne Key. *Follow Me: The Life and Music of R. Nathaniel Dett.* Composers of North America Series, no. 10. Metuchen NJ: Scarecrow Press, 1993.

Smith, Sherry L. *Reimagining Indians: Native Americans through Anglo Eyes, 1880–1940.* Oxford: Oxford University Press, 2000.

Smith-Rosenberg, Carroll. "The Female World of Love and Ritual." *Signs* 1 (Autumn 1975): 1–29.

Southern, Eileen. *The Music of Black Americans: A History.* 3rd ed. New York: W. W. Norton, 1997.

Spencer, Frank. "Aleš Hrdlička, MD, 1869–1943: A Chronicle of the Life and Work of an American Physical Anthropologist." Ph.D. dissertation, University of Michigan, 1979.

Spencer, Jon Michael, ed. *The R. Nathaniel Dett Reader: Essays on Black Sacred Music.* Special issue, *Black Sacred Music: A Journal of Theomusicology* 5 (Fall 1991). Published by Duke University Press.

Spotts, Frederic. *Bayreuth: A History of the Wagner Festival.* New Haven: Yale University Press, 1994.

Stansell, Christine. *American Moderns: Bohemian New York and the Creation of a New Century.* New York: Metropolitan Books, 2000.

Stewart, Earl L. *African American Music: An Introduction.* New York: Schirmer Books, 1998.

Stuckenschmidt, H. H. *Ferruccio Busoni: Chronicle of a European.* Trans. Sandra Morris. New York: St. Martin's Press, 1970.

Sturtevant, William T., ed. *Handbook of North American Indians.* 15 vols. Washington DC: Smithsonian Institute, 2001.

Sun's Guide to New York City. New York: R. Wayne Wilson, 1892.

Szasz, Margaret, ed. *Between Indian and White Worlds: The Cultural Broker.* Norman: University of Oklahoma Press, 1994.

―――. *Education and the American Indian: The Road to Self-Determination since 1928.* 2nd ed. Albuquerque: University of New Mexico Press, 1977.

―――. *Indian Education in the American Colonies, 1607–1783.* Albuquerque: University of New Mexico Press, 1988.

Taylor, Eugene. *Shadow Culture: Psychology and Spirituality in America.* Washington DC: Counterpoint Press, 1999.

Thompson, Gregory. "The Origins and Implementation of the American Indian Reform Movement: 1867–1912." Ph.D. dissertation, University of Utah, 1981.

Thompson, Mark. *American Character: The Curious Life of Charles Fletcher Lummis and the Rediscovery of the Southwest.* New York: Arcade Publishing, 2001.

Tibbetts, John C., ed. *Dvořák in America, 1892–1895.* Portland OR: Amadeus Press, 1993.

Tick, Judith. "Women as Professional Musicians in the United States, 1870–1900." *Yearbook for Inter-American Musical Research* 9 (1973): 95–133.

Tingey, Joseph L. "Indians and Blacks Together: An Experiment in Biracial Education at Hampton Institute (1875–1923)." Ph.D. dissertation, Teachers College, Columbia University, 1978.

Tischler, Barbara L. *An American Music: The Search for an American Musical Identity.* Oxford: Oxford University Press, 1986.

Tisdale, Shelby J. "Women on the Periphery of the Ivory Tower." In Parezo, *Hidden Scholars,* 311–33.

Titiev, Misha. *Old Oraibi: A Study of the Hopi Indians of the Third Mesa.* Papers of the Peabody Museum of American Archaeology and Ethnology, 1944. Reprint, Albuquerque: University of New Mexico Press, 1992.

Torgovnick, Marianna. *Gone Primitive: Savage Intellects, Modern Lives.* Chicago: University of Chicago Press, 1990.

Trachtenberg, Alan. *The Incorporation of America: Culture and Society in the Gilded Age.* New York: Hill and Wang, 1982.

———. *Shades of Hiawatha: Staging Indians, Making Americans, 1880–1930.* New York: Hill and Wang, 2004.

Trennert, Robert A. "Fairs, Expositions, and the Changing Image of Southwestern Indians, 1876–1904." *New Mexico Historical Review* 62 (April 1989): 127–50.

———. *The Phoenix Indian School: Forced Assimilation in Arizona, 1891–1935.* Norman: University of Oklahoma Press, 1988.

———. "A Resurrection of Native Arts and Crafts: The St. Louis World's Fair, 1904." *Missouri Historical Review* 87 (1993): 274–92.

Troyer, Carlos. *The Zuni Indians and Their Music.* Philadelphia: Theodore Presser, 1913.

Tweed, Thomas A. *The American Encounter with Buddhism, 1844–1912: Victorian Culture and the Limits of Dissent.* Bloomington: Indiana University Press, 1992.

Udall, Sharyn Rohlfsen. *Modernist Painting in New Mexico, 1913–1935.* Albuquerque: University of New Mexico Press, 1984.

United States Bureau of Indian Affairs. *Course of Study for the Indian*

Schools of the United States: Industrial and Literary. Washington DC: Government Printing Office, 1901.

Versluis, Arthur. *American Transcendentalism and Asian Religions*. Oxford: Oxford University Press, 1993.

Vickers, Scott. *Native American Identities: From Stereotype to Archetype in Art and Literature*. Albuquerque: University of New Mexico Press, 1998.

"Virginia Day." *Southern Workman* 34 (June 1905): 356–58.

Visweswaran, Kamala. "'Wild West' Anthropology and the Disciplining of Gender." In *Gender and American Social Science: The Formative Years*, ed. Helene Silverburg, 86–123. Princeton: Princeton University Press, 1998.

Voth, H. R., and George Dorsey. *The Oraibi Soyal Ceremony*. 66 Anthropological Series, vol. 13, no. 3. Chicago: Field Columbia Museum, 1901.

Wagnalls, Mabel. *Stars of the Opera*. New York: Funk and Wagnalls, 1899.

Ware, Louise. *George Foster Peabody: Banker, Philanthropist, Publicist*. Athens: University of Georgia Press, 1951.

Waters, Donald J. *Strange Ways and Sweet Dreams: Afro-American Folklore from the Hampton Institute*. Boston: G. K. Hall, 1983.

Watkins, William H. *The White Architects of Black Education: Ideology and Power in America, 1865–1954*. New York: Teacher's College Press, 2001.

Watson, Steven. *The Harlem Renaissance: Hub of African-American Culture, 1920–1930*. New York: Pantheon Books, 1995.

Weigold, Marilyn E. *The American Mediterranean: An Environmental, Economic, and Society History of Long Island Sound*. Port Washington NY: Kennikat Press, 1974.

White, G. Edward. *The Eastern Establishment and the Western Experience: The West of Frederic Remington, Theodore Roosevelt and Owen Wister*. New Haven: Yale University Press, 1968.

Whiteley, Peter. *Deliberate Acts: Changing Hopi Culture through the Oraibi Split*. Tucson: University of Arizona Press, 1988.

Wick, Michelle. "'Practical Education': Indian Schooling in the Progressive Era." Master's thesis, Purdue University, 1998.

Wiegle, Martha. "Exposition and Mediation: Mary Colter, Erna Fergusson and the Santa Fe/Harvey Popularization of the Native Southwest, 1903–1940." *Frontiers* 12 (1991): 117–50.

"William M. Semnacher." *American Art Journal* 57 (April 25, 1891).

Williams, Vernon J., Jr. *Rethinking Race: Franz Boas and His Contemporaries*. Lexington: University of Kentucky Press, 1996.

Willis, H. Parker. "George Curtis." In *Dictionary of American Biography*, vol. 2. New York: C. Scribner's Sons, 1958.

Winn, Edith Lynwood. "The Woman Musician." *Etude* 19 (September 1900): 335.

Wood, Elizabeth. "Women and Music." *Signs* 6 (1980): 283–97.

Zuck, Barbara. *A History of Musical Americanism*. Ann Arbor: UMI Research Press, 1980.

INDEX

NC = Natalie Curtis